COLLECTING, ORDERING, GOVERNING

TONY BENNETT,
FIONA CAMERON,
NÉLIA DIAS,
BEN DIBLEY,
RODNEY HARRISON,
IRA JACKNIS, AND
CONAL MCCARTHY

Anthropology, Museums, and Liberal Government

Duke University Press   Durham and London   2017

Designed by Courtney Leigh Baker
Typeset in Trade Gothic and Minion Pro by Westchester Publishing Services

Library of Congress Cataloging-in-Publication Data
Names: Bennett, Tony, [date] author.
Title: Collecting, ordering, governing : anthropology, museums, and liberal government /
Tony Bennett, Fiona Cameron, Nélia Dias, Ben Dibley, Rodney Harrison, Ira Jacknis, and
Conal McCarthy.
Description: Durham : Duke University Press, 2017. | Includes bibliographical references
and index.
Identifiers: LCCN 2016026986 (print)
LCCN 2016028134 (ebook)
ISBN 9780822362531 (hardcover)
ISBN 9780822362685 (pbk.)
ISBN 9780822373605 (ebook)
Subjects: LCSH: Anthropology—Political aspects. | Ethnology—Political aspects. | Museum
exhibits—Political aspects. | Cultural policy.
Classifi cation: LCC GN27 .B45 2017 (print) | LCC GN 27 (ebook) | DDC 301— dc23
LC record available at https://lccn.loc.gov/2016026986

Cover Art: "General view of the Asian Hall, Musée d'Ethnographie du Trocadéro, Paris,
January 1934." QB 53498, Musée du quai Branly, Paris. © Photo SCALA, Florence.

CONTENTS

AM
Australian Museum

AMNH
American Museum of Natural History

ANZ
Archives New Zealand

ATL
Alexander Turnbull Library

ATP
Musée des Arts et Traditions Populaires

AWMM
Auckland War Memorial Museum

BAAS
British Association for the Advancement of Science

BMER
Board of Maori Ethnological Research

DM
Dominion Museum

EFEO
École Française d'Extrême-Orient

HC
Hocken Library Archives and Manuscripts, Dunedin

IIEH
Institut Indochinois pour l'Étude de l'Homme

MET
Musée d'Ethnographie du Trocadéro

MH
Musée de l'Homme

MH HAN
Musée de l'Homme, Hanoi

M-O
Mass-Observation

MOI
Ministry of Information

MOO
Mass Observation Online

NAA
National Archives Australia

NMV
National Museum Victoria

NTI
Northern Territory Invention

OM
Otago Museum

POC
Papuan Official Collection

TPA
Te Papa Archives

We have, when using the general category of "indigenous," used lowercase throughout this study, reserving the use of capitals for our reference to specific indigenous peoples: Indigenous Australians, Native Americans, Māori. We follow the convention in current New Zealand English of using macrons for Māori words to indicate a double vowel. However, Māori words in the titles of books, organizations, and so on and in historical archival sources and texts have been left in their original form. *Aotearoa* is the Māori name for the North Island of New Zealand. While the country remains formally "New Zealand," we use the double appellation Aotearoa/New Zealand where appropriate to reflect increasing formal use of this term in bilingual references to national institutions and in other official state contexts.

ABORIGINAL AND TORRES STRAIT ISLANDER READERS are advised that this book contains names and photographs of deceased persons.

This book is an outcome of the Discovery Project "Museum, Field, Metropolis, Colony: Practices of Social Governance" (Award Number DP110103776), funded by the Australian Research Council. The research grant was awarded to Tony Bennett (convenor) and Fiona Cameron at the Institute for Culture and Society, Western Sydney University, as chief investigators, and to Nélia Dias (University of Lisbon), Rodney Harrison (University College London), Ira Jacknis (University of California, Berkeley), and Conal McCarthy (Victoria University of Wellington) as international partner investigators. Ben Dibley was the research fellow appointed to the project. The project was also supported by research assistance from Michelle Kelly.

In Australia our work was generously and helpfully guided by an indigenous advisory committee that included Phil Gordon, manager of Indigenous Heritage, Australian Museum (chair); Laura McBride, Australian Museum; Lyndon Ormond Parker, University of Melbourne; Garry Pappin, University of Canberra; Mat Poll, Macleay Museum; and Chris Wilson, Flinders University. In New Zealand we were helpfully advised by Professor Paul Tapsell, Te Tumu: School of Māori, Pacific and Indigenous Studies, University of Otago. We thank all of the individuals mentioned here for giving so generously of their time and knowledge throughout the duration of our research project.

We are also grateful to the many scholars whose participation in the workshops and symposia that we organized over the course of the project greatly enriched the intellectual environment for our work. Our first research workshop, Colonial Governmentalities, brought together members of the research team with an international group of invited participants, including Philip Batty (Melbourne Museum), Elizabeth Edwards (Durham University), Henrika Kuklick (University of Pennsylvania), Tim Rowse (University of Western Sydney), Paul Tapsell (University of Otago), Julie Thorpe (University of Western Sydney), and Paul Turnbull (University of Queensland). We acknowledge our debt to these individuals for their contributions to the workshop as well as to the special issues of the journals *History and Anthropology* and *Museum and Society* that we edited from the workshop proceedings. Our second event was a seminar, Reassembling the Material, hosted at Te Herenga Waka marae, Victoria University of Wellington. This brought together members of the research team with local and particularly indigenous Māori scholars: Arapata Hakiwai (Kaihautū/Māori director, Te Papa) and Paul Diamond (Māori curator, National Library of New Zealand). The third event was the symposium Museums, Collecting, Agency, held at, and jointly organized with, the Australian Museum, Sydney. The keynote speakers were Phil Gordon (Australian Museum) and Huhana Smith, Ngāti Raukawa ki te Tonga and Ngāti Tūkorehe, and the presenters included indigenous scholars from Australia and Aotearoa/New Zealand and members of the research team. We benefited greatly from the opportunity these two occasions provided for advice from Australian and New Zealand indigenous intellectuals whose work has had a formative influence on museum policies in both countries.

Our work was also enriched by the critical feedback we received from collective presentations of our work at the Cultural Crossroads conference of the international Cultural Studies Association in Paris in 2012, and especially from the incisive comments offered by Benoît de L'Estoile from the Centre National de la Recherche Scientifique (CNRS) as the discussant for our panels. We are similarly indebted to Lee Baker from Duke University for his generous but critical assessment of our work in his response to our presentation of the project's preliminary findings at the American Anthropology Association's annual conference in Chicago in 2013. The presentation was sponsored by the association's Council for Museum Anthropology and its Society for Visual Anthropology. We acknowledge our appreciation of the association's support for our work.

While the conception, development, and writing of this book have been a collective enterprise, this has also required a division of writing and editorial responses. Tony Bennett wrote the introduction and was the lead writer for chapter 1, in collaboration with Conal McCarthy. Ben Dibley was the lead writer for chapter 2, in collaboration with Rodney Harrison. Harrison was the lead writer for chapter 3, in collaboration Ben Dibley. Ira Jacknis was the lead writer for chapter 4, in collaboration with Tony Bennett. Fiona Cameron and Conal McCarthy jointly wrote chapter 5. Nélia Dias was the lead writer for chapter 6, in collaboration with Tony Bennett. Rodney Harrison was the lead writer for the conclusion, with additional input from Tony Bennett and

Conal McCarthy. Ben Dibley coordinated the compilation of the references. Conal McCarthy superintended the production of the figures and their accompanying captions across all the chapters and the conclusion. He also oversaw the process of obtaining the permissions and the artwork for the figures. Tony Bennett and Rodney Harrison were jointly responsible for the overall coordination of the book. Their work was enormously assisted by the extremely careful and detailed copy-editing input from Kim Miller. We therefore gratefully acknowledge the value of Kim's contribution in this regard.

SOME OF THE CHAPTERS DRAW on material previously published elsewhere, although in all cases this has been substantially edited and revised in the form in which it appears in the present volume.

Chapter 1 draws on material first published as Tony Bennett, Ben Dibley, and Rodney Harrison, "Introduction: Anthropology, Collecting and Colonial Governmentalities," special issue, *History and Anthropology* 25, no. 2 (2014): 137–49; and Tony Bennett, "Liberal Government and the Practical History of Anthropology," *History and Anthropology* 25, no. 2 (2014): 150–70. Chapter 2 draws on material first published as Ben Dibley, "Assembling an Anthropological Actor: Anthropological Assemblage and Colonial Government in Papua," *History and Anthropology* 25, no. 2 (2014): 263–79. Chapter 3 draws on material first published as Rodney Harrison, "Observing, Collecting and Governing 'Ourselves' and 'Others': Mass-Observation's Fieldwork *Agencements*," *History and Anthropology* 25, no. 2 (2014): 227–45; and Ben Dibley and Michelle Kelly, "Morale and Mass-Observation: Governing the Affective Atmosphere on the Home-Front," *Museum and Society* 13, no. 1 (2015): 22–41. Chapter 4 draws on Ira Jacknis, "'America Is Our Field': Anthropological Regionalism at the American Museum of Natural History, 1895–1945," *Museum and Society* 13, no. 1 (2015): 52–71; and Tony Bennett, "Cultural Studies and the Culture Concept," *Cultural Studies* 29, no. 4 (2015): 546–68. Chapter 5 includes material first published as Fiona Ruth Cameron, "From 'Dead Things' to Immutable, Combinable Mobiles: H.D. Skinner, the Otago Museum and University and the Governance of Māori Populations," *History and Anthropology* 25, no. 2 (2014): 208–26; Fiona Ruth Cameron and Conal McCarthy, "Two Anthropological Assemblages: New Zealand Museums, Native Policy, and Māori 'Culture Areas' and 'Adaptation,'" *Museum and Society* 13, no. 1 (2015): 88–106; Conal McCarthy, "'Empirical Anthropologists Advocating Cultural Adjustments': The Anthropological Governance of Āpirana Ngata and the Native Affairs Department," *History and Anthropology* 25, no.

2 (2014): 280–95; and Conal McCarthy, "To Foster and Encourage the Study and Practice of Māori Arts and Crafts: Indigenous Material Culture, Colonial Culture and Museums in New Zealand," in *Craft and Community: The Material Culture of Place and Politics, 19th–20th Century*, edited by Janice Helland, Beverly Lemire, and Alena Buis (Aldershot, UK: Ashgate, 2014b), 59–82. Chapter 6 includes material first published as Nélia Dias, "Rivet's Mission in Colonial Indochina (1931–1932) or the Failure to Create an Ethnographic Museum," *History and Anthropology* 25, no. 2 (2014): 189–207; and Nélia Dias, "From French Indochina to Paris and Back Again: The Circulation of Objects, People, and Information, 1900–1932," *Museum and Society* 13, no. 1 (2015): 7–21. It also draws on "Collecting, Instructing, Governing: Fields, Publics, Milieus," chapter 3 of Tony Bennett, *Making Culture, Changing Society* (London: Routledge, 2013).

The concerns of this study are located at the intersections of museum studies and the history of anthropology. Our primary interest with regard to the former focuses on the varied ways in which museums act on social worlds. These include, but are not limited to, their exhibition practices, which we consider alongside the ways in which museums obtain and order their collections. Our interests relating to the latter concern how its practices have been shaped by its relations to mechanisms for the governance of populations. We bring these two sets of questions together to examine the connections between museums and anthropology associated with the articulation of a new set of relations between the practices of collecting, ordering, and governing that characterized the development of anthropological fieldwork in the closing decades of the nineteenth century and the first half of the twentieth century.

We examine these practices through a set of case studies that illustrate the different social and governmental logics underlying their interconnections in different sociohistorical contexts. The historical horizon encompassed by these case studies stretches from the Torres Strait Island expeditions led by Alfred Cort Haddon in the 1880s and 1890s through to the fieldwork missions of the Musée de l'Homme (MH) in the 1930s and the influence of the Boasian culture concept on the development of American assimilationist policies in the 1930s and 1940s. We take in, en route, the fieldwork expeditions of Baldwin Spencer and Frank Gillen to Central Australia; the varied versions of Māori culture informing a connected set of collecting, ordering, and governing practices in early twentieth-century Aotearoa/New Zealand; and the role of the Papuan Official Collection established by Hubert Murray in Papua. If this last case stretches our definition of museums beyond its conventional limits, the same is true of our inclusion of Mass-Observation (M-O) among our case studies. This was, however, a project whose collecting practices partly derived from and resonated with anthropological fieldwork, while its conception as an "anthropology of ourselves" was echoed in the projects of the Musée des Arts et Traditions Populaires, which brought the methods developed by the MH in its overseas fieldwork missions to bear on the study of France's rural populations. The role of M-O in the governance of morale in wartime Britain was also partly shaped by its interactions with the wartime mobilization of anthropology in the United States.

Our purpose, however, is not to provide a comprehensive comparative analysis of the relations among museums (or similar collections), anthropology, and governing practices across these different case studies. That said, we have been surprised at the extent to which the literature available on these matters has rarely ranged across national boundaries. We therefore highlight those similarities and differences among our case studies that are most striking from the point of view of our lines of inquiry. We also stress some little-noted connections among them, particularly those bearing on the role that the Boasian culture concept played in the political projects of Māori intellectuals in the 1920s and 1930s and into the early 1940s. We are also aware that the traditions we examine do not exhaust the course of early twentieth-century anthropological fieldwork. There is, most obviously, the parallel work of Bronislaw Malinowski in Britain and Adolf Bastian in Germany, whose work, through its influence on Franz Boas, helped to shape the trajectories of American anthropology. While we draw on these where they touch on our concerns, we do not consider them in any detail.

We should also note that our focus on early twentieth-century fieldwork traditions does not imply acceptance of an unbridgeable divide between the pre- and postfieldwork moments in the historical development of anthropology. This aspect of the discipline's early twentieth-century professional rhetoric has since been called into question on numerous grounds that we shall review in due course. Nonetheless, the development of fieldwork practices at this time did have a significant impact on what was gathered from different sites of anthropological collection, on how it was collected, and on how such collections were relayed to centers of calculation. These practices also constituted, in the figure of the field-worker, a new kind of authority that called earlier forms of anthropological authority—notably that of the armchair savant—into question. We are, however, wary of the further suggestion, predicated on the strength of the connection between armchair anthropology and the so-called museum phase of anthropology, that the early twentieth-century development of anthropological fieldwork brought about a severance of this connection to the museum as anthropologists increasingly took up positions in a developing university system.

The American case represents perhaps the clearest shift in this direction. Boas is the key figure here. His departure from the American Museum of Natural History (AMNH) in 1905, his critique of the comparative method for museum displays advocated by Otis T. Mason, and his focus on postgraduate training during his years at Columbia: all of these make him the emblematic figure for those narratives that argue that by the early twentieth century anthropology had abandoned the museum for the university. Such accounts neglect the continuing commitment to fieldwork shown by Clark Wissler, Boas's successor at the AMNH. Boas's case was also far from typical internationally: the MH, for example, was the primary institutional site for French fieldwork in the 1930s; the expeditions of Spencer and Gillen set off from and returned to the National Museum of Victoria; and in New Zealand the fieldwork of Thomas Cheeseman, Henry Devenish Skinner, Āpirana Ngata, and Peter Buck (Te Rangihīroa) depended on their relations to, respectively, the Auckland, Otago, and Dominion Museums. A part of what was involved in the Australian and New Zealand cases was the displacement of the earlier flow of indigenous materials from settler-colonial contexts to London and other metropolitan centers as in situ museums became the primary sites for the collection of such materials and for the exercise of more local forms of anthropological authority.

However, if museums remained important sites for the exercise of new forms of authority, their roles in this regard also changed significantly. The connections between anthropological and natural history collections loosened; the hold of evolutionary assumptions on museum displays weakened relative to those stressing the distinguishing properties of indigenous cultures; the influence of physical anthropology declined without entirely disappearing; the increasing attention given to the collection of stories, myths, and grammars as well as phonographic recordings and films, relative to material objects and anthropometric measurements, transformed museum collections and their relations to other archives; the connections between museums and practices of colonial governance became increasingly important, while the growing popularity of "anthropology at home" projects also embroiled ethnographic museums in debates and practices directed toward the governance of metropolitan populations. The role of the field-worker as a new point of connection between colonizing and indigenous worlds also opened up new challenges and prospects for indigenous agency operating through these new forms of contact.

Our object of inquiry, then, is constituted by the connections between the processes of collecting, ordering, and governing as these were articulated across the relations between the varied sites of collection, the centers of calculation, and the practices of a range of governmental agencies involved in the management of colonized, metropolitan, and settler populations. We explore these processes by drawing on and developing the insights suggested by three related traditions of inquiry. We approach processes of *collecting* through the concept of fieldwork *agencements*, which we derive from post-Deleuzian assemblage theory and use to analyze the agency of human and non-human actors in different sites of collection and in the passage of things, texts, and data from those sites of collection to centers of calculation. We approach processes of *ordering* by drawing on the approaches to centers of calculation developed in the Latourian tradition of science studies and on the "archival turn" that has characterized recent revisionist approaches to the histories of anthropology and other collecting practices. A good deal of our attention here will focus on the ordering practices of museums and the material technologies—means of accessioning, index and file cards, and exhibition practices—through which these operated. We approach processes of *governing* through the optic of Michel Foucault's account of liberal government as a set of knowledge practices and technologies that work through the forms of freedom they organize. This provides a means of engaging with anthropology as a "liberal discipline" that has worked through its differential distribution of capacities for freedom across varied populations. Its adjudications in these regards have been crucial in distinguishing ways of governing that operate through liberal forms of subjecthood in relation to some populations and issues while favoring discriminatory biopolitical approaches in other contexts. In developing this approach, we pay particular attention to the "transactional realities" through which anthropology's role in governmental practices was organized. We borrow this term from Foucault to refer to the concepts and technologies that epistemological authorities produce and through which their forms of action on social worlds are mediated. In the case of the cultural disciplines, including anthropology, we interpret such transactional realities—of race, culture, morale, and tradition, for example—as the "working surfaces on the social" through which those disciplines engaged with the management of populations.

We offer a fuller elaboration of how we interpret and apply these concepts and the traditions of inquiry from which they derive in chapter 1. Our main concern in that chapter is, however, to give a more concrete sense of how the relationships between the processes of collecting, ordering, and governing operate across our case studies. We do so by means of four vignettes organized around emblematic museum exhibits: Spencer's display connecting the development of the Aboriginal throwing stick to that of the boomerang at the National Museum of Victoria, Boas's life group in the Hall of Northwest Coast Indians at the AMNH, the introductory vitrine in the Senegal section of the Sub-Saharan Africa Hall at the MH, and two exhibits in Wellington's Dominion Museum in 1936 that illustrate different interpretations of "the Maori as he was" and of how he or she is or should be. We show how these exhibits were informed by specific processes of collecting, how they subjected the materials they brought together to distinctive kinds of ordering, and how they formed a part of processes of governing informed by particular governmental rationalities: that is, particular combinations of the ends of governing, the means by which these should be pursued, and their distribution across varied populations.

We then look more closely at the social and historical contexts for each of our case studies. We draw on assemblage theory to engage with the ways in which, in their early twentieth-century forms, anthropological museums operated at the intersections of different sociomaterial networks: those connecting them to the public spheres of the major metropolitan powers, those linking them to the institutions and practices of colonial administration, and those constituting the relations among the museum, the field, and the university. We also consider the different disciplinary connections that anthropology entered into as its affiliations with natural history loosened: the importance of archaeology in the United States compared to its virtual absence in Australia, for example, and anthropology's relations to differently configured traditions of folklore studies in France, Britain, and the United States. The chapter then reviews the colonial formations that provided the settings for anthropological practices in different national contexts. All of our case studies are shaped by the end of the conquest period of colonialism and, in the settler contexts of Australia, New Zealand, and the United States, the cessation of warlike relations across colonial frontiers and the movement toward more regularized forms of exchange between colonizers and colonized. The French case reflects a different dynamic in being shaped by the extractive logic of France's overseas colonies. We focus particularly on the complex ways in which the governmental rationalities in evidence across our case studies were informed by different articulations of the relations between liberal and biopolitical forms of government.

Our second chapter develops this last line of argument further by exploring the contrasting rationalities for the governance of indigenous populations that were developed in the Australian-administered territories of Papua and the Northern Territory. Both modalities of rule were in operation in these territories but in rather different combinations. Our points of departure for broaching these questions are the ethnographic collections associated with two figures central to Australian "native policy": the anthropologist, museum director, and intermittent colonial administrator Baldwin Spencer, and the lawyer, anthropological patron, and long-serving lieutenant governor of Papua Hubert Murray. Spencer's notion of race helped to shape a biopolitics of assimilation whereby the indigene was to be absorbed into the national population through a program of bio-cultural "up-lift" or "whitening" through which subsequent generations would reach the threshold of liberal subjecthood. By contrast, Murray's notion of "native culture" informed a biopolitics of protection to preserve the health and wealth of native populations and so sustain an indigenous economy independent from wage labor. This involved programs of sanitation, education, and so on by which "the better brown men"—candidates for self-improvement—would be distinguished from the unredeemable savages, who would be left to die out.

Chapter 3 focuses on M-O's project of an "anthropology of ourselves." It argues that M-O's fieldwork practices were distinctive in the ways in which they brought together ethnographic methods of collecting and assembling (largely, but not exclusively, drawn from colonial anthropological contexts) with new mechanisms of collective self-watching. Drawing on arguments relating oligoptic visual economies to liberal technologies of government, we show how M-O was implicated in the development of the notion of "the mass," giving this a distinctive interpretation as a conception of the population as self-knowing and self-regulating. We also show how the concept of civilian morale, as the barometer by which the mood of the mass might be measured, acted as an example of the practical application of an "anthropology of ourselves" that aimed to manipulate the conduct of the population by acting on its milieus. What was most innovative about M-O was the way in which it emphasized new, collectivized forms of self-knowledge that sought to make the population self-governing. At the same time, M-O's practices had a biopolitical register that, in seeking to influence the affective dimension of the population, targeted the psycho-corporeality of the masses as a new surface of social management.

Chapter 4 follows the political career of the culture concept, which was initially elaborated by Boas but then subjected to reinterpretation—and to varied forms of practical use—by his successors. We focus particularly on the role played by the concept of culture areas in relation to the fieldwork missions organized by the AMNH. While these were initially organized by Boas and focused on the Northwest Coast, we look more particularly at the American Plains expeditions organized by Clark Wissler, showing how he maintained and developed the relativistic thrust of Boasian anthropology in spite of the constraints imposed by the museum's eugenicist president, Henry Fairfield Osborn, and his own eugenic sympathies. For Wissler, as for Boas, culture areas were not essentialist collections of peoples and cultures but relativistic constructions: spatial arrays that expressed historical encounters and developments. The ordering of anthropological materials by culture areas became the basic rationale for ordering the AMNH's public galleries, contributing significantly to the elaboration of the culture concept, which progressively displaced eugenic conceptions of population in providing an alternative basis for programs of cultural assimilation. Other students of Boas, notably Alfred Kroeber and Ruth Benedict, extended culture-area theory from a technique of museum ordering into broader theories of cultural patterning. We consider how these qualities of the culture concept informed white nativist conceptions according to which American society would creatively transform itself by absorbing immigrant cultures in an assimilationist logic focused on the relations between different periods of European migration at the expense of African Americans and Native Americans.

Chapter 5 investigates the connections between the processes of collecting, ordering, and governing in Aotearoa/New Zealand in relation to the rationalities of rule that emerged between the 1900s and 1945. These were organized around the notion of "the Maori as he was," a concept that referenced the preservation of pre-European Māori life and the construction of a classic Māori cultural tradition. In its varied career, this notion articulated a changing set of governmental rationalities ranging from liberal government practices detailing the freedoms and limits of the Māori population to the biopolitical governance of Māori bodies. Indigenous actors were closely involved in these intertwined histories of museums, fieldwork, and colonial government. We show how the notion of "the Maori as he was," in the first instance, was linked to salvage/memorial and racial assimilationist projects and, subsequently, to Wissler's notion of culture areas. This notion, which was also shaped by the influence of the Boasian culture concept, became a lever for developing Māori potential for liberal subjecthood within an emerging nation. These changing rationales are examined through four sets of fieldwork–museum relations that offer different takes on the project of preserving "the Maori as he was" in order to shape him or equip Māori to shape themselves as they ought to be.

Chapter 6 examines the governmental deployments of anthropology both "at home and away" in Greater France as represented by the interwar fieldwork and exhibition practices of the MH. Whereas the critical literature on the MH has mostly focused on its relations to France's West African colonies, we concentrate on its fieldwork missions in former French Indochina, and on the creation of a satellite institution, the Musée de l'Homme Hanoi. Assessments of the role played by the MH in processes of governing have varied from seeing it as a key part of a developing institutional complex of colonial governance to interpreting it as relatively detached from colonizing processes. By engaging with these debates through the Indochinese case, where museums and civic institutions coexisted with native political institutions, we examine the different logics of government at work in metropolitan and colonial contexts. At the MH in Paris the Indochinese collections were displayed for the metropolitan public in accordance with the principles of a new humanistic universalism that viewed the world as made up of different, but ostensibly equal, racial types and cultures. At the Hanoi museum such collections were primarily addressed to administrators, tourists, and colonial personnel, differentiating races in terms of their degree of development in ways that connected with local imperatives of governance by acting on the milieus conditioning ways of life. We also look at how the Musée des Arts et Traditions Populaires translated the principles of scientific colonialism into programs for managing the populations of regional France. The currency of *les petites patries* proved particularly important in this respect, designating regional homelands as key sites for the management of identities in both France and Indochina.

We conclude by reviewing the light that our organizing themes of collecting, ordering, and governing have thrown on the relationships between anthropology and practices of social governance in the first half of the twentieth century. We then explore more recent historical and contemporary concerns in which the legacies of this period are evident. We look at how these paved the way for postwar forms of multicultural governance by (to different degrees) displacing hierarchical conceptions of race in favor of more plural and cultural conceptions of difference. We also discuss the emergence of the concept of "indigeneity" as a transnational actor, and its influence on the subsequent indigenization of museum practices, especially in settler colonies. The ongoing significance of the culture-area concept in providing templates for the development of Aboriginal land councils in Australia and of Māori social governance structures in Aotearoa/New Zealand is also considered. We look finally at how the divisions between populations produced by colonial governmental rationalities have continued to inform the segmentations of populations within settler-colonial contexts. We look particularly at the contested history of Australia's Northern Territory Intervention, in which measures relating to law enforcement, land tenure, and welfare provision have been targeted at specific Northern Territory Aboriginal communities judged to lack the capacities required for participation in a liberal political community.

CHAPTER ONE

COLLECTING, ORDERING, GOVERNING

We begin with four museum displays that exemplify the connections we want to explore between how the processes of collecting in "the field" were organized, how the texts and materials brought back from such sites of collection were ordered at the centers of calculation where they were gathered together, and how these collecting and ordering practices were shaped by, and helped to shape, practices of governing. Two of the displays belong to the early years of the period covered by our study: Baldwin Spencer's conjectural series connecting the evolution of the Australian Aboriginal throwing stick to that of the boomerang, displayed at the National Museum of Victoria (NMV) in 1901, and the life group that Franz Boas arranged for the Hall of Northwest Coast Indians at the American Museum of Natural History (AMNH) in 1896. And two belong to the later years of the period: the Maori Ethnology Gallery in 1936 at Wellington's Dominion Museum (DM) and the introductory display in the Senegal section of the Sub-Saharan Africa Hall at the Musée de l'Homme (MH), which opened in 1938. There are relations of historical affiliation between these displays. The arrangements at the DM drew on the principles of typological exhibitions, which also informed Spencer's display, whereas the vitrine at the MH rejected these principles in favor of a more holistic approach to the exhibition of ways of life that testifies to Boas's influence on Paul Rivet, the director of the MH. It is, however, the qualities that distinguish these displays from one another, and the different relations of collecting, ordering, and governing that inform them, that are our focus here.

ARRESTED HISTORIES

Spencer's fidelity to the principles of typological displays thus matters less than how he adapted these to the particular circumstances of early twentieth-century Australia. Spencer had worked with both Henry Balfour and Edward Burnett Tylor in arranging the Pitt-Rivers collection in accordance with typological principles on its removal to the University Museum at Oxford (Petch 2009). These characteristically resulted in long evolutionary sequences in which each object, abstracted from its originating milieu, represented a stage in a universal sequence of development leading from the simple and primitive to the developed and complex. Such displays, in A. H. L. F. Pitt Rivers's interpretation, were driven by an aspiration toward completeness: each stage of evolutionary advancement would ideally be represented by an appropriate object so that the story of evolution might be told as one of smooth and unidirectional advancement, uninterrupted by any reversals or gaps suggesting a leap from one stage to the next.[1] Pitt Rivers's exhibition of weaponry was a case in point, telling a story of (in principle) uninterrupted evolution from the Aboriginal throwing stick to the medieval musket (Pitt Rivers 1891).

Spencer followed these principles inasmuch as his conjectural evolutionary series leading from the throwing stick to the boomerang, and thence to the Aboriginal sword, depended on the specimens selected for this purpose being brought together from varied locations as part of a pan-tribal Aboriginal developmental sequence (figure 1.1). This was, however, a self-enclosed evolutionary series that had already come to an end. In writing to Tylor, Spencer described it as a "record of the Aborigine," of a history that was past.[2] While occasionally conceding that Aboriginal culture had shown signs of autonomous development in the past, Spencer argued that it had altogether lost its momentum in the present (Bennett 2011). Spencer's (1901) introduction to the guide to the NMV's ethnographic collections interpreted these as relics of "the most primitive of existing races" (7), representative of "palæolithic man" (10) and testifying to a series of nondevelopments (no cultivation of the land, no domestic animals, no writing) that, attributed to the isolation of Indigenous Australians from the flows of competition and their subjection to the tyranny of custom, added up to a frozen history.

Frozen and done with. This was not a history that in any way connected with or fed into Australia's fledgling national culture. On the colonial fron-

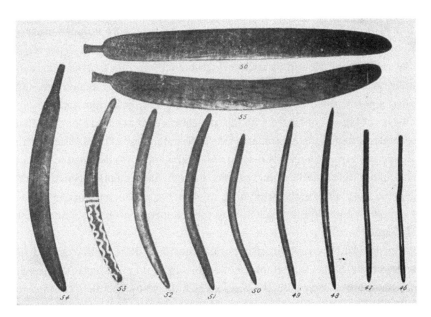

FIGURE 1.1 "Series showing possible development of boomerang from ordinary throwing stick, and of sword from boomerang." Reproduced from Baldwin Spencer, *Guide to the Australian Ethnographical Collection in the National Museum of Victoria* (Melbourne: Robert S. Bain, Government Printer, 1901), plate 4.

The exhibition constructs a hypothetical sequence for the development of the Aboriginal throwing stick into the boomerang as (moving from the right), a rough crooked stick becomes straightened, then rounded, and then curved, eventually acquiring a handle, which serves as a point of connection to the two double-handed swords running across the top of the exhibit. Some of the items had been collected by Spencer during his first extended visit to Central Australia in 1896 to work with Frank Gillen among the Arrernte, but these were exhibited alongside items gathered by other means from other sites of collection in Western Australia, Queensland, and Northern Australia. The exhibition formed part of a special gallery devoted to the exhibition of Aboriginal weapons, implements, and ceremonial objects. Each of the displays of weaponry—of clubs, shields, and spear throwers—was governed by a similar logic. Writing to Tylor on September 5, 1900, Spencer informed him that the exhibition was conceived as "a kind of record of the Aborigines which the ordinary public can understand and take an interest in" (Tylor Papers, Box 13a, Spencer S16, Pitt Rivers Museum).

tier, as opposed to the armchair distance of Oxford, the maintenance of a gap between the settler and indigenous populations had become increasingly important. For a good part of the nineteenth century this gap had been viewed as potentially bridgeable via civilizational programs designed to carry Aboriginal and Torres Strait Islander peoples across it. By 1901, however, it had come to be viewed as an unbridgeable chasm, one that was increasingly racialized.[3] While Spencer recognized linguistic, cultural, political, and physiognomic distinctions between different tribes, he minimized the significance of these compared with the consequences of a shared bloodline that separated Indigenous Australians and settlers along racial lines.[4] Faced with competition from a superior race, the Aboriginal race was destined to die out although individual Aboriginal people, through managed miscegenation and generations of progressive whitening, might serve as switch points, initiating a lineage that would eventually lead to the acquisition of Australianness (see McGregor 1997).

Spencer had been appointed honorary director of the NMV in 1899, and his arrangement of its ethnographic collections in 1901 coincided with the Act of Federation. In preparing the way for the hitherto independent colonies to become part of a political federation, this act constituted the first step in establishing a national governmental domain (Rowse 1992) that was also defined in racial terms. The Constitution reflected this by excluding Indigenous Australians from the census that was established for "reckoning the numbers of the people" of both the Commonwealth and state levels of government, and from the provision that empowered the Commonwealth to "make special laws" for "the people of any race" (cit. McGregor 2011: xviii). While these two exclusions are seemingly contradictory, Russell McGregor articulates the logic underlying them: "active measures had to be taken to safeguard white Australia against colored aliens, but not against colored indigenes, since they were expiring independently of government action or inaction" (2011: xxi). Destined for extinction, Aboriginal people no more needed to be counted than white Australia needed special laws to protect against them. They were already sequestered by a racial dynamic that needed just an administrative tweak here and there to expedite their passage into history. Spencer's display was thus emblematic of a political logic in which earlier secular and missionary civilizational strategies aimed at lifting Indigenous Australians were being progressively displaced by state-directed programs aimed at eliminating Aborigines as a race. While "full bloods" were to be assigned to reserves for such time as they continued to exist, different possibilities were opened up for half-castes in a conception of assimilation that sought to transform the racial constitution of the Aboriginal population through programs of selective breeding aimed at the progressive dilution of Aboriginal bloodlines, thereby "breeding out the color."

LIFELESS GROUPS

Boas's life group at the AMNH (figure 1.2), first exhibited in 1896, reflected a different set of relations between the processes of collecting, ordering, and governing. A critic of both the general premises of evolutionary theory and—with some qualifications—biological conceptions of race, Boas had already challenged the conceptual basis of evolutionary museum displays in his telling criticisms of Otis T. Mason's exhibitions at the Smithsonian Institution in Washington (Boas 1887a, 1887b). Rather than excerpting artifacts from their place within a particular society to represent stages in universal sequences of evolutionary development, Boas insisted that such materials derived their meaning only from their relations to one another within a particular way of life or culture. By no means his invention, the life group drew on, and mixed, the conventions of natural history habitat displays, the illusionistic techniques of dioramas and panoramas, the earlier tradition of mannequins produced for Scandinavian folk museums, the mise-en-scène of theatrical tableaux, and the emerging properties of the cinema screen (A. Griffiths 2002: chap. 1). It assembled the materials collected during fieldwork to exhibit them as interacting components of a particular cultural whole whose constituent elements derived their meaning only from their relations to one another and the uses to which they were put within a way of life that was historically, rather than essentially, connected to a particular locality. Although the AMNH's Hall of Northwest Coast Indians brought together collections that had been acquired earlier through purchases or expeditions, by far the greater part of its exhibits were collected by Boas in the course of the museum's Jesup North Pacific Expedition.[5] The items displayed in the cedar-fabrication life group—which occupied the center of the hall—derived mainly from his fieldwork among the Kwakiutl (Kwakwaka'wakw).

The procedures regulating the movement of collections from field to museum were distinctive in other ways. The preparation of life groups often involved an artist accompanying the anthropologist into the field, selecting a spot based on its scenic or aesthetic qualities as well as its scientific value, photographing the "natural" setting to provide a backdrop for the immediate

FIGURE 1.2 American Museum of Natural History, Hall of Northwest Coast Indians, ca. 1904. 351, American Museum of Natural History, New York. Courtesy of American Museum of Natural History.

———

Cedar bark being shredded and hung to dry, the implements needed for the shredding operation, the repair of fishing nets, salmon baskets in the background, a young child in a hanging cradle with cedar-bark bedding, the weave on the women's blankets, decorative ankle bracelets, the gendered division of labor between the woman shredding the cedar bark and the man beating it, the placing of the child next to the women and at some distance from the man: in these ways the relations between the artifacts and the mannequins integrate the former into specific uses that evoke a particular way of life with its distinctive internal divisions, patterns, and forms of adaptation to a natural environment.

———

scene, constructing a miniature model of the scene while in the field, and taking life casts of the faces and, occasionally, the bodies of the Native Americans selected as models for the mannequins (A. Griffiths 2002: 19–20). Boas frequently modeled the poses he wanted to be reproduced by the plaster cast makers; he also corresponded with local theatrical agencies for samples of Indian wigs to experiment with before ordering the ones that produced the effect he wanted.[6] However, the verisimilitude this produced went hand in hand with the dehistoricization of the subject: the effect of the Boasian mannequin, Bill Brown has argued, was that "of an uncannily lifelike body in motion but out of time" (2003: 95). The figures in Boas's life groups are absorbed in their work and among themselves, composing a scene that is distanced from the present: lifelike but no longer living.

In spite of their differences, both Spencer's evolutionary displays and Boas's life groups dehistoricized indigenous peoples. It was widely believed in early twentieth-century America that Native Americans were destined either to disappear, withering on the vine of history in special reservations, or to merge with the rest of the population through miscegenation (Baker 2010; Conn 2004). Boas shared this view.[7] The arrival of new cohorts of immigrants from southern Europe and Asia pressed on questions of whiteness differently, presenting a challenge to America's Nordic white nativism that elicited a succession of eugenic strategies for differentiating America's earlier and later immigrant populations along racial lines. The AMNH would later, under Henry Fairfield Osborn, play a key role in the development of eugenicist policies. While this postdated Boas's departure from the museum in 1905, its anthropology department, under Clark Wissler (Boas's successor and also a former student of his), continued to collect Native American materials and to exhibit these in ways that stressed their differences from one another in terms of the configurations of the relations between the elements making up their ways of life or cultures. This conception of cultures as plural that Boas, drawing on his German training, brought to the American anthropological scene was to become the defining concept of American anthropology through the developments and transformations to which it was subjected in the work of Wissler and a whole generation of Boas's students. Yet this was a paradoxical history. For while the culture concept was developed on the basis of fieldwork studies of Native American cultures on the Northwest Coast, in the Plains, and in the Southwest, it functioned as the key operator in an "anthropology at home and away" project that found its main sphere of governmental application in the northeastern states, where it was invoked to manage the process of assimilating new generations of migrants to the white nativist culture established by earlier generations of predominantly northern European settlers. It was a paradoxical history, too, in that the intersection between this culture concept and the continuing influence of a residual set of biological race categories operated to exclude both Native Americans and African Americans from the machineries of assimilation that the culture concept helped to establish.

ENVIRONMENTAL OBJECTS

This bears on our third display: the vitrine introducing the Sub-Saharan Africa Hall at the MH. Melville Herskovits, one of Boas's students, suggested that Boas's principles of museum exhibition had been "refined and extended—but not superseded— . . . by Rivet and his associates at the Musée de l'homme" (1953: 21). Paul Rivet, the director of the MH, also acknowledged his indebtedness to Boas. "Franz Boas was a master," he wrote. "Thanks to him I was able to imagine what a real Museum of Mankind should be, that is, a panoramic museum where the visitor would find the full portrait of races, civilizations and languages in the world" (quoted in Conklin 2008: 250). Yet it is the differences between Boas's life groups and the MH's ethnographic vitrines that most stand out. These partly reflect the relations among museum, field, and exhibition gallery that were developed at the MH to secure a particular set of capacities for its anthropological objects as distinctive objects of knowledge and public pedagogy.[8] Their scientific validation via a number of procedures—the program of instructions issued to the museum's missions (*Instructions* 1931) and the multiperspectival techniques of fieldwork observation developed by Marcel Griaule (1933), for example—distinguished those objects from both curiosities and aesthetic collections of fine-arts objects by investing them with the distinctive epistemological value of the document. This imbued them with a distinctive moral force and authority derived from what Christine Laurière calls an "environmentalist conception of the object" (2008: 416), in which the object testifies both to the force of the environmental factors that shaped it and to the creativity of human practice. When translated into the somewhat austere principles of the MH's *muséographie claire*, this conferred on its anthropological objects a distinctive pedagogic quality that aimed to foster respect for other cultures as evidencing a shared human capacity for creativity.[9] At the same time, such cultures came into view as forms of life that could be changed by reshaping their conditioning environments.

The introductory display in the Senegal section exemplifies how these principles were applied (figure 1.3). What is most immediately striking here is the lack of any attempt to create an effect of verisimilitude in the robed figure displayed in the vitrine. In contrast to Boas's life group, where tools and implements are integrated into their use in a way of life, the tools here lie inert and unused. This reflected the rational didacticism of the MH's display principles, manifested in the relegation of all large objects to the bottom of the display case so that they would not obstruct the clear lines of sight needed to ensure that everything in the vitrine would be plainly visible. If Boas's life group exhibits a way of life self-absorbedly turned in on itself, the MH's display more forcefully references a set of relations between a people and an environment.

These relations were the focus for colonial action. While paying lip service to the universal recognition of different cultures in the name of "Man," the MH formed part of an apparatus of colonial humanism that accorded the varied populations of Greater France (roughly, the population of France and its colonies) different civic statuses and political rights.[10] This usually meant no or very few rights for the indigenous populations of France's overseas colonies. These were regarded as being separated from French citizens not by innate racial characteristics, as in Spencer's differentiation of Aborigines from white Australians, but by a temporal lag, one they were judged to be incapable of overcoming by their own actions. The relations between such peoples and their environments were thus regarded as the proper focus for remedial programs of colonial improvement aimed at developing those cultures that were perceived as still lagging behind; the goal was to eventually reach a point at which they might be admitted into the polity of Greater France on equal terms. As for the skulls, these partly reflected the MH's commitment to the "solidarity of physical anthropology, ethnography, sociology and linguistics" and to the reunification of "osteological and ethnographic collections" (Rivet, Lester, and Rivière 1935: 515, 529). However, they also played a role similar to that played by the residual racial categories of the Boasian tradition in suggesting a set of anatomically grounded racial differences underlying different cultures and retaining an implicit hierarchy between them. This aspect of the MH's practice, Alice Conklin (2013: 148–57) argues, also resonated with the racialized principles of French immigration policy by drawing on such racial typologies in distinguishing between desirable and undesirable immigrants—with the evidence of skull types favoring Nordic immigrants most and Arab immigrants least.

FIGURE 1.3 "Musée de l'Homme, vitrine 71: Afrique noire, Senegal." QB53498, Musée du quai Branly, Paris. Courtesy of the Musée du quai Branly/Scala.

———

Formally opened in 1938, the exhibits of the Musée de l'Homme reflected an ongoing program of reform at the Musée d'Ethnographie du Trocadéro carried out by Anatole Lewitzky and Georges Henri Rivière under the direction of Paul Rivet. The program was oriented to the production of ultramodern and rationalized displays that would make the variable relations between humans and their environments transparent. The texts, photographs, artifacts, and skulls are arranged so that each of these is fully visible; there are no conflicting lines of sight. The exoticism of mannequins as a prop for the exhibition of costumes is jettisoned in favor of the costumes' suspension via invisible nylon strings. There are no diagonal arrangements to disrupt the horizontal lines of sight in ways that might confuse and fatigue the visitor. These principles were implemented in all of the galleries at the Musée de l'Homme except for the Hall of Treasures, which retained an aesthetic focus on the singularity of the artifacts exhibited.

———

We look next at how the concerns of American and European museums played out in New Zealand, particularly with regard to the development of new forms of indigenous agency by a range of Māori actors. On August 1, 1936, the DM and National Art Gallery opened in Wellington. The Maori Ethnology Gallery (figure 1.4) was more formally anthropological than the adjoining Maori Hall (figure 1.5). The museum's director, W. R. B. Oliver, had determined that each department should have a separate "exhibition hall" with a distinct architectural treatment "to amplify the exhibits on the floor, the object being to tell in the best way the story of the exhibits" (1944: 20). He and his colleague S. F. Markham were critical of crowded permanent exhibits and particularly lamented the "lack of technological displays" showing the manufacture of Māori objects, as these displays have "distinct educational value" (Markham and Oliver 1933: 93). The museum's "new" approach to displays and education programs was also influenced by the U.S. Carnegie Corporation, which funded museum education and libraries in New Zealand from the 1930s. This sponsorship opened up New Zealand museums to American influences, as the models employed in training workshops were drawn from both pre- and post-Boasian life groups (McQueen 1942).[11] Visitors liked the change from the traditional rows of specimens to "the modern method of making the displays instructive as well as attractive."[12] That "instruction" still clearly pointed to evolutionary ideas, but tempered by a capacity for indigenous acculturation; one critic wrote that the "the development of human society" exhibited at the DM was "epitomized" in the Māori people's development from "neolithic simplicity to civilization" (Inch 1936).

In the Maori Ethnology Gallery, tall glass pier cases and "Carnegie" table cases were arranged alternately down the center of the space, leaving the side walls largely free for the display of pictures and maps "illustrative of Maori life and customs."[13] The overall aim was to reconstruct the "Maori as he was," in line with museum ethnologist Elsdon Best's (1924b) book by that title, which was compiled from his extensive fieldwork in Māori communities. The arrangement of some objects within the cases was, however, still typological: there were cases of clothing, weapons, and gear for fishing and bird catching. Artifacts were placed on glass shelves, functioning as illustrations of the extended labels beside them. Display here was a by-product of the archive, the collections and texts that were the ethnologist's primary interest, with the public halls being treated like an excerpt from a research monograph—a book on a wall. In this case the displays were selected from the fieldwork of

FIGURE 1.4 Maori Ethnology Gallery, Dominion Museum, Wellington, 1936. B.5622, Te Papa, Wellington. Courtesy of the Museum of New Zealand Te Papa Tongarewa.

This photograph shows a typical materialist approach to the representation of native culture in New Zealand museums in the interwar period. The image of "the Maori as he was," an idealized view of pre-European Māori culture popularized in Elsdon Best's book by that title (1924b), was based on the museum's collecting and ethnological fieldwork. We see a formal, scientific display with objects grouped by type in cases, while photographs, maps, and labels on wall panels are "illustrative of Maori life and customs": clothing, weapons, fishing, and bird catching ("Guide to the Dominion Museum and National Art Gallery and War Memorial Carrillon," MU 203, 3/10, Te Papa Archives, Wellington). But the mixed typological and anthropological approach seen here contrasted in style and mood with the celebration of contemporary Māori arts and crafts in the grand Maori Hall next door (see figure 1.5).

FIGURE 1.5 Concert party in the meeting house *Te Hau ki Tūranga*, Dominion Museum, Wellington, 1936. Hall-Raine, B.13061, Te Papa, Wellington. Courtesy of the Museum of New Zealand Te Papa Tongarewa.

The members of the Ngāti Pōneke Young Maori Club are gathered around a piano practicing their action songs, dressed in traditional costume. The scene is the famous carved meeting house *Te Hau ki Tūranga* in the museum, where, along with carvers from the School of Maori Arts and Crafts, they were working on its restoration as a centerpiece of the Maori Hall in the new Dominion Museum. This was seen at the time as the museum's "central shrine," holding the nation's "priceless treasures" that showed the "advanced" culture of the Māori, treasures that were "inseparable from the story of early New Zealand" (*Dominion*, August 1, 1936). So in contrast to the style of the adjoining Maori Ethnology Gallery (figure 1.4), which focused on the past, here a lively contemporary culture is expressed by the young women depicted in this photograph.

Best and other staff who had gathered objects, photographs, notes, and films on their expeditions into tribal areas.

However, despite the impression gained from this exhibit of a museum memorial to the Other's distant past, a "tomb with a view" (Kirshenblatt-Gimblett 1998: 57), a closer analysis of the actor networks circulating around it reveals a more complicated picture of cultural heritage as a regenerative resource for contemporary maintenance and revival, a kind of womb that worked against the museum setting. Māori were indirectly involved with the DM through Best's proactive informants (Holman 2010), the research of the Māori anthropologist Peter Buck, and the work of Thomas Heberly, a Māori carver on the DM's staff (McCarthy 2007a). In addition, the member of Parliament Sir Āpirana Ngata, a keen supporter of fieldwork through the Board of Maori Ethnological Research, saw value in a "homegrown" anthropology that assembled an idealized Māori past and positioned it as a springboard for the revival of "traditional" language, arts, and culture. When visitors walked into the new DM, they found themselves in the grand interior of the Maori Hall (figure 1.5), with the meeting house *Te Hau ki Tūranga* at the center, flanked by other large carvings re-creating a pre-European village scene. The house became synonymous with the idea of classical Māori culture, evoking a celebratory atmosphere lacking the ordered regime of the adjoining Maori Ethnology Gallery. However, this display was not just about the preservation of a Māori legacy but also concerned the revival of native arts and crafts as a living practice: "Out from the past there is bequeathed to us a heritage—an art of abiding beauty peculiarly our own. . . . It is for us to-day to see to it that in our national life all that is best in Maori art will be revivified to live again in a new and better age" (W. Phillips 1943: 24).

The house and its decorative interior were primarily Ngata's work, drawing on his close connections with the Māori community in Wellington. Ever the pragmatic politician, Ngata eschewed ethnographic accuracy, changing the length and proportions of the house to create a symbolic internal space for a social role that went beyond simply being a passive museum exhibit, becoming rather a stage for a Māori renaissance.[14] *Te Hau ki Tūranga* became the model for the many new carved houses in customary style that were produced around the country over the next twenty-five years, a native-led revival of the kind that James Clifford (1988) has called "newly traditional." When these houses were opened, Ngata encouraged the performance of oral arts, which underwent a revival alongside the visual arts. In 1935–36, he formed the Ngāti Pōneke Young Maori Club, drawn from the men and women working on the restoration of *Te Hau ki Tūranga* at the DM, seen in figure 1.5 dressed in their costumes around the piano in the unfinished meeting house.

Indigenous agency is clearly articulated in this Māori participation in the museum display of "the Maori as he was," constructed in part through ethnological research flowing from the field to the museum and back out to the community. This active *revival* of Māori cultural practices was linked to the policy and practice of Ngata's Department of Native Affairs, which developed a distinctive set of practices of "anthropological governance" that repositioned the Māori social within the modern nation-state, avoiding the "common error of studying the Maori merely as a museum object, and dismissing him from the story of New Zealand as it is today, and as it will be tomorrow" (Ngata 1928).

COLLECTING . . . ORDERING . . . GOVERNING . . . COLLECTING . . .

Clearly the relations among the processes of collecting, ordering, and governing exemplified by these vignettes do not conform to a linear logic. If collections must be gathered before they can be ordered, what is to be collected is always already ordered before it is gathered; and if the processes of gathering and ordering contribute to the development of governing practices, they are, in turn, shaped by governmental logics in both their conception and their execution. The relations among these processes are not lines, then, but overlapping loops. There are a number of perspectives from which the reciprocal interactions among these processes might be broached.[15] However, Bruno Latour's account of the collection of specimens by a scientific expedition to the Amazon forest, of the work of ordering and classification that was performed on the botanical samples collected from the forest when they were brought together in a laboratory, and of the forms of action back on the sites from which those samples were collected provides perhaps the best point of entry into these questions for our purposes here. Latour summarizes the outcome of these processes as follows: "The plants find themselves detached, separated, preserved, classified, and tagged. They are then reassembled, reunited, redistributed according to entirely new principles that depend on the researcher, on the discipline of botany, which has been standardized for many centuries, and on the institution that shelters them, but they no longer grow as they did in the forest. The botanist learns new things, and she is transformed accordingly, but the plants are transformed also" (1999: 39). And not just the plants in the laboratory: the forest from which the specimens are taken is itself transformed in being subjected to programs of environmental management informed by the new grids of intelligibility produced by the laboratory orderings in which those specimens have been inscribed.

Laboratories and museums are not, of course, identical.[16] Nonetheless, both are examples of Latour's more general concept of centers of calculation as the loci of ordering practices for materials that are brought together from diverse locations. Indeed, for Latour (1987: 215–57), the natural history museum preceded the laboratory as one among a number of centers of calculation for the natural sciences. While in some respects illuminating earlier accounts of the virtues of the distanced observations of the sedentary naturalist working on the materials gathered in his cabinet, compared to the observations of the field naturalist, Latour also displaces the binary logic that often informed such accounts by stressing the two-way relations between sites of collection and centers of calculation.[17] It is, for Latour, the variable articulations of the relations between these that matters: how sites of collection are organized by the instruments, derived from centers of calculation, that are brought to bear on them; how the work conducted at such sites of collection influences what is carried back to centers of calculation; and how the practices of ordering and classification conducted at centers of calculation have implications for varied forms of action in and on both the originating sites of collection and other worlds.

In developing this aspect of Latour's work—and of science studies more generally—Peter Miller and Nikolas Rose (2008: 8–10) connect it to Michel Foucault's work in proposing the concept of "laboratories of governmentality" to engage with the role of the psy disciplines, and of the social and human sciences more generally, in producing distinctive governmental objects through the work of classification and ordering they effect on the persons, bodies, and data they bring together in varied custom-built settings. Similar concerns have been evident in the literature bringing the Foucauldian analytic of governmentality to bear on the processes through which colonial populations have been constituted as objects of knowledge and governance (Scott 1995; N. Thomas 1994; Stoler 1995; Pels 1997; Pels and Salemink 2000; White 2005; Petterson 2012). The recent material turn (Bennett and Joyce 2010) has, in some of its interpretations, brought to this literature a concern with the material techniques and devices through which the relations of knowledge and power constituting different forms of governmentality are composed.[18] This includes a concern with the operation of the sociotechnical assemblages through which the forms of authority informing the relations between governors and governed are organized.

It is helpful, in bringing these general considerations to bear on our more specific concerns, to think of collecting, ordering, and governing as practices whose interrelations are ordered through the networks that compose the "anthropological assemblages" within which those practices are enacted. Drawing on assemblage theory in ways that we shall shortly elaborate more fully, anthropological assemblages encompass

i   the relations and processes that condition anthropologists' routes to, conceptions of, and modes of entry into the field, including the role of anthropological discourses—of culture, of "Man," of the environment, of race, and so on—within such processes;

ii   the relations between anthropologists and other agents (human and nonhuman) in the more immediate fieldwork contexts in which data are collected and subjected to initial sorting and classification;

iii   the ways and means through which what is collected in the field is returned to "base," and the mechanisms through which those materials and data are subjected to institutionally specific processes of ordering and classification; and

iv   the manner in which such materials and data are connected to the institutions and networks through which, whether in relation to the tasks of colonial administration or those of social management "at home," anthropology is governmentally deployed, by either state or nonstate actors, to bring about changes in the conduct of specific populations.

The poster prepared by Anatole Lewitsky for the 1939 New York World's Fair is a telling illustration of what we have in mind here: it depicts the MH as the organizing center of a network of anthropological institutions that, through being brought together at the MH, were connected to collecting and governing practices focused on the colonies that constituted Greater France and to exhibition practices directed toward the reeducation of the French citizenry (figure 1.6).

It is with these considerations in mind, then, that we now turn to look more closely at the processes of collecting, ordering, and governing. While considering each of these in turn, we shall also keep the relations among them in view.

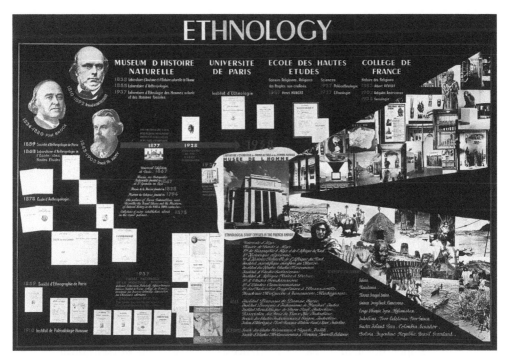

FIGURE 1.6 Musée de l'Homme poster on the organization of French ethnology produced for the New York World's Fair in 1939. 2AP5.4.3., Muséum d'Histoire Naturelle, Paris. Courtesy of the Muséum d'Histoire Naturelle.

The time arrow moving from left to right depicts the opening of the Musée de l'Homme (MH) as the culmination of a history running back through the reorganization of the Musée d'Ethnographie du Trocadéro initiated in 1928 to its opening in 1938. These earlier collecting institutions are set in the midst of the publications of a range of earlier anthropological and scientific associations. This reference to scientific predecessors bridging the divide between the natural and the human sciences is maintained in the key ancestral figures evoked at the top left, placing Paul Broca, the champion of physical anthropology, alongside Ernest Théodore Hamy, the founding director of the Musée d'Ethnographie du Trocadéro, for example. This dual orientation is continued along the top of the poster in bringing together the Muséum d'Histoire Naturelle (the MH's governing body) with the Université de Paris, the École des Hautes Études, and the Collège de France, and connecting these to the MH through the newly established Institut d'Ethnologie. The MH, located at the center of Paris (the Eiffel Tower is placed immediately behind it), radiates its influence to the rest of France through its exhibition galleries in the beam to the top right of the picture, and to France's colonies (Algeria, Indochina, Ethiopia, and the Cameroons) and the rest of the world in the beam to the bottom right, connecting with these through the colonial scientific associations and institutions that are named directly below the MH.

There is no question here, of course, of taking "the field" as either a given or a unitary object, particularly not for the period we are concerned with. It was, Michel-Rolph Trouillot (2003: 124) has argued, only from the perspective of the routinization of fieldwork associated with its large-scale professionalization as a university discipline after World War II that figures like Boas were retrospectively consecrated as archetypical field-workers. This consecration paid little heed to the fact that the working practices of the anthropologists in question were only tangentially related to those they were later cited as models for: the expectation of a period of solitary immersion in the field followed by a return to a university base for the preparation of a scientific monograph. The similarities among the so-called first generation of field-workers were also quite limited. The immersive paradigm was little practiced. Initially extolled by William Halse Rivers Rivers, partly in critique of the team-based expeditions led by Alfred Cort Haddon in which he had earlier participated (Kuklick 2011: 17–23), the ideal of an intensive period of study conducted by a single observer had relatively little traction at that time. Boas is often cited as an example, although his early experience as a solitary field-worker quickly gave way to his role as a member of teams and, in his later career, to what is perhaps best characterized as "epistolary fieldwork," which he conducted via correspondence with his "native informant" George Hunt.[19] Complemented by occasional visits to Fort Rupert, this form of collecting was organized through a complex set of relations in which conflicting claims to authority, political patronage, and a fair amount of bullying at a distance jostled uneasily with one another.[20] Spencer visited the field in episodic forays of limited duration, either as a member of a team led by others or in company with Frank Gillen, staying whenever possible at the telegraph stations that formed the nodal centers from which the reach of Australian governmental authority radiated further into Central Australia.[21] By contrast, the fieldwork missions organized by the MH were quite varied in their form.[22] The most emblematic of these—the 1931–33 Dakar-Djibouti mission led by Griaule—was distinctive in both the scale of its conception as an ongoing media event (Bennett 2013b: 100–102) and its adoption of a multiperspectival approach requiring the coordination of large interdisciplinary teams in preference to the monocular vision of the single observer (Griaule 1933; Clifford 1983, 1988).

The breaches with earlier traditions of collecting were also partial and incomplete. George W. Stocking Jr., rebutting accounts of fieldwork as a break with a "pre-promethean period when evolutionary titans, seated in their armchairs, culled ethnographic data from travel accounts" (1983: 71), places the accent on an accumulation of gradual changes initiated, in the British tradition, by Edward Burnett Tylor in the 1880s. These included the expedition to Northwest Canada that Tylor organized under the auspices of the British Association for the Advancement of Science, to which Boas was recruited. This led beyond the earlier tradition, represented by *Notes and Queries on Anthropology*, of collecting data via surveys or guides sent to travelers or to in situ collectors. These guides were intended, according to the introduction to the 1874 version, to "enable those who are not anthropologists themselves to supply the information that is wanted for the scientific study of anthropology at home" (quoted in Urry 1993: 21). The *Notes and Queries* were progressively modified in favor of having trained observers "on the spot"; after their revision under Rivers's direction in 1912, their primary purpose was to guide, direct, and assist trained field-workers (Petch 2007). This shift of emphasis followed earlier models of fieldwork pioneered by the biological sciences, as was evident in the disciplinary trajectories of the first field-workers as "academically trained natural scientists defining themselves as anthropologists, and involved also in the formulation and evaluation of anthropological theory" (Stocking 1983: 74). This involved, Howard Morphy has argued, a move away from seeking to collect "isolated facts or culture traits to be constructed into evolutionary sequences" and toward "analyzing the relationship between different components of a socio-cultural system" (1997: 42). However, even as they helped to effect this transition, early twentieth-century field-workers remained in the slipstream of the natural sciences, continuing to collect natural specimens alongside ethnographic materials, just as they remained in the tradition of physical anthropology in their concern to collect anatomically based measurements of racial types (Bondaz 2011; Laurière 2008; Cole 1999; Jones 1987; Mulvaney and Calaby 1985). And in spite of the endeavor to sever the cord connecting anthropological fieldwork to earlier voyage literatures, both the manner of the anthropologists' entry into the field and their return to base remained deeply indebted to earlier travel practices and narratives (Defert 1982; Debaene 2010).

Interpreting fieldwork as part of an ensemble of governmental practices, Peter Pels and Oscar Salemink (2000: 12) suggest that what they call the "anthropological process" comprises three phases: the *préterrain*, the anthropological occasion, and anthropological tradition. Borrowing the concept of the préterrain from Clifford (1988), they define it as comprising all those mediations—from discursive practices through modes of transport to local power relationships (of missionaries, colonial administrators, etc.)—through which the ethnographer must pass to get to her or his site of investigation. The anthropological occasion is the "situation of contact between the ethnographer and those to be described, in which they coproduce the knowledge that is to be written down in terms of essences of self and other" (Pels and Salemink 2000: 13–14). The anthropological tradition, finally, comprises the texts that are brought to bear on the constitution of the anthropological occasion. We would add, however, that it is not only the anthropological tradition that needs be heeded from this perspective. Account also needs to be taken of the relations between anthropology and other knowledge practices since these have a profound effect on the kinds of transactions that do, or do not, eventuate in the field. The relations between anthropology and sociology had a bearing on French fieldwork practices that is not found in any of our other case studies (Conklin 2013); anthropology's relations to folklore studies were significant in both France (F. Weber 2000, 2005) and the United States (Baker 2010), albeit in different ways, but much less so in Britain (Wingfield 2011) and scarcely at all in Australia, where the category of the folk had very little purchase. Similarly, while anthropology and archaeology were closely intertwined in both the United States (Kehoe 1998) and New Zealand (Cameron 2014), archaeology had little influence on anthropological practice in early twentieth-century Australia, where the conviction that Aboriginal culture had got stuck at the level of prehistory inhibited archaeological excavations: since the past was still manifest in the present, there was no need to go digging to unearth it (T. Griffiths 1996).

We shall elaborate more fully on the significance of these variable articulations of the relations between different knowledge practices at various points in the following chapters. Our more immediate concerns are the implications of the perspectives of assemblage theory that we identified earlier for our understanding of the "anthropological encounter" in the field and, more particularly, with the light that the concept of *agencement* can throw on these matters. While *assemblage* and *agencement* were introduced by Gilles Deleuze and Félix Guattari (1983) as affiliated terms, subsequent debates, particularly in the field of cultural economy, have elaborated the virtues of the concept of agencement over those of the concept of assemblage in view of the attention it accords to the configuration of agential capacities. The perspective of agencement thus refers not merely to the coming together of human and nonhuman, textual and material, institutional and technical agents and entities; it additionally stresses how the relationships among these give rise to particular spheres of action (McFall 2009: 51). Agencements, if you like, are the action-oriented end of assemblages. More to the point for our present purpose, the concept has been applied to different processes of collecting to identify the forms of agency that are exercised across the varied instruments, persons, technologies, and environments that are brought together in any given set of collecting practices.

Evelyn Ruppert's concept of a "census *agencement*" is a case in point. Applying the concept to the Canadian Census of 1911, the first to attempt a "scientific" enumeration of the indigenous populations of Canada's Far North, Ruppert (2009: 13) includes human actors (the mounted police), technological actors (steamships, trading posts), and natural forces (snow, seals) as making up this census agencement.[23] These all interacted in providing the occasions for the temporary gatherings of nomadic groups—around police patrols, visits to trading posts, and seasonal seal hunts—that formed the points of contact between indigenous groups and census enumerators. But Ruppert also stresses the role of material mediators in these exchanges: the various census instruments—the organization of the census returns on which the data collected were to be recorded, for example—and the grids of intelligibility these interposed between the enumerators and those who were to be enumerated regarding what could be asked and not asked, what recorded and not recorded. While the governmental imperatives exercised from the more distant centers of calculation of the census bureau in Ottawa clearly played a crucial role in bringing together collectors and collected, the concept of a census agencement draws attention to the relations between these imperatives and the factors organizing the forms of action and interaction that are entered into and performed on the spot.

Spencer and Gillen's (1912) account in *Across Australia* of what was collected from, and exchanged with, members of the Kaitish and Unmatjera peoples during their stay at the Barrow Creek Telegraph Station, some three hundred kilometers due north of Alice Springs, testifies to a pointed articulation of the relations between these more distant and local forces while also underlining the commingling of the practices of natural history and ethnographic collecting. It is with the former in view that Spencer and Gillen first introduce Barrow Creek, expressing their disappointment that the flash flooding that had followed a torrential storm a few days after their arrival at the station had not, as they had hoped, attracted a large number of animals. This immediately gives way to a description of the station as a site for material exchanges conducted through the mechanism of barter. Spencer and Gillen recount how they unpacked their stores of "knives, tomahawks, looking-glasses, bead necklets and pipes" before a "deputation of natives" who, hearing of Spencer and Gillen's arrival, had gathered at the station. Once these had "returned to their camps and spread the news," Spencer and Gillen were very shortly engaged in a regular trade of "a stick of tobacco or a single-bladed knife" for "a shield, spear or pitchi" (1912: 318).

The relationship between the development of fieldwork practices and the pacification of relations across colonial frontiers has long been recognized (Kuklick 2011). The role of the telegraph line running from south to north, from Adelaide to Darwin, in drawing Australia's "outback" interior more closely into an emerging national governmental domain was especially important in this regard. Spencer and Gillen's expedition across Central Australia in 1901–2 kept close to the telegraph line wherever possible, with telegraph stations constituting their main stopping places. These, alongside government waterholes, railway terminuses, and missionary stations, also functioned, with the gradual cessation of warlike exchanges across the colonial frontier, as significant contact zones for the relations between anthropologists and the Aboriginal populations of remote regions. This is reflected in the photograph of Barrow Creek—taken in 1901—that Spencer and Gillen use to evoke a past scene of "a treacherous attack by the natives" (1912: 319) on the station shortly after it opened in 1872 (figure 1.7). Interpreted correctly as extending and consolidating the power of settler Australia in regions where it had hitherto been exercised only sporadically, in 1874 Barrow Creek was temporarily seized in an act of guerrilla warfare by the Kaitish, who were resisting the intrusion it constituted.[24] Recounting this attack in some detail, Spencer and Gillen note that it was the failure of "the natives" to destroy the telegraph line that, via the "last farewell" of the stationmaster that was transmitted to his wife in Adelaide, led to rescue parties being organized from both the north and the south. When these had made the station safe, they embarked on a punitive expedition among the neighboring tribes: they "rode out all over the surrounding country, and the natives had such a lesson that they never again attempted an attack" (321).

This scene of past violence is contrasted to a pacified present in a number of ways. The courtyard is now open day and night, Spencer and Gillen write, and the loopholes in the wall that had been designed for defensive gunfire remain, "but they serve only for ventilation" (321). Past and present are also both connected and disconnected through the figure of Tungulla, once a great warrior and a participant in the raid in 1874, but now "well advanced in years and mild in manners" (321). Spencer and Gillen attached Tungulla to their staff, exchanging three meals a day and a liberal supply of tobacco for his knowledge of Kaitish lore and his authority as a respected elder. It was through Tungulla that Spencer and Gillen extended their collecting practices

Fig. 159. BARROW CREEK STATION.

The photograph is taken looking south from the hill behind the station. When it was attacked the officers were seated in front where a small tree can be seen, and had to run round to the back to enter the courtyard. The natives were grouped in the position occupied by the rain gauge.

FIGURE 1.7 Barrow Creek Station, Northern Territory, Australia, 1901. Reproduced from Baldwin Spencer and Frank J. Gillen, *Across Australia* (London: Macmillan, 1912), fig. 159. Courtesy of the State Library of New South Wales.

Built in the "early days of the overland telegraph" when "the natives were liable to be troublesome," the Barrow Creek Station was built in the form of a square onto which all rooms opened, with a fortified entrance on only one side of the square, "as a precaution against attack," according to Baldwin Spencer and Frank Gillen (1912: 319). All windows had iron bars with, at intervals, loopholes in the walls "through which, if necessary, the natives could be fired at." Three of the officers were mortally wounded, and the tally would have been greater but for "one friendly black boy, employed about the station" who "seizing his revolver . . . immediately fired upon the natives" (Spencer and Gillen 1912: 320). This description of the station as a site of past conflict served as a counterpoint to its current operation as a stage for the performance of Aboriginal ceremonies before Spencer and Gillen's anthropological gaze.

beyond "bartering our goods in exchange for native things" (318) to the collection of stories, myths, details of magic and medical practices, racial types, and customs and rituals as parts of a complex set of fieldwork agencements in which materials, instruments, collectors, and collected each exerted their influence. Spencer and Gillen's note taking in the field, for example, prompted "their boy" Jim (or Erlikilliaka), one of the Aboriginal trackers they had brought with them to Barrow Creek, to do the same thing. Although he could not write, he constantly had a pencil and paper to hand, providing hieroglyphic representations of traditional stories that Spencer and Gillen used to convey the connections between natural objects and ancestors in Kaitish belief systems.

The most distinctive material actor in the ethnographic encounters at Barrow Creek was, however, the camera. A great deal has been written, and controversies abound, in relation to Spencer and Gillen's use of photography (e.g., Wolfe 1999; Peterson 2006; Batty, Allen, and Morton 2005). One point of agreement concerns its importance as a transformative episode in the history of anthropology: it was the first sustained substitution of photography and development on the spot for earlier studio-based forms of ethnographic photography. Another notes its role in the development of new forms of ethnographic authority based on the eyewitness testimony of having "been there" and, in some interpretations, penetrated the veil of secrecy that had hitherto shielded indigenous customary practices from the anthropological gaze. Our purpose here is not to adjudicate these controversies but rather to note how the agency of Spencer and Gillen's cameras at Barrow Creek incorporated the Other within the extended reach of the governmental domain that followed in the wake of the telegraph line. Nicolas Peterson (2006) has noted the preponderance of ceremonial practices, artifacts, portraits, and sites among the photographs included in *The Native Tribes of Central Australia* (Spencer and Gillen 1899). This is also true of the photographs in *Across Australia* (Spencer and Gillen 1912), and of those relating specifically to Barrow Creek. While the portraits vary in type, including illustrations of ornate body decorations, the majority conform to the earlier conventions of studio-based anthropometric head-and-shoulder shots; these testified to the shared racial characteristics of the Kaitish and Unmatjera peoples, in a form of ordering on the spot that brought the different tribes of the region together within the framework of classifying grids derived from distant centers of calculation. The photographs of sites—there are two of Barrow Creek (figure 1.7 and a photograph taken from a different angle of the flooded creek a few days earlier) and one of a rocky gorge immediately behind Barrow Creek in which, the text accompanying the photograph tells us, "the natives secreted themselves before attacking the station"—complement Spencer and Gillen's narrative of the station's transition from the turbulence of the raid in 1874 to, a quarter of a century later, a peaceful state in which different groups of Aboriginal people could be gathered to perform their similarities to one another, and their differences from the settler, through staged presentations of their ceremonies before the cameras.

These were carefully rehearsed events, with Spencer and Gillen taking great care to excise any signs of the forty-year history of local Aboriginal interaction with settler culture. Yet, a little later, this history comes in through the back door when, returning to their initial presentation of Barrow Creek as a location for the collection of natural history specimens, they recount how the old women of the area would bring to the station curious collections gathered in a day or two's foraging that they would empty out of "sundry old jam tins, pickle bottles or bags of all kinds and sizes, made of white men's discarded socks, coat sleeves, trouser legs or anything that could serve as a receptacle" (1912: 328). Yet while chronicling settlers' presence and the quelling of earlier Aboriginal resistance to the territorial extension of colonial power within Australia, and while clearly contriving the scenes that were enacted before them for their photographic record, Spencer and Gillen act as though everything that unfolded before them was unaffected by these considerations. However, as Elizabeth Povinelli has observed in relation to Spencer and Gillen's earlier collecting among the Arrernte, the exercise of force was "the very condition of communicative action, or practical reason" (2002: 94) that informed the Arrernte's calculation, in performing their culture under the gaze of the anthropologist, "that one aspect of colonial power was being bracketed by another equal and opposing colonial force; that Spencer and Gillen were holding police, settlers, and starvation at bay" (94). These were the conditions in which indigenous agency manifested itself in detaching "a segment of their semiotic 'life-world' " as a means of building a dialogic platform with a conquering power through their relations with "these European men" (94).

ORDERING: THE ARCHIVE

The concept of agencement, then, focuses attention on the sociomaterial processes of collecting in the field as these are framed by the broader governmental imperatives mediating the relations between anthropologists and their subjects. We now turn to the processes of ordering to which the materials collected from the field—or, more accurately, from different fields—

are subjected when they are brought together in centers of calculation. In doing so, we look to recent debates prompted by the "archival turn," in which, as Ann Laura Stoler summarizes it, attention has shifted from "archive-as-source to archive-as-subject" (2009: 44), for the light these debates throw on the ways in which collections function as technologies of rule.

The archival turn was initially prompted by Foucault's conception of the archive as *"the general system for the formation and transformation of statements"* (1972: 128), a conception that has subsequently been criticized for its abstraction: as if, as Thomas Osborne (1999) puts it, the archive had a purely virtual existence rather than existing concretely in a specific place or set of places. While there is much truth in this, it overlooks Foucault's stipulation that an essential condition for statements is that they "must have a material existence" and, further, that "the rule of materiality that statements necessarily obey is . . . of the order of the institution . . . ; it defines *possibilities of reinscription and transcription* (but also thresholds and limits), rather than limited and perishable individualities" (1972: 100, 103). It is this sense of archives as socially and materially grounded that Osborne values in Jacques Derrida's (1998) conception of the archive as located in a literal place—at an address, a residence, a library, a record office—that constitutes the locus for the accumulation and exercise of power and authority through the ordering of the materials that are gathered there and, thence, through the ordering of society. With the operation of historical archives primarily in mind, Osborne likens their functioning to Latour's laboratories except that, where the latter subject the materials they bring together to procedures of statistical calculation, he sees archives as being governed by "a certain art of deposition, preservation and . . . interpretation" (1999: 52). While thus stressing the archive's ordering function, he also stresses its significance as a switch point or, in Latour's terms, "a kind of 'obligatory passage point' . . . ; the archive is the place in the network through which all the other points must pass" (52).

What light do these formulations throw on the constitution of anthropological collections as these were reshaped by the changing institutional relations informing early twentieth-century anthropological practices? Sven Spieker's account of the development of historical archives in late nineteenth-century Berlin provides a productive point of entry into these questions. "In an archive," Spieker argues, "everything has to come from somewhere, everything must act as evidence or clue, a hint at a place or site where it is not" (2008: 44). Yet what the archive collects is "not what exists in an extra-archival outside but what has already been collected, arranged, and organized *in another place*" (17). This produces new forms of authority based on the ability to "interpret texts in relation both to their place in the archive and to the place from which they emerged" (18). The "other place" that Spieker has in mind with regard to the archives of business history that are his primary focus is the registry. As a site of temporary storage and collection, the registry mediates the relations between the office—the place where papers are produced in the course of business—and the archive. It does so by classifying, ordering, and shaping the documents it collects "with a view to their future place in the archive itself" (21). "The other sphere to which the archive alludes, its beyond," is thus "not an extra-archival outside but another collection, the site where records accumulate before their transfer to the archive" (20).

The relations between anthropological collections and the field exhibit similar properties in the early twentieth century as, in displacing earlier forms and social relations of collecting, the field comes to operate as that "other place" where the ways of life of indigenes are classified and ordered—most famously in the anthropologist's tent (Schumaker 1996)—with a view to their eventual placement in a museum or colonial archive. Compared to the mechanisms through which anthropological collections had earlier been collected—through donations or purchases, for example—anthropological authority came increasingly to depend on interpreting the relationships between the materials gathered together in the archive and their provenance in the field as opposed to armchair interpretations of the place of artifacts within general evolutionary sequences.[25] At the same time, anthropological collections became increasingly archival in their composition owing to the extension of what Ira Jacknis has called the ethnographer's toolbox to collect not just "first-order tangible objects such as native-made artifacts" but also "second-order ethnographic objects constituted by the ethnographer as part of the process of ethnographic interpretation and representation" (1996: 186). While some of these second-order objects were continuous with earlier traditions in physical anthropology (anatomical and craniometrical measurements and plaster casts, for example), what most stands out is the multiplication of the textual forms through which indigenous cultures were collected: maps, drawings, photographs, films, sound recordings, musical transcriptions, native stories, ethnographic notes and observations, vocabularies, and grammars.

Jacknis's comments are focused on Boas, who represented this tendency in perhaps its most extreme form, particularly, as his career developed, in concentrating increasingly on the collection and codification of textual data. When due allowances are made for the contextual specificities of other field-work practices—Spencer's central concern with producing photographic or filmic records of rituals, which Boas came to view as a distraction and, compared with recordings of oral testimony, too staged to be authentic—the (relative) displacement of the object as the main focus of anthropological attention by an accumulating textual corpus was a generally shared tendency in which museums participated (Henare 2005).[26] For example, at the MH, where, as we have seen, the object retained a special epistemological value, the Dakar-Djibouti mission collected 3,500 objects along with a textual corpus of 6,000 photographic negatives, 200 sound recordings, notations of 30 languages, 300 manuscripts, and 1,500 *fiches d'observation* (Rivet and Rivière 1930). Perhaps more tellingly, the epistemological value of the object was elaborated by comparing it to that of the document.[27] Similarly, as we have seen, the Ethnology Gallery at the DM conveyed the impression of a "book on a wall," while, more generally, museum visitors were increasingly led into an environment in which "the meaning of things—far from standing clearly before the eye—was constantly deferred in being referred to a dense and proliferating web of words" (Bennett 2004: 167).

What was at issue in these developments, however, was not simply a matter of an accumulating textual archive supplementing collections of artifacts; the constitution and functioning of the latter were transformed by being brought increasingly into the orbit of the former. David Jenkins (1994) argues this point forcefully in his analysis of the processes through which the labeled, numbered, and described artifacts brought back from the field to the museum were subjected to a further process of rationalization and systematization via the processes of accessioning, indexing, and photographic copying. The resulting translation of artifacts into "inscriptions on paper" facilitated their "conceptual and symbolic management" (244) by simultaneously aligning them with other textual corpora.[28] This resulted, Jenkins argues, in "a kind of 'semiotic homogeneity'" (254) through which the various kinds of "primary" and "secondary" objects brought back from the field could, in Latour's (1987: 227) famous definition of immutable mobiles, be made "presentable, readable and combinable with one another." At the same time, the material form of these textual corpora made them amenable to the archival logics of collecting and ordering through which museums came to view the collection of such corpora as an extension of their mission to collect material culture. As Jacknis (1996) and others (Stocking 1968; Briggs and Bauman 1999) have noted, the priority that Boas accorded to the collection of texts in native languages was informed by a museal logic.[29] This was evident in his conception of such texts as enduring material collections that would provide an objective and accumulating basis for future research into indigenous cultures analogous to that provided by European museums and libraries for research on classical cultures.

These transformations in the composition of anthropological collections were in turn connected to the changing constellation of knowledge practices that anthropology was affiliated to as the balance of its institutional connections shifted from the museum to the university. The degree to which this was true varied. The American case represents perhaps the clearest shift in this direction, and Boas is again the key figure here. His departure from the AMNH in 1905, his critique of the comparative method for museum displays advocated by Otis T. Mason, and his focus on postgraduate training during his years at Columbia: all of these make him the emblematic figure for those narratives that argue that by the early twentieth century anthropology had, as Steven Conn puts it, "packed its bags," moving out of the museum to "new digs in the departmental structure of American colleges and universities" (2004: 191–92). Conn is, however, careful to rebut those ruptural narratives that suggest a complete severance of the relations between American anthropology and museums. Such accounts neglect the continuing connections between the AMNH and fieldwork under Clark Wissler, Boas's successor, as well as the importance of museum affiliations for many of the leading members of the generation of anthropologists trained by Boas, not to mention Boas's own continuing assessment of the importance of the relations between anthropology in its university and museum settings.[30]

Boas's case was also far from typical when viewed in an international perspective. Britain, where Haddon's expeditions had been organized under the auspices of the University of Cambridge's Museum of Archaeology and Anthropology and, in turn, contributed to the development of the university's teaching programs in anthropology, provides perhaps the closest parallel (Rouse 1998). In New Zealand the DM and Otago Museum played a significant role in the development of early twentieth-century fieldwork, while in Australia the NMV became a significant center for fieldwork only after Spencer had weakened its ties with the University of Melbourne by moving the museum into the city center, where, along with the library, it formed part of a new ensemble of civic institutions. This was reflected, in reverse, by Spencer's failure to develop an institutional power base for anthropology at the university, where his chair was in the biological sciences (Kuklick 2006: 560). And in France, as the MH became the primary institutional site for French fieldwork in the 1930s, it also came to be more closely associated with the university through its relations to the Muséum National d'Histoire Naturelle and the Institut d'Ethnologie at the Sorbonne. As Emmanuelle Sibeud (2000) has argued, the MH's accumulating archive of textual materials alongside its artifactual and osteological collections, particularly in being brought together in its "anthropological laboratory" and its *bibliothèque*, played a crucial role in mediating its relations with the various scientific associations that came to be grouped around the museum and the Sorbonne, as well as its relations with the archives of the apparatuses of colonial rule both in France and in the colonies, and of the extensive network of societies and institutes that operated alongside these.

Let's go back for a moment to Spieker, who shows how, in the 1920s and 1930s, surrealist programs for the museum frequently envisaged its future as archival in form as the value of uniqueness (whether aesthetic, historical, or anthropological) gave way to the documentary value of collections and, consequently, to a positive estimation of the bureaucratic mechanisms of classification that secured this value. For Varvara Stepanova the archive heralded the coming of the "new museum" (quoted in Spieker 2008: 106), while for Le Corbusier the "museum of our own day with objects of our own day" would need to include "a *Ronéo* filing cabinet with its printed index cards, tabulated, numbered, perforated, and indented, which will show that in the twentieth century we have learnt how to classify" (quoted in Spieker 2008: 101). Knowledge here, Spieker argues, is not a matter of step-by-step discovery, like an archaeological dig, but a matter of classification in which everything finds it place via the address it is assigned. The surrealist manifestos were, of course, poetic exaggerations of real tendencies that, nonetheless, had some points of connection with actual museum practices: with those of the MH, for example, and also those of Mass-Observation (M-O), which, drawing on surrealist conceptions, was often described by its leading practitioners as a museum-like project of collection (Harrison 2014: 231).[31]

The key point here, however, concerns the relations between the increasingly archival properties of museums and the relations between these and the development of parallel systems of classification. We can perhaps best make this point by way of a historical contrast regarding the systems of classification that anthropological museums came to be aligned with. Shortly after he joined the AMNH Boas wrote to its president, Morris Ketchum Jesup, proposing that the museum enter into an alliance with the U.S. Bureau of the Census with a view to bringing together two sets of data: the census would allow the anthropological "collection of vital statistics of the Indians" to be carried out "in a more thorough manner than has been done heretofore in anthropometric studies," thus yielding "material of a permanent value to museums" in interpreting their "photographs, casts of faces and of bodies, crania, and other objects."[32] While, as we have noted, the collection of anthropometric data continued, the increasingly archival properties of anthropological collections, orientated to the collection of beliefs, values, and ways of life, was paralleled, particularly in the 1930s, by new forms of collecting developed by the social sciences with a similar focus. The mutating archive of drawings, observations, file notes, survey responses, diaries, and photographs that M-O collected at different points in its history thus yielded a mobile set of inscriptions that, as Osborne and Rose (2008) have observed, jostled for space with the surveys produced by the fledgling disciplines of British sociology and public opinion research. The blending of anthropological and sociological forms of collection of the ways of life of small-town America that was evident in the surveys informing Robert S. Lynd and Helen Merrell Lynd's (1929) study of Middletown is another case in point. So too were the varied networks and mechanisms that the Musée des Arts et Traditions Populaires developed for collecting regional cultural resources, and for cataloging and analyzing these in its laboratory of French ethnography. These provided a centralized inventory of regional cultures enabling comparisons and contrasts to be established between them of a kind hitherto impossible (Segalen 2001, 2005).[33]

GOVERNING: POPULATIONS, PUBLICS, MILIEUS

Governing, we have suggested, forms part of a circuit in which practices of collecting, ordering, and governing inform one another. We now need to complete the circuit by looking at how the forms of ordering discussed in the previous section bear on the mechanisms through which governing practices were organized and put into effect. We are not the first to broach such questions. To the contrary, there is a rich literature exploring the connections between anthropological archives and governing practices. Nicholas Dirks's (2001) assessment of the significance of colonial archives in "textualizing tradition" and, alongside census practices, in collecting and enumerating caste to produce the caste/custom nexus as a primary site for colonial governmental action in late nineteenth-century India is a particularly signal case in point. And, although insisting that their operations are uneven, contested, and resisted—sites of epistemological and political anxiety rather than of assured authority—Stoler's conception of archives as mechanisms of "lettered governance" (2009: 1) aptly summarizes this line of argument. The contribution we intend here, then, is twofold: first, to consider how the collections that constitute our point of entry into these questions operated as switch points for "anthropology at home and away" projects, connecting governmental programs in both colonial and metropolitan contexts; and, second, to consider the variable ways in which such governmental programs operated depending on whether they worked primarily through the mechanisms of population, publics, or milieus.

Alongside Dirks and Stoler, we approach these questions through the perspectives of Foucauldian governmentality theory, albeit not in a spirit that would view this as the only valid point of departure for engaging with what Pels and Salemink (2000) call the "practical histories" of anthropology. The work of Benoît de L'Estoile (2005), for example, proposes a productive fusion of Foucauldian and Weberian approaches in linking the centralization of anthropological knowledge from dispersed fieldwork sites to rationalized forms of domination brought to bear on the administration of native bodies as a productive economic resource in French West Africa. George Steinmetz's (2007) conception of the colonial state as an autonomous field within which diverse forms of "ethnographic capital" are mobilized by the representatives of different class fractions points to a different set of questions concerning the respects in which the forms of anthropological knowledge that are acquired in situ in colonial contexts serve as distinctive forms of cultural capital facilitating access to positions of power within colonial states' apparatuses of rule. While productive on its own terms, Steinmetz's Bourdieusian focus on the role of "ethnographic capitals" in the competitive struggles of colonial elites lacks the flexibility that Foucault's concept of governmentality brings to the analysis of the relations between states and practices of governance, and the more varied role that he accords the practices of epistemological authorities within these. We also part company with Steinmetz's exclusive focus on the role of ethnography in producing an unbridgeable gap between colonizer and colonized by essentializing the difference between them. This reflects his subscription to the "rule of colonial difference," derived from the work of Partha Chatterjee (1993), which David Scott called into question in his original elaboration of the concept of "colonial governmentality." In place of such a singular conception of anthropology's deployment—but one that undoubtedly applies in particular contexts—Scott proposed a focus on its "governing-effects on colonial conduct" (1995: 204), where such effects are interpreted as the outcomes of varied governmental rationalities.[34]

This, however, is a concept that owes less to the work of Foucault directly, or to the anthropological literature on colonial governmentalities, than to the parallel work of Miller and Rose in the fields of economic and psychological governance.[35] Adapted to our purposes, *governmental rationalities* refers to the ends that are to be pursued in relation to the different populations constituting a given national, colonial, or imperial polity, as well as to the technical means through which these are pursued by varied forms of action on those populations—and/or on their milieus—by a range of epistemological authorities, which include, but not are limited to, state actors. Where we draw more directly on Foucault is in his account of liberal government (Foucault 2008), which, in becoming widely known only some time after his classic essay on governmentality (Foucault 1991), had only a limited influence on earlier applications of the governmentality perspective to the practical histories of anthropology.[36] A distinctive part of our argument, then, consists in the contention that, for the period we are concerned with, anthropology should be treated as a "liberal science" so far as the forms of its governmental deployment are concerned.

The liberal intellectual affiliations of the leading figures we examine across our different case studies have a bearing on these questions. These cleaved to the liberal side of the debates they were involved in concerning the extent to and manner in which anthropology should be placed in the service of governmental practices. Deeply shaped by German liberal political thought and by the liberal cultural technologies of the self that were fostered by the tradition of *Bildung* (Bunzl 1996; Cole 1999), as well as by the progressive liberal traditions of late nineteenth-century German anthropology in which he was schooled (Penny 2002; Zimmerman 2001), Boas reorientated the methods of physical anthropology that he inherited to extend the possibilities for freedom by demonstrating the plasticity and malleability of human attributes (Boas 1911, [1912] 1982). He was, at the same time, deeply committed to a high modernist liberal conception of science as an autonomous field of practice that should stand outside of, and resist subordination to, state authorities (Yans-McLaughlin 1986). Circulating instead in the relations between the scientific community, state, and civil society, the responsibility of science, Boas argued, was to govern through, and so to further secure, individual freedoms. Henrika Kuklick (2006) and Povinelli (2002) have similarly shown how Spencer's anthropological practice was shaped by his formation within liberal intellectual and political traditions. Spencer and Gillen's fieldwork reports, Kuklick argues, reflected an earnest engagement with the tensions of classical liberalism as they struggled to reconcile the limited evidence of a capacity for change—the mere glimpses of will and volition, and the faint glimmerings of a polity based on the principle of discussion—that they discerned amongst the Arrernte with the requirement, most influentially articulated by John Stuart Mill (1969), that a people should exhibit such capacities for freedom if they were to be governed accordingly. Indeed, Mill haunts

Spencer at almost every step in his encounters with Aboriginal people as he variously elaborates, qualifies, rebuts, and worries over the evidence he finds suggesting that they exhibit a creative capacity for change (or once did but now lack it), are completely subject to the repetitions of habit and custom (but punctuated by occasional glimpses of innovation), and show signs of an aesthetic sensitivity (albeit blunted and limited).

In its founding conception, M-O similarly aimed to provide a liberal alternative to existing forms of ruling authority by operating as a mechanism for the circulation of the opinions of the masses—giving "both ear and voice to what the millions are feeling and doing" by operating as a "receiving set" through which anyone can "listen-in to the movements of popular habit and opinion" (Mass-Observation 1939: 9–10). The MH, under Paul Rivet, was explicitly committed to the application of a reformist anthropology—molded in the Durkheimian–Maussian tradition—that aimed both to reshape French colonial administration along more liberal and humanist lines and to promote an antiracist public pedagogy in the face of opposition from the conservative anthropological tradition represented by Louis Marin (Lebovics 1992: 13–35). In New Zealand, finally, Henry Devenish Skinner's adaption of the culture-area concept as interpreted by Alfred Kroeber played a significant role in shifting anthropology's earlier association with a salvage paradigm to a focus on the integration of Māori into national and economic life (Cameron 2014).

The liberal intellectual affiliations of anthropologists are, however, only one aspect of the relations between early twentieth-century anthropological fieldwork and the practices of liberal government that, in Foucault's (2008) account, partially overlap with, but are also broader than, liberalism as a specific set of intellectual and political traditions. Rather, he argues, liberal government should be understood as referring to the operations of a series of apparatuses that, working through the regimes of truth that they deploy, make up different kinds of freedom that act as the interfaces through which the relations between governmental practices and the population are organized. If this means that freedom is not to be taken as a given, it also means that attention has to be paid to the various exclusions and limits that are placed on the different historical forms in which such freedoms are produced and, thus, to the organization of different mechanisms through which governmental practice are brought to bear on the management of populations (Rose 1999; Joyce 2003, 2013). This is the work performed by those knowledges that, in assessing the variable capacities for freedom exhibited by different populations, apportion the mechanisms for governing through freedom or, where such capacities are judged to be absent or poorly developed, bypass such mechanisms in favor of more directive or coercive ones.

Anthropology has been one of the main knowledges through which this work has been performed across the relations between metropolitan and colonized populations, and within each of these. It has, however, rarely done so in isolation; rather, its operations have to be assessed in terms of its relations to those of other cultural disciplines—and, historically, its relations to aesthetics have been particularly important here—as well as to those of the biological sciences. The considerations that are relevant to its role in these regards concern the varied discursive and technical warrants it has proposed for differentiating populations with regard to a range of attributes. These include the following:

i   Their relations to their environments, and in particular whether they are viewed as being entirely shaped by their environments or, in accordance with the logic of post-Lockean conceptions, as demonstrating a capacity to reshape their environments through agriculture and related practices.[37]

ii   Their political traditions, and in particular the weight of habit, custom, and traditional forms of political authority relative to the role of discussion as, after Mill, a defining attribute of liberal polities.[38]

iii   The position of different populations in relation to history, understood as both a developmental process (the assignation of different populations to different stages of development) and a region of discourse (the realms of historical writing and painting, for example, from which indigenous populations were progressively excluded in Australia and America but not New Zealand).[39]

iv   Assessments of racial physiognomies and of the differentially calibrated intellectual capacities these were interpreted as attesting to.

v   Assessments of sensory capacities and of the relations between these and the possession or lack of an aesthetic sensibility, which is, in turn, interpreted as an index of civilization.[40] These reflect a lineage that goes back to the civic humanists, for whom aesthetic judgment indexed a capacity for regulating and governing the self that, freed from the constraints of necessity, qualified those who possessed it to contribute disinterestedly to the civic affairs of a self-governing polity.[41]

To speak of anthropology as a "liberal science" from this perspective is to focus on it as a set of discourses and apparatuses in and through which a range of governmental options spanning the liberal–illiberal spectrum are canvassed and put into effect with different "weightings" as they are brought to bear on different populations in different historical and geographical contexts. One of the ways in which these tensions are worked through is via the different "transactional realities" that anthropology has proposed as the mediating mechanism through which its truths are brought to bear on the task of managing different populations and the relations between them. We borrow this term from Foucault (2008: 297), who proposes it to identify how the forms of knowledge and power through which governmental activities proceed give a distinctive organization and shape to the aspects of individual or group conduct they seek to act on and govern through. This argument forms a part of his disputation with the view that the objects of government—the entities to which it is applied—are pregiven to governing practices rather than the effects of those practices. Transactional realities are therefore not "primary and immediate" realities but an aspect of "modern governmental technologies," not in the sense that they are purely the fabrications of such technologies but rather in the sense that they are being produced at the fragile and contested interfaces between "governors and governed" (297).

In his course of lectures delivered a year earlier (1977–78) Foucault identified two such realities that he saw as crucial to the exercise of modern forms of governmental power: that of the public and that of the milieu. Discussing these at the moment of their emergence out of, and differentiation from, sovereign and disciplinary power, Foucault distinguishes these from each other in terms of the degree to which, and the respects in which, they constitute the populations they address as agents whose capacities for freedom are to be enlisted in the programs through which they are to be governed. The mechanism of the public seeks to shape conduct by working on "opinions, ways of doing things, forms of behaviour, customs, fears, prejudices"; it is what power seeks to get a hold on "through education, campaigns and convictions" (Foucault 2007: 75). The concept of milieu, by contrast, is a by-product of biopolitical forms of power. Instead of acting on "individuals as a set of legal subjects capable of voluntary actions," biopower, relating to humans as a species, acts on "a population," understood as "a multiplicity of individuals who are and fundamentally and essentially only exist biologically bounded to the materiality within which they live" (21). These are, however, categories operating at a very high level of generality. In his work on the governance of sexuality and madness, Foucault proposes more specific concepts identifying the mediating role played by categories—the delinquent and the pervert, for example—that are the product of the knowledge practices and technologies that are specific to them. In a similar spirit, the concept of "working surfaces on the social" has been proposed as an umbrella term encompassing those categories produced by the cultural disciplines, including anthropology, that mediate the relations between governors and governed (Bennett 2013c: 43–45). The disposition of these surfaces—the forms of conduct they identify as needing to be acted on, the forms of action that are brought to bear on them, the populations to which such actions are to be applied—is the outcome of the governmental rationalities they are set within and form a part of.

As these questions form the central concerns of the following chapters, we shall not pursue them in detail here. Instead, by way of concluding our discussion in this chapter, we outline the connections between these concerns and the relations of metropolis and colony, and of anthropologies at home and away, that are spanned by the practices of collecting, ordering, and governing that are our central concern. We note first that we do not restrict these terms to the relations between metropolitan powers in Europe and North America and overseas colonies: Melbourne is just as much a metropolitan center, when considered in terms of its role in extending the reach of settler colonialism into Australia's interior, as is New York (and the Eastern Seaboard more generally considered) in relation to the Native American populations of the Northwest Coast. The relations between anthropology at home and away also apply just as much to the ways in which the study of the Native American cultures of the West Coast and Plains Indians provided the template for the application of anthropology in the management of cultural diversity "on the home front" of the Eastern Seaboard as they do to the relations between the Torres Strait expeditions and the anthropology at home projects comprising Haddon's ethnographic surveys of the United Kingdom and, later, the projects of m-o.

Second, and no less important, while the distribution of the mechanisms of governing through publics and milieus maps roughly onto the distinction between metropolis and colony, this is by no means entirely so. In metropolitan contexts, anthropology's routes from field, to archive, to publics proceeded largely through the exhibition practices of museums. Depending on the context, the composition of these publics varied. There was little sense in America or Australia that their indigenous populations were to be counted among museums' publics, whereas in New Zealand Māori were; New York's immigrant communities were increasingly targeted as a significant audience by the AMNH, but there was no such active engagement with non-Anglo migrants at the NMV. Whatever these differences in the composition of museum publics, the means for connecting with them were, in a broad sense, pedagogic: a matter of changing hearts and minds, opinions and beliefs. Indigenous populations, by contrast, were brought into the orbit of anthropology's practical applications largely through administrative practices that subjected them to biopolitical forms of classification and management. Spencer's work, as we have seen, was informed by, and contributed to, the development of a newly emerging national governmental domain that marked Australia's increasing independence from a "Greater British" imperial domain. Rather than aiming to provide Aboriginal people with the means to acquire the mores and mentalities of Anglo-Australia, as had been the case with earlier civilizing programs, assimilation was redefined as a matter of transforming the racial constitution of the Aboriginal population through programs of selective breeding aimed at the progressive dilution of Aboriginal bloodlines. French colonialism in the interwar years was driven by a sharply contrasting imperative: that of transforming the indigenous populations of France's overseas colonies into a productive economic resource within a colonial logic governed by a drive to increase the economic value of the colonies (Conklin 1997). This involved anthropology in a rigorous disciplining of the bodies of the colonized (Dias 2010) and in educative and administrative programs that sought to transform the conditions of village life in order to detach indigenous labor from its traditional constraints in ways that would allow a greater surplus value to be extracted from it (Wilder 2005). This was complemented by the need to manage the rhetorical incorporation of the colonized within the imperial ideological formation of Greater France while, at the same time, maintaining a differential distribution of civic rights and entitlements across the populations of metropolitan France and France's overseas colonies (Lebovics 2004), as well as within the latter (Conklin 1997).

At the same time, however, related distinctions were applied to the relations between the populations of Paris and those of provincial France as the lessons of colonial science were brought to bear on the governance of France's regional populations through the collection and classification of their cultures by the Musée des Arts et Traditions Populaires (Sherman 2004). Similar equivocations between the masses as political subjects and the masses as inert forces to be managed through the manipulation of their milieus informed the projects of M-O. These "anthropology at home" projects also exemplified the logic of Foucault's (1991) conception of the governmentalization of the state. While originating outside the central apparatuses of the state, they gravitated toward these in the late 1930s, and particularly during the 1939–45 war, in ways that impacted considerably on postwar forms of governance. This is well-trodden ground in relation to M-O. Envisaged initially as a mechanism operating outside, independently of, and, indeed, in critique of the state, M-O aimed to insert anthropological expertise into the processes of governing by producing new representations of the populace that would reorganize the relations between the leaders and the led. It had considerable success in this regard, interposing a new technocratic class fraction into such relations that displaced more traditional gentlemanly forms of social authority (Savage 2010), and—although not without splits and schisms—was eventually integrated into the state as a part of the Ministry of Information. Although complicated a good deal by the accusations of collaboration with the Nazi and Vichy regimes that were leveled against Georges Henri Rivière after the 1939–45 war, the mobilization of anthropology "at home" within the prewar logics of Greater France proved a significant precursor to the postwar development of eco-museums. Their conception of the *ensemble ecologique*—a later development of the MH's environmentalist conception of the ethnographic object—was that of a regional collection of things, persons, and dispositions that were to be preserved, managed, and developed as resources for identity management.[42] And the stress that was placed on the plasticity, and therefore the malleability, of conduct in the post-Boasian development of the culture concept saw anthropologists increasingly engaged in projects directed at the governance of the American domestic population at large through the application of anthropology's techniques of observation and collection to mainstream American culture (Gilkeson 2010).

There is a further more general tendency running across our case studies. This consists in the respects in which—unevenly, and in different ways with different consequences—the concept of culture or variants of it (culture area, "mass," morale, atmosphere) begins to replace that of race as the primary "transactional reality" through which the practical history of anthropology takes place. The respects in which this shift shaped the development of postwar forms of cultural governance—as well as the limits placed on these—are questions we return to in our conclusion. We look first, though, at an earlier period, one in which the relations between metropolis and colony, home and away, were complicated by the triangular relations between Britain, Australia, and, since 1914, its new colony, Papua.

CHAPTER TWO

CURATORIAL LOGICS AND COLONIAL RULE

The Political Rationalities of Anthropology in
Two Australian-Administered Territories

In this chapter we investigate the contrasting rationalities of government
that emerged in the Australian-administered territories of Papua and the Northern Territory during the first half of the twentieth century. We explore how
ethnographic practices became implicated in the regulation of indigenous
populations in these spaces of colonial rule. Our points of departure are the
ethnographic collections associated with two figures central to Australian
native policy: the anthropologist, museum director, and intermittent colonial
administrator Baldwin Spencer and the lawyer, anthropological patron, and
long-serving lieutenant governor of Papua John Hubert Plunkett Murray.
Here we extend our earlier discussion of Spencer, comparing and contrasting the ways in which his collecting practices were implicated in colonial
government with those of the Murray regime. The collections of both men,
and the mechanisms in which they were enrolled, formed parts of contrasting transactional realities ordering the relations between the governors and
the governed. In the case of Spencer's Northern Territory this concerns
the ways in which "race" was used to advance a policy of eugenics. In the
case of Murray's Papua, it concerns the ways in which "native culture" was
implicated in a policy of salvage colonialism.[1] What is striking in this context is a particular empirical conundrum: how was it that despite sharing
the same central administrative authority, broad intellectual milieu, and

personnel, colonial rule turned to *eugenics* in the Northern Territory and to *salvage* in Papua?

Proceeding in three steps, this chapter first traces the elements composing the fieldwork *agencements* through which these collections came to be gathered, alongside the data on which the authority of ethnographic claims came to rest. With regard to Spencer, we return to his expeditions with Frank Gillen to Central Australia and the ethnographic material that was deposited with the National Museum of Victoria (NMV). With regard to Murray, we focus on the collecting practices he instituted in the Papuan colonial service, which came to form the basis of the Papuan Official Collection (POC). We anticipate this discussion with a brief consideration of Alfred Cort Haddon's Cambridge Anthropological Expedition to the Torres Strait in 1898–99. The second step moves from the field to various centers of collection and calculation, both metropolitan and colonial. Here the practices of arranging and displaying Indigenous Australian and Papuan materials are investigated with particular regard to the contrasting roles of the collected objects in relation to the respective transactional realities governing these territories. The final step makes explicit the political rationalities in which the particular transactional realities associated with each territory were enmeshed. We do this by examining the different combinations of the modalities of rule—the liberal and the biopolitical—that were in operation in these territories and the ways in which these relations displaced earlier surfaces of government. Schematically, Spencer's notion of race concerned a biopolitics of assimilation whereby the indigene was to be absorbed into the national population of the settler state through a program of biocultural "up-lift" or "whitening." By contrast, Murray's (1929a, 1929b, 1921) formulations on "native culture" informed a biopolitics of salvage, which sought to promote an indigenous economy with a degree of autonomy from wage labor so as to sustain native populations and forms of life by buffering them from the "corrosive effects" of colonial modernity. We conclude the chapter with some observations on the curatorial logics that undergird the colonial ordering effected by these different programs in these two territories.

FIELDWORK AGENCEMENTS

In tracing these relations between ethnographic collecting and colonial rule the notion of fieldwork agencements is useful for the light it throws on the various collecting practices on which this chapter focuses. A brief consideration of the fieldwork agencements established by Haddon's 1898–99 Torres

Strait expedition and its relation to his subsequent advocacy of "practice anthropology" in the service of colonial rule is helpful here, since these were to leave important traces on the fieldwork agencements that emerged in the Australian-administered territories.

THE CAMBRIDGE ANTHROPOLOGICAL EXPEDITION: TORRES STRAIT

This expedition is widely held to mark a watershed in the history of anthropological fieldwork, particularly in the British tradition (see Stocking 1983, 1985; Kuklick 1991; Urry 1993, 1998; Gosden 1999; E. Edwards 2001, 160; Barth et al. 2005). Henrika Kuklick (2011) notes that Haddon's emphasis on scientific fieldwork was rooted in his background in marine zoology, showing how this trajectory was part of a broader historical trend in the reorganization of the natural field sciences, away from the collection of specimens for armchair survey-scientists and toward a focus on grounded, field-based knowledge practices (see also Roldán 1992). Extending the concept of the "perambulatory laboratory" that had been an integral part of his vision for the Dublin-based Anthropometric Laboratory of Ireland (established in 1892) and that had underpinned his earlier attempts at ethnographic fieldwork with Charles Browne on the Island of Aran (see further discussion in chapter 3), Haddon put together a team of field-workers, each of whom would have specialist responsibility for collecting information relating to a particular discipline of the human sciences—psychology, physical anthropology, ethnology, linguistics, music, sociology, and material culture—by undertaking extensive, systematic studies of particular cultural groups in situ. This model of fieldwork would in the British tradition ultimately be supplanted by a Malinowskian methodology that emphasized extended participant observation by a single field-worker–ethnographer.[2] However, in its employment of new technologies and techniques for the production of what Bruno Latour (1987) has famously termed "immutable and combinable mobiles"—through the collection of wax cylinder sound recordings, still photographs and films, artifacts, genealogies, and other textual inscriptions—it broke new ground in a number of ways: in employing distinctive technologies of collecting and recording, in mediating encounters between anthropologists and field subjects, in organizing fieldwork through general regional surveys followed by intensive area studies, and in producing from this material distinctive modes of scientific writing that would come to characterize the discipline as it developed in the early decades of the twentieth century.

Haddon, appointed a professor of zoology at the College of Science in Dublin in 1883, was invited to participate in a field expedition to the Torres Strait Islands in 1888 to study marine biology. He himself noted, "[I] had no intention of paying attention to ethnography; indeed, before I left England, I consulted Sir William Flower about taking measurements of natives and he dissuaded me from doing so, and others seemed to think that there was little worth doing as regards the natives" (1935: xi). His comments here are somewhat disingenuous; we know he took a copy of *Notes and Queries on Anthropology* with him, had been corresponding with James George Frazer before his journey, and planned to collect objects to sell to museums on his return (Roldán 1992). Nonetheless, his change in interest and career from biology to anthropology as a result of his field experience in 1888 seems beyond question.

Sandra Rouse (1998: 56) notes that Haddon was meticulous in his selection of team members for the later expedition (see also Langham 1981). William Halse Rivers Rivers, an experimental psychologist and physiologist, was persuaded to lead the expedition's psychological investigations based on the enrollment of his former students Charles S. Myers (who was also included for his interest in ethnomusicology) and William McDougall. They were to be accompanied by Herbert Ray, a primary school teacher and linguist who had undertaken a comparative study of two Torres Strait Island languages based on materials provided by Haddon, and, as the expedition's photographer, Anthony Wilkin, a Cambridge graduate who had experience working on archaeological and anthropological expeditions in Egypt and Algeria. Charles Seligman, a physician with an interest in ethnography and indigenous medicine who funded his own involvement, completed the group.

Haddon spent much of 1896 putting together his team and lobbying for funding for the expedition, with Cambridge University ultimately funding the bulk of the cost, with additional funds from the British Association for the Advancement of Science (BAAS), the Royal Dublin Society, the Government of Queensland, the Royal Geographical Society, and others (Rouse 1998: 58). Haddon also reestablished connections with his missionary contacts in the region from his earlier visits to the Torres Strait, who helped arrange logistic details such as accommodation, local transportation, the furnishing of the team with supplies, and access to ethnographic subjects in the region. In advance of the trip, Haddon formulated a clear plan for publishing a series of technical volumes as well as a popular book to help recoup the costs of the expedition and make the results of the anthropological work more widely available. An embargo was placed on any publication preceding this popular account. A contract was drawn up that stipulated the precise roles of expedition members, made clear the intent to collect significant numbers of ethnographic objects and established the terms of ownership of those materials, and specified the terms of the funding of the expedition. Various reports were made to the media to announce the team's departure (see Rouse 1998: 60).

Throughout 1897 Haddon purchased, designed, and had built the various technical recording devices and instruments that would form the field equipment for the expedition. These included still and moving film cameras, field developing equipment, a phonograph and wax cylinders, and a range of physiological and psychological testing devices: anthropometers, Galton's whistle (for pitch perception), Lovibond's Tintometer (for color perception), Haken's E (for distance perception), a color wheel with rotating Masson's disks, Politzer's Hörsmesser (for auditory acuity), and Zwaardemaker's Olfactometer (for measuring sensitivity of smell) (see Richards 1998; Kuklick 1991: 142), to name some of them. Elizabeth Edwards (1998: 106–7) emphasizes the systematic scientific ambitions of the expedition in highlighting the "cutting-edge" nature of the recording devices in particular. The Newman and Guardia cinematograph was accompanied by thirty reels of seventy-five feet of film, and there were also several still film cameras, one of which employed the brand-new Ives and Jolly color photographic process, and two phonographs with playback and recording facilities. This was, she notes, the highest-quality and most modern equipment available. The aim was to reproduce European laboratory conditions in the field, and the technology would support the veracity of the information collected by the expedition (figure 2.1).

The rigors of life in the field laboratory on occasions exposed the limits of various technological devices and required improvisation to produce usable data. For example, Graham Richards (1998: 141) notes that Politzer's Hörsmesser for assessing auditory acuity was almost useless given the constant noise from the breaking surf and rustling palm leaves. These pragmatic decisions influenced not only which data were collected but also the forms in which data were collected and ordered. These would ultimately supply the basis for generalizations regarding the "modes of thought" of indigenous peoples (see Kuklick 1991: 139) and provide a model for the fusion of anthropological theory building and the direct observation that supported it.

That these various technical devices and associated survey techniques were integral to the production of a new anthropological field science is without doubt. But in the expedition we can also see certain patterns established

FIGURE 2.1 "Charles Myers recording the sacred songs of the Malu ceremonies during the Cambridge Anthropological Expedition to the Torres Strait. Gisu is beating the drum Wasikor, while Ulai sings into the recording phonograph." 1898. Probably photographed by A. Wilkin, P.950.ACH1, Museum of Archaeology and Anthropology, University of Cambridge. Courtesy of the Museum of Archaeology and Anthropology.

The collection of scientific data of various kinds was integral to the model of anthropological fieldwork that would be established by the Cambridge Anthropological Expedition to the Torres Strait in 1898. Various technical devices and associated survey techniques mediated the production of a new anthropological field science that would attempt to replicate the conditions of a European laboratory. The use of the recording phonograph was particularly significant in generating "immutable mobiles" in the form of wax cylinders. The phonograph created portable audio data, which could be translated into textual data and reproduced as musical scores in the published records of the expedition.

in the engagements between ethnographers and indigenous people—as components of this field itself—that would be replicated in various subsequent episodes that we discuss in this chapter.

SPENCER AND GILLEN: CENTRAL AUSTRALIA

Following Haddon's Torres Strait expedition in 1898–99, "the second revolutionary field study" in British social anthropology is widely considered to be Spencer and Gillen's fieldwork conducted in Central Australia (Kuklick 2009: 64; Stocking 1996). As discussed in chapter 1, Spencer played an important role in advancing evolutionary thought as an intellectual and exhibitionary program at the NMV. This theoretical orientation continued to organize his work as his preoccupations shifted, similarly to Haddon's, from natural history to anthropology. Pivotal here was his involvement with the Horn Expedition to Central Australia in 1894. Formally appointed as a biologist to this expedition, he took an active interest in the recording of ethnographic data, and it was in this context that he met his collaborator, Gillen, the sub-protector of Aborigines for South Australia and long-serving stationmaster for the transcontinental telegraph. Like Haddon, Spencer returned to field sites he had first studied as a biologist and in 1896–97 undertook ethnographic fieldwork in Central Australia with Gillen. The findings were published in the first of their co-authored texts, *The Native Tribes of Central Australia* (1899), which drew international attention to their work. In 1901 the pair undertook further fieldwork that took them to the Gulf of Carpentaria, leading to the publication of *The Northern Tribes of Central Australia* (1904). Spencer and Gillen's fieldwork has been positioned as an intermediary step in the movement from armchair theory to field science. Indebted to the methodological innovations of the Torres Strait Island expedition, though drawing less on survey methods and more on intensive studies based on Rivers's genealogical method, Spencer anticipated the techniques of participant observation that Bronislaw Malinowski would make famous (Stocking 1996) and, following Haddon's advice, instituted field practices that were innovative in their early application of mimetic devices, including film and sound recordings.[3]

Below we outline some of the key dimensions composing the ethnographic agencements through which Spencer and Gillen's fieldwork was performed. To extend the discussion of these matters that we began in chapter 1, it is useful to draw attention to the range of actors involved in such agencements, across which different forms of agency were distributed. The human actors who shaped the immediate ethnographic exchange included the collectors Spencer and Gillen, the Arrernte informants, the mounted troopers, and the telegraph station operators, as well as those whose support and patronage facilitated this exchange, such as Haddon via methodological advice, James George Frazer via patronage, and David Syme via financial sponsorship and media coverage. A cast of nonhuman actors was similarly significant in mediating the ethnographic event. These included the various technological actors involved in transportation and communication, in particular, the Great Northern Railway line and the Overland Telegraph line. There were also the instruments associated with various techniques of data gathering—the notebook, the still camera, the movie camera, the phonograph, and on occasions the tools of anthropometrics—along with other field equipment, including field accommodation, makeshift darkrooms, preserving spirit, and collecting containers. All of these, along with, importantly, quantities of goods used for bartering, played roles in mediating the ethnographic exchange. And there were the horses, camels, and "buggies" that moved it all from one place to the next (figure 2.2).

To draw out some of the significant relations among these actors, we focus on several key dimensions through which Spencer and Gillen's fieldwork was performed. First, there are the ways in which the field site was conceived as an object of knowledge before the fieldwork. One window onto this conceptualization is through Frazer's petitioning of the Victorian and South Australian governments in support of the 1901 expedition, which he submitted to the London agents-general for South Australia and Victoria (Mulvaney and Calaby 1985: 189–90). Signed by seventy-seven prominent politicians, scientists, anthropologists, and other academics, the document echoed the contentions of *The Golden Bough,* with a phraseology, as Mulvaney and Calaby observe, "redolent of social Darwinism" (190).

As Frazer's petition suggested, Australia was a "field laboratory," and Spencer and Gillen's fieldwork was the labor that would generate the data that it was anticipated would empirically resolve contemporary theoretical debates concerning the major preoccupations of the emerging discipline of anthropology (see Stocking 1996; Kuklick 2006, 2011). Inasmuch as these debates were framed in stadial theory, Spencer and Gillen's data were considered crucial as evidence that positioned the indigenous inhabitants of the Australian continent as an "evolutionary ground zero" (Bennett 2004; see also Wolfe 1999).

If Spencer and Gillen risked being put into service by metropolitan savants, the risks were cast in more existential terms in Melbourne's *The Age* as it promoted public interest in the expedition. Syme, the newspaper's owner, was a major financial backer of the expedition, and the paper published

FIGURE 2.2 Camp Tennant Creek, Northern Territory, Australia, between July and September 1901. Among the individuals identified in the photograph are Kite and Jim. XP15087, Museum Victoria, Melbourne. Courtesy of Museum Victoria.

———

Baldwin Spencer's ethnographic practices were mediated through a complex composition of human and nonhuman agencies some of which are captured in this image of the expedition's camp. It was through a heterogeneous network of indigenous agents and technical devices whose friction and flows performed the fieldwork *agencements* in which Spencer's own agency was enrolled. In this sense, the agency of fieldwork practices did not rest exclusively with the sovereign subject, the anthropologist, but rather was distributed across the various elements of which the fieldwork assemblage was composed and through which ethnographic practices were performed.

———

Spencer's regular reports from the field, which later served as the basis for the popular account, *Across Australia* (Spencer and Gillen 1912). With *The Age* alluding to another famous but less fortunate pair, the significance of the expedition was anticipated by the particular trope invoked in its media coverage. As Mulvaney and Calaby report, the "publicity surrounding their [Spencer and Gillen's] departure stamped them as an intrepid latter-day Burke and Wills combination" (1985: 202).[4] However, in contrast to the earlier ill-fated couple, Spencer and Gillen's journey was facilitated by a well-established, if thin, colonial infrastructure, including the Great Northern Railway line and the Overland Telegraph Line, which traversed the interior of the continent with a network of stations. These not only facilitated the pair's passage but provided points of cross-cultural exchange, in part because this infrastructure had brought with it a system of rationing that had regularized the presence of the colonial state in the lives of the Arrernte, across whose country the lines now ran (Rowse 1992, 1998).

Inasmuch as fieldwork agencements are ones of exchange, they are also ones of economy; that is, they are performances of exchange. Such exchange relations concerned the articulations of indigenous agency through which cross-cultural transactions were entered into or refused in the field, and through which the economy of the fieldwork came to be composed. In the case of Spencer's expeditions this concerned an economy of cross-cultural exchange that was implicated in different regimes of value associated variously with rations, with barter, with gifts, and with the secret-sacred. Indicative of the modes of indigenous agency articulated in this fieldwork economy were forms of conduct that unsettled the collectors. As Tim Rowse observes, the ethnographic texts from the Horn Expedition "exhibit a recurring anxiety that the parties to frontier transactions did not have the same ideas about what they were doing" (1998: 20). This led to concerns from expedition members around questions of reciprocity. Without a common medium of exchange and measure of value, the collectors were at times concerned with what constituted a fair exchange. The often opaque exchange relations they entered into produced ethical concerns around uneven reciprocity.[5]

Rowse has analyzed the distinction between rationing—"the practice which maintained a 'native' presence near non-indigenous donors"—and bartering, the "specific bargains over particular items" that the anthropologist wished to collect or over particular services they wished to secure (1998: 20).[6] In connection with the Horn Expedition, Rowse argues that it was the governmentality of rations that underpinned this expeditionary enterprise and that was implicated in the establishment of an early articulation of welfarism (16–17). Rationing was formally introduced by the federal government in 1901, the same year as Spencer and Gillen's expedition to Central Australia. However, it was a long-standing practice in that region, designed to underwrite the subsistence of indigenous populations whose traditional food sources had been disrupted by the pastoral industry, which intermittently called on their labor. In this, then, Spencer's fieldwork was implicated in practices of colonial governmentality, in which he would take on a more formal role in 1912 as the special commissioner and chief protector of Aborigines in the Northern Territory, to which we subsequently turn. As a point of contrast to Central Australia, it is useful now to turn to the ethnographic agencements associated with the Australian-administered territory of Papua.

GOVERNMENT ANTHROPOLOGY: PAPUA

In December 1914 Haddon prepared a memorandum for Atlee Hunt, secretary for the Australian Department of External Affairs. Haddon briefed Hunt on, first, the rationale for appointing government anthropologists to Australia's colonial possessions in the Western Pacific, and second, the feasibility of establishing a museum and curatorial position devoted to "Papuan ethnology." Haddon advocated both, insisting they were mutual requirements for "the good government" of "alien peoples," a view no doubt built on Haddon's expeditionary experience in the Western Pacific.[7] It was also a position he advanced in various scientific and public fora—pertinently, earlier in 1914, at the Sydney and Melbourne meetings of the BAAS (Haddon 1921).[8]

For federal bureaucrats, Haddon's expertise was no doubt enhanced by his recent visits to both Australia and Papua. After presenting on the "practical value of anthropology to administration" at the BAAS meeting in Sydney in 1914, Haddon visited Papua.[9] This further cemented Haddon's authority on Western Pacific ethnography, providing the occasion to follow up the survey work of the 1898–99 Torres Strait expedition with intensive studies and to seed more fieldwork in the region. It was on this excursion that Haddon met Murray (Campbell 1998). A significant conduit connecting metropolitan anthropology, ethnographic field sites, and colonial administration, Murray was Haddon's long-standing colonial correspondent, facilitating his Papuan expedition and likely recommending his expertise to the Department of External Affairs.[10] Murray himself had made presentations in various scientific and administrative fora and lobbied the federal government for the establishment of both the post of government anthropologist and suitable facilities for the administration's ethnographic collection.[11] For Murray, anthropology's administrative utility had been suggested by one of Haddon's Torres Strait collaborators, Seligman, who was part of the Cooke Daniels Expedition to Papua in 1904. Murray, following Seligman's work with the colonial government of Sudan, along with similar appointments in British Africa, advised Hunt that information should be sought from these protectorates if a government anthropologist was to be appointed.[12] Seligman's visit also fostered Murray's interests in material culture. Murray had a small army of collectors in the form of his government officers—the resident magistrates and patrol officers of the Papuan colonial service—who were equipped with both a budget and an extensive "shopping-list" for desirable "native curio" (Schaffarczyk 2011: 195).

Murray was in part motivated to match the legacy of his predecessor, William MacGregor, who, as lieutenant governor of British New Guinea, had amassed a considerable personal collection.[13] Posterity was not, however, Murray's sole objective.[14] Murray concurred with anthropological luminaries, Haddon among them, that ethnographic collecting would not only provide testimony to rapidly disappearing forms of indigenous life but also advance the knowledge of the territory's present inhabitants, and so contribute to "scientific administration," as he would later describe his program (Murray 1931). Unlike MacGregor, whose collection was deposited with the Queensland Museum on the close of his term of office, Murray's intention was that the POC should ultimately be for the benefit of Papuans and remain in Port Moresby as the property of the territory.[15] While no doubt an exercise in salvage predicated on his belief that Papua was rapidly changing and, therefore, that its material culture was rapidly disappearing, Murray's collecting, at least in part, rested on his view that self-government, though not an immediate prospect, would and should eventuate. The developing collection and future museum would demonstrate the distance that the Papuan population had traveled to reach its capacity for autonomous government.

In advocating federal support for government anthropology, Haddon's approach was twofold: scientific and economic. First, motivated by the propositions of social evolution whereby indigenous forms of life faced impending and inevitable extinction in the wake of the unfolding European universal, Haddon repeated the mantra of the salvage ethnography that had long driven his fieldwork: with the old order "rapidly passing away," there was, he contended, "no time to lose."[16] While for Haddon this disappearance was ethically troubling, equally concerning was the loss to science should these societies go undocumented.[17] Although there was a growing literature on the ethnology of Papua, Haddon observed that "a very great deal yet remains to be collected and recorded, for most of what has been published is incomplete." The appointment of a government anthropologist would remedy this fragmentary record: coordinating "all existing information" and making "fresh intensive studies in the ethnology of the Territory."[18]

However, this data collection project was not simply for the benefit of metropolitan savants preoccupied with the study of modernity's disappearing primitive Other as an insight into European prehistory. Rather, and this was Haddon's second prong, ethnographic knowledge had economic utility. Providing expertise on the treatment of "backward peoples . . . during the period of tutelage," anthropology, he argued, lowered the cost of colonial administration, making it more effective and efficient in the pursuit of colonial "social and material development."[19] In 1916 Murray likewise emphasized this dimension in correspondence with Atlee Hunt, contending that the "services of a trained anthropologist" would be vital to the colonial administration—providing "advice on how best to reconcile the native public opinion (so far as it exists) with the general advance and development of the territory."[20]

Haddon's advice was largely followed, and the position of government anthropologist was eventually established after the 1914–18 war. It was initially held by Walter Mersh Strong, the territory's existing medical officer, whose ethnographic interests were largely medical. However, it was Francis Edgar Williams, a South Australian–born student of the Oxford anthropologist Robert Ranulph Marett, who provided the most enduring service, holding the position from 1922 to 1943: first as an assistant before being promoted to government anthropologist after Strong's retirement in 1928.

In 1922 Williams, conducting one of his first official assignments, undertook fieldwork in the Purari Delta. He produced three reports in this connection: *The Vailala Madness and the Destruction of Native Ceremonies in the Gulf Division* (1923b), *The Collection of Curios and the Preservation of Native Culture* (1923a), and *The Natives of Purari Delta* (1924). Written in the contrasting registers of "practical anthropology" and "salvage ethnography," these documents together offer an optic on the sociotechnical agencements through which Williams's fieldwork on the delta was performed. Produced at Murray's request, the first two reports addressed particular issues of concern to the colonial authority: respectively, the emergence of a cargo cult and the impact of European collecting of indigenous material culture. As the latter part of each title suggests, the reports articulated Williams's concern with an indigenous culture under threat and in need of protection, particularly against the removal or destruction of the cultural objects that were the substrates of ceremonial life. In both reports the threat was the negative effects on indigenous life of an encroaching and unregulated modernity. The specific agents bearing this threat were, however, quite different—on the one hand, a disruptive indigenous mimicry associated with a millennial movement and, on the other, unscrupulous European collectors, exemplified by the recent expedition to the area by Alan McCulloch of the Australian Museum (AM) and the filmmaker Frank Hurley, whose collecting, particularly of bullroarers and *piforu* (preserved human heads), caused unrest among indigenous communities in the region. Formally embedded in the colonial administration, Williams offered these two reports as exercises in "practical anthropology," offering advice on native policy so as to manage the interface between colonizers and colonized in the interests of producing stable native subjects. In contrast, Williams's third report, *The Natives of Purari Delta*, offered no recommendations to the government. Following in the *Notes and Queries* tradition, as Williams saw it, this text was "purely descriptive." As an exercise in salvage ethnography, it aimed to detail indigenous social relations before, or at least when relatively untouched by, colonial modernity. Nevertheless, as the paratext to this document makes clear, relations of colonial governmentality were never far away. In his preface, Williams wrote that he hoped the volume would "contribute to a better understanding of the people . . . for the first essential toward fair, sympathetic, and kind treatment of inferiors is to know what they are doing" (1924: vii).

To know what they are doing: it was of course precisely to this end that Williams found himself employed, when Murray sent him to the Purari Delta to investigate the "Vailala Madness," which had first emerged in the region in 1919. In the early 1920s the Purari had only recently been pacified. Murray had led a punitive expedition into the region some years earlier, and the insurrectionary rumors associated with the "mania" were of particular concern to him (Bell 2006, 2010). The apparent "hysteria" engulfing the region ran counter to Murray's program of "scientific administration," which sought gradual, rational, European-led social change (Murray 1926, 1932). The Vailala Madness was manifestly contrary to this aim and thus contrary to the cultivation of a stable native subject to which his administration was committed and which needed to be secured if the colonial authority was to meet the Australian state's international obligations to guarantee the material and moral development of Papua's population. Murray commissioned Williams to provide an assessment of the movement's threat to colonial rule, as well as advice on its management and containment. Williams's brief was, as Murray put it, to "assist us in our task of fitting or, as it were dovetailing existing customs into the new civilization which we are introducing" (1924: ii).

Williams's fieldwork practices in the delta were both facilitated and frustrated by the colonial infrastructure in which he was enmeshed in his official capacity as a government anthropologist. A network of government rest houses built for the administration's patrol officers enabled his work, and he did on occasion accompany these officers to access various field sites. Yet he was regularly frustrated in his work by his association with the colonial authority, and he acknowledged how "an anthropologist's business may be obstructed by his official character and the presence of a uniformed policeman" (Williams 1924: 119). In the delta he found informants on occasions wary and uncooperative, refusing to talk and hiding objects or, indeed, lampooning him. Frustrated with "obdurate informants" in the Purari, he commented in his field notes that they were "on the whole a lying, leg pulling, secretive, suspicious lot of bastards" (quoted in Young and Clark 2001: 31). It was through these equivocal arrangements that Williams gathered his data on the Vailala Madness. The resulting report, which is cited as the first ethnographic study of what the subsequent anthropological literature termed cargo cults, charted a mytho-Christian "hysteria" sweeping through various communities in the Purari (Williams 1923b; also see Williams 1934). As he detailed it, there was a wholesale destruction of the material culture of traditional ceremony, and the institution of novel, elaborate spectacles—which included mimicking European military drills and the English habit of taking tea—all of which were conducted in anticipation of the arrival of dead relatives by ship or by plane. While seeing it as undoubtedly a chaotic disruption that appeared to draw out a psychological malady in some individuals, Williams did not find the movement politically potent. It was, however, socially and economically disruptive, disturbing, as he saw it, the delicate balance between traditional life and regimes of plantation labor deemed necessary for Papuans' accommodation to colonial modernity. He advanced possible substitutes (principally, cricket and Christianity) that might displace the mania and restore good government. This policy of substitution was implicated in a form of biopolitics. Williams shared Rivers's conviction that native psychological malaise was directly connected with the collapse of indigenous populations. For Williams, as Young and Clark noted, "ceremony had not only a social value, but also a psychological one directly related to depopulation" (2001: 16). As Williams put it: "Leave the native something worth living for, and he will live" (quoted in Young and Clark 2001: 16).

Deploying the notion of fieldwork agencement, this section has sought to draw attention to the range of human and nonhuman actors involved in the performance of anthropological fieldwork to consider the distributed agency through which anthropological practices are performed. This includes human bodies but also their prostheses—the tools, equipment, technical devices, theoretical and theological statements, and so on—that come to perform a set of distinctive anthropological fieldwork practices in each of the instances we have discussed. In arguing that anthropological fieldwork practices were performed through these heterogeneous agents, through the friction as well as the flows they engendered, the agency of fieldwork in this sense rests not exclusively with the human or sovereign subject but rather is distributed across the various elements of which the fieldwork agencement is composed and through which fieldwork practices are performed. Deploying this notion of fieldwork agencements provides the occasion to compare and contrast the various field sites and sites of collecting associated with the collections on which this chapter focuses. To map the composition of these arrangements is also to be concerned with the ways in which they came to be implicated in practices concerned with the government of the colonial frontier—be it the ways in which Spencer and Gillen's practices were located in a ration economy constitutive of a proto-welfarism, or the ways in which Williams's practices were enmeshed in policing operations designed to assert the presence of the colonial authority in "uncontrolled" zones. Such fieldwork agencements, then, were in part constituted by relations of government and in turn were consequential for the development of such relations. To draw out these connections we now turn to the particular centers of collection and calculation through which the field data gathered came to circulate.

CENTERS OF COLLECTION AND CALCULATION

In moving from the frontier relations of the field to the various centers of collection where the data gathered came to be processed and subjected to procedures of ordering, this section focuses on the practices of arrangement and display to which the materials collected by Spencer and Gillen and the materials of the POC were subjected. As discussed in chapter 1, Spencer, at the NMV, built on and qualified the typological method, which coordinated the display of indigenous objects via the logic of the developmental sequence. Williams's Port Moresby office served as a "depot" for objects belonging to the POC before their transportation to the AM. These objects were subject to Williams's (1939) self-ascribed "perfunctory" interest in material culture; he contended that his labor was better directed at the preservation of the skills of the indigenous craftsperson than at the preservation of the museum object. At the AM a life-group diorama displayed Papuan material. In part, these different orientations to the collected object between the two territories could be attributed to the changing orientation of the discipline of anthropology, from a focus on material culture as evidence for stadial theory to more relativist formulations concerned with mapping and displaying cultural wholes. While that is no doubt partly true, this contrast was also the outcome of different structures of colonialism in which the fate of the indigene was rather differently cast in each territory. In the case of Indigenous Australians the future was closed, since the logic of settler colonialism was premised on the dispossession of the native from the land and an ensuing policy of extermination and assimilation. In the case of Indigenous Papuans the future remained open, if in a qualified sense. This was so inasmuch as extractive colonialism, structured as it was on the use of native labor, relied on the maintenance of indigenous modes of production to subsidize the cost of labor to colonial capital. This, to a degree, countenanced a policy of "humanitarian colonialism" in the context of Papua. In the former case, then, museum objects were evidence justifying the inevitability of the closure of an indigenous future. In the latter, cultural objects were embodiments of indigenous labor, the capacities for which needed to be maintained and skills transferred intergenerationally to ensure the possibility of an indigenous future.

This at least is the contention we wish to advance here. It is an argument that qualifies other accounts of the difference in native policy between the two territories, which would explain it in terms of a difference in the "attitude" of the colonizers toward the colonized (N. Thomas 1994) or, relatedly, in terms of remorse for the treatment of Aborigines and a desire to be considered by the international community as a humane colonial presence (Gray 2007: 33). Rather, we suggest this difference is better accounted for in terms of the logics of colonization in which each territory was historically implicated. While both spaces came to be under the auspices of the Commonwealth government shortly after Australia's federation in 1901, the history and rationale for their establishment were quite distinctive, as were the forms of colonization they articulated: settler colonialism on the one hand and "humanitarian colonialism" on the other. The Northern Territory was annexed from the state of South Australia in 1911 and transferred to federal control in a move to foster European settlement in the region; this was intended to encourage economic development and address anxieties about the racial identity of the emerging nation and the security of the nation-state's northern border. Security concerns also played a part in motivating interests in Papua, but it was rather differently positioned in relation to questions of economic development and the new nation's self-image. Formally annexed in 1888, British New Guinea passed to the newly federated Commonwealth of Australia in 1902 and became the Australian Territory of Papua in 1906. Following the outbreak of World War I, German New Guinea fell to Australian forces. From 1919 it was administered first as a League of Nations mandated territory and later as a United Nations trust territory. In relation to the Papuan territories the federal state was concerned to demonstrate itself a benevolent colonial presence and uphold the international ideal of humanitarian colonialism. Under Murray's regime, European expropriation of indigenous land was resisted, as were labor practices that relied on the importation of non-European workers, while a program establishing native plantations sought to bring indigenous resources and labor into market relations in the interest of the "dual mandate": that is, that of developing the territory in the interests of both colonized and colonizers. Nevertheless, the economic development of the territory of Papua under Murray's regime remained limited. The collapse in copra prices following the Great Depression was no doubt a major contributing factor.[21]

ETHNOLOGICAL COLLECTION, NATIONAL MUSEUM OF VICTORIA

In anticipation of the 1914 BAAS meeting in Melbourne, Spencer organized an exhibition of ten thousand Aboriginal stone tools from the NMV's collection, which had itself significantly escalated in size under his tenure as director. However, Spencer's intention for the NMV's new exhibition was to qualify metropolitan concepts of typology and so, as he wrote to Henry Balfour, "'astonish' overseas visitors" to the meeting (quoted in Mulvaney and Calaby 1985: 306). Pitt-Rivers's series offered visual demonstrations of the movement toward increasing complexity in material culture, famously, as was noted in the previous chapter, from the throwing stick to the musket. In such evolutionary series each object displayed was imbued with an archaeological depth. This was so in that each object was an ontological entity composed of multiple layers, which were variously orientated to "time's arrow": some of the object's elements pointed to the past, others to future developments (Bennett 2010). However, at the NMV Spencer's stone tools were objects of a different ontological order. By demonstrating the shared variety of these implements, which were nevertheless used contemporaneously and did not suggest progressive technological development, Spencer posited these tools, and their makers, as entities that were "out of time," in the sense of being subjected to a limited developmental time whose duration had now ceased (N. Thomas 1996). In marshaling in this way the "immutable mobiles" he and others had gathered in the field, Spencer used the material exhibited as evidence of a single entity, an "Aboriginal race," that was historically static and, as such, had not (yet) entered the dynamic of evolutionary time. He thus posited a race that had not been exposed to the forces of competition and so displayed their technology, as exemplified by stone tools, as lacking significant progression.[22]

There are several epistemological and political dimensions to such arrangements that merit attention here. First, as a society that had not entered historical time Aboriginal people occupied an "evolutionary ground zero" (Bennett 2004). As Spencer elaborated in his guide to the NMV's ethnological collections: "The Australian aborigine may be regarded as a relic of the early childhood of mankind left stranded in a part of the world where he has, without the impetus derived from competition, remained in a low condition of savagery" ([1915] 1922: 11) As a "relic" the "Aboriginal primitive" was a "living fossil" that afforded insights into European's own prehistory. As such, it was a figure that came to occupy a central, originary position in late nineteenth- and early twentieth-century social theory, particularly, to list the pressing debates of the time, around the doctrine of survivals, the origin of religion, totemism, animism, nescience, and questions of kinship and mother right (see Wolfe 1999).

Second, this museological explication was consequential for the ways in which indigenous populations came to be governed in the Northern Territory. At the same time as Spencer was planning his exhibition in anticipation of the BAAS meeting, he was completing a special commissioner's report on Aboriginal policy in the Northern Territory (Spencer 1913). This was in partial fulfillment of his role as chief protector of Aborigines (1911–12) and detailed concerns Spencer would later return to in an advisory role on "the half caste problem."[23] In that report Spencer advanced a spatial zoning of the territory's capital, Darwin, and its surrounds, which aimed to regularize the movement of racially coded bodies. Gray has contended that anthropological expertise played a limited role in the government of such spaces. Despite the appointment of figures like Spencer, he argues, "anthropology as an informing discipline was almost absent from any matters associated with the formulation, application and implementation of Aboriginal policy" (2007: 32). Yet there was a certain shared logic by which Spencer organized his museum objects and sought to manage racialized bodies in the Northern Territory. Both were organized by a curatorial eye invested in the logic of the developmental sequence (Bennett 2004, 2011). We will return to this connection in the final section of this chapter.

In addressing the question of a "Museum for Papuan Ethnology" Haddon chastised the federal government. Bemoaning the lack of systematic collections in New Guinea and deploring the inadequate curation of Papuan collections in Australian institutions, he asserted that a "museum of carefully selected and labeled ethnological specimens is necessary for the study of a people."[24] However, Haddon did not entirely share Murray's view that such facilities should be developed in Port Moresby. Perhaps signaling anthropology's emerging intimacy with colonial law and order, a small museum had been erected in Port Moresby in close proximity to the courthouse and the police barracks, the latter of which doubled as a storage site for ethnographic material. Reporting on this arrangement, Haddon observed that this "small museum building" contained specimens "of considerable interest." However, with adequate facilities likely to prove prohibitively expensive and with a locality remote from those it would most benefit—anthropology's scholars and students—he reasoned that "an ethnological museum should not be installed in Port Moresby."[25] Rather, Haddon advised that "the ethnological collection of the Papuan Government should be installed in an Australian museum," with provisions for the appointment of a curator devoted to it. "The existing building," he contended, "should be retained as a receiving house for specimens collected by Government officers and others, and thence dispatched from time to time to the main collection."[26]

Plans for a comprehensive ethnographic museum in Port Moresby were shelved. The existing facility became the office of the government anthropologist and served as a site for marshaling and dispersing ethnographic data and personnel. In its museological role it acted as a "depot," as Murray put it, for ethnographic specimens destined, as it was ultimately determined, for the AM.[27] With no new curatorial position established, the duties fell to William Walford Thorpe, the museum's keeper of ethnography (Specht 1979). Lasting from 1915 to 1933, this arrangement saw limited exhibition of the collection. Notably, however, in 1923 the "Ravi" diorama opened (Thorpe 1926; Specht 2003).[28] This coincided with the Australian public's increasing curiosity about its Western Pacific colony as "a land of great possibilities" for scientific discovery, economic exploitation, and colonial fantasy.[29] This curiosity was no doubt fueled by the sensationalism surrounding Hurley and McCulloch's recent expedition to Papua, which, in the media's reporting, fostered an image simultaneously of the radically Other savagery of purportedly previously undiscovered tribes and of a "golden heritage" of untouched riches ripe for Australian exploitation (Hurley 1924).[30] Conceived by Mc-Culloch, the "Ravi" diorama no doubt contributed to such presentations of the territory (figure 2.3).

In addition to being the conduit through which ethnographic objects moved from the Papuan field to the AM and elsewhere, in his Port Moresby office Williams engaged in the sedentary tasks of an anthropologist: penning monographs, analyzing surveys, writing reports, cataloging photographic images, storing ethnographic objects, and planning forays into the field—be it at Murray's request to investigate special topics (sorcery, cargo cults, and so on) that threatened colonial authority, or to pursue his own academic interests in native institutions.[31] From that office, he kept up his correspondence with his administrative superiors in Port Moresby and Canberra and with his anthropological colleagues, including, as he termed them, "the Sydney savants"—Alfred Reginald Radcliffe-Brown and Raymond Firth—and those further afield, in London, Cambridge, Oxford, and so on.[32] It was also from this office that Williams mentored the territory's resident magistrates and patrol officers, fostering anthropological interests in ways that informed the exercise of their field duties (Schaffarczyk 2011: 206).[33] And the office also served to funnel "academic fieldworkers out of Sydney into appropriate sites," Beatrice Blackwood and Reo Fortune among them (Stocking 1996: 386).[34] From 1929 it was also where Williams edited a monthly newspaper, *The Papuan Villager*, which sought to engage the colonial public sphere, targeting literate "native public opinion" (Nelson 1968). This space, then, was intimately connected with other spaces both within the territory and abroad—from the network of government district stations and rest houses in the field, which served as points of cross-cultural gathering, to the networks of patronage associated with metropolitan academic and museum institutions. The Port Moresby Museum was a well-connected node in an increasingly expansive and dense anthropological-administrative network through which ethnographic data, objects, theory, opinions, and personnel circulated.

As a depot and bureau the Port Moresby Museum came to operate as a local center of collection and calculation: one located in a network of data gathering and mobilizing that circulated from the field, through administrative regimes, through academic practices and museological institutions, and back to the field via anthropologically informed modalities of colonial rule. This museum, then, was a component in an emerging anthropological assemblage through which ethnography was performed and new formulations of native culture came to be composed. These, in turn, served as mechanisms through which the colonial social came to be governed. Codified and

FIGURE 2.3 "The Ravi, or club-house, exhibit." Frontispiece, *Australian Museum Magazine*, April–June 1926. State Library of New South Wales, Sydney. Courtesy of the State Library of New South Wales.

The accompanying caption to this photograph reads:

> The Ravi, or Papuan club-house, exhibit. The ravi was described by the late Allan R. McCulloch, who conceived the idea of this exhibit, as being, in addition to a club house and fortress, a native museum and the stronghold of the village sorcerers. In the foreground may be seen a warrior in gala attire. The skulls shown in the racks are those of former enemies, beneath are rows of strangely carved boards to drive away evil influences, and near them are skulls of pigs and crocodiles. In the centre are displayed masks used in ceremonies which have for their object the increase or maintenance of the food supply. The scene represents two cubicles typical of the many comprising a ravi.

Absorbed in the ethnographic present, the manikin of the diorama presents the colonial subject to a Sydney public in an image of radical alterity, one embedded in a timeless cultural whole. This presentation contrasted with the territory's administration, which figured native culture not as a totality in need of preservation but as an entity whose various components were open to reform.

---

calibrated as an object of knowledge, native culture emerged as a target of administrative calculation: an entity that could be plugged into "new assemblages of institutions, practices, knowledges and tactics for controlling subjects and achieving security" (Lattas and Rio 2011: 1–2). It was an entity, then, that was ambivalently implicated in the cultivation of what Murray took as the moral horizon of his regime: "the better brown man."

LIBERAL GOVERNMENT AND BIOPOLITICAL ADMINISTRATION

In this section we consider how native subjects were targeted in projects of "improvement" that organized and reorganized colonial social relations to different ends—in Spencer's case, in a program of biocultural "whitening" and, in Murray's, in a program of "making better brown men." Here we offer an account of the different native policies developed in these spaces, in which Spencer advanced a racial logic that divided the Northern Territory's population into discrete subpopulations according to genetic inheritance, and Murray promoted a cultural logic that divided indigenous Papuan practices into the tolerable and the intolerable. Spencer's notion of race concerned a biopolitics of assimilation whereby the indigene was to be absorbed into the national population through a program of biocultural "up-lift" or "whitening," through which subsequent generations would reach the threshold of liberal subjecthood. In this way a biopolitical program prepared the way for the possibility of liberal government. In contrast, Murray's (1929a, 1929b) notion of "native culture" concerned a biopolitics of protection, to preserve the health and wealth of native populations and so sustain an economy independent to a degree from wage labor. This concerned programs of sanitation, education, and so on by which "the better brown man" would be cultivated. Inasmuch as it countenanced Williams's (1923b, 1939) long-held view that the indigene, as a subject of freedom, was an ontological a priori and, contra Spencer, not an evolutionary horizon to be achieved via biocultural "up-lift," it was a formulation of the colonial subject that recognized the indigene as a subject with the right to a particular way of life and so to a degree of self-determination.

"RACE" AND THE NORTHERN TERRITORY

Spencer played a leading role in the production of the "Aboriginal domain" in postfederation Australia through his activities as an anthropological fieldworker, photographer and filmmaker, collector and curator, lecturer and writer, and scientific administrator (Rowse 1992). In these roles his ethnographic authority was pivotal to the emergence of a scientific production of

Aboriginality that, displacing, at least in part, Christian formulations, positioned indigenous subjects as bearers of a racial inheritance to be administered, rather than as souls to be ministered to (Bennett 2010). In this, Spencer was central to the constitution of an Aboriginal domain in which biopolitical administration increasingly superseded pastoral salvation as the dominant modality of colonial power. In his various administrative activities directed at the inhabitants of the Northern Territory—initially in his role as the chief protector of Aborigines (1911–12) and later in an advisory role on "the half caste problem"—Spencer's racial formulations were directly folded into an administrative apparatus targeting the colonial social.[35] The report he produced in the context of his initial role was directly critical of Christian institutions, taking aim at Carl Strehlow's Hermannsburg Mission (Spencer 1913).

Bennett (2004, 2011, 2013c) has usefully situated Spencer's ethnographic practices in relation to these shifting modalities of governmentality that came to target indigenous subjects in late nineteenth- and early twentieth-century Australia. In particular, he highlights the contestations through which indigenous subjects came to be figured less as the bearers of souls in need of salvation, as they had been for missionaries, and more as members of a race in need of assimilation, as they increasingly came to be positioned under the auspices of the settler nation-state. As Bennett argues, this concerns the contrasting political logics of the missionary project and the assimilation project: the former worked through a theological-cum-governmental program in which souls to be saved for the afterlife were subjects to be civilized in this life, and the latter through a scientific-cum-governmental program directed at "life itself," in which indigenous populations were to be governed through the biological logic of race. To Bennett's analysis we add two further elements: one highlights the spatial dimension of Spencer's program to consider the ways in which Spencer instituted a form of biopolitical rule in Darwin and its surrounds; the other considers the ways in which Spencer's program was viewed as preparatory for the subsequent cultivation of liberal subjecthood. We advance this argument by drawing out four main aspects of Spencer's administrative engagement in the Northern Territory.

First, Spencer's program was implicated in practices that were simultaneously ones of "make live and let die." With the emergence of scientific racism, Michel Foucault (1976, 2003) has diagnosed a new power to kill associated, not with the sovereign's right to let live and make die, but with a power that enters into life drawing a distinction between "what must live and what must die" (2003: 254). Spencer's evolutionary conceptions were imbricated in an administrative program of "making live," which, in distinguishing between the potentiality for civility of the "half caste" and that of the "full-blood," advocated the isolation of the former to foster their intermarriage so as to dilute the percentage of Aboriginal blood and progressively whiten that population and thus increase its capacity for civilization. The corollary of this strategy was the identification of "what must die." "Full-blood" Aborigines were, in his opinion, as for many of his contemporaries, "doomed to extinction," necessarily determined by the natural mechanism of competition.[36] It was through various institutional arrangements targeting the colonial social that this biopolitical program was to be implemented.

Second, to consider how Spencer's practices were implicated in securing the colonial social, it is useful to turn to the notion of milieu. In Foucault's account of biopower what is "targeted through the milieu" is the optimization of "circulation." These interventions he described as "organizing circulation, eliminating its dangers, making a division between good and bad circulation, and maximizing the good circulation by eliminating the bad" (2007: 19). In the case of Spencer's intervention in the Northern Territory, it is precisely this concern with optimizing circulation that was at stake—one that was principally focused on drawing a line between the desirable and undesirable circulation of human bodies and other entities. For example, Spencer worked to enforce a spatial zoning of the township of Darwin and its surrounds that aimed to regularize the movement of racially coded bodies so as to achieve two aims. On the one hand, the spatial zoning was intended to eliminate the dangers of indigenous "demoralization" through association with "undesirable" whites and Asiatics and so to prevent prostitution, venereal disease, drug use, infertility, and casual miscegenation, thereby suppressing the bad circulation of opium, diseases, and dangerous bodies. On the other hand, it was supposed to maximize the opportunities for the cultural and genetic "up-lift" of the indigenous population through the training and employment of indigenous labor and through a eugenic program of whitening. Spencer's program, then, was concerned to optimize the circulation of bodies to realize the potentiality of both their labor power and their genetic inheritance so as to promote the health and wealth of the population.

The optimization of this circulation was contingent on various dividing practices by which the population of Darwin and its surrounds was split according to a racial logic, since only certain subpopulations were to be targeted in training or eugenic programs, whereas other subpopulations required different measures. For example, to govern the contact between races, Spencer (1913) constructed a fourfold taxonomy by which the indigenous population of the Northern Territory was divided into subpopulations whose respective mentalities and milieus required different modes of intervention to regulate the circulation of bodies, labor, commodities, diseases, and fecundity (1913: 14–16). These concerned, first, those "living in and around towns," who were "de-moralized" and so subject to curfews, prohibited zones, employment restrictions, and resettlement in "compounds," restrictions intended, in particular, to prevent fraternization with "Asiatics." Second, those "living on land . . . thrown open for . . . close settlement" were pristine but at risk from encroachment by white settlers and thus required the provision of "reserves," if they were to be "preserved." Third, those "living on large pastoral areas" needed to be maintained on stations to supply labor, for wages or otherwise. And, finally, there were those "living on wild, unoccupied land," of whom "practically nothing is known."

This focus on circulation—the third aspect of Spencer's program—targeted frontier sexuality, since it concerned conduct that at once presented risks to the corporeality and morality of individual bodies and threats to the prosperity and health of the social body. In his report in 1913, this administrative concern with sexuality targeted the following subjects and subpopulations: "the prostituted indigenous women," "the licentious Asiatic male," "the immoral white male," "the absent white women," "the married European couple," "the pure blacks," the "demoralized" urban indigene, "the half castes," "the Asiatics," "the whites," and "the venereally diseased." With regard to colonial sexuality Spencer's biopolitical administration sought to regularize the contact of racialized bodies so as to manage the Northern Territory's population. This concerned how these bodies were distributed in space, particularly through zones of exclusion and institutions of enclosure, and how they were distributed in time, in particular, through a eugenic program of intergenerational whitening. The former was the key to securing the latter and was to be instituted through various mechanisms. These included the various dividing practices that segregated the different subpopulations, such as the prohibition zones that separated the indigene from the Asiatic by banning Aborigines from entering Darwin's Chinatown, the "lock-hospitals" that separated the venereally diseased from the undiagnosed, the "special institutions" that separated "the half castes" from both the whites and the "pure blacks," and the "reserves" that separated the "wild native" from all other populations. There were also various legislative practices around marriage, which forbade it between different races and made it mandatory for appointment to government positions, which were to be held by white men.

Fourth, in judging Aboriginal subjectivity to lack the capacity for self-government, Spencer's report in 1913 purported that the indigene has "the mentality of a child" and thus "no sense of responsibility" (14). Spencer viewed the responsibility toward others that might be attributed to indigenous practices of resource redistribution as a hindrance to the cultivation of individual responsibility and as evidence of primitive communal, as oppose to liberal competitive, forms of social relations. He wrote, "Everything is communistic and even if a man is provided with an extra supply of food, or in recent years, tobacco, in return for something he has made or done, it is usually not long before it is divided amongst his friends, there is an equal distribution of profits quite irrespective of deserts" (14). Spencer advanced forms of training in "industrial habits" by which conduct might be responsibilized in ways that accorded with liberal subjectivity (27): this included those associated with the discipline of wage labor and the prudence of "saving money" (22). Where the discipline of employment was not kept and contractual obligations breached, Spencer urged that immediate punishment must ensue if the recalcitrant was to learn responsibility: "Punishment of natives to be salutary must be summary" (18). However, for those living on reserves or "wild" lands, Spencer recommended a certain colonial tolerance with regard to the law:

> There are many deeds committed by wild natives which are crimes, and often most serious ones under our laws, but are in strict accord with their own customs and it is manifestly advisable not to interfere with their customs so long as they are dealing with fellow tribesmen. In the case of semi-civilized natives who have some knowledge, but still a very imperfect one of our laws and are as yet strongly influenced by their own customs, considerable discretion should be exercised when a deed is committed which is a crime under our laws but is strictly in accord with their customs. (20)

 In this way colonial tolerance came to enact a form of exclusion by which "the native" was marked out by "exceptions" to the claims of liberal citizenship.

"NATIVE CULTURE" AND COLONIAL PAPUA

By contrast, for Murray's Papuan regime, governing the colonial social was concerned less with a racial logic determining the capacity for assimilation across indigenous populations based on blood percentages, and more with a cultural logic seeking the preservation and augmentation of "native culture" so as to stabilize native subjects and harness their potential for liberal rule. Reflecting on the implementation of colonial rule late in his career, Murray was adamant that the "pacification" of subject peoples "must proceed on scientific lines" so as not to "degenerate into indiscriminate terrorism" (1932: 2). Murray associated this mode of pacification with the methods of "indirect rule," whereby ethical and efficient government was to be achieved, not through overt violence (the modus operandi of the "direct method"), but rather, as Andrew Lattas puts it, by "governing through culture and tradition" (1996: 156–57). In this Murray echoed his earlier view that indirect rule was the only mode of colonialism "reconcil[able] with scientific anthropology" (quoted in Lattas 1996: 151). Over this period Murray's problematic was the application of indirect rule to acephalous societies—that is, how to govern through customary practice in a context in which there were, in contrast to the situation in British Africa, no obviously developed indigenous structures of authority and rule.[37] Murray wrote, "We believe in the principle of Indirect Rule; but how are we to apply it when there is . . . practically no system of chieftainship where there is, in fact, no one for us to rule through?" (1929a: 6).[38] It was in this situation that the ethnographic apprehension of native culture emerged as of especial import if it were to serve as a surface through which to get a hold on indigenous customs, habits, and practices so as to make them amenable to administration.

On Murray's account, anthropology was thus a prerequisite for the successful government of subject peoples if "one wanted to draw them by gentle means to a new order of living" (Campbell 1998: 70).[39] It was, then, in his self-ascribed capacity as a "semi-technical advisor" that Williams over time provided counsel on "how far it is desirable and possible to preserve" native customs (1939: 145) and how "to weave them into the fabric of . . . administration" (Murray 1929a: 11–12). In this, Murray's scientific administration exemplified the ascendancy of "rule by experts" and its corollary, the removal of questions of "the political" (Mitchell 2002). This was so inasmuch as the appeal of anthropology to colonial rule lay in its technical expertise on the native, in which the "native problem" was construed as one requiring not political but rather administrative resolution (Kuklick 1991: 189). Thus, in making his case for scientific administration, Murray warned against the idolatry of democracy, contending that, in the area of colonialism, "there is a risk that we may be led astray by an excess of devotion to our own particular fetish," which, he continued, "takes the shape of an advanced form of democracy" (1929a: 12). The implication was that it would be mistaken to assume that native subjectivity had the capacity for democratic citizenship, since it had not (yet) reach the necessary threshold of "'responsibilized' freedom" (Scott 1999: 87). This capacity was, however, to become the ostensible, but deferred, horizon of Murray's policy.

In pursuing this, Murray's administration came to participate in humanitarian colonialism, which the League of Nations in 1929 formalized as "the sacred trust," charging the colonial authority with responsibility for the material, intellectual, and moral uplift of colonial subjects.[40] Murray (1929a) was clear that this uplift did not equate with assimilation, which, in his opinion, was the erroneous policy of French colonial rule. Rather, as he characterized his aim, "we are not trying to make the brown man white; we are trying to make him a better brown man than he was before" (1932: 6). Prefiguring this objective by nearly a decade, Williams had commented similarly on the alteration of native subjectivity: "The thing is not to unmake and remake; but to improve what has been made already" (1923a: 62). This production of the subject, of the improved "brown man," then, was part of a longer strategy contingent on a particular "editing" of native culture. In this emergent program native culture was not posited as a hindrance to development in and of itself; rather, it contained impeding elements that required censoring for indigenous societies to progress. Under this regime, then, native society was not a totality destined to be eliminated and replaced by a European universal but rather an entity to be "reformed" so as to upgrade the already made. Practices deemed retrograde—those associated with the undesirable (sorcery, head-hunting, or poor sanitation) or those less advantageous (stone implements)—were to be "deleted and substituted" with those judged more progressive, be they Christianity, cricket, cleanliness, or steel chisels. As Williams opined, toward the end of his tenure, to facilitate indigenous accommodation to colonial modernity, native culture needed "tidying-up, purging, reconciling, blending and developing" (1939: 154). However, precisely which practices were worth preserving and which warranted purging was an enduring point of contention between Murray and Williams (figure 2.4).

Vital to this program's success was recognition of the limits to reform. Such limits were contingent on what were admitted to be inherent, and often unknown, qualities of native culture in whose operations it was not in the interests of the administration to intervene. Below we advance three propositions that consider how a particular politics of truth emerged in which specific anthropological contentions came to undergird the ethos of humanitarian and scientific administration, and through which native culture emerged as a particular, historically distinct interface of colonial government.

First, in recognizing the veracity of particular anthropological positions, the colonial authority came to identify the limits to government. Drawing on Rivers's (1917) contention that the lower a culture was on the evolutionary scale of humanity the greater the interdependency of its parts, Murray ac-

FIGURE 2.4 "Policeman from the Papua Armed Constabulary holding what looks like a decorated human head." 1921. Frank Hurley, 26530881, National Library of Australia, Canberra. Courtesy of the National Library of Australia.

This image was taken by Hurley on his expedition to Papua with Alan McCulloch from the Australian Museum in Sydney. The Hurley expedition caused disturbances among indigenous communities in the Purari Delta, particularly with regard to their collecting practices. Through the intervention of the Murray administration, cultural objects collected by Hurley's expedition were confiscated at Port Moresby, and some items were repatriated to villages. However, those objects associated with practices that the Murray regime sought to suppress, such as the *piforu* (preserved human heads), were not.

knowledged how such relations of interiority established the contingencies to which "good government" was exposed. He observed, "If you suppress a native custom, your action may have effects which you never contemplated, because the custom in question may be related to all sorts of other customs, with which it seemed to you to have no connection. Therefore if a custom is not positively harmful it is well to leave it alone, however foolish and trivial it may seem" (1929a: 11–12). From this anthropological conception Murray came to infer the problematic of liberal government. That is, only with proper regard to the nature of native culture could the balance be found between governing "too much and too little" (Foucault 2008: 19; see also 2007: 352–53). In thus recognizing native culture as a totality composed of its own internal regularities, the administrator could never be sure of the consequences of intervention, because knowledge of how the parts related to the whole remained incomplete. On the one hand, this was registered in concerns around the dangers of overassimilation, which, it was contended, interrupted the totality of indigenous cultures, crushed "the native spirit," and led to dramatic population decline (Murray 1931).[41] On the other, it recognized the prudence of cultural tolerance. Guarding against the contingencies that might stem from unnecessary intervention with the injunction, "if it isn't harmful, leave it alone," such tolerance set limits to government to manage its risks. In these concerns, then, Murray acknowledged the role of ethnographic expertise in deciding "what to do and what not to do" in relation to the native question and thus in establishing "the division between the agenda and the non-agenda" of native policy (Foucault 2008: 12).

Second, if indirect rule, in assuming a liberal tolerance for cultural diversity, worked to intervene in the field of indigenous relations with the lightness of touch required to preserve native custom and so avoid unforeseen contingencies and protect indigenous populations, it also served to identify those indigenous practices that required a heavier hand. British colonial administration theorist Charles Lindsay Temple wrote that exercising indirect rule "means first of all that you must shut your eyes . . . to a great many practices which, though not absolutely repugnant to humanity, are nevertheless reprehensible to our ideas" (1918: 49–50, quoted in Helliwell and Hindess 2002: 148). Here, indirect rule established the line between the tolerable, through which it sought to rule with a minimum of intervention, and the intolerable—that seen as "absolutely repugnant to humanity"—which must be governed otherwise. Murray made this (in)tolerance explicit, writing that "customs . . . which are harmless should be protected and encouraged, for, absurd, as they may seem to us, they may have been a support and comfort to many generations," but that those "which are really evil should be suppressed, and suppressed without hesitation" (1929a: 13).

This (in)tolerance of colonial rule also had a biopolitical dimension. The making live of a "better brown man" was simultaneously the letting die of the "absolutely repugnant" inasmuch as Murray's statements on the tolerant uplift of Papuans also invoked the extinction of "degenerate" populations. Here, tolerance served as a dividing practice: between those deemed to have the capacity or potentiality for self-improvement, and thus for being beneficiaries of passage up "the scale of humanity," and those who failed to reach this threshold and thus were condemned to extinction. For example, in one tract Murray attributed the declining population in one of the territory's divisions to "unnatural offences and other filthy customs," in reference to child brides and homosexual practices (1920: 19). Naturalizing their decline, Murray contended, "People of this kind must die out, whether white men come or not. . . . It is difficult to imagine that people with such habits . . . should ever increase" (19).

Third, while accepting in principle the notion of native culture as an integrated whole, the reform program to which the Murray regime was committed in fact qualified it. Murray objected that, unqualified, this notion would lead the administration to a curatorial rather than philanthropic responsibility, whereby "preservation" would outweigh "uplift." While acknowledging functionalism's importance in establishing the intrinsic worth of indigenous societies, later in his career Williams, too, was critical of its conservatism.[42] By the late 1930s, Williams viewed functionalism as, first, epistemologically flawed. While he did not reject the proposition that culture was a system, it was, in his view, "a hotch-potch and a sorry tangle," which belied the seamless integration implied by functionalists' mechanical and organic metaphors (1939: 153). Rather, recalling Edward Burnett Tylor's "survivals," Williams postulated the presence of what he termed "cultural junk"—those residual cultural elements that lacked, or had lost, meaning and utility (153). Second, he also considered functionalism as ethically flawed. Functionalists did not afford the native the self-reflexivity and autonomy in subjectivity that Williams had long been committed to recognizing. Rather, as a "prisoner of the particular," the native was positioned outside this threshold of liberal subjectivity. Both faults, in Williams's view, impacted on the native's constitution as the subject of government. Against the notion of a tightly integrated but precarious whole, native culture was, in principle, reformable. This did not ensure the inevitable collapse of native society but rather the possibility of its accommodation with colonial modernity.

However, Williams was quick to install a second principle to curtail the enthusiasm of reformist zealots. Against the notion that the native was forever trapped in the particular, Williams considered the indigene in principle a subject of freedom—one whose "liberty is no less sacred than our own" (1939: 157). It was with such appeals that limits to reformist fervor were sought. "We need," Williams wrote, "a proper sense of limitations to govern our zeal . . . [as] due precaution lest we destroy too much in our desire to build afresh" (1935: 3). Articulating this concern with the indigenous subject's "right to personal freedom and self-determination," Williams (1939: 159) contended: "The limits which we impose on native liberties are not to be dictated by our own arbitrary sense of propriety but by consideration for the rights, in fact the liberties of others, whether individuals or societies. While, then, we undertake the high sounding obligations of trusteeship, we should impose those limits with a hand as light as it is firm, recognizing that the native's way of living is his own, that he is much devoted to it and that, if it does nobody any harm, he has a right to it" (159).

CURATORIAL LOGICS, LIBERAL SUBJECTS, COLONIAL RULE

This liberal formulation of the indigenous subject as one of freedom and autonomy was not the target of Spencer's administrative concerns in that he did not conceive of the "pure black" Aboriginal body as a biocultural substrate capable of bearing such qualities. Rather, this was a potentiality that could be achieved only with the addition of "white blood" and a decisive break with indigenous tradition; this was the promise of the "half caste" if properly managed. Spencer's biopolitical concern to secure a milieu optimizing the movement of racially coded bodies was principally focused on this potentiality. His approach to Aboriginal policy and the "half-caste" question, rather than being without "anthropology as an informing discipline" (Gray 2007: 32), was, on the contrary, informed by the typological method that Spencer carried over from his practices as a curator of ethnology. This link between Spencer's museum practices and those of his colonial administration is one that Bennett (2004, 2005, 2013c) has analyzed in detail. He identifies the ways in which the collected object and the colonial subject were organized by the same sequential, developmental logic. Spencer's native policy hinged on the view that the mixed descent of "half-castes" imbued them with a possibility of development that was absent in the "pure-blood" Aboriginal. This instituted a program that, Bennett argues, "consisted in the movement of bodies through social space as if they were so many museum pieces being moved along a continuum of evolutionary development" (2005: 534).

To build on Bennett's analysis, it is important to stress the forms of spatial zoning through which Spencer sought to curate the Northern Territory's population so as to prepare it genetically over time as a biological substrate capable of bearing liberal subjecthood. In this regard the reserves, compounds, and training institutions dividing the population of Darwin and its surrounds corresponded to different locations in developmental time in which particular subpopulations were placed—between, that is, the "wild" natives on reserves, who were, in the double sense of the phrase, "out of time," and the "half-castes," who, via genetic inheritance and training, had entered into evolutionary, developmental time and so had the prospect of liberal subjecthood.

Murray explicitly juxtaposed his administrative program with that of the museum. However, in making this contrast it was the ethos of preservation, not that of the sequence, that he objected to. Shortly before his appointment as lieutenant governor, Murray asserted his ethnographic authority in competition with that of his immediate predecessor, Francis Barton. For Murray, "scientific administration" was required to ensure the "dual mandate" through which the territory would be advanced for the benefit of both colonizers and colonized, lest it become, as he retorted, an "expensive ethnographic museum" (quoted in Dixon 2001: 79). This trope proved enduring. Later in his career, responding to the preservationist mentality he attributed to academic anthropologists critical of Papuan native policy—Malinowski and Fortune among them—Murray replied that "[it is] no part of our duty of to keep . . . 'a human Zoo' " (1932: 14). Yet, despite this rhetoric, a political logic prevailed in which the Papua population was to be curated in a program of tolerance through which the native subject was to be protected, augmented, and stabilized as the "better brown man."

It was in preparing his early report *The Collection of Curios and the Preservation of Native Culture* that Williams (1923a) first articulated the native subject as the subject of freedom. Williams's ostensible concern in this document was to correct the haphazard manner in which the artifacts in his office were accumulating, and so to put the POC on a surer scientific footing. In this document he thus sought to establish procedures to ensure that objects were collected exclusively on the grounds of their anthropological worth, not their artistic merit or curiosity value. However, rather than being merely methodological, Williams's report was also intended as a moral guide.

Devoting half of it to the "ethics of collecting," he advised on how and what to collect, establishing protocols for collecting in the territory more generally so as not to disrupt customary practices and unnecessarily enflame cross-cultural tensions. Though Williams did not mention it by name, the immediate circumstance prompting this manual on intercultural conduct was the recent Hurley expedition. The expedition's collecting practices had caused unrest among indigenous communities. Through the administration's intervention, the material that had been collected was confiscated at Port Moresby and items were repatriated. However, objects associated with practices that Murray sought to suppress were not. On the metropolitan front, too, the expedition presented challenges to the Murray regime. Reports of the expedition and the confiscation presented something of a public relations crisis for the administration as it looked to manage the media reception of Hurley's expedition in metropolitan Australia and so to counter the sensationalism of Hurley's account of hereto-unknown tribes and resources (Dixon 2011; Specht 2003). This belied the public image of Murray's scientific administration, particularly its presentations of the Papuan indigene as a colonial subject capable of development, which stood in contradiction to the degrading presentation of the radical Other, which Nicholas Thomas has characterized as "Hurley's misogynist dehumanization" (1991: 184), or, indeed, to the savage alterity of McCulloch's "Ravi" diorama at the AM.

The protocols Williams sought to develop were not simply concerned with regularizing collecting practices, however. Rather, anticipating what was to become an enduring concern, they bore "upon a wider question, one which should be of paramount importance to Administration, viz., the right of the native to his own culture" (1923a: 1). For Murray, by contrast, culture remained expedient—significant less as an integrated whole, or a sphere of autonomy and freedom, and more as a surface for population management. Culture was not so much an end, "a whole way of life," as a means to an end, "a way *to* 'life'" (Gordon 1991: 5; italics added). Capturing this biopolitics, Williams observed toward the close of his career, "To the administrator, trustee for their welfare, the human animals under his care, both European and native, represent the end; their various cultures are merely means, good, bad, or indifferent, for the satisfaction of their needs and the expression of their potentialities" (1939: 154).

For Murray, native culture was strictly instrumental. As a way to the welfare of the "human animal" it constituted an administrative surface and component of what the British colonial reformer Lord Hailey described as "a benevolent type of police rule" (quoted in Young and Clark 2001: 27). By contrast, for Williams, native culture was increasingly inseparable from vexing questions linked to liberal conceptions of freedom. For him the limit of colonial reform increasingly concerned less the inherent qualities of native culture and its precarious internal regularities, and more the conception of the human subject—as one, in principle, of freedom and autonomy, one who bore rights to choose a particular way of life. In this, Williams's tenure marked a transition in which colonial rule was coming to accommodate the prospects of an indigenous future, one that had been closed, in Haddon's bleak prognosis, in the dyad of assimilation and extinction.

CHAPTER THREE

A LIBERAL ARCHIVE OF EVERYDAY LIFE

Mass-Observation as Oligopticon

This chapter considers how the "anthropology at home" project of Mass-Observation (M-O) was implicated in the political technologies of liberal government through the emergence of distinctive transactional realities ordering British wartime populations. Central to these transactional realities were the linked concepts of "mass" and "morale." We begin with a detailed examination of M-O's "anthropology of ourselves," describing its distinguishing fieldwork *agencements* in the ways in which it brought together ethnographic methods of collecting and assembling (largely but not exclusively drawn from colonial anthropological contexts) and new mechanisms of collective self-watching. Drawing on Chris Otter's (2008) arguments relating oligoptic visual economies to liberal technologies of government, we suggest that M-O's fieldwork agencements operated oligoptically in the relations of government they produced. They did this by extending the collective self-monitoring of liberal collecting institutions, such as the public museum and archive, both to the quotidian, interior lives of individual subjects and, through the new collective forms of self-knowing and self-regulating that M-O promoted, to the population more generally. In doing so, M-O was implicated in the development of new conceptions of the population through its inflection of earlier notions of "the mass" toward a conception of the population as self-knowing and self-regulating. We also show how the concept of civilian morale acted through the work of M-O as an example of the practical application of an "anthropology of ourselves" that aimed to manage the conduct of the population.

The chapter then proceeds by considering the project of M-O in relation to the notion of the "liberal museum" (see Bennett 1995, 2004) or "liberal archive" (see Joyce 1999, and also 2003). Here the contention is that M-O's ethical and epistemological credibility lay with its commitment to a museal or archival logic, which was consequential for the types of publics that it assembled and the forms of political subjectivities it hailed. Interrogating this contention, the chapter considers how M-O's practices of observation and collection, ordering and interpretation, became imbricated in programs targeting (i) the population, via what we have called the mechanism of the public, and (ii) the individual, via regimes of self-observing and self-governing. These practices are shown to be exemplified, in different ways, by both M-O's early "surrealist" work on the coronation of George V as well as its later "social science" work for the Ministry of Information (MoI) on civilian morale. Both of these drew on the techniques of the diary and epistolary exchange, among others, to solicit the subjectivity of ordinary citizens as a means by which the contours of the social might be determined and calibrated and so made legible and thus manageable.

To identify both some of M-O's continuities with the practices of earlier British anthropology at home projects and also its distinctiveness in terms of the new transactional realities it produced, the chapter begins with a brief consideration of Alfred Cort Haddon and Charles R. Browne's late nineteenth-century ethnographic survey of the Aran Islands, which served as a prototype for the failed Ethnographic Survey of the United Kingdom, conducted by the British Association for the Advancement of Science (BAAS). Here we review this project's "failure" on its own terms—conceptually in using racial logics for ordering populations, and methodologically in using amateurs to collect data—and we consider its implications in relation to the absence of a British national museum of folklife. Haddon subsequently attempted to correct both failures in the Cambridge Anthropological Expedition to the Torres Strait in 1898–99, deploying an expert team to calibrate the contours of race. The inadequacies of "race" as a transactional reality in this earlier anthropology at home project act as a point of contrast for exploring how M-O came to be articulated with the processes of the "governmentalization of the state" as practices of cultural governance were brought under the auspices of the emergent British welfare state. It also provides a point of introduction through which to explore the ways in which the governmental rationalities informing the deployments of anthropology at home were shaped by particular constructions of the relations between "home and away" in both a metropolitan (home) versus colonial (away) and an urban (home) versus rural (away) sense. Here, M-O is distinctive in that it was not focused on a concept of population that sought to identify the residuum of the "folk" still surviving from traditional, precapitalist social arrangements but instead (largely) on the working classes.[1] In describing these arrangements we introduce a distinction between anthropology at home in its conventional focus on traditional, rural European folk subjects and M-O's project of an anthropology of ourselves, focusing instead on urban laboring subjects.

RACIAL SCIENCE, AMATEUR FIELD SURVEYS, AND ANTHROPOLOGY AT HOME: THE ETHNOGRAPHIC SURVEY OF THE UNITED KINGDOM, 1892–1899

We reviewed Haddon's 1898–99 Torres Strait expedition in the previous chapter and noted its importance in providing a template for a new set of anthropological fieldwork practices at the turn of the twentieth century. On returning to Dublin from his first field trip to the Torres Strait in 1888, Haddon would pursue a very common trajectory (at least insofar as British anthropology in this period was concerned) in applying his developing interest in anthropological fieldwork practices to local subjects. In 1891 he was instrumental in cofounding (with Daniel J. Cunningham) the Anthropometric Laboratory of Ireland, modeled on Francis Galton's Anthropometric Laboratory in London. The laboratory's work would be driven by a focus on investigating the origins of the "Irish Race" (Cunningham and Haddon 1891: 36).

In contrast to Galton's *stationary* laboratory at the South Kensington Museum, Haddon's intention was to produce a "perambulatory laboratory" that could extend its reach into the "country districts" through ethnographic fieldwork (figure 3.1). Haddon, together with Cunningham's assistant, Charles R. Browne, undertook the first of his Irish ethnographic field trips to the Aran Islands in the summer of 1891, and Browne continued to visit various parts of County Galway and County Mayo in the western part of Ireland to gather further ethnographic data for the laboratory almost annually over the following decade. In their report to the Royal Irish Academy in December 1892, they noted that their work had gone beyond the strict remit of anthropometry "in the belief that the ethnical characteristics of a people are to be found in their arts, habits, language, and beliefs as well as their physical characters" (Haddon and Browne 1892: 769). Nonetheless, racial science played a central role in their expedition, which was conceived as a direct response to British

Anthropometry in Inishbofin.

FIGURE 3.1 "Anthropometry on Inishbofin, Ireland, 1892." MS 10961/4 fol. 5v, Charles R. Browne Collection, Trinity College Dublin. Reproduced with permission of the Board of Trinity College Dublin.

Alfred Cort Haddon and Charles R. Browne's anthropometric fieldwork on the Aran Islands and west coast of Ireland in the early 1890s was significant not only in forming an important background to the Torres Strait expedition of 1898–99 through its development of the notion of a mobile anthropological field laboratory but also in demonstrating the potential for an anthropology at home that might extend beyond the concerns of racial science to those of archaeology, ethnology, folklore, and material culture studies. Nonetheless, racial science did play a key part in this work, even as the usefulness of racial science was challenged by the ambiguous findings Haddon and Browne produced.

ethnologist John Beddoe's suggestion that certain parts of the Irish and Welsh populations maintained particular physical characteristics that were survivals of the pre–Anglo-Saxon inhabitants of the British Isles.[2] For Beddoe, one of the most important physical characteristics of the Celtic "race," and one that marked it out to him as "Africanoid," was the degree of prognathism, or protrusion of the lower jaw. The presence of these characteristics in certain prehistoric skulls from Ireland led Beddoe (1885: 11–12) to suggest that these "primitive" traits belonged to a pre–Anglo-Saxon population of the British Isles. Haddon and Browne recorded the hair and eye color (using Beddoe's typologies and the marking cards he developed for this purpose) of some 436 individuals, as well as seventeen additional detailed head, body, and face measurements for some 27 individuals (using a field kit comprising a Traveller's Anthropometer, a Flower's Craniometer, a modified Busk's Craniometer, and a sliding rule). A good deal of the subsequent report is dedicated to considering the degree of "Nigrescence" (Beddoe's term for darkness of complexion) of the population, drawing on the computational methods developed by Beddoe and presented in *The Races of Britain* (1885). In addition to these statistical data, Haddon and Browne illustrated their article with several half-length full-face and side-view portrait photographs—their arrangement clearly indebted to late nineteenth-century anthropological "type" photography (E. Edwards 1990; Carville 2012) of the form specified in *Notes and Queries on Anthropology*—alongside other less formally composed views of Aran Islanders (figure 3.2).[3]

While this work is remarkable enough in itself, Haddon clearly conceived of it as one of a much broader set of regional surveys that would take place programmatically across the whole of Ireland and the British Isles more generally. Delegates of the Anthropological Institute, Folklore Society, and Society of Antiquaries met in 1892 in response to Haddon's suggestion to discuss the possibility of making an ethnographic survey of the British Isles (Petch 2011; Urry 1984: 87). The three societies lacked the resources and personnel between them to assume the task of a national ethnographic survey, but Edward William Brabrook, a member of all three, took a proposal to the BAAS in January 1892 that they join forces to support the founding of an Ethnographic Survey of the United Kingdom (Brabrook 1893a, 1893b; Folklore Society 1892). Elizabeth Edwards (2009, 2012) has remarked on the synergy between the amateur photographic survey movement (itself organized into a national survey in 1897), the work of local county societies, and the increasing organization and mobilization of amateur survey work, which was overseen by the various associations and societies that came together under

5

6

7

FIGURE 3.2 Plate xxiii in Alfred Cort Haddon and Charles R. Browne, "Ethnography of the Aran Islands," *Proceedings of the Royal Irish Academy* 2 (1892): 768–830. Reproduced with permission of the Royal Irish Academy.

This is one of the series of plates that accompanied Alfred Cort Haddon and Charles R. Browne's "Ethnography of the Aran Islands," published in the *Proceedings of the Royal Irish Academy* in 1892. While plate 5 (top) shows a combination of typical full-face and side-view compositions, in the form specified by *Notes and Queries on Anthropology*, the other two photographs employ a more casual arrangement of subjects: plate 6 (middle) still full face but plate 7 (below) apparently naturalistic in composition. Indeed, the caption for plate 7 contradicts the earlier observation in the text that "the promise of a copy of their photograph was usually sufficient reward for undergoing the trouble of being measured and photographed" (778), noting that "Faherty refused to be measured, and the women would not even tell us their names" (830).

---

the auspices of the Ethnographic Survey of the United Kingdom. In proposing this survey, Brabrook noted that many groups were already voluntarily involved in collecting certain forms of information that, if collated and properly organized by an appropriate group of experts, could constitute data for the survey. Local BAAS corresponding societies were particularly singled out as candidates to assist (Folklore Society 1893). A committee was subsequently appointed, with Galton as chair, Brabrook as secretary, and Haddon, John George Garson, and Joseph Anderson as members. Subsequently, Brabrook assumed the position of chair, and various other members were added representing other allied societies, including Beddoe, Cunningham, Arthur Evans, and General Augustus Pitt-Rivers.

The association committee quickly drew up an outline of its various objects of interest. The list reflected Haddon's broad conception of anthropology as encompassing not only physical anthropology and racial science but also archaeology, folklore, ethnology, and language:

It is proposed to record for certain typical villages and the neighboring districts—

(1) Physical Types of the Inhabitants.
(2) Current Traditions and Beliefs.
(3) Peculiarities of Dialect.
(4) Monuments and other Remains of Ancient Culture; and
(5) Historical Evidence as to Continuity of Race.

As a first step, the Committee formed a list of such villages in the United Kingdom as appeared especially to deserve ethnographic study, out of which a selection was made for the survey. The villages or districts selected are such as contain not less than a hundred adults, the large majority of whose forefathers have lived there so far back as can be traced, and of whom the desired physical measurements, with photographs, may be obtained. (Folklore Society 1893: 114–15, quoted in Petch 2011)

Instructions for the collection of information were drawn up as a form to be filled out, including a series of subjects to be covered and questions to be asked, similar to *Notes and Queries on Anthropology* (see chapter 1). These instructions were published as a twelve-page brochure that was circulated to relevant societies to pass on to amateur recorders (E. Edwards 2012: 294), denoted as "observers," to ensure the standardized collection of information in the 367 priority areas identified using the criteria above (Folklore Society 1895: 111).

The brochure included detailed instructions regarding the completion of the form and the taking of photographic portraits (at least twelve more or less beardless adult males and twelve adult females in full face and in profile, with further provision made for the taking of composite portraits of groups by Galton).[4] It also contained a series of sixty-eight questions digested from the much longer list used for similar purposes by the Folklore Society ("Describe any ceremonies performed at certain times in connection with mountains. . . . Are there spirits of rivers or streams? Give their names. . . . Does the building of a house cause the death of a builder?"); a series of "Directions to Collectors of Dialect Tests"; a list of "Monuments and other Remains of Ancient Culture" to "plot on a map, describe, furnish photographs on, sketch and state measurements and names (if any)"; and a series of prompts for recording historical information ("state if any precautions have been taken by the people to keep themselves to themselves; if the old village tenures of land have been preserved") (BAAS n.d.). The instructions were adapted from a number of similar documents, including, as already mentioned, *Notes and Queries on Anthropology*, as well as the Folklore Society's *Handbook of Folklore* (Gomme 1890), various publications by the English Dialect Society, and the Society of Antiquaries's county survey notation system.

Despite the optimism of the committee members and this initial flurry of activity, by 1897 it appeared that very little of any substance had been achieved by the survey (Urry 1984: 95). Committee members continued to appeal to local BAAS members and others to take up the task, but in 1899 the committee was disbanded owing to lack of progress (see also Petch 2011). The collapse of the survey, organized as it was around a regional framework based on presumed racial variations within the British population, seems to have occurred as much because of the failure of the governmental rationalities of the racial model of variation of British populations on which it was based as because of the lack of support for, and training of, its field-workers. For example, Scott Ashley has argued that Haddon and Browne's study failed to produce findings that could "easily be marshaled into the argument either for or against Home Rule. . . . [W]hile Haddon and Browne were part of contemporary racial science in their concern to classify the islanders according to skull type and physiognomy, their restrained presentation—illustrated with photographs that ironically belie their descriptions of a single island 'type'— . . . was never about finding primitive, or 'apish,' physical features in the Irish peasantry" (2001: 16). Indeed, in the very final sentence of their report on the ethnography of the Aran Islands, Haddon and Browne were to conclude with the remarkable admission, "To what race or races the Aranites belong, we do not pretend to say, but it is pretty evident they cannot be Firbolgs, if the latter are correctly described as 'small, dark-haired, and swarthy'" (1892: 826).[5] They were forced to conclude that their physiognomic measurements of Aran Islanders alone would not produce results that could distinguish them clearly from the rest of the population of the British Isles.

That the failure of the BAAS Ethnographic Survey related not only to questions of logistic organization but also to a broader conceptual failure of the framework under which it was organized can be seen in the related issue of the absence of a British national museum of folklife during this period, despite the prominence of such national museums in Europe. Indeed, in 1904 Henry Balfour noted, "There is one type of museum in which the British Islands are singularly deficient, and, by some irony of fate, it is one which would fully illustrate the ethnology and culture of the people of Great Britain" (15).

Chris Wingfield (2011) has argued that it was only Britain's movement from an expansionist imperial power in 1860 to an actively decolonizing nation in 1960, and an ideological shift from a focus on "civilization" to a focus on the "culture" concept, that facilitated the emergence of the folklore paradigm and a "national consciousness" in the 1950s and 1960s. This paved the way for the emergence of the Museum of English Rural Life (founded in 1954) and the establishment of a number of other folk museums and equivalent collections of "English" rural material ("Scheme for the Development" 1949; Higgs 1956; P. Rivière 2010).[6] Despite the persistence into the 1920s and 1930s of race as an organizing principle for the differentiation of British populations (e.g., Fleure 1923; see discussion in Kushner 2004), it could be argued that the increasingly contested nature of the concept, confusion regarding its relationship with other regional manifestations of local culture, and arguments over the characteristics of the various racial types in question worked to deprive the racial categorization of British populations of both its museological and governmental logics at the end of the nineteenth century.

If race was increasingly falling out of favor as a model for the differentiation and governance of British populations, what other concepts or transactional realities might replace it? With specific reference to England, Oliver Douglas (2011) identifies three paradigms for the museological framing of the ethnographic materials held in disparate collections in the late nineteenth and early twentieth centuries: folklore, survivals in culture, and the neo-archaic. As Jonathan Roper (2012) notes, the "folklore" paradigm tended to be most wholeheartedly adopted in stateless nations administered by external powers in circumstances where the collection and promotion of vernacular culture could be connected directly with a particular ethnopolitical imperative; for these reasons, it seems to have failed in late nineteenth-century England. This failure can also be seen to derive from tensions between a more comparative or "world-oriented" imperial approach and nationalistic approaches to folklore studies in England at the time (Wingfield and Gosden 2012). Douglas (2011) further argues that survivalism was too abstract a concept to succeed in museological terms. Among the large nonmetropolitan industrialized population of England it seemed equally difficult to find occurrences of the neo-archaic. Nor was the distinction between rural (or "peasant") and metropolitan populations one that was able to be maintained with much vigor. While gender and class remained important categories for ordering populations (K. Hill 2005), these complicated and cut across the other categories in ways that did not necessarily make them amenable to museological schemes of classification and ordering. It was thus as much a conceptual failure of the various competing models for differentiating and ordering populations as an institutional or organizational failure that meant that no national museum of folklife was established in this period, and that the BAAS Ethnographic Survey of the United Kingdom ultimately failed to produce results.

Initiated some forty years after the failure of the BAAS Ethnographic Survey of the United Kingdom, M-O brought together both approaches: the collection of mass data using amateur collectors and more detailed studies by ethnographic "experts." But it could do so only through a process of refiguring the object of investigation—shifting from a concern with the folklore paradigm of archaic and primitive cultures to a focus on those that were seen to be both emergent and modern, with the qualification, however, that at the core of modern subjectivity lay a "primitivism" that could shape conduct in ways hitherto unknown. We will argue that this required the mutation of dominant anthropological transactional realities from a focus on race to a concern with the "morale" of the "masses," understood in broadly Freudian terms as related to the collective unconscious, as an explanatory mechanism for individual and group behavior. We also suggest that M-O supplied a partial answer to the absence of a British national folk museum, inasmuch as it presented itself in museological terms as an organization devoted to the collection and study of the everyday lives of Britain's inhabitants—a museum of "us," as the organization would come to put it.

In 1937, in the immediate wake of the Edward VIII abdication crisis, M-O was founded when the amateur anthropologist and ornithologist Tom Harrisson responded to a letter published in the journal *New Statesman and Nation* by poet (and subsequently sociologist) Charles Madge (1937). In a direct parallel with Haddon, Harrisson, recently returned from fieldwork in Malekula (then part of the British-French Condominium of the New Hebrides) and Borneo in 1936, had begun working in a factory in Bolton as an exercise in participant observation of England's "natives" (Madge and Harrisson 1937: 10). Madge's letter announcing the establishment of the Blackheath Group, whose anthropology at home sought to understand the reaction of the public to the abdication crisis and similar contemporary events, immediately caught Harrisson's eye. This group included M-O cofounder, poet, and documentary filmmaker Humphrey Jennings and photographer Humphrey Spender, who had been involved in organizing the London International Surrealist Exhibition in 1936 and whose approach was strongly influenced by surrealism and notions of the collective unconscious (MacClancy 1995, 2001; Highmore 2002, 2007). Harrisson made contact with Jennings, and the foundation of "Mass-Observation" was reported in the same periodical soon afterward.[7]

Once founded, M-O proceeded quickly along two fronts. Harrisson initially developed and directed the "Worktown" (Bolton) and "Seatown" (Blackpool) projects, which were operated out of a house rented by Harrisson for that purpose in Davenport Street in Bolton (figure 3.3). The Worktown project involved forms of relatively covert observation undertaken by a small number of paid (and sometimes volunteer) observers (generally somewhere around a dozen, although sometimes "up to 60" [Marcus 2001: 12]), who observed "others" under Harrisson's direction, taking notes and making detailed reports on their findings. Meanwhile, a national panel of part-time volunteer observers was established and directed by Madge from his home in Blackheath, London. The national panel was composed of volunteers who initially agreed to keep diaries, referred to as "day surveys," of all of their own activities and reflections on a single day, and subsequently to respond in writing to particular "directives," open-ended questionnaires sent out to the national panel by the team at Blackheath. The important distinction here is between the observation of "others" in the Worktown project and the observation of "self" in the national panel (although sometimes members of the national panel were also asked to interview colleagues and family members about particular issues in directives).

FIGURE 3.3 "Full time 'Worktown' observers planning observations at 85 Davenport Street." Bolton, April 1938. Left to right: Walter Hood, Tom Harrisson, John Sommerfield, and an unidentified man. Humphrey Spender, 1993.83.19.09, Bolton Museum and Archives. Courtesy of the Bolton Museum and Archives, Bolton Council.

The field observation and collecting practices of full-time observers in the Worktown study were influenced by Tom Harrisson's ornithological survey work, Bronislaw Malinowski's participant ethnography, Robert S. Lynd and Helen Merrell Lynd's *Middletown* study, Chicago School sociology, and the "penetrational" fieldwork methods used in the psychological research of Oscar Oeser. They focused explicitly on direct (and, initially, covert) observation and written and photographic documentation of observed activities and overheard conversations, which were cataloged in notebooks according to the time and place of observation. Despite this focus on observation, the Worktown project also occasionally used direct and indirect interview techniques and even written questionnaires and surveys to collect information about specific topics of interest.

Members of the national panel were recruited through advertisements in magazines and newspapers but also responded to radio programs and popular pamphlets and books that recounted the aims and preliminary findings of the organization, which became a subject of national interest and frequent public comment as a result of widespread media coverage of the organization and its work. The size of the national panel quickly swelled to over two thousand people (Harrisson and Madge 1940) as M-O developed into a popular social movement in the months leading up to the beginning of World War II. Following the outbreak of war, fears about disruption of the postal service forced M-O to stop sending regular directives. National panel members were instead urged to keep comprehensive diaries during this period, a task that almost five hundred people undertook sporadically or continuously throughout the war. In addition, M-O established a "war library" in an attempt to salvage print items that reflected popular responses to the conflict. Subsequently, M-O assumed an important political role when it publicly criticized government efforts to engender support for the war effort, and it was commissioned by the MoI to provide information about wartime morale.

Conflict between the various founders saw Jennings part company with Madge and Harrisson in 1938 to concentrate on filmmaking for the General Post Office Film Unit, which in 1940 became the Crown Film Unit, itself part of the MoI. It was during this period that Jennings produced *Spare Time* (1939) (which included material filmed in Bolton) and *London Can Take It!* (1940), both of which explored themes and drew on documentary styles that had been central to M-O. Madge subsequently departed in 1940, to undertake various research projects, including a study of wartime economics for the Institute of Economic and Social Research (Madge 1943), before taking up the position of first chair of sociology at the University of Birmingham in 1950. In 1949 M-O became a limited liability company primarily concerned with commercial market research, by which time all of the founding members had moved on to pursue other interests, including Harrisson, who accepted the position of curator of the Sarawak Museum in 1947. Nonetheless, the founders of M-O can all be seen to have contributed directly in their own ways to the wartime and postwar British state (Hubble 2006: 13)—Harrisson through his work with M-O and the MoI, Jennings with the production of wartime propaganda films, and Madge through his associations with John Maynard Keynes and William Beveridge and his work for the National Council for Social and Economic Research (1940–42) and the political think tank Political and Economic Planning (1943), which was influential in the formation of the National Health Service, in postwar planning, and in the development of

the African colonies. But of more lasting importance than these direct legacies were the new governmental rationalities M-O produced as a result of its
fieldwork agencements, to which we now turn.

MASS-OBSERVATION AS "COLLABORATIVE MUSEUM"

From the outset, M-O was concerned with processes of collecting, ordering, archiving, and exhibiting. In one of its earliest formative statements of
intent, Madge suggested that the aim of M-O was to create a "collaborative
museum" (1935: 16). This framing of the project was reiterated by Madge and
Harrisson in the 1937 booklet *Mass-Observation*, where they noted, "We shall
collaborate in building up museums of sound, smell, food, clothes, domestic
objects, advertisements, newspapers, etc" (35). On the pamphlet's back cover
the aim of the project was again underlined: to "*collect* a mass of data based
upon practical observation of the everyday life of all types of people and to
utilize the data for scientific study of Twentieth-Century Man in all his different environments" (italics added).

The field of collection of M-O was conceptualized in a number of ways:
geographically, thematically, and through the lens of its varied interests in
the social sciences (principally sociology, anthropology, psychology, and
economics) and artistic movements (surrealism, poetry, photography, and
documentary filmmaking). Its strong interests in class also played a role in
defining its field (e.g., Summerfield 1985; Hinton 2008; Hubble 2006; Savage
2008, 2010). It employed a range of distinctive collecting strategies, practices,
and methodologies that helped it to shape its conceptualization of this field,
with which it was interested in the aggregate, rather than in specifics: "The
field to be covered is . . . so apparently nebulous that the scientists have little
more to offer than generalizations on method. Mass-Observation intends to
work with a new method. It intends to make use not only of the trained scientific observer, but of the untrained observer, the man in the street. Ideally,
it is the observation by everyone of everyone, including themselves" (Madge
and Harrisson 1937: 10).

We have already noted that in recounting the work of M-O and its methodologies it is conventional to distinguish between the Worktown (Bolton)
and Seatown (Blackpool) projects, on the one hand, and the activities of the
national panel, on the other. A distinction is also made between the forms
of relatively covert participant ethnography undertaken by a small number
of paid (and sometimes volunteer) observers, who observed "others" under
Harrisson's direction, and the day surveys, wartime diaries, and directive

responses (and later the war library), which involved self-observation by volunteer observers. In the preface to *May the Twelfth: Mass-Observation Day Surveys*, the relationship was described in these terms: "The local survey starts with the whole-time research workers studying a place from the outside and working inwards, getting into the society, and so coming to the individual. The national plan starts from the individual observers and works outwards from them into their social surroundings. One aim of Mass-Observation is to see how, and how far, the individual is linked up with society and its institutions" (H. Jennings and Madge 1937: x–xi).

The first methods to be employed by M-O were the day surveys and the "ethnographic" surveys of Bolton and Blackpool. Harrisson's approach to ethnography prioritized direct observation over interviewing: "Basically, my idea was not to take words into very much account anyway. It was the behavior of people we had to study. I thought then (and think now) that the first training of a good observer of human behavior in your own society is by giving each person a pair of earplugs and then allowing him (her) to work out what people are doing, without him (her) knowing what these people are saying to each other. Willy nilly, though, one ends in words: thus this talk, thus the Archive I am talking about" (Harrisson 1971: 398).

The field observation and collection practices of full-time observers in the Worktown and Seatown (and later Metrop) case studies were strongly influenced by Harrisson's own experiences undertaking ornithological surveys in Oxford in his youth and fieldwork in the New Hebrides, along with the participant ethnography of Bronislaw Malinowski, Robert S. Lynd and Helen Merrell Lynd's (1929) *Middletown* study, Chicago school sociology (see Deagan 2001), and the "penetrational" fieldwork methods used in the psychological research of Oscar Oeser (Stanley 2001; Street n.d.; Hubble 2006). The observers focused explicitly on direct (and, initially, covert) observation; the recording of observed activities and overheard conversations, which were cataloged in notebooks according to the time and place of observation; and covert photography (figures 3.4 and 3.5). However, despite this focus on observation, the Worktown project also occasionally used direct and indirect interview techniques and even written questionnaires and surveys to collect information about particular themes.

May the Twelfth: Mass-Observation Day Surveys (H. Jennings and Madge 1937) sets out the range of methods that were developed by the national panel over the course of its first months of operation. The bulk of the book consists of carefully edited and juxtaposed reports from forty-three observers who had returned day surveys for the three months of 1937 preceding the coronation of George VI, directive responses from seventy-seven members of the public who had responded to a questionnaire that had been circulated by the team, and observations made by a "mobile squad" of observers who recorded their observations of what was happening on the streets of London on the day of the coronation. This occasion was presented as an important symbolic event during which the collective unconscious and repressed desires of ordinary citizens would be released (MacClancy 1995: 500). The book established the three main forms of information provided by the national panel—the day surveys (1937–38), responses to directive questions (which ran throughout the period 1937–49; figure 3.6), and, later, the war diaries (which were begun in 1939 when it was feared that the outbreak of war would make regular communication between mass observers and M-O's centers of collection difficult [Courage n.d.]). It seems likely this model of using amateur observers in undertaking a large-scale survey was again at least partially influenced by Harrisson's experience organizing large-scale ornithological surveys in his youth, as well as the *Notes and Queries* model of "armchair" anthropology. As the number of volunteer observers grew, the circulation of a regular bulletin (titled *Us*) to observers provided an important means (in addition to formal book-length publications, newspaper and magazine articles and radio broadcasts) by which new observers were recruited and existing observers developed a distinctive identity for themselves (see also Savage 2010). The bulletins fed back the statistical results of directive responses and topical or interesting examples of edited day surveys, diaries, or directive responses that had been received in previous months. As effective "inscription devices" that transformed data into text for circulation (see Latour and Woolgar 1979), they also established clear templates for observers to follow in their own writing. The importance of the circulation of these bulletins is discussed further below.

In summary, while there was a general unity in approach across both arms of M-O in the relationship between each "center" and its respective "field," the organization employed a complicated mix of techniques, and these changed over time and in relation to the particular investigators involved and the subjects being researched, ranging from observation to direct questioning, focusing on both behavior and opinion (Stanley 2001: 100). What unites these methods is their distinctive emphasis on the production of archival apparatuses that aimed to produce collectivized knowledge of both self and other. We now move on to consider how these distinctive agencements operated in organizing new relations of governance.

The funeral was that of J.J.Shaw of Davenport-street. It was held
in Heaton Cemetery, 2 to 2.15 p.m. Weather - sunny, some cloud,
cool, little wind.

Observer was at the graveside at 2 p.m. The grave was one row back
from the main path, but had a smaller path leading right to it.
The grave was covered with two planks, and a mound of earth excava-
ted from the grave was heaped on one side. Two gravediggers dressed
in floppy felt hats, brown overalls, and thick trousers, leggings
and clogs of wood, the trousers and leggings being in addition protected with canvas cloth, stood near. A third workman in the same
dress but without overall stood at the bottom of the main path and
supervised the carrying of the coffin to the grave. About 5 men and
10 women stood near also, most of them sightseers.

The cortege arrived just after two o'clock. It consisted of the
motor hearse, with wreaths of flowers on the roof, then 3 hired and
1 private cars, then another hired car with flowers on the roof,
then 6 more hired cars. They all stopped at the bottom of the foot-
path leading to the graves. (At this point observer heard a man say
"Is Aspinall here?" The reply was not audible.) The mourners got
out of the cars and formed a procession four abreast as they came up
the hill. First came the gravedigger, then the coffin, borne by six
men, then the mourners, 21 men and 8 women. All wore black or navy
blue suits, black ties. The coffin was carried to the grave and
lowered in. Each of the mourners was given a white chrysanthemum by
one of the gravediggers.

The ceremony consisted in an address read by a middle-aged man
with black hair. Observer did not notice that any earth was thrown
on the coffin, and certainly no words were spoken by anyone apart
from this address, which was original and moving, and well delivered
by the speaker. Most of the men had tears in their eyes; one or two
had obviously been weeping a great deal previous to the funeral.
Observer could not get down all of the address, but the following
fragments give an idea of its content.

"Our friend has entered into that eternal rest....Death comes as
a soothing anodyne....The penalty of life is death....The clouds over
him will weep for us,..the flowers will grow in the earth where he
lies, and the earth will produce a harvest rich with the fruits of
the earth.....This is the only immortality that we recognise - the
immortality of the great ones of the world....May the flowers bloom
over his head....Farewell, John James Shaw! A long farewell!"

The mourners each gave a last look into the grave and then moved
off. At least 10 people who were not mourners stood near the whole
time, including two women who kept peeping between the gravestones.

ˍˍˍˍˍˍ ˍˍˍˍˍˍ on a ˍˍˍˍˍˍ of green painted ˍˍˍ the property of the
ˍˍˍˍˍ.

FIGURE 3.4 Written observation of the funeral of John Shaw on September 21, 1937, by full-time Worktown-based observer Brian Barefoot. Worktown collection, Box 24/C, Mass-Observation Archive. Courtesy of the Curtis Brown Group Ltd., London, on behalf of the Trustees of the Mass-Observation Archive.

Full-time observers were initially dispatched to cover a range of different events relating to Mass-Observation's topics of interest, including work, secular and religious ceremonies, leisure activities, political activities, sports, games, and other habits and customs. Observations of activities, behaviors, and "overheards" (overheard conversations) were recorded in field notebooks, often accompanied by tables and drawings. In some cases, such as this one, written observations were accompanied by a sequence of photographs. Observations were subsequently classified and filed according to theme.

FIGURE 3.5 "Library Reading Room," Bolton, April 1938. Humphrey Spender, 1993.83.19.21, Bolton Museum and Archives. Courtesy of the Bolton Museum and Archives, Bolton Council.

The low position of the camera and slightly tilted angle of this photograph suggest Spender may have taken it from a seated position, or have "shot from the hip," so as not to draw the subjects' attention. Tom Harrisson's instructions were to take photographs in such a way that people did not know they were being observed. Other of Spender's images show more clearly his covert photography via the presence of a blur of coat lapel obscuring part of the frame. He describes his approach as "trickery, really, deceit" (Mulford 1982: 19) and notes that he often hid the camera under his coat. Spender initially used a 35 mm Leica camera in Bolton, but after it was stolen he replaced it with the Zeiss Contax 35 with which most of the Mass-Observation photographs were taken, which he generally used with a wide-angle Biogon lens. This was a very small and comparatively lightweight camera that had a very wide depth of field so he didn't have to spend a lot of time focusing when taking shots. The use of medium-fast film allowed him to dispense with flashes, which also helped him to avoid drawing the attention of his subjects. (See the discussion of Spender's photographic work for Mass-Observation in Spender, Smith, and Picton 1978; Mulford 1982; Spender 1987; and interviews with Spender recorded in 1996 and 1997, held by Bolton Museum and Archives.)

OBSERVERS OBSERVED: MASS-OBSERVATION'S METHODOLOGICAL APPARATUSES AS OLIGOPTIC TECHNOLOGIES OF LIBERAL GOVERNMENT

Bruno Latour has drawn attention to the role of oligoptica, nonpanoptic sites in which microstructures of macrosocial phenomena are assembled and from which "sturdy but extremely narrow views of the (connected) whole are made possible" (2005: 181). Oligoptica function through the associations made possible by the existence of multiple, overlapping visual spaces that facilitate rigorous inspection of the parts of a whole. Building on this notion, Otter (2008) has charted the history of the development of a Victorian oligoptic visual economy, in which the liberal subject became increasingly implicated in practices of self-observation, alongside the development of a series of materially heterogeneous technologies of illumination and visibility that facilitated interconnected practices of collective, individual, and practical inspection. He argues that the distinctive spatial, visual, and material organization that characterized Victorian British urban design, engineering, and government administration was related to the development of liberal subjectivities of visual perception that were played out in a range of different quotidian contexts, all structured around the freedom to observe the self and others. He suggests, "There is nothing intrinsically liberal about a library, but a library organized spatially, visually and practically as a partly self-governing, partly overseen institution can be described as liberal in that it expresses the particular kind of organized freedom associated with nineteenth century British liberalism" (260). Citing Bennett's (1995) work on the exhibitionary complex, Otter notes that museums represented one of the classic oligoptic spaces of Victorian Britain, in which the orderly crowd regulated itself through a process of self-monitoring (74).

Otter draws particularly on Patrick Joyce's parallel discussion of the "liberal archive." Joyce (1999, 2003, 2013) has charted the ways in which such institutions, which were centrally concerned with the formation of the liberal subject as one of self-surveillance and self-government, were necessarily "intimately concerned with collecting information about the condition of 'the people'" (1999: 40). He argues that this was so because the constitution of the liberal self as one of self-understanding was contingent on understanding society: "knowing one's society was a prerequisite to knowing one's self" (39). In this, then, the archive came to constitute its political subjects in practices that involved shifting between knowing one's society and knowing one's self. This "social" understanding of the self, Joyce contends, constituted "an 'anthropologizing' of the metropolitan archive" (40).

January 10th, 1939.

A. Saving.

1. Do you save systematically ?   By what method do you save ? –
    Bank, Savings Club, Club Cheques, Cash Boxes, Co-op etc.

2. Describe in your own way your methods for saving and attitudes
    towards the worthwhileness of providing for the future.   Give
    all your thoughts about saving, past and present.

3. What are your pet extravagances ? And your pet economies ?

4. How much cash have you on you ?

5. Did you know how much you had before looking ? – answer this
    question yourself.   Then ask five other people, giving their
    sex, approximate age and job.

6. Where do you keep the cash that you are taking about with you –
    in which pocket of clothes or bag, in a wallet or purse, how do
    you handle it when you take out money or get change ? Observe
    this also in friends and strangers.

B. Jazz.

Describe the part Jazz plays in your home life, if any.   Do you
have gramophone with dance records ? How about radio , Do you listen
to Jazz, and if so, what are the family reactions ? Talk about Jazz in
the family, and write down as nearly as possible the things different
members say about it.   Describe any incidents that have happened to your
knowledge, for example, of people leaving the room when the radio is turned
on because they hate it so much, or on the other hand, of people dancing for
joy with some particular band.

Do you go to dances, and if so, on what occasions ?   From your memory,
or from any dance that you are going to in the next few weeks, describe
what happens at such dances, what you talk about and think about, and whether
you look forward to a dance with pleasure or fear.

Then about words of dance tunes. Do you remember the words more
easily than the tune ? Of how many dance songs do you remember the words, and
what are they ? What do you think about the words of a song like "Cinderella,
Stay in my Arms", "Music, Maestro, Please", "The Chestnut Tree" ?

FIGURE 3.6 Mass-Observation directive on savings and jazz, dated January 10, 1939. SXMOA1/3/26, A19.1, Mass-Observation Archive. Courtesy of the Curtis Brown Group Ltd., London, on behalf of the Trustees of the Mass-Observation Archive.

––––––––––

Directives were sent by mail to members of the national panel of volunteer observers, who were asked to respond to a variety of open-ended questions on different topics related to current Mass-Observation areas of investigation. Responses to the directives were categorized according to the observers' place of residence, occupation, and gender and filed according to directive topic. Like *Notes and Queries on Anthropology*, and the booklets produced for the collection of information by volunteers for the Ethnographic Survey of the United Kingdom, these questionnaires were intended to facilitate the collection of large quantities of data from the approximately two thousand members of the national panel in a form that would allow the information to be considered collectively and comparatively.

––––––––––

While M-O lacked the architectural presence of the Victorian public collecting institutions, as a project it nevertheless continued in this tradition of the anthropologized metropolitan archive—now in distributed form, however—as it utilized the mechanisms of contemporary communications technologies and bureaucratic administrative apparatuses. It was launched with the following peculiar set of interests:

> Behavior of people at war memorials.
> Shouts and gestures of motorists.
> The aspidistra cult.
> Anthropology of football pools.
> Bathroom behavior.
> Beards, armpits, eyebrows.
> Anti-Semitism.
> Distribution, diffusion and significance of the dirty joke.
> Funerals and undertakers.
> Female taboos about eating.
> The private lives of midwives. (Harrisson, Jennings, and Madge
>   1937: 155)

The "Ground Plan for Research" of M-O (Madge and Harrisson 1937: 50–60) explicitly cited topics (and hence objects of collection) gleaned directly from Hadrey Cantril's (1934) article "The Social Psychology of Everyday Life," the Lynds' (1929) *Middletown* study, *Notes and Queries on Anthropology*, and a list of possible subjects sent in by observers themselves. The influence of *Notes and Queries* on M-O is significant and did not simply extend to the Worktown project. Indeed, the 1929 edition of *Notes and Queries* suggests that the field-worker should keep a diary of the day's events and, if possible, engage a "native" to do likewise (BAAS 1929: 35–36). It is possible that this influenced Madge and Jennings in their formulation of the day survey as the original methodology for the national panel, as well as M-O's subsequent suggestion that volunteer observers might undertake to keep wartime diaries after the outbreak of war made regular communication more difficult. Similarly, the form of early editions of *Notes and Queries*—a list of questions—is directly reflected in the form of the directives that were sent to members of the national panel, which generally involved a list of questions on a variety of topics of interest that the volunteer members of the national panel were asked to respond to. There is also a clear resonance in the form and topics covered in this "Ground Plan for Research" with that drawn up by the BAAS committee appointed to organize its Ethnographic Survey of the United Kingdom some forty years before (itself indebted to earlier versions of *Notes and Queries*). Interest in regional traditions, funerals, children's games, and race is found in both M-O and *Notes and Queries* in various ways.

Mirroring recent discussions of the necessity of understanding the ontologies that are generated in and through the practices of collecting as a way of "being" (e.g., Moutu 2007), Lorraine Daston has suggested that scientific observation might be productively viewed as a "trained, collective, cultured habit . . . that guarantees the sturdy existence of a world" (2008: 110). What was novel about M-O as an oligoptic program is the way in which it combined the observation of self and others with the process of collecting. In this sense, it operated both as a technology of the self through its establishment of models for self-observation and diary writing and as a collective habit through its normalization of mass surveillance and opinion polling as a popular pastime and "social" science. Central to this program were the practices, technologies, and techniques that provided M-O with its modes of ordering its masses of "facts," which in turn provided templates for knowing and governing the population.

The focus on direct observation saw M-O emphasize the use of mimetic recording devices, in particular, "cameras" (e.g., Pickering and Chaney 1986: 36; Stanley 2001, 2008, 2009). In *New Verse*, Madge and Jennings characterized the volunteer mass observer as "a recording instrument of the facts" and M-O as "(i) Scientific, (ii) human, and therefore, by extension, (iii) poetic" (1937: 2; see also Frizzell 1997: 25). Madge and Harrisson proposed a similar formula: "The observers are the cameras with which we are trying to photograph contemporary life. The trained observer is ideally a camera with no distortion. Mass-Observation has always assumed its untrained observers would be subjective cameras, each with his or her own individual distortion. They tell us not what society is like, but what it looks like to them" (1938: 66).

Similarly, the introduction to the London section in *May the Twelfth: Mass-Observation Day Surveys* draws on the language of documentary filmmaking to explain how the three types of observer reports—the forty-three day surveys, various responses to a questionnaire, and the "mobile squad" in touch with M-O headquarters by telephone—were arranged to ensure that "close-up and long-shot, detail and ensemble, were all provided" (H. Jennings and Madge 1937: 90; see also Hubble 2006: 121).

The role of technologies of recording, replicating, classifying, and ordering, in particular those technologies closely associated with the archive (see Spieker 2008), was also stressed. "Subjectivity" formed one axis along which observers were themselves ordered and classified, and the distinction between "full-time" and "part-time" observers formed another such axis. Full-time paid observers were involved not only in making field observations but also in writing reports and helping to reorganize and interpret materials for publication. The relationship between field and center, and the role of the center in reorganizing, retyping, reporting on, and interpreting materials, in "making and mobilizing cultural worlds" (see Bennett 2010: 188), was frequently underscored: "The problems of co-ordination will grow greater with time. The immediate problem is to mobilize a numerous and representative corps of observers, and to equip and maintain an efficient central organization, in touch with all other relevant research bodies, however different their methods" (Madge and Harrisson 1937: 45). In addition to observers being classified by age, gender, class, occupation, and geographical place of residence, observers were each identified by a number: "To preserve the anonymity of the observers, no names are given. Each observer will be assigned a number for purposes of filing and identification" (50).

The relationship between M-O and its technologies of storage and archiving is particularly relevant here. The technologies and techniques of filing, classifying, storing, and retrieving information by way of card catalogs, filing cabinets, and typewritten reports facilitated particular modes of collecting and ordering vast quantities of written materials and file reports. The language of the M-O archive, with its "file reports" and "directive responses," is an artifact of this technocratic machinery.

Perhaps most important, the process of M-O was itself conceived of as a participatory liberal technology that operated oligoptically (Hasenbank 2011), and in this sense it was perceived to be both transformative and emancipatory: "For this labor there are immediate compensations. It will encourage people to look more closely at their social environment than ever before and will place before them facts about other social environments of which they know little or nothing. This will effectively contribute to an increase in the general social consciousness. It will counteract the tendency so universal in modern life to perform all our actions through *sheer habit*, with as little consciousness of our surroundings as though we were walking in our sleep" (Madge and Harrisson 1937: 29; italics added).

Thus, the results were "fed back" to observers through the regularly published bulletin *Us*. Until its circulation was disrupted during wartime, this bulletin was sent to volunteer observers to report back on the collective and noteworthy results of the directive responses, so as to "give reliable information about current trends in opinion, public and private, and in social habits and mass behavior" (Mass-Observation 1940). Joyce (2013; see also Stoler

2009) has recently pointed to the importance of infrastructures of circulation, such as the postal network, to the history of the liberal government of the British state and to the making of what Latour (1987) would term *centers of calculation*, as well as the practices and material forms by which state bureaucracy is inscribed within and across those infrastructures of circulation. The relationship of the directives to the bulletin established m-o as a sort of self-regulating feedback loop. It emphasized the dual roles of the observer as simultaneously author and participant observer, informant and research subject, and curator and audience member. It was assisted in doing so by specific technologies of communication (in particular those of the postal service) for collecting and distributing information and delivering observations, and by technologies of mass communication (such as print media and radio broadcasting) for recruiting observers and replicating and disseminating the bulletins themselves. As inscriptive devices, the bulletins provided translations of, and templates for, observing, collecting, and knowing the self and others (figure 3.7). In both of the anthropology at home projects discussed in this chapter, we see the clear influences of particular documents (taking the form of lists of specific questions) on the observations that are produced, and the subsequent looping effects that are generated by a combination of the circulation of these lists and the observations made by amateur observers, which are subsequently organized according to the lists' specifications.

The use of the phrase "sheer habit" by Madge and Harrison is also relevant and warrants further comment here. It denotes the ways in which m-o operated as a liberal technology of the self in the sense that it sought to cultivate modes of self-reflection that opened up a space in the subject between unconscious, automatic, repetitive habit and conscious, reflective, deliberate conduct. m-o operated to construct a division in the self between habit and reflection, as a form of self-regulation that worked via a reflexive freedom to modify that which was habitual and automatic. Bennett (2013a) has recently shown how the significance of this concept of habit relates to different accounts of its place relative to thought, will, instinct, and memory within different historical conceptions of architectures of the person. In this regard, m-o was influenced by a broadly Bergsonian sense of personhood. Bennett notes that, for Bergson, "the relations between habit memory and memory proper produce a space in which freedoms can be delimited and distributed so as to empower a certain kind of emancipatory practice of the self on the part of those who possess the inner partitioning of the person required for this purpose, and to deny it where such a partitioning is absent" (123).

10 FEBRUARY, 1940

US2

Mass-Observation's Weekly Intelligence Service.

Published by Mass-Observation, 6 Grotes Buildings, Blackheath, London, S.E.3. Telephone Lee Green 4278. Subscription rates, 5s. per quarter or £1 per annum, post free.

This Issue Reports on

The War and US
Morale and the Future
Workers' War-Time Spending
US3 will report on Repercussions of Conscription, a Workers Week, what Painters are Painting and Selling.

The War and US

The function of this paper, and of M-O, the research organisation which issues it, is to give reliable information about current trends in opinion, public and private, and in social habits and mass behaviour.

The urgency and importance of this information is very widely admitted. The *Manchester Guardian*, for example, thought it worth while to write the whole of its first leading article on M-O's newly published survey, " War Begins at Home."

This sympathetic leading article (5.2.40), which quotes as serious evi-

(Continued on page 7)

MORALE AND THE FUTURE

You will read in US every week plenty of facts about people and their opinions. In this report, as well as giving the latest facts, we attempt to see if "morale" is a mythical abstraction or something which may win or lose the war.

More and more as the war intensifies on the Home Front, stagnates on the Western Front, authoritative people say it will be lost or won by civilian morale. What is morale ?

War morale is the amount of interest people take in the war, how worth while they feel it is. If people are left bewildered or if their leaders do not interest them (either in truthful or lying versions of the situation) then morale cannot be regarded as " good " and may easily become " bad."

The main way in which public opinion has previously been ascertained is by interviewing. But interviewing does not give information about what people *think* (morale): it only gives information about what people *say*, and say to a stranger. And in war time, when it is disloyal to oppose the status quo, an increased number of people give to a stranger a version of their opinion which is different from the one they " really hold." We may distinguish:

What a person says to a stranger.
,,   ,,   ,,   friend.
,,   ,,   ,,   acquaintance.
,,   ,,   ,,   his wife.
,,   ,,   ,,   himself.
,,   ,,   ,,   in his sleep.

It is at the level of wife, self and dream that the most honest assessment of morale can be made. From the private opinion of 1940 comes the public opinion of 1941.

FIGURE 3.7 Front cover of *Us: Mass-Observation's Weekly Intelligence Service*, volume 2, dated February 10, 1940. File Report 27, Mass-Observation Archive. Courtesy of the Curtis Brown Group Ltd., London, on behalf of the Trustees of the Mass-Observation Archive.

Although it was produced for only a few months between February and May 1940, with its printing and distribution ultimately disrupted by war, *Us* nonetheless constituted a novel solution to a problem that had been encountered in previous amateur anthropological surveys through its role in feeding back the results of directive responses and forming a template for the subsequent formatting of responses by observers. It was also far more than this, however, in that it constituted one element in the materialization of Mass-Observation's objective to transform society through informed participation. As inscriptive devices, the bulletins provided translations of, and templates for, observing, collecting, and knowing the self and others.

The techniques used by M-O for the collection and dissemination of data on the masses, it would seem, shared in this political logic of mobilizing technologies of self-fashioning that operated on the premise that knowing one's self required knowing one's society: that is, through active participation as a gatherer and interpreter of social data, the volunteer observer was to be drawn into a better, and ultimately emancipatory, understanding of herself or himself through an understanding of the mass society of which she or he was a part. In this, then, M-O continued in the tradition of the anthropologized metropolitan archive discussed by Joyce.

ETHNOGRAPHY, SURREALISM, AND THE "MASS"

Mike Savage (2008, 2010) has recently argued that M-O as a movement was instrumental in the emergence of a new *technocratic* lower-middle-class fraction in Britain, which sought to distance itself from existing "gentlemanly, artistic, highbrow motifs in favor of a more technical, 'scientific' intellectual vision" (2010: 64; see also Summerfield 1985 on M-O as a popular social movement). His work suggests that M-O must be seen as a project in which novel ways of "speaking" were developed, disseminating (and exhibiting) newly emergent forms of cultural capital and modes of authority associated with representing "the mass" in the public domain. He emphasizes the development of the social sciences in Britain within this context, associating the emergence of this new intellectual formation with, among other things, the popularity of the Left Book Club and the newly launched Penguin and Pelican paperbacks, which covered science, current affairs, and social issues in a technical manner but were nonetheless cheaply available and became widely read among this new class fraction. While M-O and its founders' (particularly Harrisson's) struggle for academic credibility in relation to contemporary British anthropology and sociology has received much attention in accounting for the relative invisibility of M-O in histories of British anthropology (e.g., MacClancy 1995, 2001; Street n.d.; Stanley 2001, 2009; Hubble 2006), we want to emphasize another adjacent field—the aesthetic—that has perhaps received less attention in relation to the question of the conceptualization of the population and the legacy of M-O in the wartime and postwar British administrative-bureaucratic apparatus. Historian of science Bernadette Bensaude-Vincent argues for the importance of exploring the mechanisms of demarcation and discrimination between science and rival forms of knowledge and "how the notions of science and the public have been mutually configured and reconfigured" (2009: 361). Similarly, understanding the ways in which forms of knowledge developed and were deployed in relation to these various fields in this period, when the modes of authority relating to the most appropriate methods for undertaking social scientific research were still very much open to question and in flux (see also Highmore 2006), might help us to account not only for the emergence of this new technocratic class fraction but also for the specific ways of understanding the population that were implicated in the development of the postwar British welfare state. We focus here on the ways in which the textual and aesthetic practices associated with the collection, reassembling, and presentation of M-O research—the carefully edited collage, montage, juxtaposition, and emphasis on the creative possibilities of *objects trouvés*—helped shape a conception of the "mass" as a population whose views could be collected as a montage and edited in such a way that a sense of a collective "atmosphere" not only would emerge but might in turn become the object of manipulation by way of the governance of morale (figure 3.8).[8] Importantly, these aesthetic practices also operated visually and in this sense relate to the broader oligoptic visual economy of M-O on which we focused in the earlier part of the chapter.

Jeremy MacClancy (1995, 2001) has already discussed James Clifford's (1981; also 1988) work on surrealism and its influence on ethnographic methodologies, along with the various criticisms of and corrections to this aspect of his work (e.g., Jamin 1986, 1991), in relation to M-O, and it is not our intention to rehearse these arguments here (see also Highmore 2002, 2006; Stanley 2001). Instead, we want to pick up on another aspect of MacClancy's (1995, 2001), Nick Hubble's (2006), and Ben Highmore's (2007) analyses of the connections between surrealism, Freudian psychology, and the material form in which M-O collected, stored, and subsequently presented its work. We have already noted the use of the language of documentary filmmaking in explaining the relationship between the observers' reports in the London section of *May the Twelfth: Mass-Observation Day Surveys*. The larger part of the book juxtaposed hundreds of edited observations made by anonymized individuals with the events surrounding the coronation of George VI in 1937. Here, as elsewhere, the emphasis is on the presentation of everyday accounts as facts en masse so that a collective sense of public opinion might emerge. This approach was consistent with an emphasis on the importance of coincidence and on the creative possibilities of juxtaposition in facilitating the emergence of distinct structures and patterns in the collective unconscious. Similarly, the logics of filing, classifying, storing, retrieving, ordering, and reordering made possible by its card catalogs, filing cabinets, and typewritten reports find resonance in Jennings's documentary filmmaking, Julian Trevelyan's

FIGURE 3.8 Julian Trevelyan, *Rubbish May Be Shot Here*, 1937. © Tate, London, 2014. Courtesy of the Julian Trevelyan Estate, represented by Bohun Gallery.

This image was produced in the same year Julian Trevelyan was invited by Tom Harrisson to participate in the Worktown study in Bolton. He produced a number of such collages while in Bolton; these artworks and others by Graham Bell and William Coldstream themselves formed the subject of a study of Bolton residents' responses to different forms of artwork. The collage shown here is clearly inspired by events following the abdication crisis, a key stimulus for the formation of Mass-Observation, and the image includes newspaper cuttings from coverage of the coronation of George VI and other pictures of the monarchy. The smiling child in the bottom left-hand corner is taken from a newspaper advertisement for breakfast cereal. The aesthetic practices of Mass-Observation—carefully edited collage, montage, juxtaposition, and an emphasis on the creative possibilities of *objects trouvés*—helped shape a conception of the "mass" as a population whose views could be collected as a montage and edited in such a way that a sense of a collective atmosphere not only would emerge but might in turn become the object of manipulation by way of the governance of morale.

---

surrealist photography and artistic montages (figure 3.8) produced during his time in Bolton, and the experimental collective poetry of Madge and the other Blackheath Group members. M-O's dream reports and directives asking observers to keep dream diaries and to note the occurrence of spontaneous mental "images" (T. Miller 2001; see also Connor 2001) also fall within this general field of interest. All demonstrate an investment in the visual aesthetic and material-textual practices of collage and montage, in the "shuffling" and juxtaposing of masses of information, to uncover hidden aspects of the collective unconscious. While M-O was large enough to accommodate a range of differing aesthetic and material-textual practices (for example, the measured realism of painter and part-time paid Bolton observer William Coldstream, which finds resonance with M-O's experiments with social scientific objectivity), it is this methodology of montage as a way of both getting a hold on and presenting "mass" culture that dominates in the early work of M-O and helps shape its distinctive conception of the population.

This conception of mass culture gained particular traction governmentally, as a novel way of conceptualizing the population, by way of the alternative it offered to class for identifying and articulating cultural difference, and hence producing new working surfaces on the social. Tony Kushner (2004) has convincingly argued against the widespread assumption that M-O's anthropological methods targeted working-class populations as de facto colonial indigenes; indeed, despite its predominantly middle-class membership it targeted and recruited members from across all classes.[9] This needs to be understood within the context of a broader refashioning of the middle class as the "ordinary" class over this period (see Savage 2010). What was distinctive about M-O's conception of the mass was its simultaneous proximity to and distance from class categories and notions of the "everyday." Participants perceived themselves to be involved in actively reworking the relationship between individuals and society, based on a belief in the emancipatory potential of participation in M-O alongside exposure to forms of high culture, in order to build a new society with the capability to reshape itself through informed civic participation (Hinton 2008: 235–36). In this way, the notion of the mass developed by M-O helped to produce novel ways of conceptualizing the relationship between governors and governed, and of conceptualizing society more generally.

We have already made note of the complicated "looping effects" (see Hacking 1986, 1995) involved in participation in M-O. What is important here is the idea of the collective unconscious as something that can be shaped, and hence manipulated, by *observation* and *collection* of the self and others. It was this sense of morale as an object of collective work, which was subject to being altered by access to particular forms of information, that may have led M-O and its founders' various side projects to assume such an important role in the conceptualization and governance of the British population. The complicated ways in which the relations between the collector and the collected were organized and ordered, and the ways in which the subjects of research could also contribute directly to the research process, were key ambiguities that might perhaps account for the relative success of M-O and its particular role in the development of a new technocratic class fraction (Savage 2008, 2010). But it seems possible that the idea of the observer as a "subjective" camera—a self-fashioning liberal subject—and the sense of morale as an object that is open to manipulation and transformation contributed directly to the large investment in wartime propaganda and the particular form this propaganda would take through the General Post Office/Crown Film Unit and elsewhere (see figure 3.9). These are the concerns to which we now turn by considering the ways in which M-O became directly implicated in the production of wartime propaganda through its involvement with the U.K. government's MoI.

MASS-OBSERVATION AND THE GOVERNANCE OF MORALE

Upon the outbreak of war in September 1939 M-O completed its first report for the MoI, and in November 1941 it delivered its final ministerial "collaboration" (Hubble 2006: 167, 187).[10] The work for the ministry represented a new kind of application for the quotidian investigations of the organization. Its various instruments that had, in peacetime, aimed to gather data on the "habit, emotion, [and] opinion" of the masses were recomposed and, as part of the MoI work, redirected at civilian morale.[11] M-O had developed a detailed approach to measuring "people's behavior, their subjective feelings . . . and fears." In 1942 Bob Willcock—then director of M-O—suggested that this "complex machinery" was in fact "strengthened by the experience of war," resulting in its increasing refinement as a method of data collection (1943: 456).

In 1940 the newly appointed director of the MoI's Collecting Division, Mary Adams, proposed the creation of a "morale barometer" (quoted in Hubble 2006: 179–80). Outlining her proposals for "the structure and functions" of this division, Adams identified that "[its] immediate tasks were to supply the Ministry [MoI] itself with routine monthly and ad hoc reports on matters of urgency and on the effectiveness of propaganda." She added, "A continuous flow of information is required . . . to study immediate reac-

FIGURE 3.9 Screenshot from the film *Spare Time* (1939), directed by Humphrey Jennings for the General Post Office Film Unit.

Spare Time was made by the General Post Office (GPO) Film Unit, to be shown at the New York World's Fair in 1939. A year later the film unit was renamed the Crown Film Unit and came under the direct control of the Ministry of Information. *Spare Time* focused on the leisure activities of British steel, cotton, and coal workers; it not only included material filmed in Bolton but also clearly adopted an approach that resonated with Mass-Observation in its abandonment of narrative in favor of largely unmediated observation. Jennings drew on both the documentary and surrealist aesthetic practices of Mass-Observation in his filmmaking; his films are noted for their naturalistic style and their use of associative montage. In contrast to the Ethnographic Survey of the United Kingdom, it was not in forgotten hamlets and rural villages but in the rituals of urban and industrial Britain, like those presented by Jennings in *Spare Time*, that Mass-Observation thought its "native" culture might be found.

---

tions to specific events as well as to create a barometer for the measurement of opinion, on questions likely to be continuously important" (quoted in McLaine 1979: 50).

There were three primary sources that the MoI drew on in its enterprise "to turn morale into writing and make it legible" (Rose 1990: 28–29): its own Home Intelligence/Collecting Division, which itself gathered data from various sources including regional staff with local contacts, the BBC Listeners' Research Unit, the postal and telegraph censors, and police duty-room reports; the National Institute for Economic and Social Research's Wartime Social Survey; and M-O, in spite of "some disquiet concerning its methods"—in fact, the initiative that led to the establishment of the Wartime Social Survey was "to act as a check" on M-O data (Hubble 2006: 179).[12] However, as Ian McLaine notes, in spite of these reservations "the Ministry placed a heavy reliance on the work performed by Mass-Observation" (1979: 52). Indeed, Adams was to convey to the Treasury that M-O reports "have now become an essential part of the whole machinery of Home Intelligence" (quoted in Hubble 2006: 182). In this, then, M-O came to make a significant contribution to this organization, assisting in the MoI's "duty . . . to [interpret] the public mind to the Government, and act as [a] clearing house for information about changing habits and beliefs."[13]

Thus M-O's work with the ministry took place in the context of, and contributed to, the processes through which citizenship "acquired a subjective form" (Rose 1990: 32). The active shaping of civilians' "wills, consciences, and aspirations" was increasingly seen as a requirement for "winning the war, and winning the peace" (32). As Nikolas Rose continues, it was over the late 1930s and early 1940s that "the psyche of the citizen was discovered as a new continent for psychological knowledge and for the deployment of the professional skills of the technicians of subjectivity" (32). Morale emerged as a key mechanism by which the governors might get a hold on this newly defined psychosocial territory, and so optimize the well-being of the citizenry while simultaneously serving the national interest and war effort. In linking up its expertise on the subjectivity of the ordinary people with the state apparatus, M-O was implicated in the conquest of this continental discovery: the psyche of the citizenry—"the mysterious, unfathomed depths of consciousness which the Government must learn to understand and exploit."[14] M-O referred to this enigmatic collective unconscious as "the public mind."[15]

In its investigations of morale, M-O was at pains to draw a qualitative difference between public and private opinion—a distinction it contended was consequential for the measurement and interpretation of morale. One report claimed, "In generalizations about morale, one must always bear in mind the vital difference between what people say, and especially what they say to a stranger (the interviewer), and what they are thinking deep down."[16] Here a methodological problematic was established that highlighted the limitations of procedures that would rely solely on public opinion to gauge morale. Refining M-O's "investigative machinery," a subsequent report to the MoI advanced an analysis precisely in terms of surfaces and depths. It contended, "[The reported] generalizations are essentially based on detailed facts, but also go below the surface layer of these facts. That is now an essential part of understanding morale. It has always been very misleading to rely on material of the interview and spoken comment type. That has never given more than public opinion[;] the done thing. . . . It is private opinion which matters."[17]

This notion of morale, then, posited the citizen-subject not only as the bearer of surfaces and depths but also as one whose psychological veracity was only to be discovered in the latter. Harrisson's academic publications of the time similarly worked to formalize this distinction between public and private opinion so that it was the interiority of the private, over the exteriority of the public, that had privileged access to the truth of morale. In contrast to the emerging methodological tools of British sociology—the social survey and the opinion poll, which offered competing cartographies of citizen subjectivity to M-O's more qualitative approaches—exponents of M-O's method laid claim to the expertise required to penetrate the interiorities of the citizen-subject, and so to lay bare the truth of what was hidden: the "unfathomed depths of consciousness" of the ordinary Briton.[18] And, with this, they aimed to reveal the precise state of the subjectivity that lay under the mask of public opinion, which the government needed to access and exploit if it was to rule effectively.

It is important to register what was at stake in this distinction between "public opinion" and that which lies beneath, "private opinion." In this formulation Harrisson looked to discredit the object of his social scientific rivals.[19] Public opinion could only ever be a poor optic on morale. Rather, the proper task of the social analyst was to understand the dynamics of private opinion and its public manifestations and implications. But more than this, public opinion had the potential to be dangerously repressive:

> Civilian morale is to-day acclaimed by Admirals, Mayors, Ministers and journalists, as A1. . . . [T]his ballyhoo sanctions only a show of pleasure or reprisal, and makes it more difficult for people to express perfectly natural feelings of depression or distress. More and more, in

recent months, emotions have been bottled up, and the [gulf] between public opinion and private opinion is again becoming dangerously enlarged. . . . The more compulsion and restriction, the more easily can tensions develop at the level of private opinion without ever being noticed on top. In such situations we have the elements of violent explosion, quite "unexpectedly" released at some crisis moment.[20]

The "good government" of morale was the management and minimization of the dissonance between public and private opinion, between external and "superficial" public expression and internal and "deep" private countenance, such that this volatile pressure did not explode in an uncontrolled manner detrimental to both the individual subject and social order. A lack of understanding and a failure to "grasp" the disposition of ordinary citizens was a recurring and prominent charge in the M-O documentation against the nation's political elites, with the governors regularly chastised for their inadequate knowledge of the governed and thus their poor management of civilian morale: "The whole situation of morale at the moment is dominated by the continuing lack of precise leadership. . . . Ministers and the Ministry of Information continue to show themselves emotionally unaware [and] administratively unready to handle or canalise the immensely powerful feelings which are surging beneath the surface of practically every individual in the island."[21]

The research of M-O thus developed a precise correspondence between an exigency of Britain's wartime government and the subject of M-O's expertise, cultivating the emergence of morale as a previously obscured object of knowledge in service of rehabilitating a nation in crisis.

The M-O documentation for the period with which this chapter is concerned was marked by a significant level of deliberation about the effective management of morale, which would necessarily walk a line between policies of persuasion and compulsion. "The State has two methods," it was contended, "persuasion and compulsion. It is rightly reluctant, at all times, to abandon the one and resort to the other" (Mass-Observation (1941: i). Here M-O's knowledge practices became imbricated in the problematic of liberal government: a problematic that, to follow Michel Foucault's characterization, must distinguish between practices of governing through liberal modalities of power that would seek to rule through liberty and practices that seek to govern through other, illiberal means, marking the limits to freedom's rule. The latter include, in this case, practices that govern through the principle of compulsion, such as conscription, curfews, rationing, and so on. We now go on to trace the logic by which M-O argued, on the one hand, for occasions where the implementation of illiberal forms of rule generated conditions counter to the aims of good government and, on the other, for instances where illiberal forms of rule ought to be implemented since they were in the interests of the effective and efficient government of the population's welfare.

In 1940 the British government campaigned and legislated against "dangerous talk" on the grounds that "those who spread gloom and despondency do definite harm" to civilian morale and the war effort generally.[22] Reviewing this attempt to control rumor and despondency through legislation, M-O contended that such a policy was demonstrative of the governors' inadequate knowledge of working-class culture. Implemented with no ethnographic understanding of the function of such talk in British society, legislation prohibiting it could only be detrimental to securing "good morale." Without this knowledge policy makers failed to recognize a key mechanism of self-regulation within that society: the role of argumentative and humorous conversation. Thus, M-O maintained that such conversation was a necessary "safety valve in our culture," and, as such, this mechanism by which affective energies were released was posited as something like a natural condition of civil society, "a British habit," a part of "the British tradition."[23] In this instance, then, illiberal rule was cast as an unwarranted interference in popular conduct. Not only ineffectual and unlikely to "defeat defeatism," it was also counterproductive to its wider aims, since it worked against civil society's own mechanisms for maintaining morale.[24] The report contended that "dangerous talk" should instead be targeted through techniques that sought to get a hold on citizens' conduct via appeals to their voluntary actions, that is, through the persuasive practices of propaganda.

While propaganda was closely involved in efforts to modulate voluntary conduct, it was also a practice that could be used to forge a connection between liberal and illiberal modalities of power: M-O reported that people were willing to forfeit freedoms when fully informed of the need for their forfeiture: "That is why this legislation has had a disturbing effect. People do not resent restrictions in wartime, so long as they know where they are and what it all means, and so long as the basic elements of freedom do not appear to be overwhelmingly involved."[25] Thus, propaganda could play a role in communicating imperatives; accordingly, the conditions under which citizens consented to coercion and were prepared to surrender freedoms in the interests of national security and welfare were a regular concern in M-O documentation of the early 1940s.

In addition, M-O was active in investigating situations where illiberal forms of rule were, in its view, in the interests of good government. It aimed to situate and quantify public tolerance for authoritarian rule, and its research sought to establish as an objective truth the existence of a demotic—if not democratic—desire for forms of compulsion in particular contexts. For example, an M-O report canvassing popular views on "the responsibility of the citizen" stated, "As the average citizen sees it, in wartime this responsibility consists mainly of doing what he is told or urgently asked to do."[26] Evidence for this claim stemmed from M-O surveys that discovered widespread support for the conscription of women's labor and other forms of compulsion in relation to evacuations, fire spotting, air-raid precautions, and so on. Such findings could translate into policy advice, and M-O urged the government to action in the case of fire spotting: "these responses suggest that the moment is ideal for the introduction of such regulations."[27] Accompanying this advice was a strategic recommendation for regulation that demonstrates M-O's dexterity in negotiating its seemingly paradoxical investment in liberal and illiberal rule: "it should continue to be stressed that compulsion is only being used where the voluntary system has been tried and failed."[28]

THE LEGACIES OF MASS-OBSERVATION

Despite the relatively minor and anecdotal place given to M-O in the history of the development of anthropology and sociology in Britain, the governmental rationalities established by M-O's conceptualization of mass society and culture had a direct and lasting influence on the postwar British welfare state. This resulted not only from its implication in the formation of a distinctive new technocratic middle class, which was subsequently central to the formation of postwar British social science (Savage 2010), but also from its extension of oligoptic visual economies from the space of the public museum to the interior and quotidian lives of ordinary people and through its particular ways of conceptualizing the mass as a population whose dispositions could be collected, edited, and manipulated as part of the governance of morale. This conception of the mass owed as much to the mixture of surrealist, "documentary," and journalistic textual and aesthetic practices by which M-O collected and presented its data as to the information generated by M-O and the work of its founders themselves. Perhaps even more important, a comparative perspective on the work of M-O sees it emerge as one among many forms of expertise impinging on governmental relations to the population in wartime Britain. These governmental relations did not equate directly with the activities of the state or with the administrative procedures of the MoI; nonetheless, the governmental rationalities they established had a long-lasting influence on subsequent practices of social government.

The oligoptic visual economy generated in and through M-O's fieldwork agencements was not limited to those aspects of its work that were directed at constituting individuals as self-governing subjects. What was most innovative about M-O was the ways in which it emphasized new, *collectivized* forms of self-knowledge that sought to make the population self-governing. These stood in contrast to a range of other contemporary and emergent instruments for knowing the population—opinion polls, surveys, census data, and so on—through the stress they placed on the need for these forms of collective self-knowing to constitute a part of the relations between rulers and ruled. Of course, these claims should not be taken at face value; they were part of the rhetoric through which a meritocratic class fraction sought to displace the leadership of traditional "gentlemanly" forms of rule. But this collectivization of oligoptic vision represented a distinctive approach to observing, collecting, ordering, knowing, and governing the population that would become an integral part of metropolitan and colonial British post-war governmental rationalities. As a form of expertise in the service of the state, M-O was concerned with discovering how, under conditions of total war, citizen-workers were amenable to, on the one hand, particular practices of persuasion that sought to get a hold on subjects' conduct through their voluntary actions and, on the other, practices directed not at free actions but at governing through the principle of compulsion. In doing so, it established certain templates for governing integral to the conception of the British welfare state as a form of *social* security that would be achieved by *material* means through cooperation between the state and the individual.

CHAPTER FOUR

BOAS AND AFTER

Museum Anthropology and the
Governance of Difference in America

In his recent account of scientific racism in America Robert Wald Sussman argues that by the 1930s the Boasian culture concept had effectively brought to an end the eugenic programs that had dominated the governance of difference in early twentieth-century America. Tracing the connections between eugenics and the longer five hundred–year history in which differences in appearances, capacities, and behaviors had been grounded in racialized biological categories, Sussman summarizes Franz Boas's significance as that of providing "an alternative explanation for why people from different areas or living under certain conditions behaved differently from one another": they "have culture" (2014: 3). Displacing the predominant influence previously exercised by physical anthropology, the culture concept defined a new intellectual program for anthropology that spilled over into adjacent disciplines—notably sociology and psychology—by producing a new set of coordinates for conceptualizing and managing the relations between America's increasingly varied populations. This did not happen overnight. Nor does Sussman suggest that it was solely Boas's accomplishment. The ascendancy of the culture concept was, rather, the outcome of a protracted history that owed as much to the refinements and extrapolations of Boas's students as it did to Boas's own formulations. Nonetheless,

Sussman interprets the culture concept as bringing about a paradigm shift by displacing race as the key category for conceptualizing human differences.

On the face of it, Michel-Rolph Trouillot reaches a similar conclusion in characterizing the culture concept as "race repellent" (2003: 100). Yet Trouillot also qualifies this assessment. While acknowledging that the culture concept prevented race from occupying the defining place it had earlier enjoyed in American anthropology, he contends that it did not effectively challenge the political relations between race and racism in America.[1] He attributes this failure to a more general shortcoming of the culture concept: that in being launched as the negation of race it also became the negation of class and history. This was most evident in its conception of "primitives" (a term that, albeit hedged with qualifications, remained an integral component of the Boasian lexicon), referring to "those who had no complexity, no class, and no history that really mattered—because they had culture" (Trouillot 2003: 100). Since each group was also believed to have "a single such culture whose boundaries were thought to be self-evident," the culture concept "reconciled the Boasian agenda with both the state-centrism of the strong social sciences and the taxonomic schemes of the even stronger natural sciences, notably zoology and biology" (102).

Yet this assessment of cultures as tightly bound to a specific locality is, Trouillot acknowledges, not the whole story, and less true of how Boas and his students construed the relations between processes of diffusion and the organization of cultural areas than of the later development of the institutional problematic of "cultural anthropology."[2] This line of argument—already a key component of George W. Stocking Jr.'s (1968: 195–233) historical reassessment of the culture concept—has since been more fully elaborated in a considerable body of work that has drawn on poststructuralist perspectives to interpret cultural areas as temporary fusions of cultural flows from diverse points of origin (see Bashkow 2004; Evans 2005). Brad Evans's work is particularly helpful here in showing how the rethinking of the concerns and procedures of folklore studies that took place in the 1890s under the influence of philology led to a view of languages and, by extension, of cultures as "public objects" whose disposition and relations to one another were shaped by processes of historical interaction and migration beyond the control of individual speakers or particular speech communities. Boas was closely related to these developments, proposing a conception of a culture as a creative fusion of diverse elements, brought together in a particular territory, which was effected by the distinctive genius of the people in question.

That said, not all peoples and cultures occupied the same relationship to these processes. This is clear in the volcanic imagery Clark Wissler used when summarizing the relationships between cultural areas and processes of cultural diffusion. Different centers of cultural creativity appear as "so many crater cones of varying diameter, all belching forth the molten lava of culture, their respective lava fields meeting and overlapping." While some "craters become extinct and new ones break forth in between," Wissler continues, "the important point is that in all of them once burned the fire of originality" (1923a: 156–57). There is, however, a crucial difference between those culture centers that have served as points of origin for the diffusion of traits on a global scale (European-American and Asian) and the tribal cultures that, although once originating centers (albeit on a more limited scale), have since been relegated to the byways of such global processes. Such peoples, Wissler concludes, have become "slackers in culture, who have slunk back into the by-ways of isolation" and for whom, since they now occupy "the chronological level of past ages," the label of "primitive" is justified (326–27).

This qualification of the culture concept needs to be viewed alongside a further limitation, perhaps first identified by William Willis ([1972] 1999) and more recently elaborated in an extended critical literature (M. Anderson 2014; Jacobson 1998): the retention of a set of hierarchically organized biological race categories (Caucasian, Mongoloid, and Negro) in which the category of Caucasian defined a new conception of whiteness as a controlling center from which the relations between America's varied populations (an "original" Nordic white native stock, Native Americans, African Americans, and new cohorts of immigrants from southern Europe and Asia) were to be managed. In what follows we explore the different and often contradictory roles played by the culture concept as it was applied to the relations between mainstream white America and new generations of migrants, on the one hand, and to Native Americans and African Americans, on the other. There is a further qualification that will characterize our approach to these aspects of the practical history of the culture concept. This has often been interpreted as an alternative to aesthetic concepts of culture. This was an aspect of Alfred Kroeber and Clyde Kluckhohn's (1952) influential interpretation of the concept, which, shaped by a fusion of nationalism and a militant scientism, construed the concept as a distinctively American and scientific break with European humanistic traditions. Although acceptance of this view has informed a good deal of the concept's appropriation into the subsequent history of cultural studies, aesthetic conceptions of creativity—attributed to a people—were an integral part of the concept's American history.[3] We see this in Melville Herskovits's contention that "it is necessary to know the 'style' of a culture—which is merely another way of saying that we must know its patterning—in precisely the same way that the student of art must know the styles that characterise the various periods of art-history in order to cope with the individual variations that are exemplified in the works of artists of a given epoch" (1938: 22). Our interest, however, will be in how this aesthetic dimension was translated into practices of governance aimed at ordering the relations between the different cultures that constituted America's melting pot.

For all that we have questioned Sussman's somewhat overemphatic sense of a complete break between the culture concept and the biological race categories of earlier traditions of physical anthropology, his discussion offers a useful point of entry into these questions by reminding us of the extent to which these different approaches to the ordering of differences were in contention in the internal politics of the American Museum of Natural History (AMNH). Sussman explores these issues in relation to the rivalry between Boas and Madison Grant, a promoter of eugenic politics in the early 1900s. These tensions, however, continued to inform the relations between the eugenic programs of Henry Fairfield Osborn, as the AMNH's president, and Wissler, as Boas's successor after the latter's departure from the AMNH in 1905. While a good deal of critical attention has been paid to the racial and eugenic coordinates of the AMNH's natural history displays under Osborn (Bennett 2004; Haraway 1992), the directions given to the museum's anthropology programs under Wissler have not been closely examined. Although Wissler is usually interpreted as having been powerless to overcome the constraints imposed by Osborn and his eugenicist allies, a closer look reveals that Wissler was able to maintain and develop the relativistic thrust of Boasian anthropology while also maintaining a strong connection between fieldwork and exhibition practices in ways that had significant implications for the development and practical history of the culture concept.

Shortly before he assumed the museum's presidency in 1908, Osborn remarked to a friend: "Between ourselves, much anthropology is merely opinion, or gossip of the natives. It is many years away from being a science. Jesup and the Museum spent far too much money on anthropology."[4] Along with Osborn's expressed disdain for the subject, Wissler noted that one unnamed trustee "actively opposed the keeping of any ethnological collections or exhibits," with the result being an "emphasis on archaeology as a museum subject."[5] The remainder of Wissler's career at the museum was circumscribed by Osborn's "containment" of anthropology, as he alternatively sought to oppose or accommodate it. In fact, a dominant theme in our story is the institutional, discursive, and even personal schizophrenia and contradiction during Wissler's tenure. As Stocking has noted, Wissler possessed "an ambivalence which permeated his whole anthropological outlook" (1974: 909). During this time of transition almost everything he did was qualified, including the balance between race and culture as explanations of human difference.

We pursue these questions by looking first at Wissler's fieldwork practices and the respects in which these retained Boas's focus on the Americas while also departing from Boas's fieldwork methods in a number of ways. We then examine the extension of the AMNH's expeditions into Africa, Oceania, and Asia, foregrounding the ways in which these moved away from the relativistic thrust of Boasian anthropology in reembracing biological conceptions of racial hierarchies. Returning to Wissler for the purpose of a closer consideration of the role that the concept of culture areas played in both his fieldwork and his exhibition practices, we go on to probe the ambiguities that informed his use and interpretation of this concept. These reflected the broader tensions between his sometimes ambivalent affiliation with the principles of Boasian anthropology on the one hand and the eugenic orientations of the AMNH under Osborn—and, indeed, his own eugenic sympathies—on the other. Nonetheless, we stress the important role that, in spite of these equivocations, Wissler's work played in maintaining and, in some respects, expanding the relativistic underpinnings of the Boasian culture concept. This provides the setting for our consideration of the broader approach to patterns of culture that informed the aesthetic readings and inflections of the concept of culture areas proposed by Edward Sapir ([1924] 1949) and Ruth Benedict (1934). These later stages in the development of the culture concept pave the way for our return, in concluding, to the role played by the culture concept in the governing of differences in America during the interwar years.

COLLECTING AS AN AMERICANIST SURVEY

In 1912, while discussing the place of the Chinese collection at the AMNH, Wissler emphatically announced, "America is our field" (quoted in Jacknis 2015a: 52).[6] As Regna Darnell (1998) has pointed out, survey and the desire to map the Native peoples of the American continent has been a defining trait for Americanist anthropology, going back at least to 1879 and Major John Wesley Powell at the Smithsonian's Bureau of American Ethnology. In sponsoring great regional surveys of the Northwest Coast, the Plains, and the Southwest, the AMNH was simply following a well-established scholarly paradigm (Cole and Long 1999). Unlike the Smithsonian, however, the museum gave this paradigm a culturalist rather than an evolutionary or materialist interpretation.

Such anthropological surveys brought with them a notion of systematic collecting: that is, filling in the gaps, and collecting from all regions, cultures, and object types, in order to have a complete, or at least representative, documentation of Native American cultures. Or such was the rhetoric. In a report to the trustees, Wissler argued that the museum's North American holdings were a type collection, a comprehensive collection of a kind that he felt was less possible or necessary for other areas.[7] The fieldwork and collection phase (1897–1905) of the Jesup Expedition to the Northwest Coast was finished by the time Boas left the museum and Wissler took over.[8] It was explicitly focused on geographical issues. Ostensibly undertaken to throw light on the original peopling of the Americas, it sought to trace the diffusion of cultural traits, as well as peoples, across the Bering Strait. At the same time, it netted huge, well-documented collections that filled the museum's galleries. In March 1898, in the midst of the Jesup Expedition, Boas proposed to the administration that it fund a vast and ambitious survey of the "Vanishing Tribes of North America" (Cole 1999: 204–7). When this survey began in January 1899, the next region to be covered was the Plains, where the fieldwork continued through 1916.[9] Alfred Kroeber, Boas's first doctoral student at Columbia, started the survey in 1899–1900 with his fieldwork among the Arapaho and Gros Ventre, which culminated in his dissertation on Arapaho decorative symbolism (1901). This was soon followed by Wissler's own collecting among the Dakota Sioux and the Blackfoot, mostly between 1902 and 1905 (figure 4.1).

Upon taking charge of the department's collecting and research in 1905, Wissler maintained the Boasian emphasis on the Americas. The Plains survey was continued the following year by another of Boas's students, Robert Lowie, who served as curator from 1909 until his departure for Berkeley in 1921. Although particularly known for his work among the Crow, he had the most comprehensive field experience of the museum's ethnographic collectors. In 1909 Wissler turned to the Southwest, which had until then been a focus for the Smithsonian and Chicago's Field Museum (Fowler 2000). The collectors of the Huntington Expedition, which continued through 1921, included Herbert J. Spinden among the Rio Grande Pueblos, Kroeber and Leslie Spier in Zuni (both ethnological and archaeological), Lowie in Hopi, and Pliny Goddard, who was the most active of the museum's ethnographers in this region, among the Navajo and Apache.[10] While the Southwestern sur-

FIGURE 4.1 Clark Wissler (?) photographing skin dressing among the Blackfoot (Blood) Indians, Alberta, 1901–5. 2A18377, American Museum of Natural History, New York. Courtesy of the American Museum of Natural History.

Like many of their anthropological colleagues, curators at the American Museum of Natural History used photography as an ethnographic tool. Their images became collectible objects in their own right, to be juxtaposed with the Native objects they brought back. Of all the museum's Plains collectors, Clark Wissler was the most avid photographer. In his monograph on Blackfoot material culture, he published a series of images documenting skin dressing. In an expression of Boasian contextualism, he sought to place these objects back into their cultural setting. Wissler's discussion, which reviews each stage of production, concludes with the relationship of the Blackfoot styles, tools, and techniques to those of their neighboring tribes on the Plains (1910: 63–70, plates I–V).

vey included some significant ethnographic work, its most important contributions were archaeological. In moving to the Southwest, Wissler vastly expanded the role and importance of archaeology in the museum's program, establishing the importance of a firmly datable, rather than presupposed and merely relative, chronology of Native American cultures in a region.

In the museum's relative balance between survey and intensive investigation one can discern the same opposing motives that Boas had explored in his exchanges with Kroeber (Jacknis 2002a). Boas had started his own fieldwork with a survey on the Northwest Coast but soon felt that it was inadequate to yield the kind of ethnographic results he desired, so he began to concentrate on a single people, the Kwakwaka'wakw (Kwakiutl). While Kroeber similarly focused on the Yurok and Mojave in California, he always maintained a deeper survey orientation (Buckley 1989). The AMNH also combined survey and intensive ethnography. Wissler made repeated trips to the Blackfoot, and Goddard did likewise for the Apache and Navajo, but, ironically, it was the scientist with the most diverse survey experience, Lowie, who also ended up doing the most intensive fieldwork, visiting the Crow first in 1907 and then every summer from 1910 to 1916 (with a final trip in 1931).[11] Although so different in many ways, each of these methods could serve to document and demonstrate cultural difference. These expeditions were characterized by a particular social organization or ordering of ethnographic activity. Employing an inherently relational and networked methodology, Wissler applied to the American Plains the basic survey method that Boas had used on the Northwest Coast: multiple field-workers investigating multiple tribes over many years. Unlike in Alfred Cort Haddon's Torres Strait expedition, however, the AMNH researchers rarely traveled together but mostly went to the field individually. Yet, unlike Bronislaw Malinowski's later model of immersive participant observation, they were not isolated in island villages. Instead, especially in the Southwest, their fieldwork frequently overlapped. For instance, when Kroeber and Spier (who did the archaeology) went to Zuni, New Mexico, in 1915–16, they were visited by streams of anthropologists.

As Boas had before him, Wissler resorted to a range of nonstaff collectors. Some, such as Kroeber and Elsie Clews Parsons in the Southwest, were anthropologists. Among the more significant of the local agents was Gilbert L. Wilson, a Presbyterian minister (figure 4.2). Assisted by his brother Frederick, Wilson worked among the Mandan and Hidatsa of the northern Plains (Gilman and Schneider 1987). Nonanthropologists also included Native agents. Wissler worked with the Blackfoot-Anglo blacksmith David C. Duvall (Kehoe [1995] 2007), just as Boas had done with the Kwakwaka'wakw

George Hunt, but such Native collaboration was less of a factor in the museum's Southwest research. As local residents, either Native or not, these nonanthropologists had the benefit of intimate knowledge of local customs. Without indoctrination in the dominant evolutionary paradigms of the time, they tended to produce detailed and relativistic cultural descriptions. At the same time, as Boas intended, a Native-generated ethnography was perhaps the most direct route to recording a distinctive Native vision.

On the other hand, some of the AMNH's acquisitions did a relatively poor job of capturing cultural difference. Especially for object-types that had already entered a craft market, such as Navajo textiles, the museum acquired many specimens from private collectors (Jacknis 2015b: 144–45). Not only were these the same people who donated to art museums, but in many cases the object-types were the same. The lack of ethnographic documentation for these specimens thus undermined their ability to record the details of distinctly Native worlds.

The expeditions returned with a huge amount of diverse objects. Wissler strove to represent a wide range of cultural domains (such as subsistence, clothing, warfare, governance, ritual, etc.) in the Native objects that were collected. These then supplied the subjects, internally ordered, for the museum's publication series as well as for its public displays. The collected artifacts were assembled in a vast network of objects and multimedia representations, including Native texts, field notes, maps, photographs, sound recordings, and plaster casts. In the face of rapid culture change, both forced and unintentional, Boas and most anthropologists of the time believed that these objects could create tangible and enduring records of the otherwise impermanent achievements of Native cultures. Where Native objects existed—such as artifacts or bodies—they could be collected, but where they did not, the ethnographer could create them using a varied array of representational tools (Jacknis 1996).

Although Boas's own privileged medium was the Native text, few of the museum's ethnographers were adept enough to extensively record cultural material in Native languages. One important exception was Goddard, a trained linguist who contributed many Native texts to the museum's publication series (e.g., Goddard 1919). The rest had to rely on their own observations and their questions to elders about past customs, transcribed in field notebooks.

While the AMNH continued the Boasian emphasis on photography and sound recording, there seems to have been relatively less of this for the Plains and Southwestern surveys. At the same time, the museum's ethnographers

FIGURE 4.2 Frederick Wilson taking notes as Buffalo Bird Woman (Mahidiwiats) weaves a basket, Hidatsa Indians, Fort Berthold Reservation, North Dakota, 1912. Gilbert L. Wilson, 286528, American Museum of Natural History, New York. Courtesy of the American Museum of Natural History.

Although he had little to do with Franz Boas, Gilbert Wilson's ethnography echoed the older anthropologist's research partnership with the Kwakwaka'wakw George Hunt in presenting a Native culture from the perspective of a single family. In contrast to a much earlier museum collection, the Boasians at the American Museum of Natural History insisted on documenting their museum specimens with Native testimony that could be obtained only through extensive field investigation. Between 1906 and 1918, Gilbert and his brother Frederick recorded in explicit detail the lives of three members of one Hidatsa family: Buffalo Bird Woman, her brother Henry Wolf Chief, and her son Edward Goodbird. This image illustrates cultural distinctions that run counter to common stereotypes: the craft of basketry was more characteristic of the primarily agricultural eastern Prairie tribes (Mandan, Hidatsa, and Arikara) than of the nomadic buffalo-hunting tribes of the western Plains.

continued to amass a collection of 2,720 wax cylinders, one of the largest at an American anthropology museum (Seeger and Spear 1987). In many ways, the phonograph was the ideal museum instrument, as it allowed one to mechanically produce an enduring objective record of an otherwise evanescent performance, even if one lacked the musical training to produce or transcribe music. These records, in turn, could help document distinctive musical traditions.

The AMNH was also a pioneer in the use of film in American anthropology. During the Southwest expedition, Goddard, along with staff artist Howard McCormick, innovated in the use of film (A. Griffiths 2002). In the 1930s, curator Margaret Mead, working with her husband, Gregory Bateson, was a methodological innovator in her massive photographic and filmic documentation of Balinese culture. Nevertheless, film remained inherently observational and descriptive. While it excelled at recording motion, which was otherwise not captured in stills, or only poorly in sequences, film, as long as it was silent, was almost incapable of rendering the cultural meanings of the Native actors, which could be obtained only from language and texts. Fully aware of this, Mead worked tirelessly to supplement the visual records with copious written notes (Jacknis 1988).

Through his work as a curator, Boas's radical perception was to shift the balance of museum anthropology away from material artifacts to the ideational world of symbolic meaning. In his summary 1907 essay on the principles of museum administration, he argued that "the psychological as well as the historical relations of cultures, which are the only objects of anthropological inquiry, can not be expressed by any arrangement based on so small a portion of the manifestation of ethnic life as is presented by specimens" (928; see also Jacknis 1985: 108; 1996). As these meanings could be expressed only in language, and even there not fully, he had argued for the importance of extensive exhibition labels and associated monographs (Jacknis 1985: 103–5).

While Boas had to struggle with the museum's administration over the balance between artifact collecting and other kinds of ethnography (Freed 2012: 657), Wissler seems to have been more open to deemphasizing collecting on his expeditions. This can be seen in both the Plains and Southwest expeditions. While both returned with enough objects to please the director and president, they actually focused on the more social complexes of political and ceremonial societies in the Plains (Wissler 1912–16; 1915–21), and on kinship and social organization in the Southwest (Kroeber 1917b). Acknowledging the research thrust of the Huntington Expedition, for example, Wissler noted that it was "a plan for a series of research projects in archaeology, ethnology and physical anthropology, all intensive research units, which might be expected to furnish data for synthetic studies in the pre-historic and historical evolution of cultures in that area, and not an attempt to secure complete collections for the area."[12]

Although Wissler avoided the public debate that greeted Boas's (1907) critical essay, to the museum administration he repeatedly, and rather provocatively, deemphasized the role of artifacts in an anthropology museum:

> Ethnological specimens hold a secondary relation to the subject matter, the origin and distribution of cultures being the real problems. Culture is the functioning of a group of people. The unit idea seems most promising in the attempt to induce in the visitor the attitude necessary to a realization of the secondary relation of the specimens to the culture. For example, spears are spears; but when properly presented under hunting the deer, [they] become mere appliances in the hands of men whose activities constitute a culture. The people can be made prominent in an exhibit of life-sized models, supplemented by smaller models and paintings.[13]

Summarizing his position, he continued, "The Curator always felt that the important thing in the exhibit was to emphasize the people themselves, so that the objects should appear in their true secondary relation." This was a bold statement for a curator, although one perhaps more palatable in an anthropology museum than one devoted to art. Thus, for Wissler, as for his mentor, the point was to document distinctive cultures, which they regarded as fundamentally mental, psychological, or symbolic phenomena. Meaning might be reflected in material objects, but it did not reside there. For both Wissler and Boas, a diverse array of representational media, in addition to Native artifacts, was necessary to document the full range of cultural difference.

In addition to ethnographic artifacts, archaeological and osteological objects were collected. Harlan Smith gathered some of both on the Jesup Expedition, and from the 1910s the museum became a major sponsor of archaeology. In fact, over time there was a gradual shift away from objects in these subfields. Archaeologists still returned with specimens, but they increasingly relied on precisely mapped features and samples of the environment. And in physical anthropology—especially with the Pacific research of Louis R. Sullivan and his successor, Harry L. Shapiro—bodies were generally measured instead of being collected (Freed 2012: 934–53). During the Wissler years the center of the museum's anthropology program also shifted decidedly, from ethnology to archaeology and physical anthropology (Jacknis 2015a). By the early 1920s, the AMNH's grand ethnological surveys had gradually declined. Archaeological collecting continued in the Southwest, as it did in Mexico and South America. Mead's hiring in 1926 facilitated important ethnological collections in the Pacific, but ethnological collecting, especially on museum-sponsored expeditions, gradually declined.

THE LIMITS OF RELATIVISTIC SURVEY: COLLECTING IN AFRICA, OCEANIA, AND ASIA

While the American collections may have followed a relativistic logic, such was not the case in forming most of the museum's Old World collections (Jacknis 2015a). In fact, two of the largest were made with substantial colonial assistance. The bulk of the AMNH's holdings from the Philippines, America's new colonial possession, were gathered for the U.S. government for display at the 1904 Saint Louis World's Fair. While technically acquired in late 1904, while Boas was still chair of the anthropology department, the Philippines collection was purchased over Boas's objections by the director, Hermon Bumpus, with funds supplied by Morris K. Jesup, the president. In its ethnic representation, however, it expressed the interests of almost every American anthropology museum at the time: focusing on the tribal, so-called Pagan Peoples of the north, and not the Christianized or Islamic peoples of the lowlands and the south. And although gathered by a crew of official anthropologists, it was unsystematic and poorly documented (Kramer 2006: 229–84).

The museum's African collections came overwhelmingly from the Belgian Congo. Its first large component came from Frederick Starr (1905–6), who had been sent to the Congo by the Belgian government in a bid to curry favorable publicity. Starr was an anthropologist but essentially untrained, evolutionist, and racist, and he was a supporter of the government of Belgium. In 1907 that government—whose King Leopold II was a friend to President Jesup—made its own donation.

Since at least the 1890s, the museum had a tradition of biologists collecting human artifacts when they had the opportunity. Thus, between 1909 and 1915 biologists Herbert Lang and James Chapin amassed an even larger collection on their museum-sponsored field expedition to the Congo (1909–15). Starr and Lang each collected about four thousand objects, but their collections were quite different. While Starr was nominally the anthropologist—he was an early curator at the AMNH (1889–91) and the first professor of anthropology at the University of Chicago—and Lang was a biologist, in fact Starr's collection was marred by poor documentation and an attempt to fit African cultures into an evolutionary scheme (when he was not defending the colonial regime). Precisely because he was *not* part of the contemporary discipline, Lang applied an empirical methodology of precise documentation and tended to treat African cultures in a more neutral fashion (Schildkrout 1998).

It is true that history was largely rejected as an explanatory framework in American anthropology at the time, but this was not entirely the case. Both the AMNH under Boas and the Field Museum under George Dorsey (Nash and Feinman 2003) were pioneers in Asian anthropology. Between 1901 and 1904, before Boas left the museum, he had Berthold Laufer collect extensively in China (Haddad 2006). Both men sought to enlighten their fellow citizens on the positive values of Chinese civilization, at a time of profound anti-Asian racism. As Boas exhorted Laufer in 1902: "You know perfectly well what we are driving at. It is to bring home to the public the fact that the Chinese have a civilization of their own, and to inculcate respect for the Chinese" (quoted in Kendall 2014: 18). Similarly, Laufer commented from China: "The Chinese culture is in my opinion just as good as ours and in many things far better" (quoted in Kendall 2014: 19). Ironically enough, these attitudes impelled Boas to work with missionaries, not known for their cultural tolerance, because he felt they could help him rapidly build a useful Asian collection (Hasinoff 2010).

Boas certainly thought that Asian objects belonged in an anthropology museum, but Wissler disagreed and the administration supported his stance. Methodologically, Wissler questioned whether contemporary American anthropology was suited for a study of literate civilizations. He raised the related concern that other museums already dealt with these regions and subjects (Haddad 2006: 141). Historical civilizations, such as China, were thus a problem, seeming to belong in an art museum (Conn 2009: 86–137). This later rejection of Asia was thus a rejection, or at least circumscription, of Boas's efforts to document the full range of human cultural difference.

Boas's Asian initiative was followed by Wissler's retrenchment to the Americas, with the exception of his interest in the Pacific. As time went on, however, the museum's administration welcomed trustee interest in Asia, acquiring large collections from Tibet and East Asia: the William B. Whitney collection from Tibet, the I. Wyman Drummond collection of Chinese and Japanese jade and objets d'art, and the Arthur S. Vernay collection from the Burmese borderlands (Freed 2012: 437–39). However, the status of these collections as cultural documentation varied; sometimes it was relativistic, as with Lang, and sometimes it was not, as in the case of Vernay (Hasinoff 2013: 65–66).

Despite his fundamental Americanist focus, during the 1920s Wissler turned increasingly to the Pacific. He supported museum research in the region by the ethnologist Mead and the physical anthropologists Sullivan and Shapiro. In his capacity as advisor to Hawaii's Bishop Museum, Wissler also worked closely with the New Zealanders H. D. Skinner and Peter Buck. Unlike in Asia, the methods developed by anthropologists in America could be applied fairly directly to observations in Oceania. While the Pacific was also a colonial milieu, unlike North America it was not a settler-colonial society, so ethnographers like Mead could observe some kind of ongoing "traditional" behavior. Clearly, such methodological transfers were important to Wissler.

As the twentieth century went on, there was a decided shift in the favored field sites of American anthropology, from an almost exclusive focus on the Native peoples of the North American continent to Latin America and then to the regions of Africa, Asia, and the Pacific (Stocking 1976: 11–12). Despite its largely Americanist focus, the AMNH's relatively early collecting initiatives in these regions were important forerunners of the discipline's mission to document a wider range of cultural diversity.

CULTURE AREAS AS CULTURAL DIFFERENCE

As centers of collection and accumulation, museums are privileged sites for the creation of artifactual and, by extension, cultural knowledge. Museum specimens are revalued and repurposed. No longer serving their original functions, they take on new ones as they are ordered in storage, re-presented in galleries, and glossed in classrooms and in publications (figure 4.3).

Boas is now well known for his debate on museum display with Smithsonian curator Otis T. Mason in 1887 (Jacknis 1985). Boas criticized the museum's arrangement of artifacts according to a universal typology, expressing a presumed evolutionary progression. In such schemes, popular in the late nineteenth century, there was no room for relative cultural differences, except as an inherent racial or cultural superiority or inferiority. Instead, Boas had argued that "the art and characteristic style of a people can only be understood by studying its productions as a whole." Thus, the meaning of an ethnological specimen could not be understood "outside of its surroundings, outside of other intentions of the people to whom it belongs, and outside of other phenomena affecting that people and its productions." Boas's "ideal of an ethnological museum" was thus one organized by a "tribal arrangement of collections" (quoted in Jacknis 1985: 79). Inherently relational, these tribal

FIGURE 4.3 Clark Wissler (?) working in the museum storage vault, American Museum of Natural History, 1908. Thomas Lunt, 32173, American Museum of Natural History, New York. Courtesy of the American Museum of Natural History.

Here the curator creates meaning from objects. As indicated by the signs attached to the shelves, once back at the museum the collections were stored by region and tribe. This order, highlighting the unique cultural characteristics of these specimens, was reproduced in the public exhibition galleries. Franz Boas was a firm proponent of what we now call "visible storage." Recounting how he came up with his interpretations of the incised decoration on Eskimo needle cases, he wrote, "Without being able to see them, I am sure the point would never have come home to me" (quoted in Jacknis 1985: 88). In his classic essay on principles of museum administration, Boas maintained that anthropological material "can only be stored satisfactorily in such a way that each specimen can be seen," owing to the multiplicity of points of view from which cultural objects can be viewed, such as size, form, or material (1907: 930–31).

units would then be juxtaposed with those of their neighbors, who had influenced them.

By the time of the World's Fair in Chicago in 1893, where Mason introduced an elaborate display of life-group dioramas arranged according to the diverse geographical regions of Native America, the Smithsonian curator had developed an appreciation for regional culture areas. While he may have invoked culture areas, however, his were defined more materially and biologically than Boas's (Jacknis 1985: 80–82; 2016). Boas's theories, derived from Germanic romantic philosophy, were more ideational and symbolic. For Boas, local meanings were a result of specific histories of development and interethnic borrowing ("diffusion").

Boas's original vision of culture areas was directly implemented in the Jesup Expedition to the Northwest Coast and Siberia, followed by the Plains survey, which he initiated with Kroeber. But it was Wissler who was to self-consciously elaborate the theory, an accomplishment for which he is today best remembered (Wissler 1917, 1927; see also Freed and Freed 1983: 811–14). Wissler developed his ideas, as had Mason before him, out of the necessity of ordering diverse artifacts in museum storerooms and galleries (Wissler 1914). In turn, these ordering schemes became the foundation for anthropological knowledge in North America throughout the first half of the twentieth century.

As Stanley A. Freed and Ruth S. Freed (1983: 814) point out, in contrast to Boas's tendency to focus on individual cultures, Wissler's concept of the culture area privileged the culture center as a locus for the diffusion of cultural traits from group to group. Thus, for Wissler and his colleagues such as Kroeber, more so than for Boas, culture areas were not essentialist collections but relativistic constructions. Growing out of Boasian premises, culture areas were seen as spatial arrays that were the residues of historical encounters and developments. For the Boasians, concerned with cultures that lacked writing and thus had an unwritten history, distribution in space implied history, a range in time. Edward Sapir systematized these notions in his classic essay *Time Perspective in Aboriginal American Culture* (1916).

The two Wissler-led expeditions were thus dominated by two alternate types of order: space and time. While today we remember the contribution to culture-area theory that was largely worked out in the Plains (figure 4.4), the Huntington Expedition to the Southwest was equally important. Although he did no archaeology himself, Wissler was critical in encouraging the development of temporal perspectives in the American Southwest (Reyman 1985), a new issue for Boasian anthropology, through Nels Nelson's stratigraphic techniques, Kroeber's ceramic seriation of Zuni potsherds, and museum associate A. E. Douglass's development of tree-ring dating (dendrochronology).

Wissler's emerging understanding was documented in a series of influential museum monographs dealing with the ethnology of the American Plains. These fell into three major publishing programs. The first was material devoted to art and aesthetics, such as one might expect in a museum. Based on new collections gathered in the field, these publications sought to delineate cultural differences or tribal styles. During the first decade of the century, the AMNH published a linked series on Plains decorative symbolism, including Kroeber's (1901) doctoral dissertation on Arapaho decorative style (figure 4.5), as well as studies by Wissler (1904) and Lowie (1922). These demonstrated a paradigm shift (Thoresen 1977). As in the sphere of museum display, the Boasians subverted an earlier evolutionary schema, based on a putative movement of designs through a universalist typology. Instead, they regarded material and formal differences (or "style") as expressions of cultural difference, produced by locally specific histories and meanings (Boas 1903).

As the editor, Wissler supervised the production of two comprehensive, multiauthor AMNH monographs, released over several years: "Societies of the Plains Indians" (Wissler 1912–16) and "Sun Dance of the Plains Indians" (Wissler 1915–21), with summarizing introductions and conclusions written by Wissler and Lowie for the former, and by Spier for the latter; these summaries also served as his influential 1921 doctoral dissertation. As Stocking felicitously phrases it, these efforts were "controlled micro-comparisons of single complexes within one cultural area" (1974: 907).

During the 1920s Wissler further elaborated and systematized the culture-area concept (Stocking 1974: 908; Freed and Freed 1983: 815–16). Based on his tabulation and mapping of cultural traits, he formulated the concept of the "age-area," which postulated that cultural complexes diffused at uniform rates in concentric circles from centers of innovation. Building on an analogy with archaeological strata, Wissler argued that the broader the distribution of a trait, the older it was. The root cause for such uniformity, he believed, was environmental. It was based on food production, which itself rested on faunal and floristic distributions, which ultimately followed ecological areas. Such notions, which resonated with Mason's formulation of culture areas, were similarly developed by Kroeber. Materiality and the distribution of discrete cultural elements remained a part of (at least some) Boasian thought.

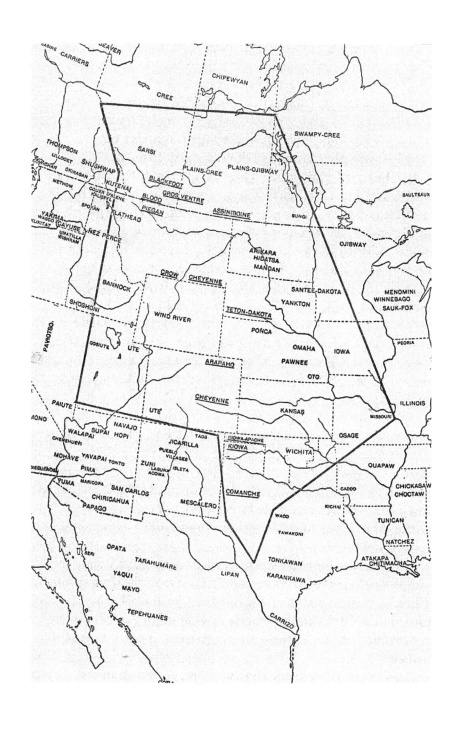

FIGURE 4.4 Map of the Plains Indian culture area: "The most typical tribes are underlined." Reproduced from Clark Wissler, *The American Indian: An Introduction to the Anthropology of the New World* (New York: Douglas C. McMurtrie, 1917), 207.

As visualizations of knowledge, maps encode the spatial distribution of cultural features. They were therefore critical to the development of a theory of culture areas. At the Chicago World's Fair in 1893, the Smithsonian curator Otis T. Mason attempted to illustrate the Smithsonian map of Native American languages prepared by the Bureau of American Ethnology in 1891. Instead, he found that artifacts seemed to follow not language but environmental and material distributions. These curatorial issues led Clark Wissler (1914) to refine a system of distinctive culture areas for Native America. The Plains region, the major area for Wissler's own research, was just one of ten continental regions he defined. This map, which came relatively early in Wissler's writing, was somewhat abstract; he did not attempt to define tribal borders, a task taken on later by his colleague Alfred Kroeber.

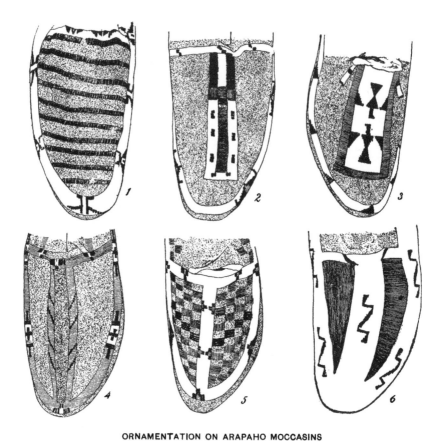

ORNAMENTATION ON ARAPAHO MOCCASINS

FIGURE 4.5 "Ornamentation on Arapaho Moccasins." Reproduced from Alfred L. Kroeber, "Decorative Symbolism of the Arapaho," *American Anthropologist* 3 (1901): plate VI.

This page from Alfred Kroeber's doctoral dissertation illustrates some of the designs found on Arapaho moccasins. The study was based on specimens Kroeber had collected for the American Museum of Natural History during 1899 and 1900. In his analysis of the kinds of designs found on moccasins and rawhide bags, he considered the balance between realistic representation and ornamental abstraction. Finding that they were about equally present, he concluded that the then-popular search for ultimate origins was futile. Kroeber's attack on a hypothesized evolutionism was based, in good Boasian fashion, on interviews with his Native consultants, conducted to discover the meanings they attributed to what would become museum specimens. He also maintained that objects and culture itself needed to be studied holistically. Kroeber's conclusion that origins could not be discovered because all such features were already given in human culture was expressed more boldly in his 1917 essay "The Superorganic."

DISPLAYS OF CULTURAL DIFFERENCE

The ordering of anthropological materials by culture areas was also expressed in the public media of exhibitions and educational programs, becoming the basic rationale for ordering the public galleries. These displays were intended to convey a message to the general public: at the AMNH, largely a narrative of cultural variation.

Just as Boas had entered American museum anthropology over a dispute concerning exhibition, so did his exit, in 1905, revolve around museum display. His resignation was driven largely by his clash with the administration over the philosophy of exhibition. In contrast to the typological and universal schemes favored by the president Jesup and the director Bumpus, Boas argued that the museum's displays should demonstrate to the visitor that culture was relative (Jacknis 1985). As he had argued almost two decades earlier, "civilization is not something absolute." "Our ideas and conceptions," he explained, "are true only so far as our civilization goes." At the time of his resignation Boas insisted to Jesup that he wanted to impress on the general public "the fact that our people are not the only carriers of civilization, but that the human mind has been creative everywhere" (quoted in Jacknis 1985: 107).

Following Boas's debate with Mason in 1887 and the latter's displays at the Chicago exposition in 1893, almost every anthropology museum in America adopted some kind of culture-area arrangement. Since Boas, continuing down to the present, the AMNH ethnological galleries have been ordered by continent or region (figure 4.6), and then within each region by bounded cultures (Wissler 1923b). In the Northwest Coast hall, for example, Boas consciously juxtaposed the regional Plateau and Coastal cultures in order to throw into relief the contrasts between these two distinctive culture areas, which bordered each other in British Columbia.

Upon assuming the anthropology chair, Wissler made plans for the department's exhibitions. If anything, he expanded Boas's regional vision: "A Museum hall should present the natural history of man for a definite geographical area. For example, we have in North America at least eight great areas in which the Indians have or had characteristic cultures." Outlining the ideal plan for each hall, he called for "one section devoted to a culture type exhibit in which life-like groups and other accessories give a concrete picture of the many features of life native to that area; the remainder of the hall, and perhaps the greater part, presenting classified exhibits of collections from the various tribes (or subcultures), their physical types and such archaeological material as is clearly associated with their past history. Thus such a hall would

Although relatively early in the Wissler period at the American Museum of Natural History, this gallery was already devoted to a single region, the Plains, and then further subdivided into cases according to local tribes. This basic order characterized the hall until its closure and renovation in the 1960s. The decorative style is rather dense, with masses of overlapping objects arrayed in many crowded upright cases; in effect, it is a book on the wall. Such conservative styles of museum display were soon supplemented, if not superseded, by dramatic life-group dioramas. This historical sequence thus fulfilled two thrusts of Boasian culture theory: the specific and local regional histories of objects, followed by the holistic integration of multiple cultural domains.

---

be a definite unit presenting the culture data or the facts for one of these geographical areas."[14]

When Dorsey, the curator of the Field Museum, visited the galleries, he immediately recognized the salience of these geographical distinctions: "It was evident that the objects on exhibition were neither placed there with the idea of their beauty nor was their arrangement such as to present primarily a beautiful picture, but rather one felt that as one passed from the exhibit of one tribe to that of another that the dominating features of each culture were so presented that they were apparent. . . . The collections revealed so far as possible the influence of environment both geographical and historical as the culture of one tribe upon that of another" (1907: 585).

Around 1906, Bumpus, the director, stimulated by the museum reform movement in America (Rader and Cain 2014), worked to systematically revise all the museum's displays to make them more appealing to the general visitor. Wissler joined in enthusiastically. The team kept Boas's cultural thrust relatively intact but simplified it. In fact, geographical ordering was made even clearer, with fewer objects in the cases, along with the general separation of ethnology from archaeology, except for the Southwest (Jacknis 2004, 2015b). The display for the Southwest not only combined the nomadic Athapaskans (Navajo and Apaches) with the settled Pueblos but also, for lack of space, included Native California. Within galleries, including the American halls and the African one, geographical order was carried down to the case level, with the layout of the halls mimicking spatial distributions from north to south and east to west. By careful planning, or perhaps just lucky accident, as one walked west in the galleries one was traveling west across the continent.

Cultural relativism was not, however, just an issue of geographical classification. The Boasian mission of re-creating the cultural context of an artifact's use would be clearly visible in some form of "realistic" or mimetic display: in the innovative life-group dioramas of costumed and dramatized mannequins, in miniature village models, or in murals. While Boas pioneered such approaches, for various reasons he curtailed their use in his galleries (Jacknis 1985), and it was left to Wissler and his AMNH colleagues to vastly expand their scope and detail (Jacknis 2015b) (figure 4.7). Wissler used some form of these mimetic devices in all of his ethnological galleries, but the most elaborate were the three large dioramas (Hopi, Apache, and Navajo) in the Southwest hall, complete with painted backdrops. Such group cases, he believed, "seem to give the observer the feeling that we have here an exhibit of the life of the people, rather than an exhibit of curious objects made by some one."[15] Again, Wissler was interested in cultural practice, not mere artifacts.

Just like the acquisition of objects, however, not all of the anthropology galleries demonstrated such relativistic principles. Several, notably those for Africa and the Philippines, pulled in the opposite direction; these were more racist and colonialist (Jacknis 2015a). The reason for this is that they were curated largely through administrative dictate. Although Lowie was asked to curate these, he clearly had little autonomy. When the Philippine collection was first displayed at the AMNH in early 1909, it was clear that much of the exhibit was arranged to explain and justify the American colonial regime (figure 4.8). For example, one section was titled "The Political and Educational Development under American Influence." According to the museum, the display "shows not only what the Filipinos were, and what Philippine agriculture and commerce were, under Spanish rule, but also what they are under American influence. It proclaims emphatically that progress has been the keynote of life in the Philippines in these ten years, despite calamities, and it suggests that in the future the prosperity of the Philippine people is to be limited only by the great productive capacity of the islands" ("The Philippine Exhibit" 1909: 129). Along with promising to display the collection at succeeding expositions (in Portland in 1905 and Seattle in 1909), the museum evidently had also committed itself to instrumental propaganda (Kramer 2006: 279–81).

As one might expect, racialism was also expressed in several halls of human biology and evolution; significantly, none of these was curated by anthropologists. Most famously, in his Hall of the Age of Man, begun in 1915 and largely completed by 1924, President Osborn advocated a more biological approach. Here Osborn depicted the extinct human races as separate species, giving distinctly Nordic features to depictions of Cro-Magnon man (Rainger 1991: 169–77). Although paleontology curator William K. Gregory opposed the racism of Osborn and Grant, he similarly included a mural, *Man among the Primates*, which depicted the white race as the furthest from the apes, in the Hall of the Natural History of Man (Rainger 1991: 231–32). Racial inferiority was even more explicit in one display in the primate hall, supervised by the director Frederic A. Lucas and the mammalogist Lang. In it, a human diorama depicting a family of Pygmies was meant to complement the monkeys and apes as presenting "a 'low,' or primitive race of man" (Lucas 1919: 66; compare Lang 1919).

Although not addressed directly in the galleries, another of Osborn's concerns was the "unrestricted immigration" that was resulting in overcrowded tenements in New York City. The president thus supported the development of a Hall of Public Health, opened in 1913, which was intended to make science socially relevant for these large local populations (J. Brown 2014; Rainger

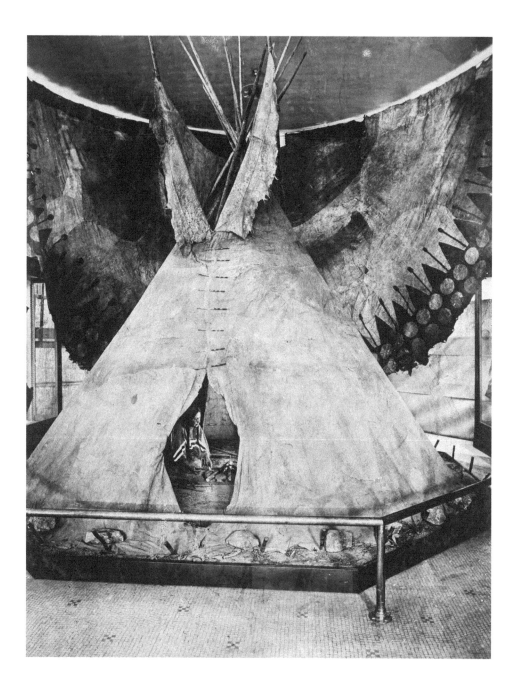

FIGURE 4.7 Blackfoot tipi, with interior mannequins, Hall of Plains Indians, American Museum of Natural History, 1907. J. Otis Wheelock, 323716, American Museum of Natural History, New York. Courtesy of the American Museum of Natural History.

————————

Around 1906 the American Museum of Natural History adopted a new style of visual drama in its anthropological displays. Instead of crowded cases of artifacts, artifactual context was illustrated mimetically. This tipi was meticulously documented. The hide cover itself had been collected by Clark Wissler on a museum expedition in 1903. According to an article in the museum's popular magazine, Wissler was "a regularly adopted member of the Blackfoot tribe" ("A Blackfoot Lodge," 1907: 92). As curator, he intended to present the lodge of a specific person: a medicine man of the Otter Clan of the Blackfoot Indians of Montana. Inside, the costumed mannequins of a man and woman illustrated tribal family life, along with beds, a family altar, a tobacco pipe, medicine bags, household utensils, food storage bags, and a man's saddle. The cases on the opposite side of the hall describe the hide preparation, which Wissler had studied in the field and documented in his Blackfoot monograph (see figure 4.1).

————————

FIGURE 4.8 Philippine Hall, section 3 ("The Development of the Natural Resources under American Influence"), American Museum of Natural History, 1909. Thomas Lunt, 32877, American Museum of Natural History, New York. Courtesy of the American Museum of Natural History.

———

This display was prepared and photographed in 1909, just before the American Museum of Natural History sent it to the Seattle World's Fair. As the collection itself had been made by the U.S. federal government for display at the St. Louis Fair in 1904, it was expressly propagandistic. When it was installed at the museum in early 1909, its colonialist messages were reinforced in the section signs. However, the fairly brutal occupation was mildly glossed as "American Influence." One case illustrated the exploitation of natural resources ("Manila Hemp: A Source of Great Wealth"), while another depicted a map of the major trading ports. Note the innovative use of colored photographic transparencies on the walls. When the display returned to the museum in late 1909, the didactic signage was removed, although the contents remained largely intact until Alfred Kroeber was asked to reinstall it according to more "traditional" anthropological concepts of regions and cultural domains in 1918.

———

1991: 152). Improved sanitation and medical care would be one solution, but another would be to limit the influx at the source (Bennett 2004: 124).

After Osborn's resignation as president in 1933 and his death in 1935, Wissler became much more openly critical of the museum's predominant display philosophy, and of many of the museum's operations in general. While he himself had been a pioneer in employing large illusionistic dioramas to portray human culture, he came to feel that the museum's large habitat dioramas, popularized by the taxidermist Carl Akeley with Osborn's enthusiastic support, were overrunning their scientific and educational utility. By the time of Wissler's retirement in 1942, museum anthropology, in the country at large and in New York specifically, was clearly coming to the end of an era.

WISSLER: RACE AS AN EXPLANATION OF DIFFERENCE

For Wissler and anthropology at the AMNH, the 1920s marked an important shift. Much of it was a consequence of the American Anthropological Association's censure of Boas in 1919. Late in that year, Boas had contributed a critical letter to *The Nation*, accusing several anthropologists of using their professional cover as scientists to hide their activity as spies in Central America during World War I (Stocking 1968, 1976).[16] As a result of this censure, the more evolutionary and racist anthropologists of Washington and Boston temporarily gained the upper hand in American anthropology. Even before the censure, however, the museum under President Osborn was becoming a strong advocate for eugenics: with the founding in 1918 of the exclusive Galton Society for the Study of the Origin and Evolution of Man, which held monthly meetings at the AMNH through the mid-1930s. Its founders included Osborn as well as his friend Grant (who was a museum trustee), along with the biologist Charles Davenport. Grant's famous *The Passing of the Great Race* (1916), which went through many editions, was one of the most influential eugenic tracts. During these years, the museum hosted two international eugenics conferences, in 1921 and 1932.

In fact, in the Osborn–Wissler years, the AMNH presented contradictory faces in the race–culture divide. As Elazar Barkan (1992: 67) maintains, the museum was an institutional mediator between the racialism of the Eugenics Society and the cultural relativism of the Columbia University anthropologists, as it was a meeting place for partisans of both camps. And Wissler was the prime example of this ambivalence. As Stocking noted, Wissler's "own mildly nativist leaning enabled him to mediate between the racialism of the hard-science establishment and the cultural determinism of the Boasian school, with which in general he identified" (1985: 118; compare 1974: 908).

Certainly, our story so far has provided ample evidence of Wissler's fundamental Boasianism. Yet there was some alienation there that became progressively more pronounced over time. Although Wissler had studied with Boas, he had earned his doctorate in psychology, a training that exposed him to racialist theories (E. Ross 1985: 391). His personal distance from Boas was compounded when his teacher resigned and Wissler agreed to assume his position (Cole 1999: 251–53).[17] After 1920, as Boas retreated to teaching more at Barnard, Columbia's associated women's college, his new generation of students developed new theoretical interests.

Personally, Wissler represents a marked contrast with most of Boas's other students. He was a Midwesterner from Indiana, of long-settled English and Pennsylvania German stock, whereas many of Boas's students were immigrants (Lowie, Paul Radin, and Alexander Goldenweiser), Jews (Sapir and Herskovits), members of other ethnicities (the African American Zora Neale Hurston and the Native American William Jones), women (Benedict, Mead, and Gladys Reichard), or some combination of these. Accordingly, Wissler was the only Boasian who was a member of the Galton Society, although there were two other members from the museum's anthropology department: the archaeologists Spinden and Nelson (Spiro 2009: 206). Lowie, in contrast, was a staunch opponent of Osborn and Grant until his forced resignation in 1921 (Spiro 2009).[18] When Wissler came to publish *Man and Culture* (1923a), his most important and widely read book for the nonspecialist, he characteristically combined a fundamental Boasian culturism with a strong dose of eugenic race theory.[19] For instance, he frequently proclaimed the inequality of the races: "So, since invention is an innate process, all we need to secure unequal groups is to separate men according to descent; and as what we call races are most surely differentiated by descent, it follows that their innate equipments will differ. Our analysis of culture traits and the unhereditary nature of the traits, show that culture is produced by the functioning of this innate equipment. If it differs, as seems inevitable, then there is no such thing as racial equality in culture" (289).

And in his conclusion he adopts Grant's views on the superiority of the Nordic race, who he thought were the most likely "to advance culture in a decisive manner" (290): "So the Nordics stand out as the new generation in the family of the world, the hope of the immediate future; it is theirs to carry forward the lamp of civilization, so that when their strength is spent, it may be safely passed to some fresh and youthful hand. Faced with such a responsibility, it would be criminal not to give the best thought of the time to the conservation of whatever virtues this stock possesses" (359).

Finally, another of Wissler's theoretical contributions, the so-called universal pattern of culture, which was highly influential at the time, rested on fundamentally evolutionary and antirelativist notions. Wissler (1923a: 78–79) argued that all cultures had to progress through a series of staged developments.

FROM CULTURE AREAS TO PATTERNS OF CULTURE

At the same time that Wissler was collaborating with the eugenicists, major changes were occurring in the AMNH's Department of Anthropology. As noted, there was a gradual but marked shift away from ethnology, with the terminations of Spinden and Lowie in 1921 and the death of Goddard in 1928, leaving as ethnologists just Mead, hired in 1926, and Wissler, who focused on administration until his retirement in 1942. On the other hand, there were some wins for the beleaguered anthropologists. The Philippines Hall was recurated in 1918 by Kroeber, who generally adopted an arrangement by ethnic group and cultural domains (weaving, pottery, weapons, etc.). When the African Hall was moved in 1931, it was only slightly revised, owing to the lack of a suitable curator, but the logic of culture areas was strengthened and the natural history elements were removed. At least in these cases, the anthropologists were able to reinstate their discursive authority and revise the exhibits in terms of relativistic culture-area theories.

This specific narrative in New York was paralleled in the country at large, which witnessed the effective end of museum anthropology in America, or at least of its "museum age"—although, as we noted in chapter 1, this occurred much later than is usually credited (Stocking 1985). Anthropology museums did not disappear, of course, but they did become static for decades (Jacknis 2004). Hit hard by the Depression, they ceased to be the cultural leaders that they had been in the early years of the century (Kennedy 1968; Rader and Cain 2014). As sponsors of anthropological fieldwork, they were supplanted by foundations and research councils (Stocking 1976: 10). With institutional shifts came theoretical transformations. Yet during the 1920s museums played a critical role in pointing the way. The AMNH may have served as a home for race-based biologism, but it continued to foster a Boasian perspective of culturally determined theories of human difference. The description and ordering of specifically cultural differences that were first expressed as culture areas in displays and publications were then "writ large," in Benedict's (1934) phrase, as "patterns of culture," in a range of professional and popular publications.

In fact, material culture theory and the museums that gave it a home were at the root of this disciplinary transition. As Stocking (1976) has argued, the history of American anthropology in the early twentieth century can be viewed largely as the successive working out of different implications of Boas's thought. Although this is often forgotten, a privileged locus was his work on primitive art (Jonaitis 1995). Beginning around 1910, and increasingly after 1920, Boas and his students shifted from tracing out tribal stylistic differences, arrayed in space, to a more psychological consideration of the relation of individuals to society. The transitional study was his monograph on Salish basketry, which took decades and a succession of authors before it was published (Boas 1928; see also Jacknis 1992), unfortunately blunting its theoretical and historical significance. Despite his premature death in 1918, the critical assistant was Herman Haeberlin, who may fairly be regarded as the first of Boas's second generation of students, those who would adapt earlier paradigms of culture areas to what became known as the theory of culture and personality. Haeberlin first expressed his interest in pattern in his doctoral dissertation, on the theme of fertilization in Pueblo culture (Haeberlin 1916). As Lowie (1959: 75) noted, Haeberlin's perception of a cultural contrast between the Pueblo and the Navajo was one of the first significant examples of the distinct cultural patterning that became the foundation for later Boasian theory.

In turn, the Salish basketry monograph was an explicit inspiration for Ruth Bunzel's (1929) study of Pueblo pottery and Gladys Reichard's (1936) research on Navajo weaving, both completed at Columbia, and Lila O'Neale's (1932) investigation of California Indian basketry, at Berkeley. Bunzel, Reichard, and O'Neale also combined the study of museum collections with their ethnographic fieldwork; in fact, both Bunzel and Reichard illustrated AMNH specimens in their path-breaking studies.

Despite the received wisdom that American anthropology had left the museum upon Boas's resignation in 1905, there was a critical exchange between the museum and university, specifically at the AMNH and Columbia University, during the Wissler period, and most especially during the 1920s. Anthropologists from both institutions met for a weekly lunch, with Goddard as a critical link (Goldfrank 1978: 17). While Wissler did not attend, his hiring of Mead in 1926 proved to be a significant connection. Columbia and its female branch at Barnard College sent a continual stream of anthropology classes to the museum. Goddard and Lowie taught in the extension division; Goddard also taught a course on technology at the museum and assisted with Columbia class trips and research funding (Caffrey 1989: 101).

While he may have been somewhat alienated from his fellow Boasians, Wissler continued to lead the way. As Stocking has noted, Wissler himself played no small role in helping to "Americanize" the anthropological concept of culture. Despite his praise of Nordic superiority, he argued that all Americans had a culture, just like tribal members. According to Stocking, "Wissler's behaviorism, his scientism, his regional-ecological orientation, and his residual biologism were quite in tune with the sociology of the post Social-Darwinist period; and his book [*Man and Culture*] played a major role in disseminating anthropological thinking about culture to the other social sciences—a role facilitated by his active participation in the interdisciplinary movements of the period" (1974: 908).

As many of the second generation of Boas's students—such as Spier, Benedict, Herskovits, and Mead—began their careers, culture-area theory was at the root of their work, just as it had been for many of Boas's first students: Kroeber, Wissler, and Lowie. The later students also picked up on yet another aspect of Boas's thought, stressing the psychological and symbolic—rather than the material and environmental—patterning of culture. From these seemingly narrow issues of artifactual ordering, they extended its theoretical insights into broader theories of cultural patterning, what came to be known as the American school of culture and personality.

Kroeber and the linguist Sapir were perhaps the only two of Boas's first generation of students to make the transition into such configurational theories. After his dissertation research in the Plains, Kroeber turned to California, where he brought the Americanist survey perspective to bear within a large and diverse region (Buckley 1989). Yet cultural contrasts, especially in the guise of the psychological contrasts that were soon to become so important for the later Boasians, became salient for him only as he worked in a completely different area, with the Zuni of the Southwest.[20] Despite his profound literary interests, Kroeber was stimulated to develop a seriation of Zuni potsherds (1916), that is, a historical reconstruction based on the relative frequency of distinctive design patterns. And in conversation with Parsons, who joined him in Zuni in 1918, he began to formulate notions of the patterning of Zuni psychology that were later developed by Benedict.

Benedict, however, represented an important contrast to such museum anthropology. Always much attuned to literature, she avoided museum work: "In her early years as an assistant to Boas, Benedict was required to teach courses at the AMNH. She never became a curator there, however (as Franz Boas, Robert Lowie, and Margaret Mead had), and she also rejected opportunities for a dual appointment" (Roffman 2010: 148).

Nevertheless, the Boasian theory of culture areas was as important for Benedict as it was for many of her cohort. Like earlier Boasians—Kroeber in California and the Southwest, Lowie in the Plains and Southwest, and Haeberlin among the Navajo and Pueblos within the Southwest—she was struck by the contrast in cultural patterning between the Plains and the Southwest, insights she developed in her dissertation (1923) and in a succession of critical articles that grew out of it (e.g., 1928, 1932). More specifically, she drew on some of Wissler's earlier formulations of patterning within culture areas, which he had first expressed in 1912 in the context of Blackfoot ceremonial bundles (Freed and Freed 1983: 819). For the museum as a center of calculation, its mission of continental survey and objective juxtaposition had thus created a site for the production of disciplinary knowledge, laying the foundation for later developments in cultural theory.

During the 1920s, a number of Boas's students extended culture-area theory beyond the Americas. Herskovits's 1923 thesis was the first application of Wissler's culture-area concept to Africa (Herskovits 1924, 1930). This, in turn, became the basis for the arrangement of the museum's revised African hall. As he later journeyed to West Africa and then to the Caribbean Basin, Herskovits expanded the Boasian cultural project to include the diffusion of African culture traits to the New World.

Mead (1928) explored culture areas in the Pacific for her library dissertation on cultural variation among five Polynesian cultures. Based partly on AMNH specimens, it was largely a study of material culture: tattoos, houses, and canoes (D. Thomas 1980: 354). When she returned to New Guinea in the early 1930s, she began applying Benedict's comparativist perspective to three cultures: the Arapesh, Mundugumor, and Tchambuli (Mead 1935). This triple comparison was structurally relativist, like culture areas, but now based on psychology rather than the distribution of artifacts.

Despite the development of her thought into cultural configurationalism, Mead never really abandoned culture-area theory. In her comprehensive ethnography of the Arapesh, she devoted an entire volume to an analysis of them as an "importing" culture, borrowing cultural traits from their neighbors (1938–49). The study was based, like all of her prewar ethnography, on her continuing artifact collections. As she began to plan for a revised Pacific Hall in 1945, she structured it according to culture areas, extending her scope to insular Southeast Asia, which was to have been a revision of the adjacent Philippines Hall (Losche 2006). Expanding the scope of culture-area theories, she intended to demonstrate the diffusion of cultural elements into the Pacific.

REORGANIZING THE FIELD OF DIFFERENCES:
THE INTERSECTIONS OF RACE AND THE CULTURE CONCEPT

We can see, then, that the concepts of culture and culture areas had significantly variable histories so far as their relations to the collecting and ordering practices of early twentieth-century American anthropology were concerned. What we encounter across the relations between Boas, Wissler, and the post-Boasians is less a set of clear-cut and absolute differences than variations of tone and shade, with the formulations of specific individuals themselves often registering significantly different emphases regarding the relations between a range of factors: the degree of mutability accorded to cultural traits in processes of diffusion, the degree of fit or dissonance they saw between the concerns of physical anthropology and those of the emerging field of cultural anthropology, and the weighting accorded to racial factors relative to cultural ones in accounting for differences within populations. As we turn now to address how these considerations affected the governance of differences, the main issue concerns the mismatch between the peoples whose cultures were collected and ordered through museum fieldwork, archival, and exhibition practices and the relations of cultural difference to which the culture concept was applied in the context of its governmental deployment. If the culture concept had its genesis in the study of Native Americans and, later, America's emerging overseas colonial territories, it had its main field of application "back home," particularly on the Eastern Seaboard and in cities like Chicago, in the development of new practices for adjudicating the relations between America's white nativists and new immigrant populations.

These formed part of a protracted process of adjusting earlier conceptions of the relationships between race and citizenship that, initiated in the transition from the Gilded Age to the Progressive Era (D. Ross 1991) and continuing through the interwar years to the conclusion of the 1939–45 war, led to a strategic redefinition of the notion of whiteness. This enlarged the self-governing political community, within which differences were to be liberally adjudicated in accordance with a distinctively cultural logic, while at the same time proposing new criteria for excluding other groups from that community. We can perhaps best appreciate the logic of this process by considering one of its more influential end points, one in which the AMNH was again implicated: the statues of *Normman* and *Norma*, initially displayed at the New York World's Fair in 1939 and subsequently at the Cleveland Health Museum in 1945 (figures 4.9 and 4.10) when the AMNH's curator of physical anthropology, Harry Shapiro, wrote a review in *Natural History* that proved

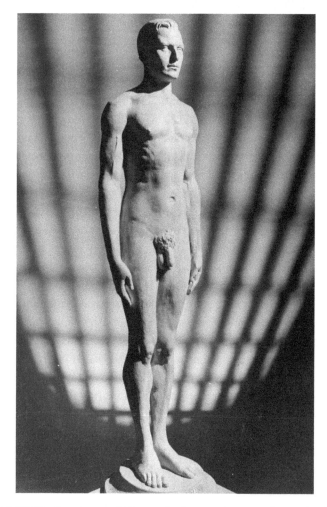

FIGURES 4.9 AND 4.10 *Normman* and *Norma*, the "average American boy and girl." Courtesy of the Cleveland Museum of Natural History.

Normman and *Norma* constituted sculptural reconstructions—originally in terracotta, subsequently in plaster—of the measurements of white patients collected by the physician Robert Latou Dickinson over the period 1910–30. In Harry Shapiro's interpretation they represented new norms of bodily perfection acquired as a result ▶

of improvements in the physical development of the American population. In being characteristic of the average American, these testified to the progress of American culture and civilization. The new vocabulary of normality represented by the figures resonated with the extension of prevailing definitions of whiteness beyond a white nativist Nordic stock to encompass all groups of European origin who had adjusted—morally, culturally, and physically—to American norms.

significantly influential in articulating the figures' public salience (Shapiro 1945).

Julian Carter (2007) relates the redefinition of whiteness represented by these figures to recent revaluations of the role played by changing conceptions of whiteness in the late nineteenth and early twentieth centuries in effecting a new distribution of civic entitlements, against the backdrop of the longer history of American republicanism. Matthew Jacobson (1998), whose work has proved particularly influential in rethinking the civic histories of whiteness, argues that whereas whiteness and citizenship were linked in an act of Congress of 1790 according to a "nativist" conception that limited citizenship to free white persons with rights of residence, the period from 1840 to 1924 witnessed a strategic redefinition of whiteness designed to address the dilemmas of American white nativism when faced with new waves of immigration from diverse sources.[21] The Nordicism of Wissler and the Galton Society represented a significant moment in this process that produced new racialized divisions within the earlier undifferentiated category of whiteness. These divisions disbarred some "white" groups from the liberal criteria defining fitness for self-government by producing new shades of darkness that differentiated groups like the Poles and the Irish from Anglo-Saxons, the privileged representatives of white nativism. The Johnson-Reed Act of 1924—prompted by the Galton Society, with Wissler playing a leading role (W. Shapiro 1985: 4)—represented the peak of this tendency in differentiating "Nordic" migrants from "Alpines," "Mediterraneans," and Asians, the main categories of new immigrants since the 1880s; these immigrants' numbers were curtailed by this measure. However, this peak—in barring Asian immigrants and establishing quotas for immigrants from southern Europe—led to a further revision of the category of whiteness that defined the political logic, and the rims, of American liberal multiculturalism from the late 1920s on. This logic, as Jacobson defines it, combined "the civic story of assimilation (the process by which the Irish, Russian Jews, Poles, and Greeks became Americans)" with "the cultural story of racial alchemy (the process by which Celts, Hebrews, Slavs, and Mediterraneans became Caucasians)" (1998: 8).

The conception of a project of assimilation organized around a newly homogenized category of the Caucasian provided the political rationality that informed the governmental mobilization of the culture concept. From the late 1920s through the 1930s and into the 1940s, the relations among the aesthetic conception of the pattern of culture, its spatial coordinates, and its malleability helped to shape a program in which cultural planners, guided by anthropologists, were to regulate the conditions under which American society would creatively transform itself by absorbing immigrant cultures in an assimilationist logic focused exclusively on the relations between different periods of European migration. The key reference point for this governmental rationality was the "third generation." This was given its most influential anthropological apologia by Mead. In applying the culture concept to define the distinguishing characteristics of the American character, Mead argued that Americans establish their ties with one another by finding common points on the road they are all expected to travel "after their forebears came from Europe one or two or three generations ago" (1942: 28). This was a road defined by the forging of new ties and by a dialectic of "remembrance and purposeful forgetting of European ancestry," as well as by an initial clinging to European ways of life in Little Italies, followed by a scattering "to the suburbs and the small towns, to an 'American' way of life" (29). In this sense, Mead argued, "however many generations we may actually boast of in this country, however real our lack of ties in the old world may be, we are all third generation" (31).

The "we" here constitutes the varied waves of migrants from Europe who were encompassed by the enlarged definition of whiteness produced by the concept of the Caucasian. The deployment of the culture concept as part of a liberal technology of governance was limited to its role in managing the relations between the members of this enlarged white community. Its distinctiveness, as John Dewey (1939) recognized, consisted in its shifting the focus for governmental action away from individuals and toward individuals conceived as members of a group.[22] The anthropological concept of culture, he argued, relativizes forms of individuality by reconceiving them as the manifestations of the ways of life of particular groups or peoples. As such, it constituted a new reality through which governmental action, guided by anthropological expertise, could seek to shape passions, interests, and desires by acting "not directly upon individuals but indirectly through their incorporation with culture" (Dewey 1939: 144). It was moreover, Dewey argued, only "through the medium of culture" (43) that science could seek to reorder the relations between different groups without trespassing on their freedom. The increasingly close involvement of anthropology in the assimilationist agendas of American multiculturalism reflected the promise it offered of being able to reorder the relations between America's varied European peoples by respecting the protocols of liberal government. This promise was premised on the distinctive fusion of the aesthetic, spatial, and temporal registers of the culture concept. The pattern of a culture, in the post-Boasian trajectory of the concept, is not, as we have seen, expressive of an essential set of relations among a people, a place, and a way of life. Rather, it is a conjunctural and pliable articulation of those relations that derives its distinctive qualities from the creative, form-giving capacity of the people concerned. The unity of a culture that results from this form-giving capacity was, however, as Benedict contended, always a fractured one given that its building blocks come from sources that "are diverse and unlike."[23] These constitute contradictory elements that either cancel each other out or are brought together in a new form of synthesis. This exactly describes the emerging logics of American multiculturalism, in which cultures brought together in America from diverse European sources were to be ordered into a new form of synthesis through the "creative genius" of anthropologically informed cultural planners. This was an exercise in cultural fusion that was to be managed from a controlling position in which the descendants of the white stock of Old America defined the terrain on which a broader Caucasian cultural synthesis was to be effected.

The residual effects of Nordicism were significant in these circumstances and by no means limited to Wissler's contention that the Nordic peoples were uniquely gifted with the creative capacities required to forge different cultures into a new and vibrant cultural formation (W. Shapiro 1985: 2–3). The post-Boasians who were most influential in translating the culture concept into a means for managing America's (European) cultural diversity— Kroeber, Benedict, and Mead—were recruited from among Eastern Seaboard elites who could trace their ancestry back to early settler families.[24] It was, however, in relation to the broader category of the Caucasian that the legacy of biological race categories was most evident. Never entirely escaping the pull of these categories, the new machineries of assimilation that the culture concept established excluded African Americans, Asians, and Native Americans. In spite of his antiracist activities and his championing of the force of culture relative to that of biology, Boas retained a distinction between the "Caucasoid," "Mongoloid," and "Negroid" as biologically differentiated stocks of humanity.[25] Although he did not organize the relations among these in hierarchical terms, these categorizations led Boas to place "the Negro" in a different position than the immigrant with regard to processes of assimilation. He interpreted this as not just a cultural process but a physioanatomical one that would likely depend on the disappearance of "the Negro" as a distinct physical type through miscegenation.

The situation with regard to Native Americans was different but scarcely more auspicious. On the one hand, in racial terms, they hardly mattered. Intermarriage between Indians and settlers, Boas argued, had not been sufficient in "any populous part of the United States to be considered as an important element in our population" ([1909] 1974: 319). Nicely distanced from the urban center of metropolitan America, Native Americans were not a part of the mix from which the future of America's population stock or its culture was to be forged. An exception to this view is found in the report prepared by Dorothea Leighton and Clyde Kluckhohn ([1947] 1969) for the Indian Research Project, conducted in 1947 by the Committee on Human Development at the University of Chicago and the Office of Indian Affairs. In reviewing the evidence for the historical plasticity of the relations between Navajo culture and personality in comparison with the Hopi, Zuni, Sioux, and Papago (Tohono O'Odham) peoples, Leighton and Kluckhohn urged the need to break with standardized and paternalistic forms of Indian administration in favor of variable ones that would, in the case of the Navajo, eventually allow them to decide how to adjust their culture so that they might "finally take an independent place in the nation and add their contribution to the American cultural heritage" (243). But this was something that was still to come and that, in the meantime, required white advisors to help steer the Navajo in the right direction.

Reflecting on these aspects of the career of Boasian anthropology, Willis ([1972] 1999: 139) has argued that the skeleton in its closet consisted in the fact that, when applied across the color line separating Caucasians from other populations, its lessons regarding the plasticity and mutability of inherited cultures were translated into the one-way enculturation of colored people into white culture. In this way, anthropology continued to perform its traditional function of making nonwhite people different human beings from white people in ways that placed them outside the mechanisms of liberal government that it brought to bear on regulating the relations between America's Caucasian populations.

CHAPTER FIVE

PRODUCING "THE MAORI AS HE WAS"

New Zealand Museums, Anthropological Governance,
and Indigenous Agency

A DISTINCTIVE ANTHROPOLOGICAL ASSEMBLAGE

In the study of the Maori as he was, in the appreciation of what he has become, and the assessment of his probable future, I ask students to interest themselves in the genealogical records of the race. —Āpirana Ngata, "The Genealogical Method as Applied to the Early History of New Zealand"

In his address to the Wellington Historical Association, the Māori politician and intellectual Āpirana Ngata urged scholars to make more use of *whakapapa* (tribal genealogies) and other ethnological records collected and preserved in archives. In contrast to Elsdon Best's vision of a pre-European Māori past, a form of salvage ethnography captured in his book *The Maori as He Was* (1924b), Ngata focused on the Māori as they *are* and *will be*. Directing his attention to the present and future, Ngata emphasized the value of anthropology and history in contributing to the development of the "brown tinge in the future New Zealander" now that Māori had "become a living subject in the history of the Dominion."[1]

If, as we showed in chapter 1, Best's vision of "the Maori as he was" found concrete expression in the Ethnology Gallery of the new Dominion Museum (DM) in 1936, the adjoining Maori Hall captured Ngata's more contemporary

FIGURE 5.1 The Maori Hall in the Dominion Museum in 1936, with the meeting house *Te Hau ki Tūranga* at the right, which was restored by carvers from the School of Maori Arts and Crafts under the direction of Āpirana Ngata. William Hall-Raine, C.1978, Te Papa, Wellington. Courtesy of the Museum of New Zealand Te Papa Tongarewa.

In the grand interior of the Dominion Museum's Maori Hall, the restored meeting house *Te Hau ki Tūranga* was at the center right, flanked by other large carved *waka* (canoes) and *pātaka* (storehouses), re-creating a pre-European village scene. The house was restored by carvers from the School of Maori Arts and Crafts under the direction of Sir Āpirana Ngata. With its composite exterior and reconstructed interior made up of new and restored fragments, it became synonymous with the idea of "classical" Māori culture, serving as a model for the carvers of the school, who produced many carved houses for tribes. During the opening ceremonies for these houses, Ngata encouraged the performance of oral and performing arts, which underwent a revival alongside the visual arts (see the Ngāti Pōneke Young Maori Club in figure 1.5).

vision of the changing Māori within New Zealand (figure 5.1). "The white man, in designing his national treasure house," declared a journalist, "has certainly given pride of place to the storied history of a proud race."[2]

The payback for Ngata's involvement in the new museum's feature display was a position on the museum board for a "representative of the Maori race." At the opening ceremony, Prime Minister Michael Joseph Savage declared support for Māori arts and crafts, describing it as a "duty" that should not be neglected and, by implication, placing Māori issues in general on the national agenda. "During a comparatively short time, Maori art has reached a very high pinnacle, and can go still higher," Savage declared, "and I am not going to lose any opportunity to help our Maori brethren in their arts and crafts, and I am sure the trustees will not be found wanting in that respect."[3] Savage referred to his governmental responsibility to facilitate the progressive uplift of the Māori population through the advancement of arts and crafts, with museums playing an important role in forming a Māori citizenry. Indeed, the day before the opening there was a lively debate in Parliament on the new museum, during which the opposition suggested that Ngata be appointed to the board to "bring the Maori people into closer association" with the museum authorities. The Native Minister, Gordon Coates, readily agreed, adding that this would be an "indication that the Pakeha [New Zealander settlers of European descent] recognizes that the Maori is part and parcel of New Zealand" (*New Zealand Parliamentary Debates* 1936: 212–29).

In this chapter we explore a distinctive anthropological assemblage over the period 1890–1940. This New Zealand assemblage comprised a varied network of actors including museums, universities, government agencies, and tribes, with each taking a position on the Māori past, present, and future: these included the Polynesian Society, the Auckland Museum (later renamed the Auckland War Memorial Museum), the DM, the Otago Museum (OM) and the University of Otago, the Department of Native Affairs, and, finally, the Board of Maori Ethnological Research (BMER). We will also examine the work of individual directors, curators, politicians, and tribal leaders who worked within and across these institutions, sometimes working together and at other times in conflict: Thomas Cheeseman, Gilbert Archey, Elsdon Best, Henry Devenish Skinner, Āpirana Ngata, and Peter Buck (Te Rangihīroa). We see these men less as authoring agents than as actors within distributed networks, which were organized around different ways of recording and producing "the Maori as he was."

The distinctive sets of relations around the notion of "the Maori as he was," which were founded on a varied assortment of ethnographic knowledge practices, actors, collections, and mechanisms, constituted a transactional reality that operated within the fragile and contested interfaces between Māori and Pakeha governors in a period of purported Māori population decline and within a milieu dominated by Social Darwinian thought, which shaped the emergence of a tradition of salvage ethnology in the later nineteenth century. This notion informed a plural and shifting set of "working surfaces on the social" that sought to mediate the relations between Pakeha and Māori by identifying the forms of conduct that needed to be acted on, the extent and limits of freedom and liberal subjecthood, and the forms of action required according to the governmental rationalities they were located within.

"The Maori as he was" was concerned with the preservation of aspects of pre-European Māori life that articulated a classic Māori cultural tradition first proposed by Cheeseman in the 1870s as curator at the Auckland Museum (Cameron 2000). In its varied career, this concept shaped and became enmeshed in a changing set of governmental rationalities: a shift from salvage/memorial and racial assimilationist projects to Clark Wissler's notion of "culture areas," and subsequently to a Boasian notion of culture that sought to promote Māori self-determination. Produced through the contestations and interplay between different conceptions of "the Maori as he was," the New Zealand assemblage examined in this chapter, in contrast to the situation in Australia and the United States, advanced the potential for indigenous liberal subjecthood and rule within and at the same time outside of a postsettler nation through the separate lines of social and economic development it authorized.

Indigenous agency played an important role in the creation of a modern liberal Māori subject, as Māori actors were intimately involved in the intertwined histories of museums, fieldwork, and colonial government. We pay particular attention to the influence of American anthropology in the New Zealand context, and to the distinctive ways in which the Boasian culture concept, mobilized through the recording of "the Maori as he was," refashioned public policy and discourses, broadly from race to culture, and from Native to Māori.

The first part of the chapter traces the elements that constituted the distinctive fieldwork agencements of the various centers of collection and calculation within this assemblage. Cheeseman deployed a distinctive typological approach directed toward the portrayal of the Māori past and evolutionary cultural history mediated through material culture, whereas Best utilized a broadly anthropological orientation with an emphasis on the more intangible aspects of cultural heritage to depict Māori social life before European contact. Skinner focused on archaeological and scientific research with an emphasis on material culture to reconstruct cultural origins and evaluate future roles and contributions that Māori could potentially make to building the economic life of the nation for Māori, in stark contrast to Ngata's and Buck's indigenous anthropological approach in which materials and practices emblematic of Māori arts, crafts, and culture were harnessed to support cultural revival and separate social and economic development initiatives. Each of these gathered and worked with distinctive collections of objects and cultural materials, human bodies, tools, equipment, technical devices, and various cosmological, theoretical, and methodological approaches to collecting, display, research, archiving, publishing, filming, recording, and the organizing of public events. In these sections the analysis moves from collecting in the field to the various centers of calculation—the OM, the Auckland Museum, the DM, the Polynesian Society, the BMER, and the Department of Native Affairs—where the data gathered came to be processed and subjected to procedures of ordering on which the authority of the respective claims of these entities came to rest. We examine the practices of arrangement and display to which the materials collected by Skinner and Cheeseman were subjected and the contrasting role of the collected object in relation to the respective modalities of rule they mobilized. Each of these actors—Best, Skinner, Cheeseman, Archey, Ngata, and Buck—were part of this assemblage through which the idea of "the Maori as he was" was produced, transformed, combined, shuffled, superimposed, recalculated, reassembled, and made legible and presentable as a series of sociotechnical configurations and arrangements.

We then analyze the processes of collecting, ordering, and governing across these centers of calculation. We discuss the political rationalities of the respective elements of the anthropological assemblage, such as different notions of traditional culture as seen in conceptions of the changing Māori and their adaptive culture, and we show how these combinations articulated different modalities of colonial government and liberal rule. The variable relations between the governed and the governors that the different elements of the assemblage facilitated produced different histories and futures for the new nation-state. For Pakeha, a Māori past created a means for Māori assimilation into the settler population, mainstream society, and modernity, but for Māori it was a tactic for their integration into the present and future on their own terms. In considering these matters, we examine how each of the elements that made up the anthropological assemblage became mobile, "able to move freely around" (Latour 1987: 227) from the field, to the museum "laboratory" and to university teaching programs, and then into wider circulation through scientific networks, publishing, policy, and colonial administrative structures.

Māori adaptation to modern social and economic life became one of the dominant narratives shared by Skinner, Cheeseman, Archey, Ngata, and Buck (Cameron and McCarthy 2015). In formulating adaptation as a form of conduct and action for mediating settler and Māori relations, underpinned by assimilationist governmental policies, both Cheeseman and Skinner worked with material culture to ascertain the level of Māori achievement and hence the population's ability and potential to adapt to modern society. Both Skinner and Ngata drew on anthropologist Raymond Firth's (1929: 471) work on Māori economic life and his conclusion "that Maori had reached the phase of adaptation"; he thus attributed to Māori a degree of self-reflexivity and autonomous subjectivity that placed them within the threshold of liberal government. In the BMER, established in 1923, we can observe a distinctive style of anthropological governance that operated with and for Māori communities as well as the state. The distinguishing fieldwork agencements of this Māori-led body are evident in how it brought together ethnological methods of collecting and ordering and yoked them to new or modified mechanisms and rationalities of rule that constituted a form of separate social development for Māori New Zealanders. In this regard, it is telling that in New Zealand the anthropological assemblage positioned the Māori past in relation to the Pakeha present not just to expedite native policy but also to locate Māori within the emerging nation, as a means to counter assimilation directives and to present a positive image of the Māori people to the majority population searching for a national identity and seeking to mark the development of the modern state: "Anthropologists tell us that to know what man is we must know what man has been. . . . Our Maori friend, with his singular institutions, his peculiar reasoning-powers and mythopoetic mentality, will do good service in explaining such advancement, and so in preparing us for further progress" (Best 1922a: 32).

The practices making up the anthropological assemblage described in this chapter—fieldwork, museums, exhibitions and events, research, and publishing—produced different forms of authority, variable images of the future nation-state, and heterogeneous modalities for managing race relations via distinctive forms of anthropological governance. They allowed, moreover, for the formation not just of the Māori (as they were, are, and will be) as liberal subjects but also for the reformation of the self in relation to this other. Best articulated these relations of self and other when he proposed that the "Pakeha knows himself by knowing his Maori countrymen better, and knows his own future by understanding the Maori past" (1922a: 32).

Furthermore, "the Maori as he was" constituted an anthropological archive that detailed the social conditions at a point in time in the past. This archive not only shaped the intrinsic worth of pre-European Māori culture but was also used in a variety of ways within government, education, academic, museum, and heritage circles for contemporary social and cultural development. This gave these activities a distinctive ethnological character in "anthropological" governance, particularly in the Department of Native Affairs, but also in welfare, education, housing, and employment. Taken together, the people, objects, ideas, nonhumans, technical devices, and practices embodied in the assemblage we examine in this chapter covered the major institutions across the country. Each provided a mechanism for taking stock of where Māori people were before their current conditions today, demonstrating social problems, and showing how they might be addressed, but also marking the progress made and noting their adaptation to modern society through politics, the economy, health, labor, and technological advancement.

AN ANTHROPOLOGICAL ARCHIVE OF THE MĀORI RACE: THE AUCKLAND MUSEUM, 1890–1930

When the Auckland War Memorial Museum (AWMM) opened in 1929, its hilltop site and neoclassical architecture suggested it was a mausoleum of the national sacrifice in World War I. But something else was memorialized within the museum's "Maori Court" (figure 5.2). Here a "traditional" Māori culture was displayed through an arrangement of a house, canoes, and a storehouse as a pre-European village: "the Maori as he was."

Cheeseman, the curator, originally conceived of his research field as encompassing all of New Zealand and therefore the totality of native culture as an integrated system. The fieldwork agencements and hybrid collectives that enacted his particular interpretation of "the Maori as he was," were formed via a series of heterogeneous human and nonhuman agential entities through which his "native culture" came to be performed. These entities included human actors: those people who mediated the collection of data and shaped the immediate ethnological exchanges for Cheeseman's archive, that is, not only Cheeseman himself but also curio and specimen collectors, private donors, ethnographers such as Best (from the DM), the French anthropologist Jean Louis Armand de Quatrefages, overseas antiquities dealers, and Māori informants and craftspeople, as well as human body parts and skeletal remains. Letters, post offices, ships, and trains constituted the modes of transportation, communication, and exchange for both objects and interactions between Cheeseman, his informants, and agents within New Zealand and

FIGURE 5.2 Thomas Cheeseman in the Maori wing of the Auckland Museum, showing on the left the *pātaka* (food storehouse) *Te Puawai o Te Arawa*, ca. 1900. PH-RES-1340, Auckland War Memorial Museum, Auckland. Courtesy of the Auckland War Memorial Museum Tāmaki Paenga Hira.

The Māori collection at the Auckland Museum at Princes Street was the largest in the country. The Auckland Museum's curator and director, Thomas Cheeseman (foreground), was a self-trained botanist who led the museum for nearly fifty years (1874–1923). In the first decades of his career, the aim was to collect and display a pan-tribal vision of Māori people and culture, rather than individual tribes, but later a concern for provenance and distinctive features of material culture is apparent. The museum's huge archive of material culture was assembled and reassembled over time and by the early twentieth century was open to new interpretations of Māori social life.

---

abroad. Notebooks, cameras, and calipers enabled the ethnological materials that would later form components of his archive to be recorded, documented, and made portable. Cheeseman's material catalog of the "ancient" Māori was gathered and compiled through techniques founded on the specification and visual analysis of form, shape and materials, the age of objects, and their manufacturing techniques and cultural context, as far as these were known. His scheme was guided by what Cheeseman described as an "old Maori style"—that is, objects manufactured by "real" Māori in the distant past or in the "timeless ethnographic present"—and the specification of specimens uncontaminated by European influences. In many instances specimens were refurbished to represent an "old Maori style" (Cameron 2000: 63).[4] These objects were regarded as the "best," most "perfect," or most "beautiful" specimens because of their design and therefore were considered as illustrative of the highest state of technical aesthetic attainment and skill by Māori. The procurement and selection of objects with distinctive cultural and magico-religious agency sought to elucidate materially the manners, customs, and modes of Māori life.

Drawing on his botanical training, Cheeseman deployed a Linnaean taxonomy, combined with French curator Edme Francois Jomard's (1777–1862) geographical system, as a strategy to direct his collecting activities and therefore shape his archive.[5] Cultural objects were organized according to categories into specimens, series, and classes. Complete sets of specimens gathered according to these criteria allowed for the accurate documentation of the manners, customs, and degree of civilization of Māori and other races (Cameron 2000: 43; Bouquet 2012). From the 1880s on, however, Cheeseman collected more common and everyday objects to complete his archive.

The particular socio-technical arrangements that Cheeseman mobilized positioned the museum as a center for collection and calculation focused on the notion of "the Maori as he was." He effectively established an anthropological archive of the Māori race, the "most comprehensive and complete in the world" (*Report of the Auckland Institute and Museum* 1889–90: 6), aimed at illustrating the manners, customs, and modes of life of the Māori race through material culture. Cheeseman referred to the Auckland Museum collection and exhibits as "a catalogue of Maori life." Here technological, nonhuman, and human actors (such as tools, technical devices, texts, bone, stone, wood, flax, manufacturing methods, Māori craftspeople, and visual analysis), combined with Cheeseman's theoretical actants, operated as parts of a system of distributed agency across these various elements to form his archive. His interest in material culture alongside his theoretical and ordering dispositions was deployed to form his definitive catalog aimed at capturing the essence of the race through outstanding pre-European specimens, arranged in classes and series, and later as regional cultures in tribal areas, as this division into units became consequential in the way it framed his "working surfaces on the social."

Cheeseman's attribution to the Māori of a high level of artistic ability, based on his assessment of objects, reflected a growing appreciation of the aesthetics of Māori design that was first seen in an art exhibition at the Canterbury Museum in 1870, where Māori works were considered examples of fine art (Cameron 2000: 58, 231) and that culminated in Augustus Hamilton's book *The Art Workmanship of the Maori Race in New Zealand* ([1898] 2001). In putting together his displays and interpretive panels, Cheeseman used his own and Best's ethnological data, in which objects were used to read the character of "the race," with the exhibits "illustrating the essence of the manners, customs and mode of life."[6]

Larger carvings were aestheticized to some extent in being displayed as freestanding forms against the plain walls, thereby showing some recognition of Māori "art." Later on, Cheeseman's theoretical, methodological, and representational strategy was also driven by an anthropological doxa similar to that of the American anthropologist Alfred Kroeber, likening culture to an organism, an integrated whole composed of interdependent parts represented by his series. By the 1920s there was a clear sense in the exhibits that objects were being understood as artifacts within an anthropological framework. After Archey became the director, the displays in the Anthropology Hall at the AWMM were *ethnographic* in the contemporary sense of giving a detailed description of a single culture, whereas the more old-fashioned DM exhibits were *ethnological* in the sense that was current in turn-of-the-century New Zealand, that of placing items in a comparative global framework. Here exhibits conveyed the use and function of objects, often employing photographs to suggest their context, as Franz Boas had done in the United States.[7] The influence of "culture areas," rather than the earlier evolutionary notion of "types," was evident in the exhibition of the localized settings created for the manufacture and use of objects from particular tribal regions—*hinaki* (eel traps) from the Whanganui River, for example.

Best visited the AWMM several times and studied the objects on display very carefully. Images and descriptions of objects are common in his published work, and he seems to have regarded that museum as a better and more comprehensive source for his ethnological construction of "the Maori as he was" than the DM. We can see from his notebooks that, on his visits to the AWMM, things on display that he liked, invariably "old," were described as "fine" or "good," but any sign of experimentation or European influence was derided as "modern" or "unorthodox." "Unusual" objects were noted with interest, sketches were made for future reference, and photographs of outstanding examples were ordered. A display might be called a "good collection" if it contained enough "good old" objects to furnish images for his research.[8] The impression is that Best saw a museum as a three-dimensional system of reference like an archive, its artifacts representing the evidence of the pre-European Māori life that was being reconstructed in his books. Indeed, the AWMM can be thought of as the archive of "the Maori as he was."

This sense of the exhibitions acting as a reference library or archive is also reflective of how Cheeseman conceived the AWMM's collections in relation to Māori people and culture and the wider colonial society, and of the ways in which the accumulated artifacts and associated information served to document and "know" the Māori, and therefore situate them within the modern nation as liberal subjects. Cheeseman's obsession with collecting was driven by the need to create a "complete picture" of Māori life, as incomplete collections or gaps provided an incorrect picture of the Māori "race" and their level of technological and artistic achievement. He aimed to represent what he considered cultural wholes to not only enable the public, scholars, and administrators to get acquainted with indigenous habits, practices, and customs through the exhibits but also change their hearts and minds by presenting Māori as a sophisticated, progressive race.

Cheeseman's anthropological archive helped create new conceptions of Māori subjecthood. In ordering these collections he sought to illustrate a Māori mentality and hence the potential of Māori as modern liberal subjects. The illustration of the character, mode of conduct, and evolutionary development of Māori culture was directed at demonstrating to the public the Māori ability to innovate and adapt. Cheeseman's and, later, Archey's collecting influenced emerging conceptions of Māori as liberal subjects and the political capacities this required them to develop. Cheeseman sought, like Skinner at the OM, to demonstrate Māori industries before the arrival of Europeans so he could insert Māori into the economic life of the nation, for example, in the trades and the textile industry.

By the 1920s objects were arranged and described to demonstrate technological achievements. This approach was reminiscent of Boas's ethnographic practices whereby each group of people was seen to constitute a unique and coherent configuration of material and intellectual features rooted in tradition (Stocking 1968: 195). Objects were used to read the race's character, activities, and technological achievements, as well as the state of Māori thought and social organization—what Ivan Sutherland (1929) referred to as their "mentality." Cheeseman and, later, Archey can be understood as accessing the Māori mind through artifacts, what they made and used, thus surmising a level of sophistication that facilitated their assimilation into mainstream New Zealand society, albeit on Pakeha terms. Māori cultural performances at the museum from the 1920s on were staged as showcases of "traditional" customs and reflected links with Ngata's cultural revival initiatives, which demonstrated an intrinsic interest in the social.

After Cheeseman's death, the zoologist Archey became the director of the AWMM, and his interest in Māori carving found expression in the museum's support of Māori arts and crafts. Even though the museum collected human remains and thus offended Māori cultural sensitivities, there was intermittent contact with Māori communities in this period (Park 1984: 19). Pakeha collector and scholar George Graham, who had close relationships with Māori, set up an Anthropology and Maori Race Section in 1922, chaired by Buck, which in turn had links to a representative body called Te Akarana Maori Association. In the 1930s the School of Maori Arts and Crafts from Rotorua spent time studying the carvings in the museum in preparation for working on the meeting house at Waitangi, completed in 1940 (Park 1986; Cameron 2000).

Alongside this performative and contemporary image of Māori, another more formal and somewhat anthropological impulse was evident in the new AWMM from 1929, which was more inclined to display Māori artifacts as evidence of a racial culture. Here the making and using of artifacts were situated in an anthropological framework depicting the ways of life of a particular people in a specific place, an approach that lent itself to public education. The influence of the American historical school and Wissler can be traced in the increasing interest in the origin of objects and in the variations of Māori culture as regionally distinctive culture areas as demonstrated through a shift to geographical groupings and culture traits in specific regions, effected by the use of Best's ethnological information on pre-European lifestyles. The gradual shift to culture areas is most clearly manifested in the education and display experiments of the 1930s and 1940s undertaken by staff like graphic designer Olwyn Turbott, funded through the U.S. Carnegie Corporation (see Cameron 2000; McCarthy and Cobley 2009; McQueen 1942). In these display cases and school programs, a new approach is discernible: the focus is now on how things are made as parts of a way of life rather than on formal typological series or groupings of objects.

Over his long career, Cheeseman's thinking shifted from salvage ethnology before 1900, when the task was to gather the vestiges of a "dying race," to a focus on culture areas and cultural adaptation in the early 1920s. This shift was in turn folded into Archey's work at the new museum, where efforts were directed toward the preservation of the skills of the indigenous craftsperson as well as the museum object, both as part of a full archive of "arts and crafts," a discourse that was comanaged by both Pakeha savants and Māori leaders such as Ngata and Buck (McCarthy 2012).

We have suggested that the anthropological archive compiled at the AWMM first operated as a memorial to a primitive race that was bound to disappear in the face of colonization by a superior culture, but as dying-race theories had been discredited by 1900 in light of a growing Māori population, the archival orientation changed to accommodate more liberal conceptions of culture and identity. After the Canterbury Museum art exhibition of 1870, Edward Treagear's (1885) *Aryan Maori*, Hamilton's ([1898] 2001) *The Art Workmanship of the Maori Race in New Zealand*, and Best's (1924b) *The Maori as He Was*, Māori came to be seen as being at a higher cultural plane compared to other "Neolithic people" thanks to evidence of proto-European ancestry, artistic skill, monotheism, and other qualities.

Museum displays, together with the loyal Māori welcome to royalty in 1901, the rise of the moderate Young Maori Party, and Māori patriotic contributions to the war effort in 1914–18 all seemed to usher in the Native population as part of the Dominion of New Zealand. This new conception of the "white" (European) Māori and the "green" (environmental) Māori, as opposed to the "red" (warlike) Māori (Belich 2001: 206–15), articulated a more sympathetic understanding of Māori capacity, with a shift away from eugenic conceptions of a dying race toward a perception of a capacity for ongoing survival and the potential for further development within modern New Zealand. Thus, by collecting, ordering, and exhibiting a different vision of the Māori past, the Auckland Museum constructed a different narrative of the nation-state and its relations with settler and indigenous populations, as well as a way to manage those relations (see Joyce 1999: 36).

FROM THE FIELD TO THE ARMCHAIR: THE DOMINION, 1910–1931

Best was the best-known "field-worker" of the early twentieth century in New Zealand, and one of the last of the self-taught amateur ethnologists, in contrast to a later generation trained in professional anthropology, such as Skinner, a student of Alfred Cort Haddon. Best lived in the isolated Urewera district for fifteen years, from 1895 to 1910, ostensibly working as a quarter-master on a road being built through the forest, and later as a health officer, but essentially using this position to conduct research among the Tūhoe people. Then, in 1910, Best moved to a clerical position at the DM in Wellington, where he worked steadily for twenty years until his death in 1931, turning his many notebooks from the field into a voluminous series of publications. Best also took part in the other activities of the DM: periodic expeditions, collecting, and display (figure 5.3).

His store of knowledge, added to by ongoing communication with his informants, usually by letter but sometimes through interviews or short trips out of Wellington, underpinned the museum's exhibitions of Māori material culture and the public images it presented of Māori social life in the past, which in turn shaped popular perceptions of their place in the national present. Here we concentrate on *The Maori as He Was: A Brief Account of Maori Life as It Was in Pre-European Days* (1924b) to demonstrate the way Best framed, gathered, ordered, and assembled pre-European Māori culture and the multifarious ways in which this shaped the governing (and self-governing) of populations. This monograph was produced to meet the demand from a Pakeha audience, as well as tourists and travelers, for a concise study of the Māori (v, xiii). We first examine Best's fieldwork agencements relating to this seminal text. Best conceived his ethnographic field areas—the Urewera, the Whanganui River, and the East Coast (the latter two locations as part of DM expeditions)—as geographical and tribal locations where "the Maori as he was" was least influenced by European culture. Best assembled his archive by working closely with local *iwi* (tribes; the Tūhoe in the Urewera); Māori informants, interpreters, and performers; and scholars, anthropologists, and museum curators, all of whom contributed to the collection of his data. New roads that penetrated deep into these isolated regions and the advent of telecommunications technology such as phone lines enabled Best to access his subjects and describe and record oral histories and cultural activities using cameras, film, sketchpads, and wax cylinders. The ethnographic specimens—examples of weaving, carvings, weapons, and meeting houses made from materials such as bone, wood, feathers, stone, and flax—and the documentation of their manufacture were used to chronicle Māori arts and crafts. Cultural phenomena and religious and divination rituals, such as mythology, songs, and poetry, were recorded and used as examples of his "mythopoetic Maori mentality" (Best 1922a: 32). Best's fieldwork was driven by the notion of a classic Māori culture of which remnants still existed, a view that was underpinned by discourses of salvage colonialism.

FIGURE 5.3 An unidentified Māori speaker is being recorded on a wax cylinder at the Dominion Museum by (from left) Johannes Andersen, Te Raumoa Balneavis, and Elsdon Best. James McDonald, 0.011963, Te Papa, Wellington. Courtesy of the Museum of New Zealand Te Papa Tongarewa.

Elsdon Best's book *The Maori as He Was* (1924b) formed the template for the public image of the Māori past that could be found on display in the Dominion Museum. It was assembled from ethnological data gathered in the field, in the form of photographs, films, manuscripts, notes, objects, songs, and other material. This work was funded by the Board of Maori Ethnological Research. These records of speech and the performing arts, as seen here, were preserved not just to reconstruct a historical vision of "Maoriland" but also, for the Māori intellectuals, artists, and performers involved, to create a platform for contemporary social and cultural development through the preservation and revival of those art forms.

The agency of these heterogeneous actors mixed, matched, and intermingled to produce Best's archive of "the Maori as he was," on which his particular ethnographical claims of what native culture had been came to rest. The monograph comprised a range of material drawn from Best's previous and ongoing fieldwork. For example, the section on fishing contains firsthand observations from the ethnological expedition to Whanganui in 1921: descriptions of net making (Best 1924b: 248–49, fig. 126) and of the construction of a lamprey weir (263). The term *ethnological* was used widely in New Zealand to describe fieldwork activities, as opposed to *ethnographical* in other Anglophone national contexts during this period; its associations, however, were different from those it had in French usage (see chapter 6). The same trip produced films of divinatory rites, staged scenes with Māori men dressed in traditional costume performing ritual practices, and several stills from this footage shot by McDonald were reproduced to illustrate various "charms" (*karakia*) associated with warfare and so on.(Best 1924b: 21, 201).

The overall impression gained from reading *The Maori as He Was* is that although the author constructs the Māori past as an idealized realm sealed off from the technological advancements of the European present, he is at pains to present the Māori in a favorable light to the public of the day. "Evidence is given that shows the forebears of the Maori to have been a people possessed of a vivid imagination and a mythopoetic turn of mind," wrote Best in the preface, "while their higher concepts point to powers of introspective thought that neolithic folk are not usually credited with" (1924b: v). This book and several others (Best 1922a,b,c) are notable for their lengthy and, for the time, relatively sensitive exposition of Māori customary concepts, such as *mana*, *tapu*, whakapapa, *mauri*, and *wairua*, which convey a strong sense of the Māori worldview, very different from that of Europeans, and Māori ontologies, showing connections between people and the natural world, and the animacy of material objects. The Māori have no writing, Best explains later, but "we must be impressed by the evidence of his powers of reflection and his ideality. . . . The Maori is mentally acute, and possesses remarkable powers of comprehension" (1924b: 8).

Best supported this claim by pointing to outstanding intellectual features such as the apparent cult of the supreme God (*Io*), which suggested monotheism and the possession of higher forms of abstract thought (1924b: 40). Other scholars at this time were working in a similar vein: Julius von Haast, the director of the Canterbury Museum (Cameron 2000: 231), and later Hamilton (1901) elevated Māori carving to the status of "fine art" and "art handicraft," while Percy Smith (1913–15) actively promoted ideas about the *whare wānanga* (schools of esoteric learning) and, famously, the arrival of a "great fleet" of Polynesian canoes in 1350. These theories were questioned by later scholars, but as historian Jamie Belich (1996: 213–15) put it, Māori at the time seemed to be quite prepared to go along with these fancies if they provided a more sympathetic view of their past, and demonstrated their fitness not just for survival but also for fuller participation in national life. In this sense, Best's book is similar to an earlier volume, Treagear's *Aryan Maori* (1885), which disseminated an entirely erroneous, but nevertheless very influential, view of Māori racial origins as similar to those of Europeans, which assumed a capacity for social advancement (Belich 2001: 206–10).

Indigenous agency was an important factor in Best's production of "the Maori as he was." Today Māori readers of this and other books by Best regard them as essential bodies of knowledge collected from elders, but there is a good deal of suspicion about Best's relationship with iwi and offense at the archaic language that refers to the "barbaric" Māori, even when they are compared favorably with "other peoples of his culture stage" (1924b: 8). However, the ethnologist's interactions with *kaumātua* (elders) were much more equitable than many contemporary critics have allowed. Certainly the books, as well as Best's original notes and manuscript material in the archives, openly acknowledge his numerous sources, the enthusiastic collaborators who were evidently anxious to see their knowledge written down.[9] For example, in Best's first DM monograph, on stone implements, he acknowledges Te Whatahoro for providing access to old manuscripts and "much oral information" (1912: 10). In *The Maori*, a two-volume work published by the BMER in the same year as *The Maori as He Was*, Best listed the "authorities" quoted; alongside eminent anthropologists and local writers he listed the names of ten Māori scholars (Best 1924a: 1:481–83). In one example he described the Ngāti Porou chief, Tuta Nihoniho, who had been actively involved in DM activities as well as the Christchurch exhibition of 1906, as an "enthusiastic contributor of Maori lore" (1:482).

Given this extensive input to Best's research, it is little wonder that Jeffrey Paparoa Holman has concluded, after a close study of Tūhoe elder and scholar Tūtakangahau's coauthorship with Best of the tribal history of Tūhoe, that "Māori had given Best his material and Māori were fully involved in seeing it through to the public arena" (2010: 195, 244). This was, Holman continued, a combination of Pakeha "ethnographic impulse" and Māori "preservationist anxiety" (190). It is clear from Tūtakangahau's own letters to the Māori newspapers of the time that he supported tribal preservationist campaigns to record whakapapa and Best's efforts to write down oral traditions

(189–90). He even seems to have anointed Best as a successor who would hold his knowledge in trust until such time as his descendants were ready to appreciate it (160; see also 137–41).

So whatever the accuracy of parts of the book, *The Maori as He Was* was immensely influential in shaping the public view of the "traditional" pre-European Māori past, which can be seen reflected in wider society through museum displays, arts and architecture, government policy, and later calls for separate economic and social development.[10] In fact, the DM aimed to sell copies at the Wembley and Dunedin exhibitions in 1925.[11] Quite apart from the impact of Best's work as a book read by exhibition goers, Best's fieldwork underpinned the museum display of "the Maori as he was," not just at the DM but also, and even more completely, at the international exhibit in Dunedin in 1925–26 and, most effectively of all, in the Maori Ethnology Gallery in the new DM that opened in 1936 (see figure 1.4).

This new museum and the adjoining National Art Gallery, together with the adjacent National War Memorial, were described as an "Antipodean Parthenon" that commemorated the sacrifice of local soldiers in World War I. But, far from announcing an independent national identity, it expressed New Zealand's loyal Dominion status within the empire. The new museum was lauded by the minister of education, Peter Fraser, as a "noble building for a noble purpose."[12] Its internal design was influenced by the modern educational philosophy shaping American museums.[13] The idea of culture areas, rather than the earlier evolutionary notion of types, was exhibited through the life group, in which figures and the objects they used were staged in a realistic setting as if frozen in time. Concurrently, didactic exhibits sought to educate visitors by setting objects within the discursive framework of explanatory text, images, diagrams, and other graphic elements to foster respect for and understanding of the indigenous population in an effort to foster harmonious relations between the races (Best 1922a: 32).

The Maori Ethnology Gallery was more formally anthropological in layout compared to the Maori Hall next door (see chapter 1). The gallery was, in short, a three-dimensional version of Best's book, which was in turn compiled from his work in the field. This book on a wall made concrete "the Maori as he was" and was somewhat at odds with the hall next door, where Ngata exhibited "the Maori as he is" (see figure 5.1). Meanwhile, far to the south, in a region of New Zealand with a very small Māori population that was outside the influence of Māori leaders, another model of museum collecting and display was being developed that owed more to the latest archaeological theories from overseas than to local, national, or indigenous forces.

CULTURE AREAS, MATERIAL CULTURE, AND ARCHAEOLOGY: OTAGO MUSEUM AND THE UNIVERSITY OF OTAGO, 1919–1940

At the University of Otago in Dunedin, on New Zealand's South Island, a course in ethnology, the first in the British Empire outside Great Britain, was taught in 1919 by Skinner, a New Zealand–born Cambridge graduate. A version of this course was delivered to the public in "popular" evening lectures. Skinner explained anthropology to his audience as the study of the "culture and physical characters of the races of mankind," pointing out that it used the same methods as the natural sciences—just as zoologists study different kinds of animals, anthropologists study the various races. Ethnology, he suggested, was therefore very useful for government agencies in training staff for the administration of "backward races," as was shown in places like the Australian territory of Papua (see chapter 2).[14]

In this section we examine Skinner's work at the OM and the University of Otago and trace the ways in which his anthropological and archaeological archive of "the Maori as he was" was put to work in the adjudication of forms of governmental regulation and the social reform of Māori populations in the context of nation building and economic development in the early twentieth century (Cameron 2014). Skinner drew attention to the practical significance of understanding "the Maori as he was" in arguing that "a right understanding of the childhood of a race is essential before any thorough plan of social reform is drawn up."[15] However, the links that are evident here between anthropology and governance, through which Māori were included within a national social domain, were not of the liberal kind pursued by Māori scholar-politicians in the North Island. The work of Skinner and others in the south reflected a more conservative position in which Māori people as a "race" were perceived to exhibit a capacity to adapt but were destined to be regulated by Pakeha administrators and not by and for themselves.

The first professionally trained anthropologist in New Zealand, Skinner was appointed to the roles of assistant curator in ethnology and lecturer in anthropology at the University of Otago in 1918. He went on to conduct fieldwork among the Moriori people in the Chatham Islands, eight hundred kilometers to the east of New Zealand, and also published his findings as a monograph with the Bishop Museum in Honolulu (Skinner 1923). Dubious about the value of oral tradition, Skinner disputed Best's and Smith's theories of Māori origins, emphasizing instead the close study of material culture and the "science of the spade" (in other words, archaeology).[16] For Skinner, ethnology entailed the close analysis and classification of artifacts based on their morphology and distribution. His comparative taxonomic analysis of southern Māori, Moriori, and Polynesian material culture, for example, his typology of adzes, was immensely influential and, diffused through his teaching and publishing (not to mention the exhibits at the museum where he became director in 1937), set the local pattern for research for the next fifty years (A. Anderson 1998).

Skinner's links to American anthropology strongly influenced his work in New Zealand. As a Rockefeller traveling scholar he took a graduate course with Wissler at Yale in 1927 (A. Anderson 1998), heard Boas teach at Columbia in 1928, and was friendly with Margaret Mead at the American Museum of Natural History, which had significant collections of Pacific and Māori material. This American influence can be seen in his lectures through comments on contemporary social issues, and it informed how he shaped policy and practice in the social governance of Māori people within New Zealand society. "Anthropology then is the whole study of man," Skinner told his students, "whether it looks backward towards his origin, or forwards towards his destiny." In support of his views he cited William Henry Holmes, who defined anthropology as "historical" and "practical."[17]

Skinner was heavily influenced by the American historical school, and particularly by Wissler, Kroeber, and Edward Sapir (Cameron 2014). He introduced and popularized Wissler's (1927) theory of culture areas in New Zealand and used it to create a template of regional tribal characteristics that has persisted to this day. "A culture area is a geographical region within the bounds of which all groups of inhabitants show a strong family resemblance," explained Skinner in the *Journal of the Polynesian Society* in 1921 (71). "The best way of working out the boundaries of a culture area is through "material culture, by which is meant dwellings, clothes, implements, ornaments, weapons made by inhabitants; in brief, all objects which fall within the scope of a museum collection" (71).

To this end Skinner conceived of his field as a historically organized cultural and geographical space and as a series of distinctive subcultures that extended beyond the modern nation. He sought to capture "the Maori as he was" through Wissler's (1917, 1923a, 1926) and Kroeber's (1917a, 1923) "culture-area" concept, the German American Sapir's (1916) methods, and British archaeologist Flinders Petrie's analysis of material culture as cultural evolutionary signifiers. The agency of material objects was mobilized through Wissler's and Kroeber's "culture area arrangements" and Sapir's methods to identify trait complexes underpinned by a social evolutionary view of human cultural development (figure 5.4). Using Wissler's (1923a: 289) idea that dif-

FIGURE 5.4 School group in Henry Devenish Skinner's Maori Ethnology Gallery at the Otago Museum, Dunedin, 1937–38. 0970_01_017A, Hocken Collections, Dunedin. Courtesy of Hocken Collections.

At the Otago Museum, objects were examined, measured, and described on the basis of their physical attributes. Decorative motifs on objects were recorded according to locality, and culture traits inferred from ethnographical sources. Henry Devenish Skinner then combined these objects with linguistic forms, images, and maps and put them in what he considered their proper relations to one another to depict eight different Māori cultures and their cultural complexes. He attempted to pinpoint a cultural center where each culture was most typical, drawing on field observations to support his work. Skinner followed Clark Wissler's (1927: 886) scheme by developing his culture areas according to constituent tribal groups, and he verified them against known tribal boundaries (Skinner 1974: 21–22). The culture-area concept had a significant impact on the later development of anthropology and archaeology in New Zealand, rendering invisible anthropology's overt racist underpinnings, and also shaped the work of Māori scholars such as Hirini Moko Mead, whose categories of Māori visual art draw on the culture areas to define regional styles of carving (Cameron and McCarthy 2015; S. Mead 1986).

ferent races had different inherent potential for cultural achievement, he sought to formulate his own "working surfaces on the social" by detailing the inherent capacity of Māori to invent cultural traits and advance culture by rating and evaluating their cultural elements (Skinner 1921: 72). Skinner was also committed to collecting forms of Māori society and culture to illustrate Pakeha influences on Māori life and society since contact (Smith 1942), the degree to which Māori had responded to Western civilization, their ability to modify their lifestyles and technologies and adapt to new circumstances, and the ways in which processes of adaption were already occurring in specific areas of culture.[18] Such examples contributed to the possibility that the predicaments of Māori could be improved because of their aptitude for innovation. This information was then used to demonstrate their ability to integrate into colonial economic and social life, as well as to detail their capacities and hence their potential contributions to present-day New Zealand, such as the deployment of Māori populations in the rural and later the urban labor force (Cameron 2014; Cameron and McCarthy 2015).

Skinner's courses in ethnology and anthropology were deemed the best way of accruing "ethnographic capital" for the colonial administration. Courses were designed to aid the successful administration of the Māori and other indigenous populations. Through his courses Skinner sought to educate administrators to sympathetically discover, understand, and appraise the disposition of Native races; their mind and modes of thought; their cultural, social, and religious customs and habits; and their history and developmental trajectories. Skinner's role in deploying these ideas of the Māori past and present acted on the social in ways that were related to, but at times in tension with, the different governmental rationalities informing the programs of Māori social development enacted by Māori politicians of the day. Consequently, there were tensions between Skinner and his colleagues in Wellington who were linked to Ngata's programs. The self-trained amateurs Smith and Best from the Polynesian Society dominated the field and regarded the younger, academically trained Skinner as "an armchair man without fieldwork experience," whose lack of fluency in Māori language was a serious shortcoming (Cameron and McCarthy 2015).[19] Skinner for his part was critical of the outdated methods of the older generation and their faith in oral tradition (Sorrenson 1992). We turn now to Wellington to take a closer look at this very different node in the network examined in this chapter: the alliance of sympathetic ethnologists and Māori scholar-politicians that gained control of government research and steered it toward Māori and tribal ends.

THE CHANGING MĀORI: THE BMER, 1923–1940

The bald description of Museum objects leaves me cold, such as Skinner delights in with his amulets. It [material culture] is . . . somewhat of a drudgery to describe but remains dead unless it is woven into the living culture of the people. —Peter Buck to Johannes Andersen, November 19, 1934

In a letter to his friend Andersen, quoted above, Buck criticized Skinner's work, which he felt was unconnected to ongoing cultural practices, the very area where he and Ngata focused their energies as "empirical anthropologists advocating cultural adjustments" (Ngata quoted in McCarthy 2014a). The contrast between these actors within the different parts of the overall anthropological assemblage is at times stark. Buck and Ngata thought that Skinner's work was dry and academic and that his lack of Māori language skills was a serious shortcoming compared to older field-workers like Best. While Skinner's approaches to cultural analysis tended to support the idea of the changing Māori and cultural adjustments, his approach was structured within an assimilationist rationality that sought to detail Māori skills and expertise largely through material culture complexes that could support Pakeha industry and economic development. Ngata and Buck conceived their national cultural field along iwi (tribal) lines. The BMER employed a different set of theoretical actors and adopted a more malleable Boasian notion of culture as something that could develop and change—"cultural adaptation," as they called it—and that was connected to a more independent vision of Māori social development (McCarthy 2014a). Despite the similarities and overlaps between different objects, institutions, and ideas, overall it appears that Wissler's ideas and approaches to collecting and ordering practices resonated with more conservative Pakeha such as Skinner and Cheeseman, while the employment of Boasian ideas was strongest with Māori and their allies around the BMER.

Ngata and Buck's style of "applied" or "empirical" anthropology was concerned with a different range of fieldwork, material culture, cosmological, policy, and governmental administrative actors that were also intimately connected with tribal communities. Participating enthusiastically in the DM expeditions, becoming very influential in the Polynesian Society, and wielding considerable power within government through the Department of Native Affairs, Ngata and Buck assembled a range of ethnological material though the museum, publications, and events; this material was employed in a distinctive anthropological rationality of rule that McCarthy has described elsewhere as "anthropological governance" (McCarthy 2014a). Allied with Best's book, which constructed the public image of "the Maori as he was," the BMER ordered data in the form of photographs, films, manuscripts, notes, objects, songs, and other materials not just to reconstruct a historical vision of Māoriland but also to create a platform for contemporary social and cultural development, and for the revival of visual and performing arts (figure 5.5).

This remarkable episode in indigenous anthropology had its origins in two overlapping movements: Māori community interest in preserving their cultural heritage, and scientific interest in ethnology and history among Pakeha savants of Maoriland. Just before World War I this concern to look into customary knowledge and practices found allies within the government in the Young Maori Party's objective to "preserve the language, poetry, traditions and such of the customs and arts of the Maori . . . by promoting research in the Anthropology and Ethnology of the Polynesian race."[20] Outside the government, a community drive to collect Māori history sprang up in the Ngāti Kahungunu tribe at Pāpāwai in the Wairarapa district near Wellington, the scene of the Kotahitanga movement, which ran an independent Māori parliament at the time (McCarthy 2007a). Here the tribal history committee Tāne-nui-a-rangi gathered whakapapa and records of tribal whare wānanga (schools of learning) for publication, and tried to set up a museum, led by the energetic figure Tūnuiārangi (Major Brown), who later collaborated with Best in gathering historical information for the museum.[21] He was one of the people who initiated a major *hui* (meeting) in 1911 at Te Kuiti, attended by Ngata and Native Affairs Minister James Carroll (Timi Kara). At the meeting the modern idea of *Māoritanga*, or Māori cultural heritage, was popularized.[22]

The DM had become involved in this campaign when its director, Augustus Hamilton, became a trustee of the museum at Pāpāwai and attended hui where he was presented with the historical records that the Tāne-nui-a-rangi committee wanted published. When Best arrived at the museum in 1910, this contact with tribal experts increased through his language skills and extensive networks. Meanwhile, museum staff members independently became interested in ethnology, particularly with the arrival of the new director, J. Allan Thomson, who had taken classes at Oxford with Henry Balfour, and they began to think about how the institution could do more fieldwork using phonographs and other technology to assist in the collecting of data (Thomson 1915).[23] Best, in a report to Thomson about his planned research and publications, also pointed out the urgent need for fieldwork to consult the few elderly Māori knowledgeable about these practices while they were still living. The enterprising display artist James McDonald, who had already experimented with moving pictures in the Department of Tourism and Health

FIGURE 5.5 Āpirana Ngata and Peter Buck (Te Rangihīroa) making a *tukutuku* (lattice-work) panel at Ngata's house in Waiomatatini, during the Dominion Museum's ethno-logical expedition to the East Coast, 1923. James McDonald, 1/2-007887-F, Alexander Turnbull Library, Wellington. Courtesy of Alexander Turnbull Library.

The Dominion Museum's annual report of 1923 records the "keen interest shown by leading members of the Māori race in the Māori work of collection and preservation of the rapidly vanishing arts and crafts and tribal lore and songs of bygone days" (12). In fact, the East Coast expedition was initiated and supported by Ngata himself, and local Māori scholars participated enthusiastically in the recording of cultural practices and the visual and performing arts. Dr. Tūtere Wi Repa wrote that ethnological fieldwork encouraged the tribe to gather and preserve its own heritage using new technology. The "Poetry" of Ngāti Porou was captured by "scientific phonograph," and thus the "living voices" of the tribe could be heard "whenever desired" by asking the museum for records, so that the "living traces of them will be preserved for the benefit of their relatives" (*Evening Post*, April 18, 1923).

Resorts, was keen to go out and work in Māori communities (Dennis 1996). With the help of Ngata and his secretary, Te Raumoa Balneavis, they had already attended the Hui Aroha in Gisborne in 1919, where they recorded songs, dances, and speech as well as other cultural practices performed by the tribes gathered to welcome Māori soldiers home from the Great War. This was followed by larger expeditions to Whanganui in 1921 and the East Coast in 1923 (Henare 2005), which Ngata, Buck, and others enthusiastically supported and participated in.[24]

Next door to the museum, in the Parliament buildings, the Māori members of Parliament were mobilizing to secure state funding and resources for the research on Māori topics they had set out to advance. Ngata, Māui Pōmare, and Tau Henare approached reluctant Pakeha ministers seeking funds to buy recording equipment to capture songs and speech, and to publish Best's manuscripts, which were languishing at the museum without funds to get them into print.[25] In August 1923 Ngata convened a meeting to consider his "proposals for the creation of a fund to assist research into Maori and Polynesian History and Ethnology." However, he felt that the DM and the Polynesian Society were not up to the task and that there was an "urgent need for the creation of a fund devoted to the special purpose of Maori and Polynesian research."[26] This led to the formation of the BMER as part of the Native Land Amendment Act in 1923, followed in 1924 by the Maori Purposes Fund Board. The purpose of the BMER was the "study and investigation of the ancient arts and crafts, language, customs, history, tradition, and antiquities of the Maori and other cognate races of the South Pacific Ocean." The Maori Purposes Fund was also directed to research and cultural programs, such as the School of Maori Arts and Crafts, established in 1926–27, in addition to education, training, welfare, and other Māori "purposes."[27]

Through this "intervention," the "forceful and energetic" Ngata and his Māori colleagues took over the management and funding of Māori research, moving the Polynesian Society and its library to Wellington from New Plymouth, restructuring its governing council, and increasing the membership (Māori members trebled). With grants of several hundred pounds a year, the society was able to expand and improve its journal and to publish Best's Tūhoe book and several other Māori manuscripts (Sorrenson 1992: 60–63, 71). Because these grants came from Māori funds, Māori land boards, unclaimed rents, and funds held by the Native Trustee (60), the Māori members of the BMER insisted that it "devote serious attention to collections of tribal traditions and history, genealogical tables, Maori songs, and poetry, the recording of Maori music, and of features in the culture of the people—matters of greater interest to the Maori tribesmen than the generalizations and abstractions of scientists."[28] This generous assistance was welcomed by the old guard of the Polynesian Society, such as the amateur Pakeha ethnologist William Henry Skinner, but reading between the lines it was seen as a Māori takeover—Best told a friend privately that the board "does not want us Pakeha to control activities."[29] Even Skinner's son, H. D. Skinner, the only professionally trained anthropologist in the country, was added to the board only at the last minute and was somewhat marginalized (Cameron and McCarthy 2015). There was also tension with the Department of Internal Affairs, which resented the board's "interference" with the staff of the DM.[30]

"It is a highly gratifying thing to note," Best wrote in 1926, "that our Maori friends have at last seen the desirability of putting their racial and tribal lore on permanent record" (Condliffe 1971: 147–49). Buck himself later wrote that Best's writing exerted a "profound influence" on the "inarticulate students of lore who had Maori blood in their veins." He continued, "Ngata, Pomare and myself felt we should do something to carry on the work begun by Best, Percy Smith and others. . . . The result was the establishment of the BMER" (1932: 19). Johannes C. Andersen said of the BMER, which he erroneously but revealingly called the *Maori* Board of Ethnological Research, that it was a "tower of strength," and he looked forward to Māori scholars taking the lead in Polynesian research: "they themselves are striving for a renaissance of their arts; and when the Polynesian workers themselves enter the field, as they surely will, we stammering, thumb-fingered pakeha may stand aside and rejoice in the day-dawn" ([1928] 1969: 6–7).

What were the outcomes of this unprecedented indigenous intervention in government ethnological research? The BMER's early achievements were impressive: the backlog of material was effectively cleared through an "efficient and expeditious" program of publications.[31] This included, besides Best's *The Maori as He Was*, five DM bulletins, two memoirs of two volumes each for the Polynesian Society, four memoirs in the board's own series, and reprints of several out-of-print studies, including one by Buck.[32] The board was focusing now on editing and printing original Māori-language material that, they hoped, "will afford scope for writers other than expert ethnologists, and provide the original material for future research work" (8).

This wider community engagement was clear in the board's magazine, *Te Wananga*, which, apart from scholarly articles, reviewed "various branches of Maori work or endeavors on behalf of the race."[33] So was the effort to publicize the board's work with politicians, the press, and the general public. "If what is on record of Maori life were more fully known to the white population of New Zealand," wrote Sutherland, "their present situation would be better understood" (1935: 123). This position was put eloquently in relation to schooling in the book *Maori and Education*:

> Further; what is the reason for the comparatively recent energy displayed by the Maori in putting on record the history and poetry of his own people? I do not particularly refer to the thousand page history of the Tuhoe tribe written at their request by Elsdon Best; but to the material being printed by the Maori Board of Ethnological Research [*sic*]; the original mss of Nepia Pohuhu in *Te Wananga*, and the two hundred annotated songs . . . edited by Apirana Ngata. These are all in the Maori tongue, and practically without English notes. Does this not indicate an ardent desire on the part of the Maori for the preservation of the best in his literature, and its preservation in his own tongue? Cannot we then, who have hindered him so much in the past[,] . . . cannot we now assist him by educating his children in a way that will teach them to appreciate, not only the best in the English people and English literature, but the best in the Maori people and Maori literature also? (Andersen, quoted in Jackson 1931: 13)

The board also facilitated the collecting and recording of genealogical records, tribal histories, music, and performing arts, as well as carving and other visual arts that were being revived in the new meeting houses constructed by the School of Maori Arts and Crafts. Thus, we can see that from the late 1920s, and particularly after Ngata himself became the minister of Native affairs in 1928, state-funded political and cultural heritage programs were interwoven through a framework that retained cultural difference and resisted assimilation (McCarthy 2014b). In these schemes covering many aspects of Māori life, modernization and preservation went hand in hand (R. Hill 2004: 149, 146–50).

For example, the board funded a large hui in 1928 at Motuiti *pā* (village) in the Manawatū district, where aspects of "ethnological" research were discussed alongside more practical matters such as farming—social and economic development was always paired with cultural aspirations. It recommended that the BMER set up university departments of ethnology to train field-workers in "Maoridom and also native races in Island dependencies," a "practical laboratory" for both races that would serve "to guide and co-ordinate the constructive movements, external and internal, affecting the Maori people" (Keesing 1928: 182). This account comes from Keesing's *The Changing Maori*, a remarkable study published by the board that explored Ngata's policy of "cultural adaptation" (1928: 17) through the ways in which dairy and sheep farming policies in Ngata's own East Coast district were underpinned by aspects of customary culture drawn from ethnological research. How do leaders like Ngata "utilize the ethnic past as a basis for present re-construction?" he asked. Their goal was not the "passive absorption" of Māori into Pakeha society but "the reassertion of Maori *mana*" [reputation, respect, power, authority]. To preserve "racial character" and "renew pride and purpose among their people," he concluded, "the young leaders seek now to restore the best in their ancestral past: language, lore and history, arts and crafts" (169).

Ngata himself attached this idea of cultural adaptation to his policy and practice in the Department of Native Affairs. He argued for the gradual acceptance of the norms of European civilization through an understanding of the "elements" of Māori "mentality" that had survived colonization, but also for the maintenance of "aspects of indigenous culture and tradition" (1929: 32):

> I maintain that the function of Government in this country, as applied to the Maori race, has been to discover and appraise these elements, and especially to judge whether in their nature they are detrimental to progress on the lines newly laid down, or worth preserving in a modified form. It is in the disposition shown by legislators, educationalists, reformers, churchmen, and all who have had to do with the administration of Maori affairs to examine sympathetically these elements in the Native culture and to provide for them so that New Zealand may be regarded as the best example of success in the government of a Native race not only in the Pacific, but perhaps the world. (32)

This revised construction of "Maori mentality" prompted Ngata to advance more evolved and abstract ideas of Māori intellectual capacity. This can be seen in Ngata's (1931) report to Parliament on the land development schemes run by the Native department under his leadership; in this report, he reworked Firth's ideas about Māori adaptation to modern life, citing Buck's observation that Māori were "maintaining their individuality as a race and molding European culture to suit their requirements" (14). As Buck had told him in a letter: "It is the recognition of certain survival features in native culture that has largely contributed to any success we may have attained amongst our own people as empirical anthropologists advocating cultural adjustments" (quoted in Sorrenson 1987: 211).

Through Buck's later career as an anthropologist, the network described here was extended out into the administration of the colonies in New Zealand's fledging empire in the Cook Islands, Niue, and Samoa. As mentioned above, the BMER was set up with the express desire to conduct fieldwork on "cognate races of the Pacific"; in fact, by 1933 Buck thought it should be renamed the Board of *Polynesian* Research (Sorrenson 1988: 77). It funded Buck's trip to the Cook Islands, which in turn led to an offer to join the Bishop Museum's five-year expedition to the South Pacific. Buck, who eventually became the director of the museum and a professor of anthropology at Yale, saw his work on material culture in the Pacific as a natural extension of his Māori research on weaving and other topics at home (Buck 1927). Aside from the many parallels in culture and society that were explored in Buck's published work, there were clear contemporary affinities and interests between Māori and Pacific Island people in terms of their responses to European technology, particularly this theme of cultural contact, change, and adaptation.

While Buck was conducting research around the Pacific from the late 1920s on, and intermittently acting as a government registrar or magistrate, back in Wellington Ngata was in the center of government, at the helm of the Department of Native Affairs and also responsible for the Cook Islands. Up to the late 1930s Ngata and Buck's close relationship was maintained through a lengthy correspondence, which shows how their mutual interests in anthropology shaped, and were shaped by, problems of cultural adaptation, identity, and race. Buck told Ngata that, as Māori, they had an insider view of the field of study, which gave them an advantage over their European colleagues. "In Polynesian research," Buck wrote, "it is right and fitting that the highest branch of the Polynesian race should be in the forefront and not leave the bulk of the investigations to workers who have not got the inside angle that we have." He added, "They miss things that are significant to us" (quoted in Sorrenson 1986: 48).

The lessons for colonial administrators from Buck's research in the Pacific were the same as in New Zealand: the gradual adjustment of native people to European culture through sympathetic knowledge and understanding while retaining the "best" of their ancestral culture. On a visit to New Zealand in 1936, Buck told a reporter about his anthropological research in the Pacific, stressing this theme of the persistence of cultural forms that Ngata also preached: "Speaking about the culture being manifested by the native peoples in the Pacific, Dr Buck said it was really strange that the new culture was really native in spite of European food, clothes, utensils and manners.

There was a change in the material and economic life, but the spirit at the back of it all was thoroughly Polynesian."[34]

If we can see the anthropological archive compiled by the BMER at work in the Pacific, back in New Zealand it helped shape the work of Māori administrators, who sought to support their people while working within government structures. For example, Edward Pohau Ellison (Erihana), a doctor and the director of the Division of Māori Hygiene, cited contemporary social data, including a rising population, as "Factors of Regeneration" that operated toward "uplift and preservation of the race," a phenomenon that the Māori people themselves had taken responsibility for: "The clash of cultures following colonization having brought about conditions inimical to the preservation of the race, it remained for the Maori to take stock of the root-causes inducing his decay, and then take action. He is doing so. The same inherent qualities of adaptability and plasticity previously mentioned have been summoned up to combat the forces of a superior culture. If he were to win through, he was to help himself. He is winning through" (Ellison 1931: 289).

However, despite these successes in influencing governance and governing, Ngata ultimately seems to have felt that exhibitions and public events had more potential than museums to project the collecting and ordering of the Māori past into a public representation of the Māori present and future. A little after the DM opened in 1936, Wellington hosted the Centennial Exhibition in 1940 celebrating a hundred years since the Treaty of Waitangi (figure 5.6). Here Ngata had a freer hand to shape the final form of the Maori Court, which had a much more contemporary feel to its celebration of arts and crafts in national life than the museum did. The centerpiece of the court was a modernized meeting house, assembled from various sources including the collections of the DM and new carvings from the School of Maori Arts and Crafts. The souvenir booklet explained that this "blend of a beautiful ancient form with modern adaptations" reflected the "Maori renaissance." Māori people did not see these cultural treasures as "curiosities" or "relics" but as "symbols of their social life" that demonstrated that "the Maori people still retains after one hundred years an individuality of its own."[35]

The performances of the Ngāti Pōneke concert party were an even more important vehicle for this message of modern adaptation (figure 1.5). As with the revival of visual arts fueled through ethnology and museum collections, customary Māori performing arts had undergone a spirited revival in the 1920s and 1930s fostered by the board's "fieldwork," which recorded speech, songs, and cultural practices such as *pōwhiri* (welcomes), opening ceremonies, and so on. Like the other areas of "traditional" cultural heritage, *kapa*

FIGURE 5.6 Image on the mural at the entrance to the Government Court, New Zealand Centennial Exhibition, Wellington, 1940. Frontispiece, *Official Guide to the Government Court: New Zealand Centennial Exhibition 1939–40* (Wellington: Centennial Exhibition Company, 1939), n.p.

———

This photograph of Prime Minister Joseph Savage and a Māori warrior shaking hands was displayed as a mural facing viewers as they entered the Government Court at the Centennial Exhibition, which celebrated a hundred years of nationhood since the signing of the Treaty of Waitangi. The year 1840 appears above the warrior, and the year 1940 above Savage, suggesting that Māori represented the past and Pakeha (European New Zealanders) the present and future. This image appears to be a classic statement of assimilation. However, at the time Māori leaders thought differently. At the opening ceremony, tribal speakers stated that, through the treaty, they became one with the Pakeha people, but they also asserted the survival of Māori culture. It seems that Māori saw the treaty, as they saw museums, anthropology, and government, as a means to maintain their identity and forge a more independent future. Indeed, after the 1935 election, Māori voters were newly enfranchised as independent Rātana Party candidates swept into all four Māori seats in league with the Labour Party (Walker 2004: 339).

———

haka (action songs) were clearly a combination of older elements reworked into contemporary form with Western harmony, guitars, and theatricality. They were nonetheless regarded by tribal elders as authentic *taonga*, treasures or expressions of Māoriness. In a letter to Ngata after the Waitangi celebrations in February 1934, Eru Ihaaka described the haka as a taonga that had been overlooked in ignorance but now was "dear to my heart," as with "all my children."[36]

Aside from cultural revival and tribal pride, Ngata's motivation in putting on a show (which he sometimes referred to as a "stunt") for external audiences—not just for the Pakeha public but especially for government officials and overseas dignitaries—was to impress on them the progress of Māori development and their continuing need for official support, funding, and resources. He orchestrated enormous public displays: in Ngāruawāhia for the opening of *Mahinaarangi* in 1926, in Rotorua for the visiting Duke of York in 1927, and in Waitangi in 1934 for the celebration of the gifting of the treaty house (the occasion also marked the declaration of independence by the united tribes in 1834), culminating in the centennial celebrations of the signing of the Treaty of Waitangi in 1940 (figure 5.7).

COLLECTING, ORDERING, AND GOVERNING THE MĀORI: FROM ASSIMILATION TO INTEGRATION IN INTERWAR NEW ZEALAND

You cannot understand material culture without some knowledge of the psychology of the minds that found expression from their physical needs and social, sexual and religious aspirations, in material artifacts. . . . It is a pity that our one professional anthropologist in New Zealand has a complex that stands in the way of whole-hearted co-operation. —Peter Buck to Johannes Andersen, November 19, 1934

In the letter quoted above, Māori anthropologist Buck confided in his friend, the librarian Johannes C. Andersen, his criticisms of H. D. Skinner, which illuminate for us the differences and similarities between the parts of the anthropological assemblage described in this chapter. For Buck, objects in museum collections had to be connected to "the living culture of the people."[37] He thus suggested that Skinner's work at the University of Otago and OM was out of touch with Māori concerns for *taonga tuku iho* (treasures handed down), which were seen as living embodiments of ancestral mana (power, authority, reputation). Buck and Ngata were even at times critical of Best, because they thought he was long-winded and apt to fanciful theories. Though they valued his fieldwork, they put the data he collected to work in

FIGURE 5.7 Āpirana Ngata leads a *haka* (posture dance) in front of the recently completed meeting house on the hundredth anniversary of the signing of the Treaty of Waitangi, Bay of Islands, 1940. MNZ-2746, Alexander Turnbull Library, Wellington. Courtesy of Alexander Turnbull Library.

At a major festival at Waitangi in 1940, the first time New Zealand's founding document, the Treaty of Waitangi, was publicly celebrated, the Māori Member of Parliament Sir Āpirana Ngata made sure that the symbols of nationhood included both treaty partners: Māori and Pakeha. Alongside the restored treaty house, symbolizing the Crown, was the carved meeting house *Te Tiriti o Waitangi*, representing the Māori signatories, whose equal status was recognized through the treaty. This house was constructed by the School of Maori Arts and Crafts under Ngata's leadership based on models in the Auckland Museum. A major festival of performing arts at its opening proved that Māori culture was alive and well, and the defiant haka in front of the meeting house, led by Ngata himself, declared in no uncertain terms the Māori demand for inclusion in modern New Zealand.

different ways. "The Maori as he was" was valued by Māori political activists as far as it went, but ultimately it was more useful in throwing light on the Māori present and future: the Māori as they are and will be.

Between 1890 and 1940 the transactional reality formed by the shifting employment of "the Maori as he was" moved from salvage (Cheeseman and Best) to the definition of capacity and future potential (Skinner and Buck) to development and revival (Ngata and Buck). Cheeseman and Skinner's "dead" material culture approach was clearly visible at Auckland and Otago, while Buck and Ngata's emphasis on the "living culture" and performing arts could be seen in Wellington. The ways in which these were woven into public culture were also quite different. At the AWMM Cheeseman looked back to an earlier naturalist, evolutionary, and typological style of collecting and display that lingered on in all of these museums. Best was also a product of older discourses of conquest, salvage, and eugenics, but just as his work was overtaken by new, more liberal discourses of culture and society, so was his work at the DM, which became caught up in the plans of Māori politicians, on the one hand, and resurgent Māori communities, on the other. Meanwhile, in Dunedin, Skinner worked through museum displays, university teaching, and the training of government administrators in a largely patronizing model of social governance, whereas for the BMER the knowledge, collections, and ethnological data about weaving, carving, and the performing arts were simultaneously aimed at changing government policy to allow for a degree of self-government, as well as preserving and developing these living arts in tribal regions.

At this point we turn to consider the major themes emerging from this analysis across the different parts of the New Zealand assemblage. We make a series of general observations. The first concerns the question of changing native culture. There is abundant evidence of the Antipodean career of the Boasian culture concept, which came into New Zealand from America and gained traction locally, in tension with another strand of American anthropology that retained traces of evolutionary science. Second, the New Zealand case reveals interesting theoretical and historical parallels with, as well as differences from, Australia and the other national contexts discussed in this book in terms of armchair–field relations, the organization of actor networks across these, and the relations between centers of collection and centers of calculation. In contrast to our other cases, the museum is decentered, particularly in Wellington. There, Ngata controlled affairs across and through several related bodies; Best retreated from the field to his office at the museum and library, where he writes up his work; and Skinner occupied a museum-university position simultaneously mixing teaching, fieldwork, and publishing. We might say that OM and the University of Otago constituted both a center of collection and a center of calculation in view of how these practices straddled the university and museum, thus collapsing the distance between metropole, colony, museum, and field in the context of a small country.

Third is the pervasiveness of the concept of the "Maori mind." The concept emerged as an apparatus and surface for administrative calculation through which different modalities of liberal rule were formulated and used to calibrate different forms of freedoms (and their limits) and therefore different formulations of the relations between Māori and Pakeha populations and governing practices. A key point of contention between Skinner and the Māori cohort was the evidence used to calibrate the state of the "Maori mind": the former relied on material culture, and the latter on a combined approach utilizing material culture alongside more intangible forms of heritage to elucidate cultural practices (Buck 1934).

From these evaluations of the Maori mind, the extent to which freedoms and the constraints on those freedoms could be conferred on the population could then be ascertained. Hence, the assessment and calibration of the state of the "Maori mind," and more specifically of Māori intellectual capacity, equated with governing through the conferment of freedom. Interestingly, in each of these calculations freedom is not taken as a given; rather, attention has to be paid to what the evidence suggests, and claims must be put forward to support the respective governing rationalities.

Throughout the early twentieth century, we find Māori intellectuals appealing to the Native "mentality" in advancing their claims for some indigenous control over their own affairs, positioning themselves as a subject of freedom within the colonial administration. Anthropology and museums provided the ethnological evidence for a distinctive Māori mental outlook thanks to the "new psychology" that was then becoming popular overseas and had been introduced to New Zealand by Sutherland. Influenced by the work of William Halse Rivers Rivers and Paul Radin, particularly the latter's *Primitive Man as Philosopher* ([1927] 2008), which dismissed the idea of primitive mentality, Sutherland in his article "The Study of Maori Mind" (1929) disputed the idea that Māori were not capable of abstract thought, drawing in large part on the sophisticated tribal traditions being collected and published by the BMER (O. Sutherland 2013: 152–53, 157–58). Ngata quickly picked up this idea, which fueled his subsequent policy and government reports in reinforcing the need to take account of Māori difference, which was clear in the way they had *adjusted* to modern civilization but *remained* Māori because their outlook was different from that of Europeans (Ngata 1931). In a speech in Parliament in 1929 seeking more state funding for Māori farming, Ngata stated boldly that "the whole of the Native problems are bound up with what the scientists call the problem of cultural adaptation" (quoted in I. Sutherland 1950: 313).

Meanwhile, in Auckland, Cheeseman's archive supported the concept of a distinct Māori mentality and individuality, but he did not support separate development as such and was much more conservative than the others canvassed in this analysis. Despite their differences, Skinner and Ngata shared these governing orientations within the existing political system; by detailing dispositions and forms of expertise rooted in "old" ways of life that could be redeployed for the modern nation, each sought clues on how Māori could adapt their culture to modern life.[38] Cheeseman sought to detail all these things through his complete archive and his focus on the state of the Māori mind through his material illustrations of aesthetic achievement, technical capacities, and therefore intellectual acuity, while Skinner did so through his trait lists of material culture, his documentation of the material manifestations of the Maori psychological condition, and the writing of cultural histories using theories of independent invention, diffusion, and affiliation. Ngata, on the other hand, sought to find these clues to the Māori mentality through the recording of living cultures, not just written accounts of tribal tradition but also speech, proverbs, and visual and performing arts.

Despite an epistemological divide between Buck and Ngata, on the one hand, and the other Pakeha scholars, on the other, particularly around attitudes toward history, culture, and language, there were similarities. In fact, "the mind" is used by all of the actors across the New Zealand anthropological assemblage, and the notion of Māori mentality is reassembled in different but related ways, all creating a platform for the integration of Māori into public life, as opposed to earlier discourses of administration based on race and eugenics. Skinner and Cheeseman calibrated the Māori mind through their close analysis of artifacts and archaeological evidence, exploring capacity and potential, and level of sophistication, whereas for Best access to the mythopoetic Māori was gained through their myths and legends. Whereas Best thought the material culture of his Native friends was relatively crude and "barbaric," he was certain their spiritual beliefs were on a higher plane, a religion in fact. While Skinner articulated his position by stating that New Zealand's greatest socioeconomic problem was the *incorporation* of Māori people into the body of New Zealand society, with his analysis of artifacts demonstrating their ability to adapt and assimilate, the more liberal adaptation discourses articulated by Ngata and his colleagues referred to an *adjustment* of Māori society to the modern day in an *equal* relationship with Pakeha, on one hand referring to social evolutionary notions of adaptive potential and on the other reflecting a more independent notion of Māori self-determination that was post-assimilationist (I. Sutherland 1940).[39]

THE MĀORI AS LIBERAL SUBJECT

It is clear from the foregoing discussion that the organization of the relations between the practices of collecting, ordering, and governing played out in distinctive ways in New Zealand. *Collecting* took many forms, not predominantly through artifacts but rather through the recording of social practices and intangible heritage; *ordering* was a varied, porous, and at times contradictory activity with several schema operating at once; and *governing* included everything from paternalist government assimilation policies for the indigenous population to the incorporation of Māori imagery into a national imaginary and moves toward self-government by and for Māori. The last point draws attention to one key theme that emerges from the analysis of this assemblage: indigenous agency. This is evident in the partnerships between Best and his informants or coauthors, in the role the BMER played in publishing Best's fieldwork as well as Māori-language material for Māori audiences, and, clearest of all, in the links between this collecting of diverse material and the anthropological governance steered through the Department of Native Affairs (by no less than the *Native* minister of Native affairs). Last, as well as collecting, ordering, and governing, *exhibiting* operated laterally *across* the country in a distributed fashion not accounted for in previous linear studies of individuals and institutions: for example, the AWMM's Maori Court was duplicated around the country, and Best's nomenclature for objects, using Māori names and concepts, was adopted in labels on display throughout the museum sector.

In the comparative transnational framework of our research, it is the indigenous intervention in colonial museums, anthropology, and liberal government that is most striking. This Māori interpretation of "the Maori as he was," what Ngata called "the appreciation of what he has become, and the assessment of his probable future" (1928: 8), aimed to support cultural revival and to underpin tribal social and economic development through the blending of Māori and Pakeha culture. In its advocacy of this conception, the BMER adopted a more flexible Boasian notion of culture connected to a more independent vision of Māori social development. In that sense, in

New Zealand the rationalities afforded by a Boasian conception of "culture" had greater traction with Māori intellectuals intent on reshaping government policy in a more tolerant direction, in contrast to the more reactionary ideas about race and culture from Wissler and others that were espoused by Pakeha anthropologists like Skinner. This vision of past and present-becoming-future—what we referred to as "becoming Māori" in chapter 1—can be seen in a wide public domain: museum display, ethnological research, public policy, and the performing arts. It took on quite a different look from the work of the dry academics and dilettante gentleman collectors, in the form of lively public events, spirited cultural revival, and community engagement.

We should not understate the intervention of Ngata and his cohort in this overall context, although it was admittedly short, limited, and partial in its achievements. Yet much was achieved in comparison with other settler colonies. As historian Richard Hill has demonstrated, the Native Land Amendment and Native Claims Adjustment Act of 1929 funded Māori farming, effectively "underpinning a communal way of life based on tribal values and organising principles" and in so doing "sustaining the nexus between the quest for *rangatiratanga* (chieftainship, sovereignty) and the viability of retaining . . . land based self-determination" (2004: 117). Through the land development schemes, tribal leaders were placed in key positions and revived their traditional roles, preserving the "communal ethos" of Māori society (118). By 1930 Ngata's restructured Department of Native Affairs was indisputably the "ultimate corporate entity for regulating and controlling Māori affairs" (149) in social and economic development, not to mention arts and cultural heritage (see also Butterworth 1990).

By the mid-1930s Ngata's career as a cabinet minister may have been over, but many of his policies lived on (I. Sutherland 1940). As Hill (2004: 149) argues, Ngata resigned to save the land settlement schemes, which, far from being scrapped after the commission of enquiry, were maintained and even expanded under the progressive Labour government that came to power in 1935. Even in the 1940s and 1950s, areas of government policy and practice such as state housing, health, welfare, education, and employment reflected the liberal principles and aspirations of the Young Maori Party, for example, the Maori Social and Economic Advancement Act of 1945 (Hill 2004).

After World War II, when the Maori Battalion's sacrifice in Europe was recognized as "the price of citizenship" (Ngata 1943), the Department of "Native" Affairs became Maori Affairs, and the last discriminatory laws and regulations were removed. In the postwar period, the official government approach—even with right-wing National Party government—was now integrationism, announced in the Hunn report of 1961 (Hunn 1961). Even later, in the 1970s and 1980s, this moderate policy of integration was overturned by pressure from liberal Pakeha and Māori protests articulating aspirations to greater self-determination, resulting in the policy of "biculturalism" (two peoples, one country), which advocated public institutions as vanguards of cultural diversity—such as the new national Museum of New Zealand/ Te Papa Tongawera, which opened in 1998 (R. Hill 2009; Bönisch-Brednich and Hill 2009; Fleras and Spoonley 1999). These developments in bicultural state formation and the accommodation of difference within modern New Zealand can be traced back to the early years of the twentieth century, which were discussed in this chapter. Both Ngata and Buck were committed to the survival of Māori and Pacific Island peoples and the maintenance of their culture, what they called "the efforts to save the worthiest in our past while seeking elements in the new culture applicable to our conditions" (Buck in Sorrenson 1987: 42). Their historical research and political and economic work as leaders and scholars was ultimately directed at the problems of the present. It aimed to construct a Polynesian past as a platform for the future, through pride in the achievements of ancestors. Producing "the Maori as he was" through books, displays, events, architecture, museums, and other media was the means to this end.

CHAPTER SIX

ETHNOLOGY, GOVERNANCE, AND GREATER FRANCE

Our concerns in this chapter focus on the project of ethnology, and its constitutive contradictions, as it was shaped by the political logics of Greater France—initially in the interwar years, most particularly during the period of the Popular Front, and subsequently during the Vichy period. In pursuing these we probe the relations between the practices of collecting, ordering, and governing that were articulated across a network of institutions connecting Paris, Indochina, and provincial France. The impetus for these developments can be traced to the period immediately before World War I—when concerns about imperial competition raised pressing questions about the role anthropology could and should play in French colonial projects—and to the war's immediate aftermath in view of the revised conceptions of colonial powers' responsibilities under the League of Nations' mandate system. However, our concerns are centered more closely on the institutional developments through which the project of ethnology was shaped from the mid-1920s onward, and particularly after 1928—the year Paul Rivet was appointed director of the Musée d'Ethnographie du Trocadéro (MET) and, in close collaboration with his deputy, Georges Henri Rivière, initiated a program of reform that radically transformed the MET's practices.

This program was developed through the projection of two new museums—the Musée de l'Homme (MH) and its sibling, the Musée des Arts et Traditions Populaires (ATP)—that were eventually established in their own right, albeit under separate administrations, in 1938 and 1937 respectively.[1] It was during the period of their incubation in the MET, however, that the distinctive signatures of both museums were forged, and we shall follow convention in referring to them by their names during this period even though they had no legal or administrative status separate from that of the MET. That said, our choice of the MH's satellite museum in Indochina—the Musée de l'Homme, Hanoi (MH HAN)—as the primary locus for our engagement with the political trajectories of French ethnology does focus mainly on the post-1938 period. Although largely neglected, the MH HAN (figure 6.1) provides a strategic point of entry into the practices of the MH and ATP that we wish to highlight: the parallels and interrelations between practices of collecting in the metropolitan center of Paris and in French colonies, the interrelations between the practices of ordering characterizing archival and exhibition practices in both contexts, and the transference of governmental rationalities across the relations between France's colonial and regional populations.

The developments that we shall trace across the period from the mid-1920s to the late 1930s constituted the key phase in the catch-up program for French ethnography that Marcel Mauss had proposed in 1913 when he compared its current state unfavorably with that of its British, American, Dutch, and German counterparts. And the comparison was unfavorable in all regards: ethnography in France was backward in its practices of collecting owing to its lack of a developed fieldwork tradition; inadequate in its practices of ordering, as evidenced by the muddled confusion of its exhibition practices and the lack of any clear differentiation of a scientific "laboratory" function from ethnography's public education role; and deficient in its contribution to the tasks of colonial administration (Mauss [1913] 1969). The program of reform that Rivet initiated operated on each of these three dimensions. It aspired to develop a program of fieldwork that would establish the MH's collecting practices on a scientific footing on an empire-wide basis. It sought to rationalize exhibition practices, drawing on the models of popular democratic instruction represented by museums in the United States, Scandinavia, and Soviet Russia, in order to transform the ramshackle MET into a beacon of rationalized public instruction.[2] And it sought to endow the MH with an archival and laboratory function, a locus for the scientific training of future field-workers and colonial administrators, which would make it a center of and for colonial governance.

In pursuing these objectives, the MH formed part of the development of a new institutional ensemble—reviewed in chapter 1—centered on the triadic

FIGURE 6.1 "The Musée de l'Homme, Hanoi, Vietnam, 30 November 1938." EFEO VIE 04249, École Française d'Extrême-Orient, Paris. Courtesy of the École Française d'Extrême-Orient.

———

This photograph was taken after the official visit of the governor-general of Indochina on November 30, 1938, the day of the inauguration of the Musée de l'Homme, Hanoi. Georges Coedès, the main force behind the Hanoi museum, is pictured in the foreground. The museum was created as an anthropological and ethnographic section of the economic museum, the Musée Maurice Long. This is reflected in the written text on the door "École Française d'Extrême-Orient. Musée de l'Homme. Exposition de recherche anthropologique et ethnographique récentes." The Musée Maurice Long was located in a neoclassical building designed by André Buissy for the 1902 Hanoi Exposition; the building itself was modeled on the Grand Palais (Paris) with a facade more than a hundred meters long. The Musée de l'Homme, Hanoi was envisaged as a replica of the metropolitan museum, a sign of the mutual mirroring characterizing the relationship between metropolis and colony.

———

relations between itself, the Institut d'Ethnologie de Paris, established in 1925, and the university. This ensemble, however, far from including the whole of French ethnography, represented only a specific wing of it—and one that, for reasons we will come to, defined itself as ethnology in contradistinction to those traditions that went under the heading of anthropology. It was, moreover, initially subordinate to these latter traditions, which for most of the first three decades of the twentieth century had the preponderant political influence. The details of this period need not detain us. Suffice it to say that after Paul Broca's death and the demise of a radically secular and social reform–orientated conception of anthropology's political vocation that he represented (Hecht 2003), Louis Marin, director of the École d'Anthropologie, was a force to be reckoned with. As president of the right-wing Fédération Républicaine and its leader in the Chamber of Deputies, Marin occupied a prominent position in the political field from the early 1900s through to 1937, when he played a role in fusing the Fédération Républicaine with the fascist Parti Populaire Français to establish the Front de la Liberté as a right-wing alternative to the Popular Front and as a counter to Rivet's influence as a founding member of the Comité de Vigilance des Intellectuels Antifascistes. Strongly opposed to the scientific rationalism of the Durkheimian–Maussian tradition in favor of the enrollment of amateurs in the networks of collecting that he presided over, Marin articulated a racialized conception of—as Herman Lebovics (1992) calls it—"True France" as a singular and defining norm of Frenchness to which local identities (provincial and colonial) were to be conformed within the political logics of Greater France. This conservative conception of anthropology's political vocation was the vis-à-vis against which the project of ethnology—comprising a distinctive fusion of the physical anthropology of the Broca tradition and the ethnography of the Durkheimian–Maussian tradition—pitched itself and which, by the late 1930s, it had outflanked by dint of its greater professionalism and the footing it had secured in the university sector, the institutions of colonial governance, and a reformed museum sector. However, the revived currency of Marin's conception of anthropology was also an aspect of the changed political and intellectual environment the project of ethnology had to contend with in the Vichy period.

This background offers a brief sketch of the contexts in which the practices of the three institutions we shall look at—the MH, the MH HAN, and the ATP—developed. In Australia and, to a lesser extent, New Zealand, the early twentieth-century relations between museums and anthropology formed part of the emergence of national governmental domains that had acquired a greater degree of autonomy from the imperial domain of Great Britain. The project of French ethnology, by contrast, was shaped by a conception of Greater France that, exceeding the boundaries of the nation-state, aspired to bring the peoples of its colonies and its regions together as bearers of a shared set of identities while at the same time differentiating them in terms of their economic, social, and civic roles and entitlements.

We enter into these issues first by exploring the light that the establishment of the MH HAN in 1938 throws on the intersecting political and epistemological trajectories that shaped the relations between metropolitan France and Indochina during the period of the MH's and the ATP's incubation in the MET. We then look more closely at the circulation of objects and ordering practices between the MH and the MH HAN. In doing so, we draw on Kapil Raj's (2013) "circulatory perspective" to indicate the respects in which Bruno Latour's (1987) account of the relations between centers of calculation and sites of collection needs to be qualified to account for the particular pattern of the two-way flows between them that was instanced by the relations between the MH and the MH HAN. We continue this line of argument in moving on to consider the relations between the exhibition practices of these two institutions, which, in turn, instantiated the ambiguous relations between race and culture as overlapping transactional realities informing the governmental programs of ethnology. This line of inquiry also shapes our discussion of the MH HAN's construction of "Far Eastern Man." We conclude, however, by returning to mainland France to consider the respects in which the project of colonial ethnology informed the practices of the ATP and the ways in which these both resembled and differed from the historically parallel project of an "anthropology of ourselves" that was represented by Mass-Observation.

THE MUSÉE DE L'HOMME, HANOI'S NETWORKS IN THE METROPOLIS AND IN FRENCH INDOCHINA

A photograph taken in February 1939 at the MH HAN shows miniatures of Indochinese houses (figure 6.2). Metropolitan museums quite often commissioned models of houses or temples because they were easily transportable to Europe and could help visitors visualize the actual forms of the buildings. Yet, in this case, the models were displayed in a museum located in a French colony. They were accompanied by a written panel: "Smoking prohibited. Touching prohibited" (Défense absolue de fumer. Défense absolue de toucher). That these two phrases were written both in French and in *quốc ngữ* (the Latin-based orthography for Vietnamese) suggests that the museum took

FIGURE 6.2 "Vietnam. Musée de l'Homme: Models of Indochinese houses, 14 February 1939." The signs in French and in *quốc ngữ* (the Latin-based orthography for Vietnamese) remind visitors not to smoke or touch the models (Habitations indochinoises. Défense absolue de fumer. Défense absolue de toucher). EFEO VIE 04259, École Française d'Extrême-Orient, Paris. Courtesy of the École Française d'Extrême-Orient.

———

Located between the "Archaeology and History in Indochina" section and the Indochinese anthropology section of the Musée de l'Homme Hanoi this so-called ethnographic display did not provide any specific information about the miniature houses featured in the exhibition. The models functioned as object lessons by means of which visitors could learn through their senses. In contrast to the other two sections, which contained written texts and charts, the miniatures were deemed to speak for themselves. The raw materials used for constructing the houses had economic value, thus reinforcing the presumed links between the economic museum and the ethnographic one within the Musée Maurice Long.

———

account of its relations with its local population. But who was the MH HAN addressing? For Rivet the value of ethnographic centers and local museums in the colonies was that they would allow tourists, colonials, and civil servants to document in situ the customs of the populations they visited, with whom they worked, or who were under their administration (Rivet 1936: 7.08.5). But who were the MH HAN's visitors? And how did they experience the museum's displays? There is very little information on these matters. We know that the MH HAN was open six days per week and that it recorded 3,763 visitors in 1939; that in 1940 there were between three to four hundred visitors per month, mostly students; and that in 1941 the number of visitors was estimated at 2,657.[3] Does this mean that the prohibitions regarding smoking and touching were addressed to Indochinese students, or that the museum's organizers expected a larger contingent of indigenous visitors who did not show up?

These two prohibitions constituted specific techniques for regulating the conduct of local visitors within the museum's space. Examining how particular forms of power are constituted within museum practices, even by means of mundane details, such as labels and captions (Bennett 2004: 5), sheds light on the operations through which subjects are governed and regulated. It could be argued that the miniatures of houses were not displayed inside showcases—as was the case with other objects on display—so that it was necessary to remind visitors that touching was prohibited. As for the prohibition of smoking, it could also be argued that the nature of the materials—wood and bamboo—used for the miniatures presented a risk of fire. These two pragmatic explanations might provide a partial answer, but they leave aside the question of why this was the museum's only text written both in French and in quốc ngữ. One plausible answer might be that this presumed "ethnographic" section was deemed to attract local visitors who were familiar with the types of houses represented by the miniatures and thus did not need any further information about the objects. The only information provided by the museum that was directed to local visitors concerned how one should behave in a public space. The very fact that there was no general indication of the section's content—no written panel on the wall—suggests that the miniatures of houses played the role of object lessons, speaking for themselves. By contrast, the caption accompanying the photograph of the miniatures—"Indochinese houses" (*habitations indochinoises*)—was undoubtedly addressed to the metropolitan public, aiming to give an imaginary representation of the colony and of its inhabitants.

The designation *Indochina* is itself a colonial construct, or, to use Pa-nivong Norindr's terms, an "imperial fantasy[,] an elaborate fiction, a mod-ern phantasmatic assemblage invented during the heyday of French colonial hegemony in Southeast Asia" (1996: 1). The term *Indochina* covered diverse ethnic groups and regions subjected to French rule, and one of the ways of making visible this colonial invention was precisely by and through the practices of collecting, ordering, and display both at the MH in Paris and at its satellite in the colony.[4] The caption "Indochinese houses" refers to what Barbara Kirshenblatt-Gimblett (1991: 389) calls "putative cultural wholes": on the one hand, the museum displayed miniatures of houses rather than "real" houses; on the other hand, "Indochinese houses" existed only as museum artifacts created within a particular colonial context, referencing a projected conception of Indochinese-ness that was the product of a specific set of metropolitan–colonial relations.

The MH HAN was opened in 1938, a year after the official opening of the MH in Paris, as part of Rivet's strategy to provide an ethnographic center with a museum attached to it in each French colony. Although an ethnographic museum in Indochina under the joint directorship of the École Française d'Extrême-Orient (EFEO)—the main research center focused on the archae-ology and linguistics of ancient Asian civilizations (Singaravélou 2009)—and the governor-general of Indochina had been planned since the 1920s, this initiative took concrete shape only in the wake of Rivet's mission to Indo-china in 1932 (Dias 2014). That said, the MH HAN was not established as a distinct institution but rather as a part of the Musée Maurice Long, a com-mercial and industrial museum named after a former governor-general of Indochina (Le Brusq 2007). The creation of the MH HAN was largely due to the efforts of Georges Coedès (the EFEO's director from 1929 to 1947), who took advantage of the Hanoi Fair that was scheduled to open in November 1938 to suggest that an ethnographic section be set up at the Musée Maurice Long. According to Coedès there would be no discontinuity between the two museums. Since the Musée Maurice Long was devoted to economy and con-tained local products such as raw materials used for housing construction, it was already a sort of "ethnological museum" in which "visitors could move naturally from ethnology to economy."[5] This conception of a smooth transi-tion from ethnology to economy reflected their close governmental articula-tion in a colonial project that aimed to increase the economic productivity of colonial labor through "sympathetic" action on colonial milieus guided by ethnological expertise.[6]

The establishment of the MH HAN was not an isolated event. To the contrary, it formed part of a wide array of institutions and events, in both France and Indochina, that, through 1937 and 1938, debated the role ethnology could play in colonial governance. As Alice Conklin has pointed out, 1937 "proved a turning point in 'selling' ethnology as a necessary colonial science to public authorities in the metropolis and overseas" (2013: 227). A conference organized by the Association Colonies-Sciences that was held in Paris in 1937 led to the formation of the Comité Consultatif des Recherches Scientifiques de la France d'Outre-Mer to coordinate research initiatives useful for colonization and to allocate public funds for this purpose on an empire-wide basis. It was also in 1937 that the Service Ethnologique (Ethnological Service) was created at the EFEO under the direction of Paul Lévy (Clémentin-Ojha and Manguin 2001: 176–78). This service was responsible for conducting surveys and organizing several ethnographic museums and/or ethnographic sections in archaeological museums. Lévy himself helped to found a new learned society, the Institut Indochinois pour l'Étude de l'Homme (IIEH), also in 1937, and was the director of the MH HAN.[7] In other words, the Service Ethnologique, the IIEH, and the MH HAN were part of a general plan conceived by Rivet to establish the MH as the coordinating center of an institutional network of museums and research institutes operating in the French colony.

These, then, are among the institutional networks specifically focused on the relations between France and Indochina that formed a part of the wider anthropological assemblage that had the MH as its organizing center, which we discussed in chapter 1. We should, however, properly refer to this as an *ethnological assemblage* in view of the distinctive meanings and political affiliations of the terms *anthropology* and *ethnology* in the French context. Anthropology in France in the second half of the nineteenth century was conceived as a broad science, a natural history of Man, incorporating physical anthropology, prehistoric archaeology, and ethnography. This conception of a totalizing and synthetic science, which was sustained by Broca, soon gave way to a more restricted notion of anthropology as physical anthropology, in which the study of cultural traits was subordinated to the analysis of anatomical characteristics. As for *ethnology*, this became the preferred term, in the late 1920s, for a new conception of a totalizing and synthesizing discipline encompassing physical anthropology, ethnography in the Maussian tradition, and prehistoric archaeology.

Two traits characterized French ethnology: first, it remained primarily a museum-based discipline, although, in the case of the MH, with developing connections to the university (Jamin 1989; Debaene 2010). As we have seen in earlier chapters, the view that anthropology moved out of museums and into university settings in the early twentieth century rides roughshod over a number of different articulations of the relations between museums and universities in the conduct of anthropological practices in Anglophone settings. And it has little purchase in the French context. Here, the greatest contrast is with the American case, where, as have seen in chapter 4, the relations between museum-based anthropology and its conduct in universities were significantly divided along political lines: its eugenicist variants retained a significant foothold in the former, while the latter affiliated itself more with the liberal Boasian tradition. This pattern was reversed in France, where the MH provided the primary institutional basis for ethnology as the heir to the earlier liberal and humanistic values of museum-based traditions. The first French ethnographic museum, the MET was founded in Paris in 1878 in the wake of the Universal Exhibition of that year. Like other ethnographic museums of this time, the MET aimed to display human difference, particularly racial and cultural difference, and the development of human civilization through the linkage of race and progress (Dias 1991). It is worth emphasizing that the conception of physical difference, that is, of *natural* inequality between human groups, was developed not by conservatives but by liberal anthropologists committed to the secular values of the French Third Republic. By displaying non-European and European objects (in other words, "primitive" and European popular rural artifacts and traditions) side by side, the MET drew on evolutionary theory to make visible the differences between nineteenth-century urban European cultures and "others," whether as primitives or as peasants. The assumption that non-European cultures as well as popular European ones were different from and inferior to French (urban) culture was based on the supposed universalizing dimension of French civilization. This helps to explain the central paradox of the MET: it displayed cultural difference at the same time that the Third Republic's politics were aimed at eradicating such differences both externally (through colonialism) and internally (by, as Eugene Weber [1976] has famously put it, turning peasants into Frenchmen).

When Rivet was nominated as director of the MET in 1928, it became institutionally affiliated with the Muséum National d'Histoire Naturelle, leading to a series of major refurbishments and a wide-ranging program of curatorial reform and modernization culminating, in 1938, in the establishment of the MH as an independent institution and, a year earlier, in the establishment of the ATP. The former was dedicated to European and non-Western cultures, the latter to the diverse cultures of regional France. The separation between the study of the primitive and that of the French popular was made spatially visible: the two museums were located in separate wings of the Palais de Chaillot. French ethnography had earlier been dissociated from natural history, belonging to the realm of folklore and conducted under the auspices of the Direction des Musées de France, while overseas ethnography remained closely linked to natural history and to the notion of race. The development of the MH and ATP reconfigured these relationships.

Dedicated to the study of humankind as a whole, the MH aimed to combine physical anthropology, ethnology, and prehistoric archaeology. For Rivet, strongly committed to the Popular Front and opposed to racist theories, the museum's mission was to make visible the unity of humankind. In contrast to his predecessors, who emphasized racial difference, Rivet sought to demonstrate racial equality, although, as Jean Jamin (1989) has pointed out—and as we noted in chapter 1—he never seriously questioned the category of race. The museum's dependence on a natural history paradigm helps to explain the limits of Rivet's move away from biological race categories. This constituted a limit on the MH's conception as a cultural and scientific space committed to defending the equal value of all cultures in order to challenge current prejudices and reshape public attitudes toward France's colonial subjects (Laurière 2008).

This was complemented by a further limitation. French ethnologists during the 1930s argued for the diversity of non-European societies; the latter, they argued, were not inferior, just different. At the same time, such differences were attributed to a temporal lag that distinguished colonized peoples, not essentially or biologically, but historically, from their French contemporaries. By refusing to use terms such as *inferior* and *uncivilized*, French ethnologists stressed the dignity of all human societies and peoples. Their insistence on fundamental respect for cultural difference among human societies was thus an early and influential articulation of the principles of cultural relativism. But this was a cultural relativism with limits. Hence, Conklin (2013) highlights the tension between a humanistic approach celebrating the fundamental unity of humankind and the equal value of all cultures and the continuing exhibition of anatomical parts, particularly skulls, which testified to the continuing force of biological racial categories. The value-laden assumption that colonized peoples needed to catch up with Europe before they could be regarded as equivalents played a similar role, one that had significant governmental implications since this assumption was closely connected to questions of citizenship.

The MH's focus on the dignity of all cultures and peoples was in these regards part of a specific form of colonial governance, termed *colonial humanism* by Gary Wilder (2005). As an "administrative-scientific complex" (Wilder 2005: 61), colonial humanism operated both in the metropolis and in the colonies through procedures, institutions, discourses, and practices that aimed to bring together two apparently contradictory aspects—republicanism and empire, or universality and particularity—that were, however, constitutive of the French imperial nation-state. French colonialism and Third Republic republicanism were grounded in a common epistemological framework and constituted two aspects of the same system of governmentality.

Also during this time, new governmental conceptions of the relationships between France and its colonies took shape under the notion of Greater France, which regarded colonies as integrative parts of the French nation that were to be valued for their contribution to the cultural diversity of the colonial power (Wilder 2005: 29–36). Far from being confined to the Hexagon, France was conceived as a nation made up of different cultures, peoples, and lands, thus implying an extended conception of nationhood. Yet, as Wilder noted, the notion of Greater France articulated a logic of both inclusion and exclusion: "while binding natives to Empire," it sought to dissociate nationality from citizenship (33–39). The process of differentiating colonial populations was not homogeneous either across all French colonies or even within the same colony. In the case of Indochina, for example, there was a wide diversity of legal categories—*sujets français* and *protégés français*—for the indigenous populations according to the administrative and juridical status of the territories (colony and protectorates) under French rule (Goscha 2012). Here again, then, we encounter a central contradiction of liberalism in the coexistence of a discourse of equality and humanistic universalism with practices of regulation that discriminated between governors and governed based on race; as Ann Laura Stoler has aptly pointed out, these discriminatory practices "were reactive to, coexistent with, and perhaps inherent in liberalism itself" (1992a: 514). Perhaps more to the point, though, these discriminatory practices were a product of the system of mandate colonialism established under the League of Nations. For this was a system designed to defer colonized peoples' rights to self-government "by designating them as populations whose rights were suspended because they were in need of 'development'" (Mitchell 2013: 82).

The notion of Greater France also informed the ATP's main program under the directorship of Rivière, the former assistant director of the MET.

Although devoted to the display of French regional cultures, the ATP promoted the idea that France was a nation made up of many regional cultures whose diversity contributed to the rich tapestry of what was nonetheless conceived as one national culture. The focus on France's cultural diversity goes back to the 1930s, when, in the wake of the World's Fair in Paris in 1937, as Shanny Peer has pointed out, "the cultural pluralism embodied in the diverse provincial cultures came to be embraced as quintessentially French: national authorities desired to recuperate and recast provincial folk traditions as a cultural bulwark against a new menace: that of mechanical, standardized, industrial civilization" (1998: 143).

Once absorbed by the French nation, "the diverse cultures of provincial France were proudly reclaimed as France's national patrimony in 1937" (Peer 1998: 97). The logic governing such conceptions of the relations between France's colonies and its regions within Greater France was the same: everyone, as Lebovics (1992: 7–10) has put it, had two *pays*; each had their own *petit pays* while sharing in the destiny of Greater France.

While the MH was promoting the cultural diversity of France's colonies, the MH HAN was advocating both ethnic diversity and political unity in French-ruled Indochina. The MH sought to demonstrate that Indochina, as a political entity, was made up of different countries—Vietnam, Cambodia, and Laos—conceived as *petites patries*, similar to the *petits pays* of Greater France. Regional homelands became key sites for the management of identities in Indochina. As Lebovics has pointed out, the notion of Greater France implied a "kind of mutual apprenticeship in citizenship: on the one side natives learning to be French while of course retaining their local customs; on the other European French recalling their own apprenticeships as Gascons or Bretons, learning to welcome the new French" (1992: 79). The cultural diversity of France's colonies and of Indochina thus mirrored the diversity of French regions as seen from the organizing centers of the MH and the ATP in the capital of Greater France and the MH HAN in the capital of French Indochina.

At the same time, something more than mutual mirroring was involved in the relations between metropolis and colony. The manner in which collections were gathered, ordered, and circulated between the MH and the MH HAN testified to the reciprocal interactions of these practices, which, although structured by the dominance of the MH, nonetheless complicate the center–periphery logic on which its conception as a center of calculation rests. It is to these matters that we now turn.

COLLECTING, COLLECTORS, AND EPISTEMIC CIRCULATION

From December 18, 1931, to April 1, 1932, Rivet traveled throughout French Indochina collecting objects for both the MH and the forthcoming ethnographic museum that was projected for development under the auspices of the EFEO. Since the MH was short of Asian collections, one of Rivet's aims was to fill these gaps in the museum collections. He collected around four hundred objects and gave money directly to collectors to purchase artifacts for the MH. Part of the collection gathered by Rivet was displayed from August to October 1932 in the *Exposition de la Mission Rivet en Indochine* at the MH. In January 1934, the MH opened its Asian Hall partly as a result of the intensive collecting carried out during the previous two years. The inauguration of Rivet's exhibit and of the Asian Hall took place between 1932 and 1934 at a moment of heightened criticism of colonial policies in both the metropolis and French Indochina, in addition to the emergence of the Vietnamese nationalist movement (Dias 2014). While "pacification campaigns" were conducted in the colony, the MH's Indochinese collections constituted a form of symbolic capture and mastery of that space.

During his mission in Indochina, Rivet spent two to three days in each of the places he visited mainly to collect objects and to set up a network of local collaborators. This contrasted with the MH's Dakar-Djibouti mission, which, although the most emblematic and most studied of the MH's various expeditions, was in many respects the least typical. Assembling a team of researchers under the direction of Marcel Griaule, the Dakar-Djibouti mission conducted a program of intensive ethnographic inquiries (from May 1931 to February 1933) across French western and equatorial Africa, the Belgian Congo, the Sudan, Abyssinia, and Cameroon. Mobilizing the techniques of "plural observation" (Jamin 1982: 91), this mission modified the immersive paradigm developed within Anglophone anthropology, bringing together the theoretician and the collector in the field but stressing the multiperspectival benefits of a team encompassing different specialisms compared to the singular vision of the lone anthropologist. Whereas the Anglophone tradition tended to marginalize the role of in situ collectors in colonial contexts— aptly summarized in Bronislaw Malinowski's conception of the anthropologist escaping the administrator's office, the "closed study of the theorist," and the "veranda of the missionary compound" to step into the "open air" of the field (quoted in Stocking 1983: 112)—the MH model aimed to effect a more efficient organization of the relations between in situ collectors (administrators, soldiers, missionaries, local scientific associations, etc.) and to bring these under the direction of the MH as a coordinating center performing bureaucratic, archival, and laboratory functions (L'Estoile 2007: 103–16).

Rivet traveled all over Indochina not only to collect objects but also to establish in each place key collectors who were willing to collaborate with the MH and the EFEO, and to set up a hierarchical team with local informants at the base, coordinated locally by Jean-Yves Claeys (in charge of the EFEO's archaeological section) but subordinated, ultimately, to his personal direction. The organization of ethnological research was thus built on a pyramidal and centralized model, as a form of "rational domination" (L'Estoile 2005). The correspondence between Rivet and Claeys provides useful information about what criteria were used to select local collectors, how collectors were recruited, what kinds of objects were collected, and what methodological procedures were applied to order the collecting practices, including how the practices of labeling and filing index cards were standardized and which kinds of textual and visual information were judged relevant to complement the artifacts.

After Rivet's departure, Claeys conducted an intensive tour throughout French Indochina in May 1932 to strengthen the links with existing collaborators and to establish new collaborative arrangements with *résidents* and colonial personnel. Claeys's activities in centralizing the ethnographic collections assembled by the network of collaborators, as well as distributing them through that network, contributed to the EFEO's development as a coordinating center among the colonial sites of collection. Local collectors were supposed to collect two examples of the same object, one for the MH, the other for the projected MH HAN. This involved two types of circulation: a local circulation (from the field to the local museum or to the EFEO's headquarters) and a global circulation (from Indochina to Paris). By keeping the doubles of the index cards and sending their shelf numbers to the MH, the EFEO constituted an archive for both the metropolis and the colony. While the EFEO at Hanoi coordinated collecting activities in the north of Indochina, the Institut Océanographique at Nha-Trang played a similar role in the south, gathering artifacts, making inventories, and sending them to the MH.

If artifacts circulated from Indochina to Paris, visual and textual information associated with them was constantly requested by the MH from the local collectors; in other words, there was a back-and-forth movement of index cards, drawings, and photographs (Dias 2015). The most important collector was undoubtedly Madeleine Colani; a regular contributor to the EFEO's *Bulletin* who had a doctoral degree in science, Colani had been collecting objects for the MH since 1931. Claeys's and Colani's correspondence with, respectively, Rivet and Marcelle Bouteiller, the curator of Asian collections at the MH, provides useful information about how ethnologists and local collectors were involved in a chain of activities: from collecting in the field, through describing objects and sharing information, to mounting exhibits. In her report on the arrival of a collection sent in July 1933, Bouteiller started by describing the physical conditions of the films, the photographs, and the 205 objects (whether they were broken, damaged, or in need of conservation or repair, for example). The issue of the physical stability of the collections was a constant preoccupation for local collectors, who had to ship objects for long voyages, and also for metropolitan curators, who had to repair, classify, and display the objects. The EFEO designed specific boxes for the shipments since objects had to travel long distances. In her report Bouteiller identified how the objects received could complement and/or fill the gap in the MH's collections and how they were put in the showcases. Finally, she requested additional textual and visual information, asking for actors' photographs, for example, in order to illustrate theatre costumes on display in the showcases.[8]

There was thus undoubtedly a hierarchy between the collectors in the field and the curators at the MH, who organized and interpreted the objects, index cards, photographs, and films and by doing so created new systems of relationships among them. However, it would be misleading to conclude that the MH placed no value on the knowledge produced by the EFEO's collaborators and that local collectors were considered to be mere providers of objects to the metropolitan museum. Local collectors, mainly French ones, contributed their knowledge and expertise to the development of Indochinese ethnology both in the metropolis and in the colony. Although the influence of the MH was predominant, the exchanges ran in both directions. Shortly after his return to France, for example, Rivet sent Claeys the index cards for the objects kept at the MH and asked for information about the provenance, use, and fabrication of the objects to which they referred. Colani's advice was similarly crucial for mounting the Asian Hall at the MH. In a detailed letter to Colani in 1934, Bouteiller described how the materials Colani had sent to the MH were processed through its accessioning arrangements, how objects and photos were classified, and what sort of information was attached to them and inscribed on the labels.[9] In other words, Bouteiller specified the mechanisms of translation by which the information collected in the field was organized at the MH, with a view to making Colani an active and more efficient collaborator in these processes. Bouteiller's advice showed her appreciation of the mutual imbrication of the relations between collecting practices in the field and the museum. The circulation of objects and information from the field to the metropolitan museum and back again was made possible through the use of common methodological protocols and standards. The methodological procedures made it possible for information and objects to circulate between colony and metropolis, inscribing collections in new networks through which a range of governing effects were produced. The standardization of conventions for naming and classifying objects, on the one hand, and for filing index cards, on the other, played a crucial role in this circulation of objects and information.

As the director of the EFEO's Service Ethnologique and cofounder of the IIEH, Lévy pursued Rivet's collecting practices by managing a network of local collectors. With a background in ethnology as well as in the history of religion and Sanskrit, Lévy both created new and reorganized existing local galleries of ethnography when traveling to Saigon, Phnom Penh, and Hue in 1938 to gather materials for the forthcoming MH HAN.[10] He spent a month in Yunnan (China), bringing back sixteen boxes of ethnographic objects for the MH HAN.[11] Although most of the collaborators and collectors were French scholars, such as Georgette Naudin (the curator of the Musée Blanchard de la Brosse at Saigon) and Suzanne Karpelès (the director of the Royal Library at Cambodia), indigenous collaborators were also named in the EFEO's publications. These included Cong Van-Trung (who made the inventories and the drawings of the objects collected by Karpelès) and Nguyen Van Huyen. However, Indochinese scholars were discriminated against in the EFEO's research activities until 1939, when a decree allowed protégés français of Indochinese origin to become part of the EFEO's scientific personnel (R. Thomas 2006). Thanks to this decree, Nguyen Van Huyen, who held a PhD from the Sorbonne and was in charge of an ethnographic mission in 1938, became a full-time employee at the EFEO.[12] Van Huyen assisted Lévy in conceiving and organizing the MH HAN, and he was also on the advisory board of the IIEH.

As the EFEO's director, Coedès acknowledged the work of Indochinese scholars in his 1938 address, which was published in the first issue of the IIEH's *Bulletin*: "In Indochina, the collaboration between European specialists can only be achieved thanks to the exchange with our Indochinese colleagues: Annamites, Cambodians and Laotians. We are lucky to have at Hanoi a small group of Annamites, trained in our methods and able to advance our inquiries with observations that Europeans would gather only with extreme difficulty."[13]

In 1943, during the Vichy period in Indochina, the IIEH's statutes were reformulated, with the stress placed on putting "European and Indochinese collaborators on an entirely equal footing" (sur un pied de complète égalité).[14] This reflected a shift in governmental rationalities during the Vichy period in

Indochina (1940–45), when measures were taken to increase the number of Indochinese in the high levels of the colonial administration in order to "provide them with a stake in the colonial state, to ensure their loyalty" (Goscha 2012: 130). With a population of between 25,000 and 39,000 in 1940, the European community represented only around 0.2 percent of the overall population of Indochina (E. Jennings 2001). Thus, for both administrative reasons as well as a means of preventing the enrollment of indigenous populations in nationalist movements, the Vichy government in Indochina implemented a series of measures to modify the status and rights of the colonized. Yet there remained a clear distinction between the contributions of European and indigenous scholars to the pages of the IIEH's bulletins. While French scholars were referred to individually by their own names, Indochinese scholars were grouped together under the rubric of "collaborators," with their names coming after the French ones.

These collecting practices, the networks of local collectors, and the circulation of objects and information were informed by a complex set of overlapping power relationships—between colonial officials and the colonized, between centers at the metropolis and those located in Indochina, and between diverse sorts of colonial personnel within the same colony. As Stoler has shown, if it is crucial to take into account the distinctions between colonizer and colonized, it is also important to consider distinctions between colonizers, distinctions that "should make us wary of taking 'Europeans' and 'colonizers' as synonymous categories" (1992b: 339). The colonial context of collecting shaped collectors' views on the objects they acquired and on the roles ascribed to native informants; conversely, collectors' colonial experiences and knowledge also affected the ways in which objects and information were selected and assembled. The manner in which objects and information were circulated highlights the active role that local collectors, native informants, administrators, and scholars played in the making of ethnological knowledge. Index cards, labels, lists, and inventories went back and forth, and in the process they were endlessly transformed through the different inscriptions they entered into. A close analysis of this "epistemic circulation" that "drew trajectories that were not necessarily coincidental to the physical movements of objects" (Roque 2011: 15) sheds new light on the workings of ethnology in the colonial context.

This is not to dispute that the MH played a significant role as a center of calculation, in Latour's term (1987: 215–57): that is, as a place where objects, photographs, films, and index cards collected and assembled in the field were classified, combined, collated, interpreted, displayed, and turned into organized scientific data. It was not, however, the only site of knowledge production. The EFEO also played a significant role as a center of calculation that operated both within and across the relations between the place of colonial administration and the metropolis. This qualifies Latour's (1987) distinction between sites of collection and centers of calculation as well as the implicit center–periphery logic underlying it. As Raj has recently argued, the "circulatory perspective" provides "rich theoretical alternatives to the center-periphery trope" (2013: 347). Located in a colonial setting that was at the same time a site of collection, the EFEO—by gathering and centralizing objects, texts, films, and photographs and dispatching them to the MH as well as to other museums in French Indochina, in places such as Hanoi, Hue, Laos, and Saigon—was also involved in the process of knowledge production. If the MH played the role of a coordinating research center located in the metropolis, the EFEO played a similar role in the colony, where it provided methodological expertise, conducted inquiries, and constituted collections that were duplicates of those of the MH. Thus, "the circulatory perspective allows one to see science as being co-produced through the encounter and interaction between heterogeneous specialist communities of diverse origins" (Raj 2013: 345).

The collecting practices in the colony also informed exhibition policies at the metropolitan museum, most obviously in furnishing the materials for the opening of new galleries but also by shaping the ways in which displays were mounted, and objects and textual and visual information assembled. However, the flow of influence ran more strongly in the opposite direction, from the MH to the colony, so far as exhibition practices were concerned. It is to these questions that we now turn, initially by considering the relations between the MH's Asian Hall, opened in 1934, and the MH HAN's exhibits in 1939.

DISPLAYING INDOCHINESE CULTURE IN PARIS AND HANOI

Opened in 1934, the Asian Hall (figure 6.3) was renovated in 1938 with a double system of analytic and synthetic cases: "In keeping with the double-circuit principle, all the ethnographic galleries contained not only the large and detailed analytic cases on one side, but smaller synthetic cases—for specific regions or races, with accompanying wall panel—on the other side. The panel usually included the geographic region, the local race(s) or ethnic group(s), several maps and photographs, and a typed text with the rubrics 'geographic description, political divisions, material life, populations'" (Conklin 2013: 153).

FIGURE 6.3 "General view of the Asian Hall, Musée d'Ethnographie du Trocadéro, Paris, January 1934." QB 53498, Musée du quai Branly, Paris. © SCALA, Florence.

The Asian Hall, curated by Marcelle Bouteiller, opened its doors to the public on January 20, 1934. The general view of the Asian Hall shows the alignment of metal cases containing objects, drawings, maps, texts, and photographs; deliberately overcrowded, the hall was deemed to demonstrate the achievements of French missions. The Indochinese section contained two kinds of vitrines: some dedicated to ethnic groups, others to examples of cultural traits shared by several groups, such as chewing betel nut.

The panels, photographs, cases, drawings, and maps shown in figure 6.4 demonstrate the main principles guiding the MH HAN's presentation. The caption at the top of the left-hand panel—"Sites and human remains"—is illustrated by three distinct features: photographs of the sites from which the remains were collected, two photographs of human remains (skulls), and one drawing of a skull and three photographs of human types, which, in being brought under the rubric of human remains, are presented as if they belonged to, or were at least the vestiges of, prehistory. The panel thus emphasizes the ways in which humankind and its environment are inter-related in the past as well as in the present, as well as human adaptations to diverse ecological settings. A map of Indochina in the middle separates these archaeological depictions of prehistory from more recent history. To the right of the map, photographs of ancient buildings are used to illustrate Indochinese history. Visitors were thus invited to see, in a sequence moving from left to right, first the environment (sites) with human remains, then the territory occupied by France (implicitly in order to admire France's colonial grandeur in terms of mapping Southeast Asia), and, finally, the cultural historical achievements represented by iconic buildings. Material objects (tools) displayed in the showcase running along the bottom of the exhibit illustrated the close links between humans and their environment. The prehistoric and historical panels of this exhibit prepared the way for the "Indochinese habitations" as the next section on the visitors' itinerary (figure 6.2).

The exhibits of the MH HAN were thus conceived along the same princi-ples as those governing the MH's exhibition practices, yet privileging synthetic cases over analytic ones. Indeed, for an ethnographic section de-voted to nonspecialists, it was more important to summarize "the sociocultural traits of major ethnic groups"—the main principle of the synthetic cases— in contrast to the "'annex' displays" that "were to be installed with objects organized analytically by 'techniques, functions, or representations' for the better-informed and initiated visitor" (Conklin 2013: 138). As the EFEO's di-rector Coedès acknowledged, speaking about the MH HAN exhibition prac-tices more generally, "Regarding the presentation of the objects, I wish to adopt . . . the same methods as in Paris: numerous maps, charts, photographs explaining the distribution and the use of the objects."[15]

As for the objects, they were mainly musical instruments, weapons, jewelry, agricultural tools, models of transportation and habitation, and clothing sup-posedly representative of each "ethnic group" and presented in relation to their contexts by means of graphs and photographs.[16] Panels representing

FIGURE 6.4 "Prehistory and history in Indochina: abstract of the graphic panels, photographs and maps, Musée Maurice Long—section Musée de l'Homme, 16 May 1939." EFEO VIE 04251, École Française d'Extrême-Orient, Paris. Courtesy of the École Française d'Extrême-Orient.

Mobilizing the modern strategies of display (objects, photographs, maps, panels, and drawings), the Musée de l'Homme, Hanoi adopted the museography of the Musée de l'Homme in Paris. The caption in both the panel and the photograph reads, "Prehistory and history in Indochina." The use of the preposition *in* is worth noting—it specifies the work carried out by prehistory and history within spatial limits, in this case within French colonial rule. Compared to "prehistory and history of Indochina" (implying a reference to a provenance or an origin) or "Indochinese prehistory and history," the title with *in* makes an implicit reference to the archaeological and historical achievements of the École Française d'Extrême-Orient in Indochina.

---

the ethnolinguistic distribution of the population, their ways of life, the main prehistoric and historical sites in Indochina, and the somatic characteristics of different ethnic groups were displayed on the walls. The focus on photographs and graphs served not only to confer on the objects an epistemological value as documents (in light of Mauss's and Rivet's precepts) but also to emphasize the importance of the environment. The "environmentalist conception of the object" (Laurière 2008: 416) that presided over the MH's displays was transported to Hanoi for the purpose of demonstrating that native ways of life could be changed by reshaping their conditioning environments, as we noted in chapter 1 in relation to the vitrine introducing the Sub-Saharan Africa Hall at the MH.

Like the Asian Hall in Paris (Conklin 2013: 154), the MH HAN was arranged according to "ethnic groups": the Moï (a pejorative term used by the French to designate the hill and forest-dwelling people of central Vietnam), the Cham, the Cambodians, the Annamites (the French name for the ethnic Vietnamese), the Vietnamese highland minorities, and the Thais. Countries and human groups were conflated under the designation of "ethnic groups," and in some cases new ethnic groups were created both administratively and ethnographically. For example, throughout the 1930s the Montagnards (the highland population) were considered "a separate ethnic group," sharing "an essential cultural unity" regardless of their linguistic differences (Salemink 1999: 297). Rivet's collection contained around eighty objects from the Moï, mainly weapons (lances and bows) and agricultural tools, particularly machetes (Dias 2014). The MH HAN held an exhibit on the Moï in May 1940, displaying objects collected by Paul Guilleminet, the *résident* (local governor) of Kontum province.[17] Along with objects from everyday life and those for funeral ceremonies, this exhibit displayed ethnolinguistic maps, photographs, and excerpts from the books of Henri Maitre, a famous explorer of the central highlands who had played a key role in the penetration of the region and its subsequent pacification.

The focus on salvaging "primitive" cultures informed French collecting practices in both the metropolis and Indochina. Rivet's collecting efforts in the early 1930s were concentrated mainly in Indochina owing to the presumed endangered status of its cultures, in contrast to "China and India, whose transformation is relatively slow" (Rivet, quoted in Conklin 2013: 152). Similarly, the ATP's fieldwork practices, which focused on French regional cultures during the interwar period, aimed to make it possible for the ATP to "observe *in extremis* certain archaic aspects of a civilization in the way of transformation" (G. Rivière 1947: 8).

The displays at both the MH and the MH HAN, with their overcrowded cases and panels on the wall, conveyed a message of objectivity and authorized knowledge. It was the combination of textual and visual information that conferred on the artifact the status of an ethnographic object worthy of being displayed. Moreover, objects accompanied by visual and textual information had the status of archives equivalent to written documents. In a lecture in 1939 dedicated to the prehistory and ethnology of Indochina, Lévy emphasized the need to constitute, for a scientific point of view, archives on ancient and contemporary Indochinese populations; these archives, he noted, were also crucial in political terms because colonial authorities needed to have scientific knowledge of the peoples' lives both in the past and in the present in order to guide them in the future (Lévy 1939: 49). Hired at the EFEO as an "ethnographer-prehistorian" (Lévy, quoted in Conklin 2013: 229), Lévy was fully familiar with the long, rich history of the Indochinese peoples and conscious that its neglect by colonial authorities might have unforeseen consequences for their governance. Thus, the administrative goal was not merely to preserve cultural traditions but to ensure their continued existence as a necessary conduit for governmental action on the colonial social—an argument we develop more fully in the next section.

For these reasons the task of organizing archives on non-Western cultures was one of the chief priorities of French ethnology. The first methodological guide, the *Instructions Sommaires pour les Collecteurs d'Objets Ethnographiques*, elaborated by the MH for the Dakar-Djibouti mission of 1931, particularly emphasized the notion of the object as a *document* itself and of ethnography as "the science that deals with the archives of man" (Jamin 1982: 81). Consequently, ethnography's aim was "to assemble the documents for the study of material civilization" (*Instructions* 1931: 4), a documentary concern that presupposed the gathering of artifacts, photographs, films, sound recordings, and maps. In addition to the *Instructions*, Mauss's courses at the Institut d'Ethnologie de Paris (where he had taught since 1925 a course entitled Instructions in Descriptive Ethnography) were compiled in his *Manuel d'Ethnographie* ([1947] 1967); they were aimed at "constituting scientifically the archives of archaic societies" (Mauss [1947] 1967: 7). Thus, according to Mauss, "the museography of a society consists of establishing material archives, museums are the archives" (16).

The archival dimension ascribed to ethnographic museums in particular and to ethnology in general was part of the humanistic discourse assigned to ethnology; the focus on constituting the "archives of man" and the very name of the museums dedicated to housing those archives illustrated what was supposed to be the universalistic dimension of ethnological knowledge. We have already indicated how this universalistic discourse was interrelated with, and constitutive of, discriminatory administrative practices. Museums and colonial-administrative governance were thus not separate spheres. The career of Jules Brévié—an active supporter of the creation of an ethnographic museum and the governor-general of Indochina during the Popular Front—illustrates the closeness of their interconnections. Brévié attended the inauguration of the MH, as well as the first session of the IIEH, and served as honorary president of this institution. Before his career in Indochina, Brévié was the governor-general of Afrique Occidentale Française between 1930 and 1936. There, he supported the creation of a research center at Dakar, the Institut Français d'Afrique Noire (E. Jennings 2001: chap. 1). In his address at the opening of the IIEH, Coedès acclaimed Brévié's career as demonstrating a perfect comprehension of indigenous mentalities and of the ways in which ethnography might solve social problems. Although devoted to "pure science," he argued that the IIEH's research would also be of service in administrative and governmental spheres in terms of the practical uses to which it might lend itself.[18]

That colonial administrators acknowledged the relevance of ethnological research is not surprising; conversely, that ethnologists sought to justify the legitimacy of their discipline by pointing out its "practical uses" is also not surprising. Assessments of the role played by the MH in processes of governing have been more varied, ranging from its conception as a key part of a developing institutional complex of colonial governance to interpretations of it as relatively detached from colonizing processes.[19] We have queried the latter view by exploring how museums and research centers that were apparently detached from the direct practicalities of colonial governance nonetheless helped to shape these practices through their exhibition practices and subjects of inquiry. Ethnographic knowledge produced by fieldwork practices of collecting converged with rational administrative practices for managing colonial populations. As Gwendolyn Wright has perceptively noted, the colonial administrators of Indochina drew on ethnographic fieldwork in using "urban culture as a cornerstone of their political endeavors" (1987: 291); Ernest Hébrard, the architect of the museum of the EFEO (the Musée Louis Finot), which was completed in 1931, and of several administrative buildings in French Indochina, similarly "relied heavily on vernacular motifs from the region" and "spent much time photographing and sketching indigenous architecture, from the high art of Angkor-Vat or Buddhist pagodas to simple rural habitations" (Wright 1987: 306).

Museums in Paris and in Indochina thus functioned as governmental technologies for acting on social worlds. The two displays at the MH and the MH HAN contributed to the production and circulation of particular conceptions of Indochinese culture through which governmental action was brought to bear on the task of managing the relations between colonizers and colonized. But if the cultures of the different groups that made up Indochina constituted one conduit through which such action was mediated, race continued to provide another. However, although sharing the same name—Musée de l'Homme—the orientations of the MH in Paris and in Indochina differed in this regard. The metropolitan museum was devoted to all humankind but particularly to the population of the French empire, whereas the Indochinese museum was essentially focused on the Far-Eastern Man. One of the IIEH's aims was precisely to promote knowledge of "the Far-Eastern Man as a physical and social being."[20] Consequently, this research center assembled scholars from several fields of knowledge ranging from anatomy, pathology, and ethnology to history, human geography, and sociology: in short, all the disciplines involved in the colonial governance of Indochina. While the MH proclaimed universalistic values and encompassed all humankind, its satellite in the colony operated a double reduction: on the one hand, it concentrated on Indochina and its inhabitants under the rubric of Far-Eastern Man; on the other hand, the so-called Far-Eastern Man was a condensation of diverse ethnic groups and nations conceived as part of Greater France. Once again, we take a display from the MH HAN exhibition in 1939 as our point of entry into these questions.

"THE FAR-EASTERN MAN AS A PHYSICAL AND SOCIAL BEING"

Figure 6.5 shows a section of the MH HAN dedicated to Indochinese anthropology that provides an overview of the IIEH's main topics of research. Combining texts, photographs, maps, casts, charts, drawings, and bones and skulls, the aim of this section was to grasp the main physical and physiological characteristics of the Indochinese population in general and of the "Annamites" in particular. Three aspects of the exhibit merit attention. First, although the introductory panel is dedicated to Indochina, the other panels and the showcase are devoted specifically to Annamites (particularly their noses, mandibles, and skulls), as if the Annamite epitomized Far-Eastern Man. Second, anatomical and physiological features are presented in an equal balance as a means of differentiating human groups. The focus on weight and height reflects a concern with the environmental dimension (milieu) that

FIGURE 6.5 "Showcases of Indochinese anthropology. Musée Maurice Long—section Musée de l'Homme, Hanoi, 16 May 1939." EFEO VIE 04250, École Française d'Extrême-Orient, Paris. Courtesy of the École Française d'Extrême-Orient.

———

At the left, a map shows the distribution of the heights of different ethnic groups across Indochina; next to it, a panel with photographs represents the deformity of the great toe (hallux varus), photographs of individuals with this affliction, drawings of Annamite noses, and charts of the weight and height of newborns of *différents pays* of Indochina. The wooden showcase displays an "Annamite brachycephalic" skull, drawings of a monkey's and a "man's" skull side by side, casts of brains, drawings of Annamite mandibles, charts of the cephalic index in Asia, and bones such as femurs and tibias, all accompanied by captions.

———

played a central role in the debates around the definition of legal categories, particularly around the issue of métis. In the wake of a decree in 1928 that regulated the status of the métis (a person of mixed blood) in French Indochina, an important anthropological, juridical, and educational debate took place focused on the category of métis (Saada 2007). Third, the depiction of the Annamite skull as brachycephalic ("Un crâne Annamite brachycéphale")—that is, as short-headed, with a corresponding widening and flattening of the skull—and its positioning next to drawings of a monkey's and a man's skull raises a set of questions. On the one hand, this arrangement suggests that humans are distinct from nonhumans and that all humans share the same anatomical configurations: the caption just says, "Skull of man." But what is the relationship between the "skull of man" and the "Annamite brachycephalic skull"? Was it a way of differentiating the Annamite's skull from the man's skull, or of pointing out the similarities between the two? A consideration of these questions will help illuminate the role played by race in the interface between governors and governed.

The IIEH was cofounded by Lévy and the anatomist Pierre Huard, the director of the Institut Anatomique (Hanoi). The creation of this institute resulted from a "spontaneous desire" to bring together the EFEO's members whose work was devoted to ethnographic and sociological research with the members of the Institut Anatomique of the École Supérieure de Médécine de Hanoi.[21] The IIEH's directorship included the EFEO's director (Coedès), as president, and two vice presidents: the director of the Institut Anatomique (Huard) and the chief of the EFEO's Service Ethnologique (Lévy). As for the list of honorary members, it included prominent scholars such as the Abbé H. Breuil, L. Lévy-Bruhl, H. Maspéro, Mauss, and Rivet. In the first issue of the IIEH's *Bulletin* Huard published with Nguyen-Xuan-Nguyen a study on the brains of the inhabitants of Tonkin (the northernmost part of Vietnam) in which the authors argued that these brains were predominantly brachycephalic—a racially loaded classification given the contemporary association of dolichocephalic, or long-headed, skulls with Nordics. But it was also in this first issue, published in 1938, that Coedès praised the collaboration between European specialists and "a small group of Annamites, trained in our methods and able to advance our inquiries."[22] Lévy also recognized, in a letter addressed to Rivet written in 1937, the anthropological competences of Vietnamese doctors: "There is a smart group of doctors here, full of zeal and talent for anthropology" (quoted in Conklin 2013: 230). In short, at the time when indigenous scholars were involved in scientific ac tivities, particularly anthropological ones, considerable political sensitivities were attached to the claim that Vietnamese were biologically inferior to Europeans. In these same years, "Indochinese physicians" became "Indochinese doctors," a change that, as Pierre Brocheux and Daniel Hémery noted, was meant as an acknowledgment of "the irreducible originality of local civilizations" (2009: 218).

Huard himself devoted his entire career to examining the ancient and actual Vietnamese populations from an anatomical and physiological perspective. He commended to his students a series of descriptive studies on different parts of the Vietnamese skeleton—scapula, fingers, clavicles, femurs—reserving for himself the study of the noblest parts, the skull and the brain (Chippaux and Olivier 1983). In his retrospective review of the anthropological inquiries that were conducted in Indochina and particularly in Vietnam at this time, Huard, G. Lanchou, and Tran-Anh (1962: 431) emphasized the joint importance of anatomy and physiology and, in the wake of Louis Bezacier and Hubert Marneffe's (1942) article, argued that the analysis of blood type could not be considered as the unique feature for individualizing a race, insisting that other ethno-anthropological characteristics should also be taken into account. The analysis of blood type was crucial for determining the legal status of individuals and for assigning them to categories according to their nationality and/or citizenship.

This focus on the biological study of the Indochinese population was undoubtedly related to the issue of métis (Huard 1940) and to mixed marriages, which increased during the Vichy period in Indochina (Huard, Lanchou, and Tran-Anh 1962: 428). As Stoler (1992a) has remarked, the juridical, political, and scientific debates about making the métis a legal category reflected anxieties about blurring the boundaries between Europeans and indigenous peoples. The métis question was a sensitive issue in Indochina because it embodied the contradictions of the colonial system in terms of the criteria for granting citizenship and subject status; it was also of the utmost importance for defining Frenchness according to either physical features, as determined by a medical legal expert, or "moral certainty" (related to the cultural surroundings or cultural milieu, that is, having a French name and being of French descent, living in a European milieu, and having a European education) (Stoler 1992a: 532–33). Race—by means of the question of the métis or in terms of defining biologically who had an "Indochinese origin"—was crucial at the IIEH and more generally in operating as a transactional reality that was "central to the practices of regulation of colonial contacts" (Saada 2002: 382).

The categorization of Indochina's population was above all a process implying forms of inclusion, exclusion, and differentiation that have constantly changed. By coining the notion of "imperial formations," Stoler and McGranahan sought to depict the "active and contingent process of . . . making and unmaking" the empire (2007: 8). This grasps "what has long marked the technologies of imperial rule," the "sliding and contesting scales of differential rights" (9). The diversity of legal categories used in Indochina reflected its emergence as a colonial invention made up of diverse countries and groups. As Christopher Goscha has pointed out, "rather than creating and imposing one Indochinese nationality for their Indochinese colonial state, the French created a variety of legal identities for the 'indigenous' (*indigènes*) living within the Indochinese Union. Those born in the French colony of Cochinchina . . . became French 'subjects' (*sujets français*), not French citizens . . . those coming from the protectorates . . . were considered legally to be *protégés français* (French-protected subjects; again not French citizens)" (2012: 99).

There was, Goscha argues, no such thing as an Indochinese colonial citizenship "for all those residing within this space," but "significantly, inside the Indochinese colonial state, each *pays* was given its own colonial nationality" (100). This diverse range of legal categories encompassing the distinction between citizenship and nationality entailed an unequal distribution of rights: indigenous populations were deprived of political rights (associated with citizenship) and could only benefit from social rights. Along with these legal distinctions, the category of "Indochinese" was subject to varying definitions and interpretations. According to Huard and Alfred Bigot (1938), the category was defined in terms of a specific bio-anthropological content. Paradoxically, at the same time that Huard was attempting to demonstrate the physical characteristics of the Indochinese, his definition of a homeland was primarily political rather than racial. The continuous debates about the definition of legal categories and their constant shifts attest to the "fundamental contradiction of imperial domination: the tension between a form of domination simultaneously predicated on both incorporation and distancing" (Stoler 1992a: 520).

Under the Vichy period in Indochina between June 1940 (when the government of Indochina swore its allegiance to Marshall Pétain) and March 1945, the judicial authorities "sought to draw the precise legal delimitation of three distinct categories: French, métis, and Indochinese" (E. Jennings 2004a: 605).[23] Wishing to incorporate the natives into the French empire, the Vichy regime was sensitive to both race and culture as criteria for defining national identities; at the same time, the IIEH developed a series of studies focused on Indochina's population, the number of Europeans and of Eurasians (Huard and Hop 1943) and the métis. Huard's works as well as the IIEH's research undoubtedly contributed to the definitions of the categories that were used for the management of populations, particularly after 1940. Along with physical features, the cultural traits that were shaped by the milieus of different groups were key elements for categorizing populations. These variable milieus and the traits associated with them served, as Stoler puts it, to fix "the boundaries of the European community and identified threats to it" (1992a: 535n74). Acting on the milieu to shape habits, customs, and practices was made visible at the MH HAN's displays and by means of the IIEH's publications.

Paradoxically, Huard, who spent his entire life examining the biological characteristics of the Indochinese population, proclaimed in a lecture "What Is the Homeland?" in 1943 that a homeland "was not a product of race, language or soil . . . but of a common experience" (quoted in Raffin 2002: 374). Rejecting the definition of *homeland* based on racial categories, he argued that racism was incompatible with the responsibilities of those European states that owned colonies, and particularly with the French colonial system. "If racism can theoretically become the national doctrine of uniquely European states," he argued, "it can only be completely adopted with difficulty by a white state owning colonies." And he added, "Our colonial system . . . does not know unequals or inferiors in relation to others, but only different civilizations and sister humanities" (quoted in Raffin 2002: 375). Huard's lecture was undoubtedly an apologia for a French colonial system that was supposedly based on the rejection of racial hierarchies and on the acknowledgment of colonized cultures as "sister humanities." This discourse of a presumed kinship among colonizers and colonized and the rejection of racial hierarchy went hand in hand with anti-Jewish measures throughout Indochina. Thence stems another paradox outlined by Anne Raffin: "at the very same moment that France was contributing to the Holocaust, it was celebrating multi-racialism in Indochina" (2002: 365). The anti-Semitic legislation was implemented in Indochina around November 1940, but with certain officials "granted exemptions"—Coedès, himself of Jewish descent, was allowed to pursue his activities at the EFEO (369). In contrast, Karpelès was, "with the collusion of Georges Coedès," forced to renounce her position as the director of the Royal Library (P. Edwards 2007: 235). Far from being contradictory, the exclusion of the Jewish population from Indochinese citizenship and the inclusion of natives in France's extended notion of nationhood were complementary. Vichy's Jewish statutes were, Eric Jennings argues, "actually used as the basis for the new legislation which for the first time sought to define an 'Asian' in the eyes of French colonial law" (2004a: 605).

Physical anthropology was one of the topics of research at the IIEH along with ethnography. The IIEH's *Bulletin* thus also published Nguyen Van Huyen's articles on burial practices and on the names of imperial Annam families, Claeys's articles on fishermen's songs, and Colani's lecture on stone disks and metal gongs; in subsequent issues there were articles on the practices of tattooing, fishing techniques, divination tables, and the conceptions of the beauty of human bodies among the Bahnar. In short, ethnography was as central as physical anthropology to the work of the IIEH, with culture as well as race providing the transactional realities through which the relations between the governors and the governed were mediated.

As Vichy's governor-general of Indochina between July 1940 and March 1945, Admiral Jean Decoux introduced Pétain's ideology, namely, respect for hierarchy, a return to traditions, the love of the *patrie*, and the revalorization of ancestral customs and moral values (E. Jennings 2004b: 30). Echoing the revival of provincial folk culture in France, Decoux established a "highly erudite cultural team," headed by Coedès (P. Edwards 2007: 231), whose aim was to promote the importance of ancient Indochinese civilization, and consequently "to root the 'Indochinese Nation' on firmer 'historical' ground in the future" (Goscha 1995: 51). Thus, an article published in *Indochine, Hebdomadaire Illustré*, a Pétainist publication, proclaimed that the knowledge accumulated by the EFEO on the country and its inhabitants was at the disposal of the administration and that the institution's aims were "to preserve the vestiges of the past," "to return to the Indochinese their history," and to "awaken in them a national sentiment."[24] Decoux also implemented a series of measures in order to strengthen both regionalism and nationalism (E. Jennings 2004a). A love for the local region, the *petite patrie*, was a means of expressing love for the French empire and the patrie. By stressing the ways in which "each *pays had the right and the duty* to claim its patriotism, to pay allegiance to its sovereign, religion and history," Decoux (1949: 388) emphasized the ways in which cultural particularisms were interrelated with nationalism, transposing Pétain's message to the colonial sphere. As Eric Jennings has noted, "the stratification of imagined communities in colonial Indochina in many ways mirrored the duality of identification in modern France, where . . . the cult of the *petite patrie* was considered not just compatible with but actually necessary for the cult of the greater *patrie*" (2004a: 620).

Decoux "officially banned the term 'indigène' and replaced it with the word 'Indochinois'" (Goscha 2012: 130) and promoted the recruitment of natives in the higher levels of the administration (Decoux 1949: 397). He encouraged the revival of traditional cultures and promoted the development of local crafts, thus contributing to the confection of native identities. The goal was to stimulate patriotic feelings toward Vichy France and to counterbalance the nationalistic movement by integrating natives into the French empire. While, in the metropolis, French people were invited to accept an imperial sense of Frenchness, in Indochina natives were invited "to return to their traditions so that by becoming more native they could become more French" (Lebovics 1992). At the same time as France was conceived internally and externally as a patchwork of diverse cultures, Cambodia, Laos, and Vietnam were envisioned as *petites patries*, as regions akin to Brittany and Gascogne, somehow miniatures of the nation.

The MH HAN and the IIEH pursued their activities during the Vichy period in Indochina. The number of Vietnamese scholars increased, constituting about one-third of the institute's membership. The IIEH lasted until 1943, and although it had to cease publishing in 1943, it "continued to hold meetings in secret until the Japanese coup of March 1945, at which time the Institute had on hand sufficient material to publish five or six volumes, in addition to the four brought out between 1938 and 1943" (Thompson and Adloff 1947: 417). The IIEH's allegiance to the Vichy regime goes back to the regime's beginnings as attested to by the presence of small blue cards containing Pétain's aphorisms in its *Bulletin*; from 1942 on, Pétain's aphorisms were incorporated in the *Bulletin* itself. During World War II the MH HAN was moving in a distinct ideological direction that, on the one hand, contrasted with the MH's humanistic and antiracist messages (at a time when the MH's staff were engaged in the battle against fascism, with some being deported, while Rivet himself was in exile [Laurière 2008]), while, on the other hand, sharing significant intellectual and ideological affinities with the ATP (Fabre 1997).

Although devoted to physical anthropology, the IIEH developed its research separately from that carried out by the Société d'Anthropologie de Paris, even during the Vichy period, when both institutions were committed to the Pétain régime (Staum 2011: chap. 9). Personal allegiances and loyalties seemed to play a determining role. Rivet's theoretical influence shaped the IIEH's beginnings, and during the Vichy period in Indochina his name appears in the list of the IIEH's honorary members until 1943. Rivet's rival for the chair of anthropology at the Muséum National d'Histoire Naturelle, Henri Vallois, had been the secretary of the Société d'Anthropologie de Paris and the editor of the journal *L'Anthropologie* since 1938. As Emmanuelle Sibeud noted, Vallois "loudly applauded the creation of the Anatomic Institute of the School of Medicine in Hanoi but neglected to mention the Indochinese Institute for the Study of Man. . . . This omission was significant in view of the gap existing between commitments to anthropological research in some colonies and his rearguard fight against cultural ethnology and very conservative understanding of race" (2012: S91). Vallois replaced Rivet as the MH's director during the war period, and his name appears as an honorary member of the IIEH in June 1941 along with Rivet's, as a strategic compromise. As for another physical anthropologist, George Montandon, who was committed to the Pétain regime and overtly eugenic and anti-Semitic, his writings on racial classification are barely mentioned in the IIEH's publications. Montandon was hired in 1932 by Marin, the director of the École d'Anthropologie, to teach ethnography in this institution, in a explicit move to counterbalance the Durkheimian–Maussian tradition.

The development of physical anthropology in Indochina thus seems to have taken a distinctive trajectory from that which it evinced in France. Detached from the eugenic discourse of the Société d'Anthropologie de Paris, the IIEH carried on studies on mixed races, métis, cultural traditions, and ethnic diversity. Loyal to the Vichy regime, it developed a theoretical and epistemological framework within which native Vietnamese scholars felt comfortable. Thus, one of the paradoxes of anthropology in Indochina in the Vichy period is that while its practitioners were mainly indigenous, they espoused many of the values of the Vichy regime—the return to traditions, the importance of ancestral values, the valorization of rural life and of the land. What accounts for this paradox? Jennings argues that this "Vietnamese undermining and appropriation of Pétainist topoi were unwittingly facilitated by a new colonial regime bent on rekindling folkloric regional identities in France and the colonies" (2004a : 619).

Conceived as satellites of both the Institut d'Ethnologie de Paris and the MH, the IIEH and the MH HAN took quite distinctive paths that led, sometimes, in directions that ran contrary to the values and principles of French ethnology. Far from being mere copies of the metropolitan model, the ethnological institutions in Indochina, and particularly the museums, appropriated, pursued, and also challenged the epistemological and political principles of the colonial power.

ETHNOLOGY AT HOME

We noted at the beginning of this chapter that the location of the MH and the ATP in separate wings of the Palais de Chaillot made spatially visible the differentiation of the study of French popular rural cultures from the study of "primitive" cultures. This was, in Fabrice Grognet's (2010) estimation, an event of both epistemological and governmental significance: the former in disconnecting popular rural cultures from the study of natural history and comparative anatomy; the latter in distinguishing the developmental objectives that were to be pursued in relation to the regional and colonial populations of Greater France. These differences reflected the differential distribution of these populations along the time line of modern civilization. If popular rural cultures were identified as pre–machine age practices that had, with adaptations, survived into the industrial age (G. Rivière and Tardieu 1953), the primitive cultures of the colonized represented survivals from much earlier phases of development. The former were to be subjected to a modernizing program in which the old was to be both retained and transformed in being blended with the new; the latter, having endured long past their use-by date, according to conceptions of backwardness that were still racially articulated, as we have seen, were to be superseded, left behind, if the colonized were ever to catch up and earn a place in Greater France on an equal footing with their mainland compatriots.

While conceding the reasoning involved in these claims, Daniel Sherman (2004) has stressed the respects in which the projects of the MH and the ATP nonetheless remained connected at an institutional, scientific, and methodological level. Like the MH, the ATP espoused a strong commitment to the project of ethnology, differing only in bringing its reforming mission to bear on a different component of the intellectual field: that defined by the conservative tradition of folklore studies, which idealized an unchanging French culture rooted in traditional country life and identified, as Lebovics (1992: 141) summarizes it, in the figures of *la terre*, the church, the village, the peasant, and the soldier. The ATP differentiated itself from this tradition in two main ways: its subscription to the principles of scientific professionalism developed in the project of colonial ethnology in opposition to the amateurism of folklore studies, and its commitment to a dynamic conception of rural cultures as components of an antiessentialist conception of Frenchness as "a cosmopolitan, multicultural, syncretic, and ever-changing product of the lives of diverse populations" (Lebovics 1992: 140).

Mass-Observation (M-O) provides an instructive contrast with regard to the first of these questions. As we saw in chapter 3, in its original conception M-O presented itself as a vehicle for articulating the views and sentiments of the masses, interposing itself as an intermediary between governors and governed in order to make the former more responsive to the latter. It thus expressed its concern at "the voicelessness of everyman and the smallness of the group which controls the fact-getting and the fact-distributing," declaring its aim as being "to give both ear and voice to what the millions are feeling and doing" (Mass Observation 1939: 9). We have also seen that, in practice, M-O instituted a set of divisions between observers and observed, serving as a vehicle for the recruitment of a new stratum of intellectuals who mobilized new forms of technical expertise in challenging traditional forms of British ruling-class authority. The ATP's project of "ethnology at home" served the same purpose in the French context but without the democratic and populist register that was embodied in M-O's participatory rhetoric of an "anthropology of ourselves." To the contrary, it was pitched precisely against the amateur forms of collecting and interpretation represented by the conservative folklore traditions it took issue with.

The ATP was, in this respect, heir to the earlier project of scientific cooperation represented by the Commission des Recherches Collectives du Comité de l'Encyclopédie Française, established by André Varagnac. In urging the need for a national network of researchers to investigate rural folkways, Varagnac extolled the virtues of teams of permanent professional researchers. However, he settled, on grounds of cost, for the recruitment of local volunteers, but only with the proviso that these be recruited from local notables (mainly teachers) and that their work—largely that of responding to open-ended surveys—be superintended by a central committee consisting of the leading ethnologists and sociologists of the day (Varagnac 1935). In the event, the commission had a short and largely unsuccessful life. But its conception fed into that of the ATP (F. Weber 2005: 92–93) partly via Rivet, who was a member of the commission's central committee. Conceived, on the model of the MH, as both a museum and a laboratory, the ATP was envisaged and developed as a center of calculation. While involving regional museums and local folklore associations, it was to play a strong directive role in relation to these, bringing them under the influence of the principles of scientific ethnology in that it was committed, in accordance with Mauss's directives, to the collection of the typical rather than of rare or exceptional items (Segalen 2005: 23).

This connects with the second main line of cleavage between the ATP's project of "ethnology at home" and the conservative tradition in folklore studies: its commitment to a centrally directed program of modernization for the cultures of the *petits pays* of regional France. In contrast to conservative idealizations of the peasantry as the authentic bearers of the spirit of a singular True France, the ATP more typically depicted popular rural cultures as cultures in movement, in the process of being brought into the age of machinery. Lebovics cites, as an emblematic example of this tendency, the Norman farmhouse that Rivière curated for the La France Européenne exhibition in 1941 at the Grand Palais, in which old carvings and furniture were complemented by a modern desk, telephone, and radio. Nina Gorgus (2003: 99–111) interprets Rivière's exhibition of village life at the Musée de Terroir de Romenay in 1937 as effecting a similar rapprochement of tradition and modernization. These exhibition practices in part reflected Rivière's aesthetic modernism, which, combined with his endorsement of the principles of social planning informing the politics of the Popular Front, resulted in his support for the incorporation of the rural peasantry into a centrally directed program of modernization rather than their preservation as tourist curios who were, as Rivière and Marcel Maget, the ATP's head of research, put it, to be preserved like "Indians on their reservation" (quoted in Lebovics 1992: 183).

It is important to add that both of these characteristics of the ATP continued into and through the Vichy period, albeit with some equivocations and strategic concessions to the conservative revalorization of the peasantry that characterized the Pétain regime. Many of the issues here have been clouded by debates as to whether or not the charge of collaboration that was brought against Rivière after the war was merited. More recent critical assessments have viewed this as a red herring, preferring instead to focus on the array of positions that it was possible for museum workers and ethnologists to take up during the period of the occupation (Segalen 2005; F. Weber 2005). The consensus is that Rivière and Maget sought, by and large successfully, to effect a strategic accommodation to the imperatives of the Vichy period that would at the same time retain a commitment to the two key planks of the project of ethnology that we have identified above: its professionalization and its subordination of regionally dispersed cultures to the direction of a Paris-centered program of rationalization and modernization.

In his survey of the historical development of French museums, Dominique Poulot (2005: 147–50) includes the ATP among those institutions that he classifies as "active museums": that is, museums with an explicit commitment to act as agents of social change, a tradition that, in France, can be traced to the establishment of the Musée Social in 1894. Although founded as a museum, this rapidly became a research institute with a collecting, archival, and activist function focused—in the spirit of Frédéric Le Play—on improving the conditions of life of the urban masses (Horne 2002). If, as Poulot contends, late nineteenth-century attempts to establish museums with a regional focus largely failed, the ATP's role in producing regional cultures as a framework within which to collect, order, and act on France's rural populations also contrasts with the failure to establish a major museum focused on British rural cultures until well into the postwar period. We have argued, in chapter 3, that this reflected the failure to replace race as a transactional reality for differentiating and governing populations with an actionable set of distinctions between rural and metropolitan populations at a time when gender and class articulated more salient distinctions, albeit not in ways that connected significantly with museum practices. The case of the ATP presents a different trajectory in which—however much socialist intellectuals like Marc Bloch had in the 1930s urged the need to pay attention to the class divisions of rural life (Segalen 2005: 40–41)—regional cultural ecologies were produced as the conduit through which rural populations were to be ordered, governed, and acted on. Its influence in this regard reached far into the postwar period. The same is true of all of the other practices of collecting, ordering, and governing that we have considered in the previous chapters. It is to these matters that we now turn.

Our concerns in this book have centered on the role of anthropology in mediating the relations between the collecting practices of fieldwork, the ordering practices of museums, and practices of social governance. In pursuing these, we have sought to qualify those accounts that pigeonhole the "museum phase" of anthropology in a past that, by the interwar period, had been largely superseded. We have also questioned a similar ruptural narrative relating to the development of museum practices. One of the key concerns of contemporary museum studies has been to explore and critique the international transformations of museum practices and policies designed to promote their use as civic institutions for fostering cross-cultural understanding in culturally diverse societies (Karp et al. 2006). These museum practices are commonly presented as breaking with the roles played by museums in the nineteenth and early twentieth centuries, when cultural differences were represented in racialized hierarchies. While this is true in some respects, one of our aims has been to show how this way of presenting the history of museums neglects the varying conceptions of cultural difference associated with the new relationships between museums, anthropological fieldwork, and programs of colonial and metropolitan governance that were developed over the first half of the twentieth century, and the legacy of these developments in the second half of the twentieth century and the early decades of the twenty-first. With this in mind, we conclude by briefly reviewing some of the more recent historical and contemporary concerns in which the legacies of this period have been, and remain, powerfully evident. In particular, we look at how the various transactional realities that we have discussed paved the way for postwar forms of multicultural governance by (to different degrees) displacing hierarchical conceptions of race in favor of more plural and cultural conceptions of difference, albeit ones in which racialized conceptions of difference have never been entirely superseded. We look first at the emergence of UNESCO and the new globalized and globalizing practices of social governance that came to characterize the postwar period through an exploration of the governmental rationalities that informed the UNESCO Statements on Race—*The Race Question* (Montagu 1950)—and the revisions of the UNESCO *Statement on the Nature of Race and Race Differences* (Dunn 1951). In the context of this emergence of new, global transactional realities that came to partially replace, but also overlapped with, earlier conceptions of race as a governmental template for differentiating populations, we also discuss the appearance of the concept of "indigeneity" as a transnational actor. We look, finally, at how the divisions between populations produced by colonial governmental rationalities have continued to inform the segmentation of populations within settler-colonial contexts. We consider the ongoing significance of the "culture-area" concept in providing templates for the development of indigenous social governance structures in Australia and Aotearoa/New Zealand. We also examine the limits of the liberal problematics of governing through culture exemplified by the restitution of racial logics of governance represented by Australia's recent Northern Territory Intervention, in which measures relating to law enforcement, land tenure, and welfare provision have undermined the role accorded to culture and custom within the forms of autonomy previously won by Northern Territory Aboriginal communities.

"IN THEIR BODIES IS THE RECORD OF THEIR BROTHERHOOD": UNESCO, POSTWAR ANTIRACISM, AND GLOBALIZED PRACTICES OF (MULTI-)CULTURAL GOVERNANCE

If, as we argued in chapter 4, the anthropological culture concept continued, in the postwar period, to differentiate populations in ways that placed non-white peoples outside the mechanisms of liberal government that it brought to bear on regulating the relations between America's "Caucasian" populations, we now also need to note the significant differences between this approach and that which emerged through the deployment of the culture concept in the cultural relativism of UNESCO and its globalizing projects. It is clear that race continued as a primary organizing principle in many different national and transnational medical, political, social, and bureaucratic contexts throughout the postwar period.[1] However, in this period the culture concept also came to officially replace or stand in for race in a range of new international discourses that emerged from the various organizations that developed out of the United Nations (UN) and Bretton Woods Conferences, in particular through the work of UNESCO. This is not to suggest that

North American anthropology did not have a clear and significant influence in shaping what Martin Barker (1983) has termed the "UNESCO tradition" of antiracism and its replacement of hierarchical conceptions of race with nonhierarchical conceptions of culture (Hazard 2012).[2] Indeed, Margaret Mead's work was particularly influential in this regard.[3] But it is also clear that the antiracism program pursued by UNESCO, which brought postwar North American anthropology into dialogue with the French conceptions of cultural difference that had developed around the projects of the Musée de l'Homme, produced significantly different mechanisms for acting on the social than those found in North American anthropology; these have had important and long-lasting influences on contemporary national and international practices of social governance.

The need to address the applications of scientific racism was a central part of the rationale for the establishment of UNESCO in the immediate aftermath of World War II.[4] The Second General Conference of UNESCO in 1949 adopted three resolutions: "to study and collect scientific materials concerning questions of race," "to give wide diffusion to the scientific material collected," and "to prepare an educational campaign based on this information" (UNESCO 1949). Accordingly, an expert meeting was held in December 1949, involving a number of anthropologists and sociologists, including Claude Lévi-Strauss and Ashley Montagu.[5] The statement agreed on by this meeting was published in April 1950 as *The Race Question* (Montagu 1950). The *UNESCO Courier* reported its publication with the headline "Fallacies of Racism Exposed" and declared the statement "a practical weapon—to all men and woman of goodwill who are engaged in the good fight for human brotherhood" ("Fallacies" 1950: 1). This notion of human brotherhood was important in denoting a particular vision of a collectivized, international humanity in which humans shared certain fundamental needs, wants, and reciprocal obligations and which directly underpinned UNESCO's rationale as a global (and actively *globalizing*) organization. The hierarchical concept of "race" would be replaced directly with the nonhierarchical concept of "culture" or "ethnicity." Moreover, each culture contributed to what Lévi-Strauss (1952)—drawing on both the French and American anthropological traditions (Visweswaran 2010: 75–76)—described as a unique and "distinctive" path toward human diversity.[6] As such, human progress, understood in its most fundamental terms as entering into the experience of modernity, was to be measured in terms of the interactions of different cultural groups, rather than being conceived as the outcome of any cultural, biological, or technological trait inherent to any of them. Progress was a function of intercultural knowledge, and thus cultural diversity was integral to progress. But here, as Alana Lentin (2005: 387) points out, lay a contradiction, because such intercultural dialogue would ultimately lead to the *erosion* of cultural distinctiveness, and hence of cultural diversity, rather than strengthening it. She also notes that the implication of the UNESCO statement on race is that racism came to be seen as a problem of *individual* ignorance based on incorrect scientific information. As such, it occluded an understanding of racism as "a consequence of . . . the political conditions brought about by the institutionalization of nationalism in the modern European nation-state [and] the need for populations of these units to be defined vis a vis external Others" (381); in short, it hindered a view of racism as being institutionally embedded within the very experience and practice of modernity and the modernizing project that lay at the heart of UNESCO itself.

The aftermath of the first statement on race and the circumstances prompting a revised version a year later are outlined in the UNESCO publication *The Race Question: Results of an Inquiry* (1952). Serious criticisms of the first UNESCO statement, from a number of prominent British and American physical and social anthropologists (among them the evolutionary biologist and then director of UNESCO Julian Huxley), were published in a number of locations, perhaps most stringently in the October 1950 issue of the journal *Man*. Critics defended race as a meaningful biological category and criticized ethnicity as a concept beyond independent and scientific verification, suggesting the statement was flawed owing to the lack of expertise in physical and social anthropology among the expert panel that had drafted it. Another expert meeting took place in June 1951, which resulted in the publication of the revised UNESCO *Statement on the Nature of Race and Race Differences* (Dunn 1951).[7] While much could be said about the differences between the two documents (e.g., see Selcer 2012), the main point we wish to draw out here is the way in which the second document contradicted the first, not only in arguing for the maintenance of the term *race* to describe physical differences between human populations, but also in emphasizing differences in intelligence and personality test scores between "nonliterate" and "more civilized" peoples. Where the first version stated that "national, religious, geographic, linguistic and cultural groups do not necessarily coincide with racial groups: and the cultural traits of such groups have no demonstrated genetic connection with racial traits. . . . [I]t would be better when speaking of human races to drop the term 'race' altogether and speak of ethnic groups" (quoted in UNESCO 1969: 31), the revised version stated that experts agreed to preserve the term *race* to describe "groups of mankind possessing well developed and primarily heritable physical differences from other groups" (quoted in UNESCO 1969: 38).

There are two significant implications of these revisions. The first consists in the persistence of the biological identification of race as a legitimate means for differentiating populations and, indeed, the addition of new ways of differentiating populations through the introduction of supplementary axes of difference in the form of culture and/or ethnicity. The second is the implication of racial inequality that is maintained by the statement on intelligence and personality testing. These two combined to produce significant discursive effects in relation to the work of UNESCO (see figures C.1 and C.2). For if, as Lévi-Strauss believed, human diversity was fundamental to human progress and modernization but was simultaneously threatened by the intercultural dialogue that would sustain it, then such inequalities would require the recognition of certain special, ambiguously racialized categories of vulnerable persons who embodied this human biological and cultural diversity but required special forms of support if this diversity was to be preserved. We can see the emergence of one such category of endangered personhood in the new transnational concept of "indigeneity."

The category of "indigenous people" was first used in the Covenant of the League of Nations in 1920 and subsequently found definition through the work of the UN's International Labour Organization in the 1930s in relation to the potential of "native" labor and the idea that responsibility for the welfare of Aboriginal peoples should be removed from the nation-state and entrusted to an international body (Rowse 2008). As such, the term *indigenous* became synonymous with a vulnerable form of temporalized racial difference that required careful management through international intervention. With the emergence of international indigenous rights movements in the mid-1970s, Rowse argues, indigeneity in settler-colonial nation-states (such as Australia, New Zealand, Canada, and the United States) came to be defined through an ambivalence toward national labor markets, which contributed to the ongoing maintenance of difference between indigenes and settlers and the emergence of what might be perceived as a new "indigenous modernity." Key to the definition of indigeneity was the delineation of a series of threats and forms of vulnerability. Ironically, given the emphasis on the local within discourses of indigeneity, "indigenousness" largely came to be defined through the work of various international conventions, in particular, the International Labour Organization's Indigenous and Tribal Populations Convention (1957) and its revision, the Indigenous and Tribal Peoples Convention (1989). Culture was thus simultaneously understood to represent

FIGURES C.1 AND C.2 Two screenshots from the film *Brotherhood of Man* (1946), directed by Robert Cannon for United Productions of America.

———

The short animated film *Brotherhood of Man* (1946) was financed by the United Auto Workers Union as a "contribution to the American people." It was based on Ruth Benedict and Gene Weltfish's (1943) Public Affairs Committee pamphlet *The Races of Mankind*. In the first screenshot (above), reified and sterotypical representations of a series of different cultural groups are each goaded by their "racist" alter ego to focus on the differences among themselves and to fight. In the second shot (below), representatives of three biological "races," identified as Caucasian, Negroid, and Mongaloid, are shown to be equally physically able. Benedict's work here exemplifies UNESCO's postwar approach to the culture concept, within the context of broader international antiracism campaigns, in identifying culture as the primary site of difference but continuing a modified form of racialized discourse in an insistence on certain fundamental biological differences, here seen to be the result of historical isolation of different human populations, alongside a series of newly identified "cultural" differences. The shared "brotherhood of man" becomes the justification for a universalized conception of individual and collective human needs, the creation and maintainence of forms of supranational social governance, and the connection between culture, education, and development, which are embodied by UNESCO and other international organizations.

———

the key to modernization and to act as an impediment to it. We look next at the contradictions that this engendered.

CULTURE AREAS, "SELF-DETERMINATION," AND THE EMERGENCE OF NEW INDIGENOUS GOVERNANCE STRUCTURES

What collecting, ordering, and governing practices came to be associated with these new conceptions of indigeneity? There has been much discussion of the UNESCO World Heritage List, the International Union for the Conservation of Nature Red List, and other similar apparatuses that have allowed groups of endangered "natural" and "cultural" objects, places, and practices to be collected in situ while simultaneously being mobilized and governed at a distance. The role of such apparatuses in articulating and specifying new forms of biological, linguistic, and cultural endangerment has also been noted (Vidal and Dias 2016; see also Harrison 2013a; Rico 2014). The governmental rationalities of indigeneity were simultaneously interventionist in the relations they established between international organizations and nation-states, and were based around principles of self-determination in the relations between nation-states and the indigenous peoples who occupied their territories. As such, they required the emergence of new indigenous governance structures, albeit structures that were formed around preexisting templates. Here, to illustrate these developments, we look briefly at how these new indigenous governance structures drew on anthropological work relating to the culture-area concept in Australia and Aotearoa/New Zealand.

As Gillian Cowlishaw (1998), Elizabeth Povinelli (2002), and others have shown, the concept of self-determination emerged in the wake of Australia's referendum in 1967, which introduced a constitutional clause that allowed laws to be targeted specifically at indigenous populations, and recognized them as part of the national population. At the same time, there were a number of prominent requests from Indigenous Australians themselves to develop new structures for self-administration, relating partially to movements toward the recognition of indigenous land rights and drawing on the UN's recognition of self-determination as a fundamental human right as a function of the UN International Covenant on Civil and Political Rights in 1966. Following the referendum, the anthropologist W. E. H. Stanner, who had been prominent in lobbying for indigenous self-determination, was invited by the Holt government to form a Commonwealth Council for Aboriginal Affairs, along with senior bureaucrats Barrie Dexter and H. C. ("Nugget") Coombes.[8] Between 1932 and 1936 Stanner had held an appointment in the

Department of Anthropology at the University of Sydney, where A. P. Elkin, a strong advocate of the role of government anthropology and indigenous assimilation policies, was chair. In 1936 Stanner moved to London to complete his PhD at the London School of Economics under the supervision of Bronislaw Malinowski. In the postwar years his views came to diverge strongly from Elkin's, and in his role on the Council for Aboriginal Affairs, he, Dexter, and Coombes outlined a radical agenda for indigenous self-determination based around the granting of land rights, the facilitation of movement to "outstations" within indigenous territories, and increased social welfare and the development of community-based economies. Central to these reforms, which began to be implemented by the Whitlam government in the early 1970s, was a system of indigenous land councils, based around traditional "cultural" boundaries. An appropriate template for these boundaries was found in anthropologist Norman B. Tindale's map of "tribal" boundaries, several versions of which had been published over the five decades it took to research it, but which achieved its final form in the map and accompanying catalogue *Aboriginal Tribes of Australia: Their Terrain, Environmental Controls, Distribution, Limits, and Proper Names* (Tindale 1974). This, in turn, was a direct cartographic manifestation of Alfred Kroeber's culture-area concept.

Tindale, who was originally employed as an entomologists' assistant in 1919, oversaw the South Australian Museum's field expedition to Groote Eylandt and the Roper River in the Northern Territory in 1921–22. While his primary objective was to make entomological observations, he was also tasked with collecting ethnographic specimens and making observations of local Aboriginal people, and in 1921 he was sent by the museum director to meet with Spencer at the Museum of Victoria to receive informal instruction for this purpose (Jones 1987). While on Groote Eylandt he was "introduced" to the concept of Aboriginal tribal boundaries by the interlocutor Maroadunei, a Ngandi man who accompanied Tindale throughout much of the twelve months he spent living with Aboriginal people in the region (Tindale 1974: 3). Tindale subsequently assumed the position of curator of ethnology at the South Australian Museum in 1927; he held this position until his retirement in 1965. His position at the museum gave him the vantage point from which to assemble what would become his life work: a map of the entire continent of Australia showing its tribal territorial boundaries at "the time of European contact" (Tindale 1974: 1; see figure C.3). The map was assembled through extensive ethnographic field research, as well as historical and archival study. A major impetus in its production was the 1938–39 joint Harvard and Adelaide Universities Anthropological Expedition to Central Australia with Joseph

Birdsell, from which the first version of the map was produced and published by the Royal Society of South Australia in 1940. Tindale (1974: 3–4) cited the direct influence of Kroeber's culture-area concept on this work and on the later edition. The 1974 map represented the result of substantial revisions and further clarification through fieldwork and archival research undertaken during the 1950s and 1960s. It was completed after Tindale was granted an honorary doctorate by the University of California and had assumed a visiting professorship there in 1967.

It is difficult to overestimate the importance of Tindale's map in promulgating the idea that Aboriginal people were not unconstrained "nomads" but that indigenous social organization was instead territorially organized around principles of kinship, language, and culture that were established genealogically. But in the 1970s, at a time when Australian federal and, subsequently, state governments were seeking a template for organizing new indigenous-led governance structures, the map had a major influence in determining the spatial nature, and the geographical boundaries, of a series of new Aboriginal land councils that would come to take increasing responsibility for matters of indigenous welfare, health, and political organization (see figure C.4). Further, the map itself would have a major influence on the development of indigenous land rights in Australia and the notion of a pre-existing, territorially based system of law, which was central to the Mabo Decision of 1992 and the Native Title Act of 1993. The map provided not only evidence for territorial organization but also a spatial and discursive template underpinning indigenous claims to land tenure. In the connection the map provided between culture, language, territory, and genealogy, it provided a ready prototype for the newly emerging governance structures intended to facilitate indigenous self-determination.

The ways in which the present system of local, regional, and, in some cases, state Aboriginal land councils developed varied significantly from state to state. To take the New South Wales system as an example, the New South Wales Aboriginal Land Council was formed out of an existing land rights lobby group as a result of the passage of the Aboriginal Land Rights Act (NSW) in 1983. This act established a three-tiered system of elected local, regional, and state Aboriginal land councils, organized geographically, which would assume responsibility for a range of functions, including the acquisition and management of land, the administration of locally run enterprises, community development, and the organization and provision of housing and financial aid. The boundaries of these local and regional land councils were not predetermined by the legislation, and they do not in every case map directly onto the boundaries of the Tindale map. Nonetheless, the two sets of boundaries relate very closely to one another, not only in the precise details of the tribal boundaries and Local Aboriginal Land Council boundaries, but, more importantly, in the assumption that the correct way of organizing such administrative structures of self-government was based more or less on local culture and language area boundaries.

In considering the governmental rationalities established by a policy of Australian indigenous self-determination, it is clear that this was simultaneously a progressive state modernizing project and one in which new categories of colonial-liberal subjecthood were generated. As Cowlishaw notes, "while the state ostensibly tried to hand Aboriginal people control over their own domain, it did not in fact relinquish anything. The success of this policy depended on Aboriginal people wanting the ends determined by the state, and in a sense they did" (1998: 165). These new forms of self-management were to be realized by recognizing, if not valorizing, specific forms of cultural difference that were constructed around a notion of indigenous communities as culturally and geographically bounded entities. Spatially, these entities were conceived of as geographically remote from metropolitan centers. Politically, they relied on a notion of cultural difference that was at once both relativist and abstract. While culture was seen as a form of "glue" that held such groups in bounded autonomy, it also constituted an impediment, or at least a series of limitations on the exercising of responsibilized freedom, that, on an individual level, would require Aboriginal people to overcome its constraints (see further discussion in Kowal 2008). These definitions clearly drew on Kroeber's culture-area concept, which had found significant administrative traction in the pre– and post–World War II periods in a range of different national contexts.

It was, however, precisely this traction that was among the key issues at stake in the Northern Territory Invention (NTI). Prompted by the report *Little Children Are Sacred* (Northern Territory Board 2007), which urged the need to protect indigenous children from widespread sexual abuse and victimization, the NTI—launched by the conservative government led by John Howard a few days after the report's release—sought to roll back the limited forms of autonomous self-government that had earlier been promoted under the auspices of the culture-area concept, challenging the role it accorded to customary law and culture. The NTI consisted of a range of prohibitions and restrictions articulating a varied set of concerns. The prohibition of alcohol and pornography and the quarantining of welfare provisions rested on the revival of earlier assessments of Aboriginality as still lagging behind as far

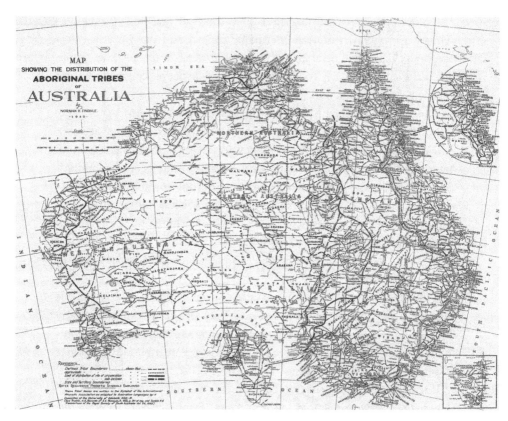

FIGURE C.3 Map showing the distribution of the Aboriginal tribes of Australia, by Norman B. Tindale. NLA MAP G 8961.E1 1940, Adelaide: Government Photolithographer, 1940. Courtesy of the National Library of Australia.

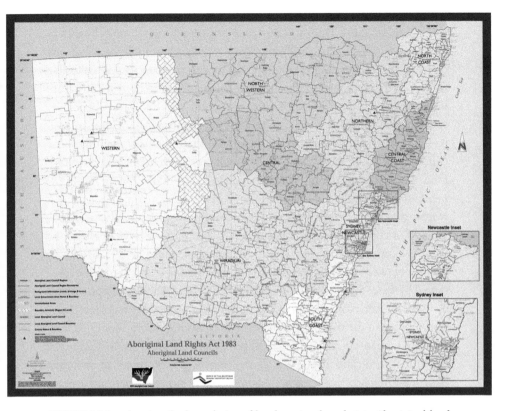

FIGURE C.4 Map showing the boundaries of local, regional, and state Aboriginal land councils in New South Wales. Courtesy of Land and Property Information NSW and NSW Aboriginal Land Council.

The culture-area concept, developed and refined in the North American context by Clark Wissler and Alfred Kroeber (see figure 4.4), was directly adopted and deployed in a range of administrative contexts in Australia and New Zealand in the pre- and postwar period. In this image, we see the ways in which the anthropologist Norman B. Tindale's map of the locations of Aboriginal tribal boundaries in Australia formed both a discursive and a cartographic template for the formation of various levels of Aboriginal land councils in the Australian state of New South Wales. Similar processes can be observed in Aotearoa/New Zealand, where Henry Devenish Skinner's work on tribal cultural areas influenced government administration but also moved toward Māori self-determination in the postwar period.

---

as the traditional attributes of liberal personhood were concerned, which required an adequate degree of will formation capable of bringing the passions under control. Measures directed at taking community land, organizations, and assets out of the hands of Aboriginal organizations and subjecting them to directive forms of state administration rested on a similar logic, but one directed at perceived shortcomings in Aboriginal capacity for collective forms of self-governance rather than at the inadequate character structure of individuals. These prohibitions and restrictions were, however, made possible only by the third aspect of the NTI: the significant limitations placed on the degree to which the courts could take account of customary law and cultural practice in their sentencing procedures. Heather Douglas and Mark Finnane (2012) note the respects in which the NTI, in developing this argument, followed in the slipstream of a long history in which violence against women and children within Aboriginal communities has served as a threshold authorizing government intervention within intra-Aboriginal affairs. Its use in the context of the NTI, they argue, has been legitimated by a distinctive alliance between a revisionist school of anthropology, most notably represented by Peter Sutton, and an influential current of Aboriginal opinion led by the Cape York community leader and indigenous intellectual Noel Pearson. This led to the distinguishing features of Aboriginal culture ("egalitarian social organisation . . . traditional power structures . . . family loyalty . . . traditional medical beliefs . . . [and] the lingering background of an originally semi-nomadic economy with its appropriate but minimal hygiene practices . . . demand sharing, and its general rejection of accumulation" [Sutton, quoted in H. Douglas and Finnane 2012: 204–5]) being interpreted not as sites of tension between indigenous and settler culture but as dysfunctional adaptations to modernity that could be overcome only through struggles conducted at the level of the individual.

At both an individual and a collective level, then, Aboriginality is understood to serve as a marker of a backwardness that must be overcome, a task that requires outside intervention until Aborigines—as both individuals and communities—have matured sufficiently to become governors of themselves. As such, it is a marker, Alissa Macoun (2011) argues, that is both cultural and racial in its ascription of specific cultural traits to a flawed racial constitution still governed by the legacies of the primitivism that provided the initial warrant for the exclusion of Aborigines from the liberal political community. If the NTI is thus premised on an eventual overcoming of the temporal gap separating remote Aboriginal communities from political modernity, there is a spatial logic in play too in the need to overcome the disorder constituted by the dysfunctionality of those communities by reintegrating them within the settler governmental domain and thus repairing the threat to its territorial sovereignty constituted by their earlier conception as quasi-autonomous self-governing cultures.

We see similar patterns in the trajectories toward self-determination that were shaped by the legacy of the Young Maori Party in postwar Aotearoa/ New Zealand, despite significant differences in the institutional arrangements and colonial histories of Australia and Aotearoa/New Zealand.[9] From the 1980s, the notion of biculturalism, which came to be exemplified in museums like the Museum of New Zealand Te Papa Tongarewa (opened in 1998), was said to have recognized Māori cultural difference, in contrast to the integration policies of the postwar period and the prewar assimilation policies.[10] But Māori self-determination was not uniquely a creation of this decade of protest, social change, and the Māori renaissance; rather, its roots can be traced back to the interwar period and the concept of cultural adaptation that was developed through the anthropological governance of Āpirana Ngata, Peter Buck, and others (who in turn borrowed it from the anthropologist Raymond Firth) and put to work in the Department of Native Affairs. As we showed in chapter 5, the notion of cultural adaptation favored by Māori scholar-politicians provided a more malleable interpretation of culture along Boasian lines than was offered by the culture-area concept. Although this intervention was short, limited, and partial in its achievements, it was distinctive when judged in relation to fledgling indigenist movements in other former settler colonies.[11] As historian Richard Hill has demonstrated, the Native Land Amendment and Native Claims Adjustment Act of 1929 funded Māori farming, thereby effectively "underpinning a communal way of life based on tribal values and organising principles" and in so doing "sustaining the nexus between the quest for rangatiratanga (chieftainship, sovereignty) and the viability of retaining . . . land based self-determination" (2004: 117). Through the land development schemes, tribal leaders were placed in key positions and revived their traditional roles, preserving the "communal ethos" of Māori society (118).

A modern post-assimilationist Māori consciousness emerged in this period from several interrelated networks that competed, crossed, and converged around heritage, science, government, and race. Buck and Ngata moved both inside and outside government, working for the state but also with and for their own people. They were certainly not rebels seeking liberation from the yoke of colonial culture, but neither did they simply tolerate assimilation. Ranginui Walker (2001: 213–14) has referred to Ngata's "rapprochement" with the state, and James Belich (2001: 206) has described his policies as a "brilliant strategy of subversive cooperation," which achieved a state of "benign segregation" rather than assimilation.

Taking the long view, then, we can see that in the period from just before World War I up to the end of World War II, New Zealand society was at a crossroads in terms of what Belich (2001: 29–30) calls its "re-colonial" orientation to Mother England, with the reformation of settler identity, incorporating elements of Māori heritage, and the Māori relationship with the state moving to a post-assimilationist phase (Sissons 2000; R. Hill 2009). This transition from earlier assimilationist discourses to Māori-influenced ideas of cultural adaptation in the 1920s and 1930s paved the way for subsequent Labour government reforms in the 1930s and 1940s, which in turn sowed the seeds for policies of integration in postwar New Zealand and then self-determination from the 1980s on (Walker 2004; R. Hill 2009).[12] Meanwhile, the notion of culture areas introduced by Skinner at Otago Museum and the University of Otago, which combined with and at times was in opposition to the notion of cultural adaptation (Cameron and McCarthy 2015), found its way into postwar discourses of government administration (Department of Maori Affairs), tribal self-governance (Rūnanga or tribal trust boards), and even schema for styles of Māori art (S. Mead 1986). In this way, the transactional realities of "culture" and "culture area," and the empirical material on which they were developed in both the Australian and Aotearoa/New Zealand contexts in the interwar and postwar periods, imprinted themselves clearly onto the organizational structure of subsequent practices of indigenous self-government in both countries.

Clear resonances of these new practices of indigenous self-determination and their relationship to earlier transactional realities that emerged in the interwar period can be seen within the contemporary museum sector in all of the Anglophone settler societies with which we are concerned here. These are manifest, for example, in the increasingly common practice of providing identified indigenous positions within national and state museums in Australia, New Zealand, and elsewhere, and in consultations and partnerships with "source communities" globally over the management and exhibition of museum objects (e.g., see A. Brown and Peers 2003, 2015; Lonetree and Cobb 2008; R. Phillips 2011; Clifford 2013; Golding and Modest 2013). Similarly, practices relating to the repatriation of indigenous human and cultural remains, and the proliferation of indigenous-run "keeping places" as alternative repositories of ethnographic material (often collected during the "museum phase" of anthropology), alongside a contemporary focus on indigenous cultural and intellectual rights and "digital repatriation" of ethnographic materials, also represent the extension of practices of self-determination, drawing in an Australian and Aotearoa/New Zealand context on models of self-government, based on the concept of culture areas, which have subsequently been brought to bear on the contemporary museum sector.[13]

CODA

There is, though, another aspect to the tangled histories of the relations between the categories of race and culture and the ordering of differences as these stretch across the pre- and postwar periods. These are perhaps clearest in the American context in the logic informing W. E. B. Du Bois's oft-noted refusal to embrace the culture concept in spite of a degree of personal interaction with Boas and Boas's personal antiracist credentials (see, notably, Zumwait 2008). As Kamala Visweswaran (2010) interprets it, this reflected Du Bois's unwillingness to jettison the conceptions of race that, preceding the biological construction placed on it in the late nineteenth century, rested on a more social logic in which "blood," as the mechanism of racial inheritance, was understood as a metaphysical rather than a biological category, and one that operated above the differences of culture that would eventually inform the postwar language of ethnicities. If, as we have seen, African Americans, Native Americans, and Asian Americans were excluded from the mechanisms of assimilation established by the culture concept through the operation of a residual set of biological racial categories, Du Bois proposed a counter to this in his conception of race and racial identities as "coalitional, contingent, and performative" responses to shared experiences of discrimination (Visweswaran 2010: 71). It is worth quoting Visweswaran's assessment of the dynamics at play here more fully: "The Middle Passage, slavery, and the experience of racial terror produce a race of African Americans out of subjects drawn from different cultures; genocide, forced removal to reservations, the experience of racial terror make Native Americans, subjects drawn from different linguistic and tribal affiliations, a race; war relocation camps and legal exclusion, the experience of discrimination make Asian Americans, subjects drawn from different cultural and linguistic backgrounds, a race" (2010: 71).

A similar logic informs the ongoing process of forging a pan-Australian Aboriginal and Torres Strait Islander identity across the divisions between different languages and cultures, between urban and remote Aboriginal communities, and between Aborigines and Torres Strait Islanders (McGregor 2011: 173–82), and, indeed, the formation of a pan-indigenous identity as a result of global indigenous rights movements.[14] These are not, however, purely defensive strategies. To the contrary, they constitute the reorganization of transactional realities through which such "races," in refusing the status of an assigned ethnicity, seek to reorder their relations with, and to act on, dominant cultures globally. In many ways, this phenomenon constitutes the most radical way in which earlier logics of race have been reworked and transformed in the latter part of the twentieth and the early twenty-first century.

CHAPTER ONE. Collecting, Ordering, Governing

1. For a fuller discussion of the stress placed on the need for evolutionary displays to exhibit smooth and continuous developmental sequences, and its relation to the concerns of post-Darwinian liberalism, see Bennett 2004: chap. 4.

2. Spencer to Tylor, September 1, 1900, box 13A, fol. s16, Tylor Papers, Pitt Rivers Museum, Oxford.

3. Bain Attwood (2003) offers a useful general overview of these questions, while Jane Lydon (2005) explores their implications through a more particular history of the Corranderrk Aboriginal Station on Melbourne's outskirts.

4. Spencer 1914 is the key text here. Its racializing discursive traits are discussed by Bennett (2010).

5. For the most detailed account of this expedition, see the essays collected in Kendall and Krupnik 2003. See also Freed 2012.

6. See Boas's correspondence, Department of Anthropology, box 12, folder 2, Division of Anthropology Archives, AMNH, New York.

7. Addressing the lessons of anthropology for race relations in America, Boas (1911: 252–53) discounted Native Americans as too insignificant to be of much practical concern, both in terms of their overall numbers and in terms of their contribution to the racial composition of the American population through miscegenation.

8. We are concerned here with what became the dominant institutional conceptions of the MH. More complicated stories would need to be told to fully disentangle the relations between these and the aesthetic conceptions informing both contemporary surrealist practices and the intellectual formation of France's main anthropological field-workers. Hollier and Ollman (1991) and Debaene (2010) discuss these questions.

9. From his initial appointment as the director of the Musée d'Ethnographie du Trocadéro in 1928, Paul Rivet, joined shortly thereafter by Georges Henri Rivière, launched a sustained critique of the principles of display that then prevailed at the Trocadéro (Rivet and Rivière 1930). This critique was conducted in the name of a rationalizing modernism that would make the scientific ordering of the relations between different cultures publicly comprehensible. See Gorgus 2003 for further details of this muséographie claire.

10. For probing discussions of the position of the MH in relation to these processes, see L'Estoile 2007 and Wilder 2005.

11. McQueen's book advocated a didactic approach to display, with objects mounted within graphic elements and photographs to tell a story to the general visitor. These approaches, seen in the Field Museum's new Plains Indians Hall opened in 1936, used commercial techniques showcased at Chicago's Century of Progress exposition in 1933.

12. "Miscellaneous Museum Labels 1923–56," MU 2, 11/1, Te Papa Archives (TPA), Wellington.

13. "Guide to the Dominion Museum and National Art Gallery and War Memorial Carrillon," MU 203, 3/10, TPA.

14. The generous proportions belie Oliver's original instructions that the house should be built "in the old Maori way" with "low side walls and low front door." See Oliver to the architects William Henry Gummer and Charles Reginald Ford, March 16, 1931, Oliver miscellaneous files, MU 208, 2/1, TPA. For Ngata's proposals see Ngata to Oliver, October 29, 1935, MU 208, 2/1, TPA.

15. For a helpful overview of these questions, see Harrison 2013b.

16. For an overview of similarities and differences, see Bennett 2005.

17. Driver (2001) offers a detailed discussion of these questions, focusing particularly on their implications for the different perspectives of Georges Cuvier and Alexander von Humboldt. The historical background to these is discussed by Outram (1984).

18. There are a number of different interpretations of the concern with the role of material agents that has been evident for some time now across the social sciences and humanities. These do not all point in the same direction. The "material turn" we identify here has different implications from the "new materialisms" (Coole and Frost 2010) that derive their main impetus from a revived interest in vitalist thought and philosophy.

19. For details of Boas's early fieldwork practices—initially conducted mainly under the auspices of the British Association for the Advancement of Science and subsequently as chief organizer of the AMNH's Jesup Expedition—see Cole 1999, Kendall and Krupnik 2003, and, for a more probing assessment of the relations between Boas's museum and fieldwork practices, Jacknis 1996. While Boas's initial fieldwork experience involved a period of close to twelve months living among the Eskimo of Baffin Island, his role in the Jesup Expedition involved only two relatively short periods "in the field." After his move to Columbia University, his collecting practices were increasingly mediated via his relations with Hunt.

20. Briggs and Bauman (1999) offer a searching assessment of the power relations informing Boas's correspondence with Hunt. Focusing on the meta-discursive properties shaping Boas's letters, they argue that these contributed to a modernist shaping of the other that was influenced by the early twentieth-century dynamics of U.S. state formation. One is struck, reading this correspondence, by a grating (lack of) contact between two different worlds as Boas, driven by his scientific interests and professional pressures, harries and cajoles Hunt to provide him with the materials he wants,

frequently threatening to cut off his funding, while Hunt negotiates the contending pressures created by his relations with his local Native American communities, the Indian Office, local missionaries, the Canadian authorities responsible for Indian affairs, Boas, and the New York museum and university world. His letter to Boas written on March 20, 1905 (Boas Papers, Hunt Folder 12, Library of the American Philosophical Society) is a moving testimony to his sense of being caught in an impossible bind between two worlds.

21. See Morton and Mulvaney 1996 for an account of Spencer's role in the Horn Expedition into Central Australia in 1894. Mulvaney and Calaby 1985 and Mulvaney, Morphy, and Petch 1997 remain the most detailed accounts of Spencer and Gillen's subsequent expeditions to Central Australia.

22. Grognet (2010) offers the most detailed assessment of the differences among these, particularly in noting the different roles accorded to women in the MH's missions.

23. But see also Vokes (2007), who, although not drawing on the concept of agencement, advances similar arguments, as do Tomas (1991) and Olsen et al. (2012).

24. See Reynolds 2013 for an application of the concept of guerrilla warfare to Aboriginal military strategies during this period.

25. With regard to the mechanisms of collecting, see Alberti 2009 and Gosden and Larson 2007 for assessments of the consequences of the different ways in which the Manchester Museum and Pitt Rivers Museum, respectively, acquired different components of their collections.

26. Jacknis (1996: 199) cites passages from Boas's diary describing participation in potlatch ceremonies as a nuisance, interrupting his work centered on the collection of texts, whereas, for reasons that Wolfe (1999) has argued, Spencer was centrally preoccupied with rituals.

27. The concept of the document played a number of somewhat ambivalent roles in the projects of the MH. Hollier and Ollman (1991) offer a detailed discussion of these.

28. See Jolly 2001 for a discussion of related questions in connection with the archival legacies of Griaule's missions.

29. Boas also collected oral testimony in order to access the subjective meanings informing the use and interpretation of artifacts as a means of deciphering the distinctive patterning of a culture. His famous instruction to George Hunt to forgo the collection of objects if he could not also provide the stories accompanying them is often cited to this effect (see, for example, Jacknis 2002b: 49). Of the red bands on the handle of a cooking ladle, Boas lectured a Yale audience that "we get no idea" of what this means "simply by the red decoration of the object, unless the Indian would tell us what it really means." Lecture "The Art of the Thompson Indians," given at the Psychological Laboratory of Yale, December 27, 1899, Correspondence, 1894–1907, box 1, folder 1, Department of Anthropology Archives, AMNH.

30. Boas wrote to Robert Lowie, one of his students, to this effect in 1918. Boas to Lowie, March 8, 1918, Boas Papers, B61, Library of the American Philosophical Society, Philadelphia. The respects in which Boas's departure from the AMNH represented a critique of the contribution that the museum as such might make to anthropology,

as distinct from his assessment of the shortcomings of the AMNH in this regard, are also clear from a letter he wrote to Haddon to explain the particular circumstances that prompted him to leave the AMNH. He did so because he was anxious that, otherwise, in view of the importance of museums to ethnology, Haddon might view his resignation as "almost unintelligible" or "hardly to the advantage of ethnology." Letter to Haddon, June 25, 1905, Boas Papers, B61, Library of the American Philosophical Society.

31. Connections between surrealism and the MH have, however, often been exaggerated. See Jamin 1986 for both a summary of the arguments made concerning the relations between surrealists and the MH and a pointed assessment of the specific and limited nature of these connections. With regard to the relations between surrealism and Mass-Observation, see Hubble, Jolly, and Marcus (eds.) 2001.

32. Boas to Jesup, May 7, 1897, box 9, folder 19, Anthropology Archives, AMNH.

33. Although short-lived, the attempt to set up a national network of observers for the collection of French ways of life—a project bearing some resemblances to M-O—is also relevant here: see Varagnac 1935.

34. Pels and Salemink (2000: 29–31) make a similar point in their introduction to *Colonial Subjects*.

35. See, for their original formulations of governmental rationalities, Miller and Rose 1989, and for their account of how this connects with—but was developed to some degree independently of—Foucault's account of governmentality, see their introduction in Miller and Rose 2008.

36. This is particularly true of Anglophone debates given that an English translation of *The Birth of Biopolitics* (Foucault 2008), in which Foucault elaborates his conception of liberal government (see especially his lecture of January 24, 1979), was not published until seventeen years after the English translation of his governmentality essay.

37. The implication of Australian anthropology in maintaining the doctrine of *terra nullius* way past its due date is the most relevant case here. Nancy Williams (1986) presents the first sustained assessment of the role played by this doctrine in denying Aboriginal conceptions of property in the land.

38. Although frequently treated as the same, the roles accorded habit and custom in these regards often differed significantly in their conception and their consequences. For relevant discussions, see Dirks 2001; Valverde 1996; White 2005; and Bennett 2011.

39. See K. Anderson 2007 and Conn 2004 for accounts of these processes in Australia and North America respectively.

40. See in particular Nélia Dias's (2004) account of the role played by the supposed lack of ability of "primitives" to perceive the color blue in the color spectrum, and the translation of this into fieldwork techniques for measuring this capacity. Martin Nakata (2007) offers a telling discussion of the relationships between these concerns and the relations between freedom and necessity in his discussion of the Torres Strait expeditions. Spencer and Haddon both worried over whether their subjects exhibited these capacities and, if so, to what extent. Spencer equivocated on these questions,

clearly struggling to reconcile the negative expectations of liberal aesthetic theory and his assessment of Aboriginal peoples' insensitivity to shades of color difference (Spencer 1921) with the evidence of aesthetic capacities present in body designs and bark paintings. Haddon (1895) interpreted the predominance of copying over creativity in primitive art as evidence of a lack of a capacity for freedom, whereas for Boas a capacity for aesthetic judgments of the perfection of form was a universal testifying to "the fundamental sameness of mental processes in all races and in all cultural forms of the present day" ([1927] 2010: 1).

41. Mary Poovey (1994) has explored the relations between the aesthetic theories of the civic humanists and the early development of the problematics of liberal government in eighteenth-century England. The rule of aesthetic judgment in differentiating populations with regard to their capacity for freedom has remained a constant, if contested, aspect of its subsequent history (Bennett 2013b: chap. 6).

42. For a discussion of the complex and divided relations between French anthropology and folklore studies and the Vichy regime see F. Weber 2000; for an assessment of the longer-term trajectories of the forms of "anthropology at home" associated with the Musée des Arts et Traditions Populaires, see Segalen 2001. And see Poulot 1994 on eco-museums and regional cultural ecologies.

CHAPTER TWO. Curatorial Logics and Colonial Rule

1. Throughout this chapter we use the term *native culture* in the singular. While this reflects how the term was used in the historical literature, in that usage it does not foreclose on the tremendous diversity across the colony in the cultural practices that were registered by the administration and whose distinctions were consequential for questions of rule. In using this term we are primarily concerned to designate a "style of thought" on the part of the governors, rather than an existent, particular lived experience of the governed.

2. Ironically, this position owed much to William Halse Rivers Rivers, a team member on the expedition, who came to the view, as Kuklick puts it, "that the observations of a lone anthropologist [were] more scientific than those of a research team" (2011: 19). As she continues, this was so, since "the anthropologist's body" itself was in Rivers's view was the primary, reliable measuring instrument in the field (19). There is a connection here with Mass-Observation in the ways in which Mass Observers were viewed as more or less objective recording instruments, as metaphorical "cameras" or "barometers." See further discussion in chapter 3.

3. Haddon wrote to Spencer on October 23, 1900, recommending that he use Rivers's genealogical method and that he take a cinematograph and a phonograph. PRM1E_02, Pitt Rivers Museum, Oxford.

4. In 1860–61 Robert O'Hara Burke and William John Wills led a nineteen-strong expedition from Melbourne to the Gulf of Carpentaria, the first European exploration of the continent's interior. Through a combination of bad luck and bad management a large proportion of the party died en route, including the expedition's leaders, who on the return journey succumbed to malnutrition.

5. And later around the violence caused by the transgression of the secret-sacred in acts of theft (see Povinelli 2002: 93).

6. See Rowse 1998: chap. 1 for a discussion of Edward Charles Stirling and Spencer's collecting practices on the Horn Expedition.

7. *Memorandum to Atlee Hunt Esq. from Dr. A. C. Haddon Concerning an Ethnologist for Papua, an Ethnologist for "German New Guinea," a Museum of Papuan Ethnology and a Curator for the Same, December 19, 1914,* A 453 1959/4708, National Archives Australia (NAA), Canberra.

8. Haddon, "The Practical Value of Anthropology to Administration," paper read before the Anthropological Section of the British Association at Sydney, 1914, A 453 1959/4708, NAA.

9. Haddon, "Practical Value of Anthropology to Administration," paper read before the Anthropological Section of the British Association at Sydney, 1914, A 453 1959/4708, NAA. For an account see Bell 2009b.

10. See correspondence in A 453 1959/4708, NAA.

11. See A 453 1959/4708, NAA.

12. A 453 1959/4708, NAA. This established a pattern where, as Donald Denoon argues: "The Australian Commonwealth often saw Melanesian affairs through an African lens" (1999: 285). Later Murray followed the development of the International Institute of African Languages and Cultures, with Malinowski forwarding him issues of *Africa*. See CRS G69 16—14, NAA.

13. Mulvaney and Calaby have suggested an early connection to the Western Pacific in Spencer's thinking on questions of anthropology and colonial administration, observing that when Spencer returned to England in 1904 "he spent the voyage in company with the retiring Lieutenant-Governor of British New Guinea, Sir William MacGregor, from whom he obtained firsthand advice on native administration" (1985: 185).

14. On the MacGregor Collection, see Quinnell 2000.

15. On the POC, see Schaffarczyk 2006, 2011.

16. *Memorandum to Atlee Hunt Esq. from Dr. A. C. Haddon Concerning an Ethnologist for Papua, an Ethnologist for "German New Guinea," a Museum of Papuan Ethnology and a Curator for the Same,* December 19, 1914, p. 2, A 453 1959/4708, NAA.

17. For discussions of this aspect of Haddon's work, see Herle and Rouse 1998; E. Edwards 1998; and Bell 2009b: 151–52.

18. *Memorandum to Atlee Hunt Esq. from Dr. A. C. Haddon Concerning an Ethnologist for Papua, an Ethnologist for "German New Guinea," a Museum of Papuan Ethnology and a Curator for the Same,* December 19, 1914, p. 2, A 453 1959/4708, NAA.

19. Haddon, "Practical Value of Anthropology to Administration," paper read before the Anthropological Section of the British Association at Sydney, 1914, p. 2, A 453 1959/4708, NAA.

20. A 453 1959/4708, NAA.

21. The development of coconut plantations, particularly "native plantations" that were intended to be developed in the interests of local communities, was a central plank of Murray's administrative regime.

22. Other alternatives for the arrangement of indigenous materials were potentially available. During this period Spencer experimented with "habitat and life group" exhibits of Australian avi-fauna (Mulvaney and Calaby 1985: 256). This would seem to open up the question as to what Spencer's views might have been with regard to this "life-group" style as an alternative approach to the display of indigenous materials, particularly as it shares something with Boas's presentations of North American indigenes as regionally distributed, holistic cultures at the American Museum of Natural History. By 1915 the NMV did include one diorama-type display, a composite view of a "scene illustrating Australian Aboriginal life" (Spencer [1915] 1922: 136; Petch 2009: 260).

23. Baldwin Spencer, *Report on the Half Castes and Aboriginals of the Southern Division of the Northern Territory, with Special Reference to the Bungalow at Stuart and Hermannsburg Mission Station*, 1923, CRS A1 1930/1542, NAA.

24. Haddon, "Practical Value of Anthropology to Administration," paper read before the Anthropological Section of the British Association at Sydney, 1914, pp. 3–4, A 453 1959/4708, NAA.

25. Haddon, "Practical Value of Anthropology to Administration," p. 4.

26. Haddon, "Practical Value of Anthropology to Administration," pp. 4–5.

27. Murray to Minister of State for External Affairs, February 23, 1915, A 453 1959/4708, NAA.

28. Murray negotiated with Robert Etheridge, the director of the AM, for the collection's accommodation. When the museum withdrew its offer, Murray arranged, with Williams's assistance, for the collection to move to Canberra's Institute of Anatomy (A 453 1959/4708, NAA).

29. "Papuan Exploration," *The Argus*, February 6, 1923.

30. For commentaries see Bell, Brown, and Gordon 2013; Dixon 2001, 2011; Specht and Fields 1984; and Specht 2003.

31. Williams's posting was remarkable for his duration in the field. With two decades in the role, Williams "spent more than a quarter of his time in the field"; as Young and Clark note, this was "more than any anthropologist before and, with a few modern exceptions, by any since" (2001: 35). For accounts of Williams, see Bell 2006, 2009a, 2009b, 2010; Dibley 2014; Schaffarczyk 2011; Schwimmer 1976; and Young and Clark 2001.

32. CRS G69 16–17, NAA. Williams spent time with Malinowski at the London School of Economics on a Rockefeller scholarship in 1933–34, and he was in regular correspondence with other luminaries, such as Haddon, Seligman, and Marett.

33. For accounts of patrolling, see Humphries 1923 and Schieffelin and Crittenden 1991.

34. Stocking contends that Williams and his counterpart in the mandated territory of New Guinea, Ernst Chinnery, were "gate-keepers to the New Guinea field" (1996: 386). On Blackwood, see Knowles 2000; Larson 2011; and Gosden and Larson 2007: 165–72. On Fortune, see Gray 1999.

35. For his report in his advisory role, see Spencer, *Report on the Half Castes and Aboriginals of the Southern Division of the Northern Territory, with Special Reference to the Bungalow at Stuart and Hermannsburg Mission Station*, 1923, CRS A1 1930/1542, NAA.

36. McGregor usefully draws out Pitt Rivers's distinction between race and population around the question of miscegenation in settler-colonial contexts. Glossing Pitt Rivers's position, McGregor writes that miscegenation "could contribute to the survival of a population, while at the same time destroying the essential racial character of a people (1997: 108). In relation to questions of biopolitics in colonial Australia this distinction makes clear that the making live of a population was simultaneously the letting die of a race. Wolfe (1999: 11) captures this logic in his distinction between ethnocide and genocide, attributing the former to programs of assimilation such as those advocated by Spencer. See also Rowse's (2014) discussion of the different currency of the narrative of "the dying native" in different settler-colonial contexts and the ways in which indigenous intellectuals have articulated the relations between the notions of a population and a people to refuse this colonial trope.

37. For Murray this situation was in contrast to the northern Nigeria of Charles Lindsay Temple (1918), on whose text he drew.

38. The acephalous problematic did not, however, correspond universally with the Papuan socialities. For example, within the Purari Delta there was a system of hereditary chiefs, and similarly in Orokolo, in the Trobriand Islands, and among the Mekeo. Mark Mosko (2012) has detailed the translation between these chiefly positions and those of the village constables established by the Murray regime.

39. While the indirect method was desirable, it was not always deemed the most expedient exercise of power. Should cultural power fail, Murray had little hesitation in turning to the judicial, enforcing laws enacted in 1919 on housing, sanitation, food production, and burial, with prison sentences for offenders.

40. The notion of the "sacred trust" was deployed in Article 22 of the Covenant of the League of Nations.

41. On this direct link between cultural production and the biopolitics of population decline see the contemporary debates: Murray 1923, 1932/33; Rivers 1922; Pitt-Rivers 1927; and Williams 1932. Murray was involved in public debate over Pitt-Rivers's criticisms of his administration. See CRS G69 16–19, fols. 1-1, NAA.

42. See Young and Clark 2001 for an assessment.

CHAPTER THREE. A Liberal Archive of Everyday Life

1. Although, importantly, not entirely—see further discussion in Hinton 2008.

2. Scott Ashley notes that far from being the geographically and intellectually remote location that they might be imagined to have been, "by 1892 the Aran Islands, despite having a population of under 3,000 . . . and being of marginal economic or political value, were one of the most written about places in Ireland" (2001: 8).

3. In the 1892 edition of *Notes and Queries on Anthropology*, John George Garson wrote, "Only two views are of any use in anthropography, namely, the full face and the profile" (BAAS 1892: 11). Haddon himself would go on to write the photography section of the 1899 revision of *Notes and Queries* (BAAS 1899; see also A. Griffiths 2002: 91–92).

4. The composite portrait was a technique developed by Galton. It uses photographs from a large series of subjects to build the distinctive characteristics or profile of a particular class of person, famously, "the criminal" and "the academic."

5. "Firbolgs" were reputed to be one of the indigenous, pre-Christian groups that inhabited Ireland. Beddoe notes, "The people of the Aran Isles, in Galway Bay, have their own strongly marked type, in some respects an exaggeration of the ordinary Gaelic one. . . . We might be disposed, trusting to Irish traditions respecting the islands, to accept these people as representatives of the Firbolg, had not Cromwell, that upsetter of all things Hibernian, left in Aranmore a small English garrison, who subsequently apostatised to Catholicism, intermarried with the natives, and so vitiated the Firbolgian pedigree" (1885: 267).

6. We note the somewhat earlier but still comparatively "late" establishment of "national" folk museums or folklife departments and/or collections within national museums in Scotland (the Highland Folk Museum was established in 1935), Ireland (as part of the work of the Coimisiún Béaloideasa Éireann [Irish Folklore Commission], established in 1935), and Wales (where a subdepartment of folk culture and industries was established in the National Museum in 1932 and a Welsh Folk Museum was opened in 1949), as well as on the Isle of Man (in the folklife collection at the Manx Museum, opened in 1922; Harry Kelly's Cottage in Cregneash, opened in 1932; and the Manx Folklife Survey, founded in 1948) during this period (see Kavanagh 1990).

7. For secondary accounts see Calder 1985; Pickering and Chaney 1986; Jeffrey 1998; Marcus 2001; Highmore 2002; Hubble 2006; Hinton 2013.

8. On "atmosphere" as the ambience in which one feels the affects of others, see Brennan 2004: 1. For further discussion of the ways in which M-O sought to measure the affective atmosphere of wartime Britain with the intention of managing it through the manipulation of civilian morale, see Dibley and Kelly 2015.

9. This is not to imply that the concept of race did not occupy a significant place in the work of M-O and its founders (see further discussion in Kushner 2004), nor that differences in the ways in which colonial and metropolitan populations were conceived were not implicated in the development of its field methodologies, as we have shown.

10. Hubble (2006: 167) observes that the first M-O report for the MoI, in September 1939, was on the subject of ministry posters. It appears that it was not until April 30, 1940, that M-O started to produce dedicated reports on general morale ("Morale in 1941 . . . ," Report P, February 4, 1941, p. 68, File Reports 1937–1972, Mass Observation Online, Adam Matthew Digital and the University of Sussex [MOO]), and on May 18, 1940, the organization commenced a series of daily morale reports that later evolved into weekly reports.

11. "Mass-Observation and Home-Front History," Report 2116, June 22, 1944, File Reports 1937–1972, MOO.

12. On the Wartime Social Survey, McLaine writes, "In the initial stages of planning, the Survey was conceived of as a supplement to the work of Mass-Observation rather than a substitute for it. And, since Mass-Observation's broad task was to assess civilian morale, the Survey was intended to do a similar job with different means. . . . The

Survey was placed under the supervision of the London School of Economics in order to avoid the appearance of 'inquisitorial' activity by the Government" (1979: 103–4).

13. "Provisional Principles for Home Planning," Report 507, November 28, 1940, p. 4, File Reports 1937–1972, MOO.

14. "Report on The-Rout-the-Rumour-Rally," Report 298, July 26, 1940, p. 12, File Reports 1937–1972, MOO. The same document reported the problem faced by the MoI as "one of the deepest and most complex . . . in the world to-day; the problem of understanding and getting into contact with the underlying mass ideas of ultra-civilised working men" (11). The implication here would seem to be that beneath the surface of "the ultra-civilised" lies an irrational, primitive depth. The establishment of a primitive structure as the kernel of modern subjectivity is a key development for British Freudians. It might be said that this relativizing gesture—that moderns and nonmoderns share a primitive kernel of subjectivity—established a connection between the knowledge practices of M-O and formulations of colonial governmentality. There are parallels here between M-O's description of "the shock" of the air raid as a "shattering psychological blow" for working-class subjects and the impact of colonization on the indigene, which led to radical upheaval of the native quotidian. Here, similarly, those figured with limited material and intellectual resources were posited as vulnerable to psychological collapse in the face of crisis. The link here is William Halse Rivers Rivers, whose work on "culture contact" in Melanesia and on shell shock in World War I soldiers established a universal primitive core to subjectivity that was revealed, and to which subjects reverted, in times of extreme crisis. See Kuklick 1991.

15. "Report on What Is Public Opinion?," Report 361, August 19, 1940, p. 8, File Reports 1937–1972, MOO. Freud, it will be recalled, was the self-described "conquistador" who discovered the workings of that great "dark continent," the unconscious. Peter Gurney (1997: 288) has suggested that Sigmund Freud's work *Group Psychology and the Analysis of the Ego*, published in 1921, "uncritically adopted many of [Gustave] Le Bon's ideas, including the supposed similarity between the 'group mind' and 'the mental life of primitive people and of children.'" The relationship between the "public mind" of M-O and the "group mind" of Freud and Le Bon may repay attention. Le Bon and Freud's work on crowds would also bear on the critical importance of crowds for M-O, among whose files can be located at least two reports filed by participant observers at political rallies, celebrating "group feeling" and "the crowd as a united whole" ("Woodford Rally Report," Report 345, August 13, 1940, p. 11, File Reports 1937–1972, MOO), and defining "a successful mass meeting" as one where there is "only one type of person; the type for which the meeting has its message" ("Report on The-Rout-the-Rumour-Rally," Report 298, July 26, 1940, p. 9, File Reports 1937–1972, MOO).

16. "Morale Now (30/4/40)," Report 89, April 30, 1940, File Reports 1937–1972, MOO.

17. "General Points in Morale," Report 2222, June 22, 1940, p. 16, File Reports 1937–1972, MOO.

18. "Report on The-Rout-the-Rumour-Rally," Report 298, July 26, 1940, p. 12, File Reports 1937–1972, MOO. For a critical engagement with M-O's methodology by a contemporary, see Firth 1939.

19. "Report from M-O on Morale Today, July 2nd 1940," Report 242, July 2, 1940, File Reports 1937–1972, MOO. Stanley described M-O as "a radical social science research organization on the borders and 'other' to institutionalised sociology" (2008: 536). See Osborne and Rose 1999 for conceptual distinctions between the notions of "opinion" and "attitude" in the British social sciences of the 1930s and 1940s. For an account of the development of M-O's methods in relation to the emergence of various disciplinary formations in the British social sciences, see Stanley 2001, 2008. For accounts of the development of the social survey see Bulmer 1985; Bulmer, Bales, and Sklar 1991; and Osborne and Rose 1997.

20. "Morale in 1941 . . . ," Report 568, February 4, 1941, pp. 56, 66, File Reports 1937–1972, MOO.

21. "Home or Foreign?," Report A16, April 17, 1939, p. 3, File Reports 1937–1972, MOO. In Harrisson's work the political elite are repeatedly upbraided for their disconnection from "that vast majority" of the population that "left school at 14." George Orwell displayed a certain ambivalence toward M-O's vigorous criticism of the ruling classes, implying there could be certain ideological blind spots in the organization's conception of civil society. Orwell ([1940] 1998: 17) suggests that just as M-O's first publication, *May the Twelfth* (Jennings and Madge 1937), failed to register the existence of any "royalist sentiment" in Britain at all, *War Begins at Home* (Harrisson and Madge 1940) is similarly unperceptive, as "the one thing that the compilers do not seem to have encountered is the sentiment of patriotism."

22. Quoted in "Prediction, Restriction and Jurisdiction," Report 286, July 18, 1940, p. 13, File Reports 1937–1972, MOO.

23. "Prediction, Restriction and Jurisdiction," Report 286, July 18, 1940, p. 14, File Reports 1937–1972, MOO.

24. "Prediction, Restriction and Jurisdiction," Report 286, July 18, 1940, p. 20, File Reports 1937–1972, MOO.

25. "Prediction, Restriction and Jurisdiction," Report 286, July 18, 1940, p. 28, File Reports 1937–1972, MOO.

26. "Morale in 1941 . . . ," Report 568, February 4, 1941, pp. 9–10, File Reports 1937–1972, MOO.

27. "Report from Mass-Observation on Fire Spotters and Compulsory A.R.P.," Report 536, January 3, 1940, p. 4, File Reports 1937–1972, MOO.

28. "Report from Mass-Observation on Fire Spotters and Compulsory A.R.P." Report 536, January 3, 1940, p. 4, File Reports 1937–1972, MOO.

CHAPTER FOUR. Boas and After

1. While Sussman also notes the dissonance between Boas's theoretical categories and his personal involvement in antiracist campaigns, Mark Anderson (2014) offers a more rounded assessment of this question in his discussion of a widespread tendency among the Boasians to dilute the specificity of racism by interpreting it as merely a particular manifestation of a more general form of prejudice.

2. A tightening up of the connections between territory and culture was particularly true of the wartime mobilization of anthropology when the relations between nation and character tended to be essentialized in the conceptions of national character proposed by both Ruth Benedict and Margaret Mead. See Mandler 2013 and Price 2008.

3. See Bennett 2015 for a critical assessment of the uses of the concept in the subsequent history of cultural studies.

4. Osborn to William Berryman Scott, May 22, 1908, quoted in Kennedy 1968: 163.

5. Wissler, "Survey of the American Museum of Natural History: Made at the Request of the Management Board, 1942–43," unpublished typescript, 1943, p. 209, Rare Book Collection, Research Library, AMNH, New York.

6. Wissler to Frederic A. Lucas, May 27, 1912, file 499, folder, 1906–12, Central Archives, Research Library, AMNH. Wissler was seconding the opinions of both Jesup and Osborn; see Haddad 2006: 141.

7. Wissler, "Survey of the American Museum of Natural History: Made at the Request of the Management Board, 1942–43," unpublished typescript, 1943, pp. 419–20, Rare Book Collection, Research Library, AMNH.

8. For comprehensive reviews of the Jesup North Pacific Expedition, see Krupnik and Fitzhugh 2001; Kendall and Krupnik 2003; Freed 2012: 164–383.

9. For summaries of the museum's Plains research see DeMallie and Ewers 2001: 33–37; Freed 2012: 403–7, 603–51.

10. Sources on the museum's Southwest collections include Fowler (2000: 233–40, 243–44, 275–84, 288–93) and Freed (2012: 407–13).

11. In addition to his visits to the Crow, Lowie worked among the Assiniboine, Plains Shoshone, Santee Dakota, Mandan, Hidatsa, Arikara, Ute, Comanche, and Kiowa, as well as the Shoshone speakers of the Great Basin and the Hopi in the Southwest.

12. Wissler, "Survey of the American Museum of Natural History: Made at the Request of the Management Board, 1942–43," unpublished typescript, 1943, p. 193, Rare Book Collection, Research Library, AMNH.

13. Wissler, "Report of the Department of Anthropology for the Quarter ending June the 30th, 1908," folder 14, Quarterly and Annual Reports (1903–30), Division of Anthropology Archives, AMNH.

14. Wissler to Hermon C. Bumpus, November 24, 1905, with "Plans for the Exhibition Halls, 1905–6: General Plan for the Development of the Department of Anthropology," folder 5, Quarterly and Annual Reports (1903–30), Division of Anthropology Archives, AMNH.

15. Wissler, "Report of the Department of Anthropology for the Quarter ending June the 30th, 1908," folder 14, Quarterly and Annual Reports (1903–30), Division of Anthropology Archives, AMNH.

16. In fact, this group included one of the AMNH curators, the archaeologist Herbert J. Spinden.

17. The antipathy between Wissler and the Boasians is well documented. Wissler referred to them as "queer foreigners or half foreigners," a common perception among

the Galtonians (Deacon 1997: 104, 421; see Spiro 2002: 45). And the feeling was recip-
rocated among many, such as Wissler's colleague Goddard.

18. Nevertheless, even Osborn and Lowie were able to find some common ground,
a situation that could not apply between their mutual friends and colleagues of Grant
and Boas, respectively, who saw each other as extremists (Regal 2002: 125).

19. The principal sources on Wissler's racism include Stocking (1968: 270–
307), E. Ross (1985), W. Shapiro (1985), Barkan (1992: 108–12), and Spiro (2002,
2009). Interestingly, there is no mention of this aspect of Wissler's thought in the
work of his principal contemporary scholar (Freed and Freed 1983, 1992; Freed
2012).

20. This was best demonstrated in his unpublished essay "On Zuni" from around
1919 (Alfred L. Kroeber Papers, Bancroft Library, University of California, Berkeley),
as well as his correspondence with Parsons and Benedict.

21. But see also M. Anderson 2014; Visweswaran 2010.

22. See also on this Mandler 2013: 20–28.

23. Benedict, "The Growth of Culture," 1947, p. 1, unpublished paper, folder 54.7,
Ruth Fulton Benedict Papers, Vassar College Library, Poughkeepsie, New York.

24. See on this Banner 2004. Banner also throws useful light on the aesthetic
properties that informed Benedict's and Mead's interpretation of the culture concept,
discussing their preanthropological backgrounds in literary studies.

25. Benedict distinguished the "real races" of Negroes, Caucasians, and Mongoloids
from the cultural factors the marked the distinctiveness of Celt and Jews; see W. Shapiro 1985: 4. Boas's differentiation of European migrants from African American and
Asian populations also had a significant influence on the founding members of the
Chicago school of sociology—particularly William I. Thomas and Robert Parks, who
contended that the racial characteristics of the latter prohibited their inclusion within
liberal mechanisms of assimilation. See D. Ross 1991: 361.

CHAPTER FIVE. Producing "The Maori as He Was"

1. Āpirana Ngata, "The Genealogical Method as Applied to the Early History of
New Zealand (to Be Read before the Wellington Branch of the Historical Association)," 1928, pp. 3–4, 8, qMs-1587, ATL.

2. "New Zealand's Treasure House," Dominion, August 1, 1936.

3. Quoted in Dominion, August 3, 1936.

4. The discussion of Cheeseman's work at the Auckland Museum draws heavily on
Cameron's (2000) doctoral thesis.

5. Jomard was the curator in the Department of Geography at the Royal Library in
Paris.

6. Report of the Auckland Institute and Museum, 1889–90.

7. The staff at the DM, who preferred the term ethnology and resisted revisionist
theories of New Zealand prehistory, moved gradually to the latter position from the late
1930s to the 1950s (McCarthy 2007b). On ethnology/ethnography, Boas, and cultural anthropology in the United States, see Barfield 1997: 17–18. The Field Museum in Chicago

led the way in museum anthropology through its display of Native American "culture areas" in dioramas and life groups (Belovari 1997; see also Jenkins 1994: 262–66; Jacknis 1985: 92–105).

8. Best corresponded with Cheeseman for many years, and while he was still in the Urewera he provided specimens and information for the AWMM as he did for Hamilton at the DM (Cameron 2000: 53). For Best's visits to Auckland, see Best, "Notes on Museum Artifacts: Māori Notebooks," MS 188, 189, 197, 199, ATL.

9. After this death, Māori interested in ethnology and history paid tribute to Best's work. "He saw things with their eyes," said Buck later, "and felt things with their feelings." Buck 1932: 161. Carver Hurae Puketapu addressed Best as a "retainer" of the "works of the ancestors" who have passed on (te kai-pūpuri i ngā mahi a ngā tīpuna kua ngaro atu nei ki te pō). Puketapu to Best, Apr. 4, 1915, Māori letters, Betty McFadgeon files, MU 47 1/26, Te Papa Archives, Wellington.

10. Here *separate economic and social development* refers to post-assimilationist government policy in the 1940s–1960s, which accorded a degree of independent management of Māori affairs or "integration."

11. *Dominion Museum Bulletins of the Maori*, general file, July 1, 1925, "The Maori as He Was," C420 734: IA1 2281, 113. 3.2, Archives New Zealand (ANZ), Wellington.

12. Peter Fraser, "National Group: Opening Tomorrow," *Evening Post* (Wellington), July 31, 1936.

13. The ethnology halls of the British Museum, with their old-fashioned typological displays, were criticized in a report by the British Royal Commission that was cited in New Zealand (Bledisloe 1934: 14).

14. Lecture 2, folder 1219, Skinner Papers, Hocken Collections (HC), Dunedin.

15. "Correspondence Etc. Collected by Skinner 1861–1943, 1, July 31, 1953," Skinner Papers, MS 1218, HC.

16. Skinner set up an archaeology section in the Otago branch of the New Zealand Institute in 1924, and he was the founding chair of the New Zealand Archaeological Association in 1955 (A. Anderson 1998).

17. "The Past and the Present—Popular Lecture," 1920, Skinner Papers, MS 1219/071, HC. Holmes was curator of the U.S. National Museum and Field Museums and head of the Bureau of American Ethnology. Holmes's *Handbook of Aboriginal American Antiquities* (1919) established, Skinner contended, "the place of archaeology in human history."

18. See Ngata to I. L. G. Sutherland, June 17, 1936, "Board of Maori Ethnological Research drafts etc.," ACIH 16068 MA51/2 22, ANZ.

19. See also Gathercole papers relating to H. D. Skinner, notes for HD Skinner file PG 5/11/63, Skinner Papers, MS 1842, HC.

20. Ngata, "Draft Statement of the Aims and Objectives of the Young Maori Party (Northern Division) in Amplification of Clause 2 of the Constitution," 1909, Maori Purposes Fund Board Papers, MS Papers, 189/11, ATL.

21. Tūnuiārangi's offer was recorded in a memo from Thompson to Internal Affairs, June 12, 1917, MU 1, 17/60, TPA.

22. Haari Hemara Wahanui, Ormsby mss. MSY-5005 1911, ATL.

23. Thomson (1915) gave high priority to Best's ethnological research and advocated comparative displays of Polynesian objects. See also *Annual Report of the Dominion Museum* 1917.

24. The Dominion Museum's annual report of 1923 records the "keen interest shown by leading members of the Maori race in the Maori work of collection and preservation of the rapidly vanishing arts and crafts and tribal lore and songs of bygone days." "The Dominion Museum," H-22: 11–12, *Appendices and Journals of the House of Representatives*, Wellington: Government Printer.

25. "Maori Ethnological Research Board (Drafts, Etc)," 1920–25, ACIH 16068 MA51/2 22, ANZ.

26. Ngata, "Proposals in Regard to the Finance and Organisation of Maori and Polynesian Research," "Maori Ethnological Research Board (Drafts, Etc)," 1920–25, ACIH 16068 MA51/2 22, ANZ.

27. Maori Purposes Fund Control Board. MA1-1445, ANZ.

28. Balneavis, Henare (Te) Raumoa Huatahi. "Board of Maori Ethnological Research: Report of operations." 1927, p. 5, MA51/3 23, ANZ.

29. Elsdon Best to T. W. Downes, MS Papers-8051, ATL.

30. See Elsdon Best to T. W. Downes, MS Papers-8051, ATL; correspondence between Ngata and W. H. Skinner, MS Papers-80-115-04A/05A, Polynesian Society further records, ATL; and Best to Balneavis, undated, "Maori Ethnological Research Board (Drafts, Etc)," 1920–25, ACIH 16068 MA51/2 22, ANZ.

31. "The Board of Maori Ethnological Research: A Review by HRH Balneavis (Te Raumoa) Secretary to the Board." 1927, 8. MA51/3 23 ANZ.

32. "The Board of Maori Ethnological Research: A Review by HRH Balneavis (Te Raumoa) Secretary to the Board," 6–7.

33. "The Board of Maori Ethnological Research: A Review by HRH Balneavis (Te Raumoa) Secretary to the Board," 9.

34. "Pacific Culture: The Island Races: Intensive Study: Dr Buck's Visit," *Evening Post* (Wellington), February 4, 1936.

35. *New Zealand Centennial Exhibition: The Maori Court: Souvenir* (Wellington: Native Department), 4–5, 11. This was probably written by I. L. G. Sutherland with input from Ngata himself.

36. Eru Ihaaka to Ngata, February 19, 1934, MS Papers 189/002, Āpirana Ngata: Correspondence in Māori 1920–34, ATL.

37. Buck to Tarawhai (Johannes Andersen) from Magareva, Gambier Islands, November 19, 1934, MS Papers 148/015, Andersen Papers: Correspondence—Peter Buck, ATL.

38. Sutherland Papers, folder 1234-1, ATL.

39. Skinner, "The Inauguration of the Teaching of Anthropology in the University of Otago," lecture delivered at the Annual General Meeting of the Anthropology Society, October 15, 1961, H. D. Skinner Correspondence, MS1218, HC; Ngata to I. L. G. Sutherland, June 17, 1936, "Board of Maori Ethnological Research Drafts etc.," ACIH 16068 MA51/2 22, ANZ.

CHAPTER SIX. Ethnology, Governance, and Greater France

1. The MH was established under the direction of the Muséum National d'Histoire Naturelle; the ATP was subsequently brought under the Direction des Beaux-Arts of the Ministère de l'Éducation Nationale.

2. Rivière was the key mediator of these influences, undertaking (on Rivet's prompting) study tours of the United States, Russia, Germany, and Scandinavia. The establishment of the Office International des Musées in 1926 played a key role in French interest in international museum practice. Established under the auspices of the Commission internationale de coopération intellectuelle, a section of the Society of Nations, the Office International des Musées focused attention on the possibilities of museums as instruments of popular education. See Gorgus 2003: 72–82.

3. For the 1939 data, see "Musée de l'Homme—Musée Maurice Long," *Bulletin de l'École Française d'Extrême-Orient* (hereafter *BEFEO*) 1940: 467–69; for the 1941 data, see "Musée de l'Homme (section ethnographique du Musée de l'École Française d'Extrême-Orient)," *BEFEO* 1942: 209–10.

4. French-ruled Indochina encompassed a federation of administratively distinct colonies and protectorates, including the colony of Cochinchina (the southernmost part of modern Vietnam) and the protectorates of Laos, Tonkin (in northern Vietnam), Annam (the central region of present-day Vietnam), and Cambodia.

5. Coedès to P. Pagès, June 11, 1938, dossier 10–17, Archives EFEO, Paris.

6. In fact, such actions were usually far from sympathetic: see Dias 2010.

7. "Musée de l'Homme, Hanoi," *BEFEO* 1938: 404.

8. Marcelle Bouteiller, "État d'arrivée de la collection expédiée en juillet 1933," carton 15, dossier 19, Archives EFEO, Paris.

9. Dossier Colani, April 13, 1934, XV-DP. P107, Archives EFEO, Paris.

10. "Musées ethnographiques d'Indochine," *BEFEO* 1938: 403.

11. *Cahiers de l'École Française d'Extrême-Orient* 16 (1938): 10.

12. In his mission's report dated 1939, Nguyen Van Huyen pointed out the reasons underlying Vietnam peasants' resistance to French colonialism; he joined the anticolonialism movement and became the Vietnamese minister of education from 1946 to 1975. On Nguyen Van Huyen's career, see Clémentin-Ojha and Manguin 2001: 177; *Cahiers de l'École Française d'Extrême-Orient* 15 (1938): 11.

13. Georges Coedès, "Allocution," *Bulletin de l'Institut Indochinois pour l'Étude de l'Homme: Compte Rendu des Séances de l'Année 1938*, 1938: 10–11.

14. "Statuts de l'Institut Indochinois pour l'Étude de l'Homme," carton 23, dossier 34, Archives EFEO, Paris.

15. Coedès to Naudin, July 5, 1938, Carton 14, dossier 17, Archives EFEO, Paris.

16. "Musée de l'Homme—Hanoi," *BEFEO* 1938: 404.

17. Carton 14, dossier 17, Archives EFEO, Paris.

18. Coedès, introduction to *Institut Indochinois pour l'Étude de l'Homme: Compte Rendu des Séances de l'Année 1938*, 1938: 10–11.

19. As Conklin pointed out, "Yet for all Mauss's and Rivet's embrace of the empire in the 1930s—from the launching of the Mission Dakar-Djibouti and association with

the Colonial Exposition to the cultivation of overseas outposts—they and their team remained detached from the actual work of colonizing" (2013: 231).

20. "Section ethnologique," *BEFEO* 1938: 397.

21. "Institut Indochinois pour l'Étude de l'Homme," *BEFEO* 1938: 397.

22. Coedès, "Allocution," 11.

23. Another paradox of the Indochinese case is that the Vichy period in Indochina lasted until March 1945, whereas in France the Pétain regime collapsed in the summer of 1944.

24. "Note sur l'orientation générale de l'activité de l'École Française d'Extrême-Orient durant les dernières années," *Indochine, Hebdomadaire Illustré*, no. 113, October 29, 1942.

CONCLUSION

1. See, for example, the introduction to Morning 2011.

2. Barker describes UNESCO's position as the assumption that racism equates with the belief in racial superiority; it follows that racism is to be countered by empirical challenges to the notion of racial difference on which such assumptions are founded.

3. Mead's (1947) report to UNESCO was influential in the development of its Fundamental Education program and of the connection between education and empowerment through forms of social, economic, and community development that has been an integral part of UNESCO's linking of culture and heritage with international development. See further discussion in Mandler 2013: 256–58.

4. Race was one of a series of issues at the heart of UNESCO's mission that have a bearing on the topics we address in this book. The question of the relationship between (individual) "universal rights" and (collective) "cultural rights," and in particular "indigenous rights," was also a topic of some debate at this time. These debates famously coalesced around the American Anthropological Association's criticism of the notion of universal human rights, published in 1947 in the journal *American Anthropologist*. See further discussion in Engle 2001.

5. We draw closely here on Perrin Selcer's (2012) historical account of the production of these two statements.

6. Michel Leiris (see chapter 6) was also commissioned by UNESCO to write on these topics, and his *Race and Culture* (1951) was published the year before Lévi-Strauss's *Race and History* (1952) in a series titled "The Race Question in Modern Science." See further discussion in Conklin 2013: 329–31.

7. The statement issued in 1951 gives the following explanation for the issue of a revision the following year:

> The reasons for convening a second meeting of experts to discuss the concept of race were chiefly these: Race is a question of interest to many different kinds of people, not only to the public at large, but to sociologists, anthropologists and biologists, especially those dealing with problems of genetics. At the first discussion on the problem of race, it was chiefly sociologists who gave their opinions and framed the "Statement on race." That statement had a good effect, but it did

not carry the authority of just those groups within whose special province fall the biological problems of race, namely the physical anthropologists and geneticists. Secondly, the first statement did not, in all its details, carry conviction of these groups and, because of this, it was not supported by many authorities in these two fields. (quoted in UNESCO 1969: 36)

8. On Stanner's legacy in Australian indigenous affairs, see chapters in Hinkson and Beckett 2008; on the legacy of Coombes, see Rowse 2000, 2002.

9. For example, New Zealand was originally part of the process of forming a federation of Commonwealth states that would originally have included the six self-governing British colonies in Australia, as well as Fiji, but it opted out of this process; there were also significant differences in the recognition of indigenous sovereignty, with New Zealand's Treaty of Waitangi and the absence of such a treaty in Australia. For a comparison with regard to some of these issues, see Havemann 1999 and McHugh 2004.

10. The term *biculturalism* was a Canadian import and was introduced into the country's academic discourse by the anthropologist Eric Schwimmer in his book *The Maori People in the Nineteen Sixties* (1968). See further discussion in Sissons 1995. On the development of Te Papa Tongarewa, see McCarthy 2011. Also see Dibley 2007.

11. See, for example, Goodall 1996 for an account of the history of indigenous land rights struggles in the Australian state of New South Wales.

12. This recapitalization of tribal Māori also needs to be seen in the context of a period of radical economic restructuring that the fourth Labour government began in 1984. Under the supervision of the International Monetary Fund, it shed the trappings of the Keynesian welfare state and devolved public services to community organizations. Similarly, these moves toward self-determination need to be understood in relation to the repositioning of the Treaty of Waitangi, signed in 1840, as a foundational document and a legal contract, with the passing of the Treaty of Waitangi Amendment Act in 1985.

13. For a detailed investigation of questions of the relationship between contemporary indigeneity and cultural and intellectual property rights, see Geismar 2013.

14. For a history of indigenous rights movements, see Anaya 2004.

ARCHIVES CONSULTED

Alexander Turnbull Library, Wellington.
Alfred L. Kroeber Papers, Bancroft Library, University of California, Berkeley.
Anthropology Archives, American Museum of Natural History, New York.
Archives École Française d'Extrême-Orient, Paris.
Archives New Zealand, Wellington.
Central Archives, Research Library, American Museum of Natural History, New York.
Division of Hocken Collections, Dunedin.
Library of the American Philosophical Society, Philadelphia.
Mass Observation Online, Adam Matthew Digital and the University of Sussex.
National Archives of Australia, Canberra.
Pitt Rivers Museum, Oxford.
Rare Book Collection, Research Library, American Museum of Natural History, New York.
Ruth Fulton Benedict Papers, Vassar College Library, Poughkeepsie, New York.
Te Papa Archives, Wellington.

WORKS CITED

Alberti, Samuel J. M. M. 2009. *Nature and Culture: Objects, Disciplines and the Manchester Museum*. Manchester: Manchester University Press.
American Anthropological Association. 1947. "Statement on Human Rights." *American Anthropologist* 49 (4): 539–43.
Anaya, S. James. 2004. *Indigenous Peoples in International Law*. Oxford: Oxford University Press.
Andersen, Johannes C. (1928) 1969. *Myths and Legends of the Polynesians*. Rutland, VT: Ruttle.
Anderson, Atholl. 1998. "Skinner, Henry Devenish." In *Dictionary of New Zealand Biography*. Vol. 4. http://www.TeAra.govt.nz/en/biographies/4s29/skinner-henry-devenish.
Anderson, Kay. 2007. *Race and the Crisis of Humanism*. London: Routledge.

Anderson, Mark. 2014. "Ruth Benedict, Boasian Anthropology and the Problem of the Colour Line." *History and Anthropology* 25 (3): 395–414.

Annual Report of the Dominion Museum. 1917. Wellington: Government Printer.

Annual Report of the Dominion Museum. 1923. Wellington: Government Printer.

Ashley, Scott. 2001. "The Poetics of Race in 1890s Ireland: An Ethnography of the Aran Islands." *Patterns of Prejudice* 35 (2): 5–18.

Attwood, Bain. 2003. *Rights for Aborigines.* Sydney: Allen and Unwin.

BAAS (British Association for the Advancement of Science). 1892. *Notes and Queries on Anthropology.* 2nd ed. London: Royal Anthropological Institute.

BAAS (British Association for the Advancement of Science). 1899. *Notes and Queries on Anthropology.* 3rd ed. London: Royal Anthropological Institute.

BAAS (British Association for the Advancement of Science). 1929. *Notes and Queries on Anthropology.* 5th ed. London: Royal Anthropological Institute.

BAAS (British Association for the Advancement of Science). n.d. *Forms of Schedule Prepared by a Committee of the British Association for the Advancement of Science, Appointed to Organise an Ethnographical Survey of the United Kingdom.* London: Spottiswoode.

Baker, Lee D. 2010. *Anthropology and the Racial Politics of Culture.* Durham, NC: Duke University Press.

Balfour, Henry. 1904. "Presidential Address: The Relationship of Museums to the Study of Anthropology." *Journal of the Anthropological Institute of Great Britain and Ireland* 34:10–19.

Banner, Lois W. 2004. *Intertwined Lives: Margaret Mead, Ruth Benedict, and Their Circle.* New York: Vintage Books.

Barfield, Thomas, ed. 1997. *The Dictionary of Anthropology.* Malden, MA: Wiley-Blackwell.

Barkan, Elazar. 1992. *Retreat of Scientific Racism: Changing Concepts of Race in Britain and the United States between the World Wars.* Cambridge: Cambridge University Press.

Barker, Martin. 1983. "Empiricism and Racism." *Radical Philosophy* 33:6–15.

Barth, Fredrik, Andre Gingrich, Robert Parkin, and Sydel Silverman. 2005. *One Discipline, Four Ways: British, German, French, and American Anthropology.* Chicago: University of Chicago Press.

Bashkow, Ira. 2004. "A Neo-Boasian Conception of Cultural Boundaries." *American Anthropologist,* n.s., 106 (3): 443–58.

Batty, Philip, Lindy Allen, and John Morton, eds. 2005. *The Photographs of Baldwin Spencer.* Melbourne: Miegunyah Press/Museum Victoria.

Beddoe, John. 1885. *The Races of Britain: A Contribution to the Anthropology of Western Europe.* Bristol: J. W. Arrowsmith and Trübner.

Belich, James. 1996. *Making Peoples: A History of the New Zealanders from Polynesian Settlement to the End of the Nineteenth Century.* Auckland: Allen Lane, Penguin.

Belich, James. 2001. *Paradise Reforged: A History of the New Zealanders from the 1880s to the Year 2000.* Auckland: Allen Lane and Penguin.

Bell, Joshua A. 2006. "Losing the Forest but Not the Stories in the Trees: Contemporary Understandings of the Government Anthropologist F. E. Williams' 1922

Photographs of the Purari Delta, Papua New Guinea." *Journal of Pacific History* 41 (2): 191–206.

Bell, Joshua A. 2009a. "Documenting Discontent: Struggles for Recognition in the Purari Delta of Papua New Guinea." *Australian Journal of Anthropology* 20 (1): 28–47.

Bell, Joshua A. 2009b. "For Scientific Purposes a Stand Camera Is Essential: Salvaging Photographic Histories in Papua." In *Photography, Anthropology and History: Expanding the Frame*, edited by Chris Morton and Elizabeth Edwards, 143–70. Farnham, Surrey: Ashgate.

Bell, Joshua A. 2010. "Out of the Mouths of Crocodiles: Eliciting Histories in Photographs and String-Figures." *History and Anthropology* 21 (4): 351–73.

Bell, Joshua A., Alison K. Brown, and Robert J. Gordon, eds. 2013. *Recreating First Contact: Expeditions, Anthropology and Popular Culture*. Washington, DC: Smithsonian Institution Scholarly Press.

Belovari, Susan. 1997. "Invisible in the White Field: The Chicago Field Museum's Construction of Native Americans, 1893–1996." PhD diss., University of Illinois at Urbana-Champaign.

Benedict, Ruth. 1923. "The Concept of the Guardian Spirit in North America." *American Anthropological Association Memoirs* 29:1–97.

Benedict, Ruth. 1928. "Psychological Types in the Cultures of the Southwest." *International Congress of Americanists Proceedings* 23:572–81.

Benedict, Ruth. 1932. "Configurations of Culture in North America." *American Anthropologist* 34:1–27.

Benedict, Ruth. (1934) 2005. *Patterns of Culture*. New York: Mariner Books.

Benedict, Ruth, and Gene Weltfish. 1943. *The Races of Mankind*. Public Affairs Pamphlet No. 85. New York: Public Affairs Committee.

Bennett, Tony. 1995. *The Birth of the Museum: History, Theory, Politics*. London: Routledge.

Bennett, Tony. 2004. *Pasts beyond Memory: Evolution, Museums, Colonialism*. London: Routledge.

Bennett, Tony. 2005. "Civic Laboratories: Museums, Cultural Objecthood, and the Governance of the Social." *Cultural Studies* 19 (5): 521–47.

Bennett, Tony. 2010. "Making and Mobilising Worlds: Assembling and Governing the Other." In *Material Powers: Cultural Studies, History and the Material Turn*, edited by Tony Bennett and Patrick Joyce, 188–208. Abingdon, UK: Routledge.

Bennett, Tony. 2011. "Habit, Instinct, Survivals: Repetition, History, Biopower." In *The Peculiarities of Liberal Modernity in Imperial Britain*, edited by Simon Gunn and James Vernon, 102–18. Berkeley: University of California Press.

Bennett, Tony. 2013a. "Habit: Time, Freedom, Governance." *Body and Society* 19 (2–3): 107–35.

Bennett, Tony. 2013b. *Making Culture, Changing Society*. Abingdon, UK: Routledge.

Bennett, Tony. 2013c. "The 'Shuffle of Things' and the Distribution of Agency." In *Reassembling the Collection: Ethnographic Museums and Indigenous Agency*, edited by Rodney Harrison, Sarah Byrne, and Anne Clarke, 39–59. Santa Fe, NM: SAR Press.

Bennett, Tony. 2014. "Liberal Government and the Practical History of Anthropology." *History and Anthropology* 25 (2): 150–70.

Bennett, Tony. 2015. "Cultural Studies and the Culture Concept." *Cultural Studies* 29 (4): 546–68.

Bennett, Tony, Ben Dibley, and Rodney Harrison. 2014. "Introduction: Anthropology, Collecting and Colonial Governmentalities." *History and Anthropology* 25 (2): 137–49.

Bennett, Tony, and Patrick Joyce, eds. 2010. *Material Powers: Cultural Studies, History and the Material Turn*. London: Routledge.

Bensaude-Vincent, Bernadette. 2009. "A Historical Perspective on Science and Its 'Others.'" *Isis* 100:359–68.

Best, Elsdon. 1912. *The Stone Implements of the Maori*. Dominion Museum Bulletin 4. Wellington: Government Printer.

Best, Elsdon. 1922a. *Some Aspects of Maori Myth and Religion*. Dominion Museum Monograph 1. Wellington: Government Printer.

Best, Elsdon. 1922b. *Spiritual and Mental Concepts of the Maori*. Dominion Museum Monograph 2. Wellington: Government Printer.

Best, Elsdon. 1922c. *The Astronomical Knowledge of the Maori*. Dominion Museum Monograph 3. Wellington: Government Printer.

Best, Elsdon. 1924a. *The Maori*. 2 vols. Memoirs of the Polynesian Society 5. Wellington: Board of Maori Ethnological Research, Harry Tombs.

Best, Elsdon. 1924b. *The Maori as He Was: A Brief Account of Maori Life as It Was in Pre-European Days*. New Zealand Board of Science and Art: Manual 4. Wellington: Government Printer.

Bezacier, Louis, and Hubert Marneffe. 1942. "Les Groupes sanguins en Indochine du Nord." *Bulletins et Mémoires de la Société d'Anthropologie de Paris* 3:1–25.

"A Blackfoot Lodge, or Tepee." 1907. *American Museum Journal* 7:92–94.

Bledisloe, C. B. 1934. *The Proper Function and Scope of a National Art Gallery and Museum*. Address Given When Laying the Foundation-Stone of the National Art Gallery and Dominion Museum at Wellington, April 14, 1934. Auckland: Wilson and Horton.

Boas, Franz. 1887a. "Museums of Ethnology and Their Classification." *Science* 9:587–89.

Boas, Franz. 1887b. "The Occurrence of Similar Inventions in Areas Widely Apart." *Science* 9:485–86.

Boas, Franz. 1903. "The Decorative Art of the North American Indians." *Popular Science Monthly* 63:481–98.

Boas, Franz. 1907. "Some Principles of Museum Administration." *Science*, n.s., 25 (650): 921–33.

Boas, Franz. (1909) 1974. "Race Problems in America." In *A Franz Boas Reader: The Shaping of American Anthropology, 1883–1911*, edited by George W. Stocking Jr., 318–30. Chicago: University of Chicago Press.

Boas, Franz. 1911. *The Mind of Primitive Man*. New York: Macmillan.

Boas, Franz. (1912) 1982. "Changes in Bodily Form of Descendants of Immigrants." In *Race, Language and Culture*, 60–75. Chicago: University of Chicago Press.

Boas, Franz. (1927) 2010. *Primitive Art*. Mineola, NY: Dover.

Boas, Franz, ed. 1928. "Coiled Basketry in British Columbia and Surrounding Region." With Herman K. Haeberlin, James A. Teit, and Helen H. Roberts. *Bureau of American Ethnology, Annual Report for the Years 1919–24* 41:119–484.

Bondaz, Julien. 2011. "L'Ethnographie Comme Chasse: Michel Leiris et les Animaux de la Mission Dakar-Djibouti." *Gradhiva* 13:162–81.

Bönisch-Brednich, Brigitte, and Richard Hill. 2009. "Fitting Aotearoa into New Zealand: Politico-Cultural Change in a Modern Bicultural Nation." In *Historical Justice in International Perspective: How Societies Are Trying to Right the Wrongs of the Past*, edited by Manfred Berg and Bernd Schaeffer, 239–63. Washington, DC: German Historical Institute; Cambridge: Cambridge University Press.

Bouquet, Mary. 2012. *Museums: A Visual Anthropology*. London: Berg/Bloomsbury.

Brabrook, Edward William. 1893a. "Ethnographical Survey of the United Kingdom." *Science* 21 (518): 5.

Brabrook, Edward William. 1893b. "On the Organisation of Local Anthropological Research." *Journal of the Anthropological Institute of Great Britain and Ireland* 22:262–74.

Brennan, Teresa. 2004. *The Transmission of Affect*. Ithaca, NY: Cornell University Press.

Briggs, Charles, and Richard Bauman. 1999. "'The Foundation of All Future Researches': Franz Boas, George Hunt, Native American Texts, and the Construction of Modernity." *American Quarterly* 51 (3): 479–528.

Brocheux, Pierre, and Daniel Hémery. 2009. *Indochina: An Ambiguous Colonization, 1858–1954*. Berkeley: University of California Press.

Brown, Alison K., and Laura Peers, eds. 2003. *Museums and Source Communities*. London: Routledge.

Brown, Alison K., and Laura Peers. 2015. *Visiting with the Ancestors: Blackfoot Shirts in Museum Spaces*. Athabasca, AB: Athabasca University Press.

Brown, Bill. 2003. *A Sense of Things: The Object Matter of American Literature*. Chicago: University of Chicago Press.

Brown, Julie K. 2014. "Connecting Health and Natural History: A Failed Initiative at the American Museum of Natural History, 1909–1922." *American Journal of Public Health* 104 (10): 1877–88.

Buck, Peter. 1927. *The Material Culture of the Cook Islands (Aitutaki)*. New Plymouth, New Zealand: Board of Maori Ethnological Research.

Buck, Peter. 1932. "The Late Mr Elsdon Best." *Journal of the Polynesian Society* 61 (141): 1–49.

Buckley, Thomas. 1989. "Kroeber's Theory of Culture Areas and the Ethnology of Northwestern California." *Anthropological Quarterly* 62 (1): 15–26.

Bulmer, Martin, ed. 1985. *Essays on the History of British Sociological Research*. Cambridge: Cambridge University Press.

Bulmer, Martin, Kevin Bales, and Kathryn Kish Sklar, eds. 1991. *The Social Survey in Historical Perspective, 1880–1940*. Cambridge: Cambridge University Press.

Bunzel, Ruth L. 1929. *The Pueblo Potter: A Study of Creative Imagination in Primitive Art*. New York: Columbia University Press.

Bunzl, Matti. 1996. "Franz Boas and the Humboldtian Tradition: From *Volksgeist* and *Nationalcharakter* to an Anthropological Concept of Culture." In *Volksgeist as Method and Ethic: Essays on Boasian Anthropology and the German Anthropological Tradition*, edited by George W. Stocking Jr., 17–78. Madison: University of Wisconsin Press.

Butterworth, Graham Victor. 1990. *Maori Affairs: A Department and the People Who Made It*. Wellington: Iwi Transition Agency and GP Books.

Caffrey, Margaret M. 1989. *Ruth Benedict: Stranger in This Land*. Austin: University of Texas Press.

Calder, Angus. 1985. "Mass-Observation." In *Essays in the History of British Sociological Research*, edited by Martin Bulmer, 121–36. Cambridge: Cambridge University Press.

Cameron, Fiona Ruth. 2000. "Shaping Maori Identities and Histories: Collecting and Exhibiting Maori Material Culture at the Auckland and Canterbury Museums from the 1850s to the 1920s." PhD diss., Massey University, Palmerston North.

Cameron, Fiona Ruth. 2014. "From 'Dead Things' to Immutable, Combinable Mobiles: H.D. Skinner, the Otago Museum and University and the Governance of Māori Populations." *History and Anthropology* 25 (2): 208–26.

Cameron, Fiona Ruth, and Conal McCarthy. 2015. "Two Anthropological Assemblages: New Zealand Museums, Native Policy, and Māori 'Culture Areas' and 'Adaptation.'" *Museum and Society* 13 (1): 88–106.

Campbell, Ian Christopher. 1998. "Anthropology and the Professionalisation of Colonial Administration in Papua and New Guinea." *Journal of Pacific History* 33 (1): 69–90.

Cantril, Henry. 1934. "The Social Psychology of Everyday Life." *Psychological Bulletin* 31 (5): 297–330.

Carter, Julian B. 2007. *The Heart of Whiteness*. Durham, NC: Duke University Press.

Carville, Justin. 2012. "The Deviant Face: Photography of Alfred Cort Haddon and Charles R. Browne's Anthropometric Survey of the Irish Race. In *The Irish Headhunter: The Photographic Albums of Charles R. Browne*, edited by Ciarán Walsh, 33–41. Dublin: The Stationery Office.

Chatterjee, Partha. 1993. *The Nation and Its Fragments: Colonial and Postcolonial Histories*. Princeton, NJ: Princeton University Press.

Chippaux, Claude, and Georges Olivier. 1983. "Pierre Huard (1901–1983)." *Bulletins et Mémoires de la Société d'Anthropologie de Paris* 10 (2): 155–57.

Clémentin-Ojha, Catherine, and Pierre-Yves Manguin. 2001. *Un siècle pour l'Asie: L'École française d'Extrême-Orient, 1898–2000*. Paris: Les Éditions du Pacifique.

Clifford, James. 1981. "On Ethnographic Surrealism." *Comparative Studies in Society and History* 23:539–64.

Clifford, James. 1983. "Power and Dialogue in Ethnography: Marcel Griaule's Initiation." In *Observers Observed: Essays on Ethnographic Fieldwork*, edited by George W. Stocking Jr., 121–56. Madison: University of Wisconsin Press.

Clifford, James. 1988. *The Predicament of Culture: Twentieth-Century Ethnography, Literature, and Art*. Cambridge, MA: Harvard University Press.

Clifford, James. 2013. *Returns: Becoming Indigenous in the Twenty-First Century*. Cambridge, MA: Harvard University Press.

Cole, Douglas. 1999. *Franz Boas: The Early Years, 1858–1906.* Seattle: University of Washington Press; Vancouver: Douglas and McIntyre.

Cole, Douglas, and Alexander Long. 1999. "The Boasian Anthropological Survey Tradition: The Role of Franz Boas in North American Anthropological Surveys." In *Surveying the Record: North American Scientific Exploration to 1930,* edited by Edward D. Carter II, 225–49. Memoirs of the American Philosophical Society 231. Philadelphia: American Philosophical Society.

Condliffe, John Bell. 1971. *Te Rangi Hiroa: The Life of Sir Peter Buck.* Christchurch: Whitcombe and Tombs.

Conklin, Alice L. 1997. *A Mission to Civilize: The Republican Ideal of Empire in France and West Africa.* Stanford, CA: Stanford University Press.

Conklin, Alice L. 2008. "Skulls on Display: The Science of Race in Paris's Musée de l'Homme." In *Museums and Difference,* edited by Daniel Sherman, 250–88. Bloomington: Indiana University Press.

Conklin, Alice L. 2013. *In the Museum of Man: Race, Anthropology, and Empire in France, 1850–1950.* Ithaca, NY: Cornell University Press.

Conn, Steven. 2004. *History's Shadow: Native Americans and Historical Consciousness in the Nineteenth Century.* Chicago: University of Chicago Press.

Conn, Steven. 2009. *Do Museums Still Need Objects?* Philadelphia: University of Pennsylvania Press.

Connor, Steven. 2001. "'A Door Half Open to Surprise': Charles Madge's Imminences." *New Formations* 44:52–62.

Coole, Diana, and Samantha Frost, eds. 2010. *New Materialisms: Ontology, Agency, and Politics.* Durham, NC: Duke University Press.

Courage, Fiona. n.d. "The National Panel Responds." Mass Observation Online, Adam Matthew Digital and the University of Sussex. http://www.massobservation.amdigital.co.uk/essays/content/TheNationalPanelResponds.aspx.

Cowlishaw, Gillian. 1998. "Erasing Culture and Race: Practising 'Self-Determination.'" *Oceania* 68 (3): 145–69.

Cunningham, Daniel John, and Alfred Cort Haddon. 1891. "The Anthropometric Laboratory of Ireland." *Journal of the Anthropological Institute* 21:35–39.

Darnell, Regna. 1998. *And Along Came Boas: Continuity and Revolution in Americanist Anthropology.* Amsterdam: John Benjamins.

Daston, Lorraine. 2008. "On Scientific Observation." *Isis* 99:97–110.

Deacon, Desley. 1997. *Elsie Clews Parsons: Inventing Modern Life.* Chicago: University of Chicago Press.

Deagan, Mary Jo. 2001. "The Chicago School of Ethnography." In *Handbook of Ethnography,* edited by Paul Atkinson, Amanda Coffey, Sara Delamont, John Lofland, and Lyn Lofland, 11–25. Los Angeles: Sage.

Debaene, Vincent. 2010. *L'Adieu au Voyage: L'Ethnologie Francaise entre Science et Littérature.* Paris: Gallimard.

Decoux, Jean. 1949. *À la Barre de l'Indochine: Histoire de Mon Gouvernement 1900–1945.* Paris: Plon.

Defert, Daniel. 1982. "A Collection of the World: Accounts of Voyages from the Sixteenth to the Eighteenth Centuries." *Dialectical Anthropology* 7 (1): 11–20.

Deleuze, Gilles, and Félix Guattari. 1983. *Anti-Oedipus: Capitalism and Schizophrenia.* Translated by Robert Hurley, Mark Seem, and Helen R. Lane. Preface by Michel Foucault. Minneapolis: University of Minnesota Press.

DeMallie, Raymond J., and John C. Ewers. 2001. "History of Ethnological and Ethnohistorical Research." In *Handbook of North American Indians,* edited by William C. Sturtevant, vol. 13, part 1, *Plains,* edited by Raymond J. DeMallie, 23–43. Washington, DC: Smithsonian Institution.

Dennis, Jonathan. 1996. "McDonald, James Ingram 1865–1935." In *Dictionary of New Zealand Biography,* http://www.teara.govt.nz/en/biographies/3m5/mcdonald-james -ingram.

Denoon, Donald. 1999. "Black Mischief: The Trouble with African Analogies." *Journal of Pacific History* 34 (3): 281–89.

Derrida, Jacques. 1998. *Archive Fever: A Freudian Impression.* Chicago: University of Chicago Press.

Dewey, John. 1939. *Freedom and Culture.* New York: G. P. Putnam's Sons.

Dias, Nélia. 1991. *Le Musée d'Ethnographie du Trocadéro (1878–1908): Anthropologie et Muséologie en France.* Paris: Éditions du Centre National de la Recherche Scientifique.

Dias, Nélia. 2004. *La Mesure des Sens: Les Anthropologues et le Corps Humain au XIXe siècle.* Paris: Aubier.

Dias, Nélia. 2010. "Exploring the Senses and Exploiting the Land: Railroads, Bodies and Measurement in Nineteenth-Century French Colonies." In *Material Powers: Cultural Studies, History and the Material Turn,* edited by Tony Bennett and Patrick Joyce, 171–89. London: Routledge.

Dias, Nélia. 2014. "Rivet's Mission in Colonial Indochina (1931–1932) or the Failure to Create an Ethnographic Museum." *History and Anthropology* 25 (2): 189–207.

Dias, Nélia. 2015. "From French Indochina to Paris and Back Again: The Circulation of Objects, People, and Information, 1900–1932." *Museum and Society* 13 (1): 7–21.

Dibley, Ben. 2007. "Antipodean Aesthetics, Public Policy and the Museum: Te Papa, for Example." *Cultural Studies Review* 13 (1): 129–49.

Dibley, Ben. 2014. "Assembling an Anthropological Actor: Anthropological Assemblage and Colonial Government in Papua." *History and Anthropology* 25 (2): 263–79.

Dibley, Ben, and Michelle Kelly. 2015. "Morale and Mass-Observation: Governing the Affective Atmosphere on the Home-Front." *Museum and Society* 13 (1): 22–41.

Dirks, Nicholas. 2001. *Castes of Mind: Colonialism and the Making of Modern India.* Princeton, NJ: Princeton University Press.

Dixon, Robert. 2001. *Prosthetic Gods: Travel, Representation and Colonial Governance.* St. Lucia: University of Queensland Press.

Dixon, Robert. 2011. *Photography, Early Cinema and Colonial Modernity: Frank Hurley's Synchronized Lecture Entertainments.* London: Anthem.

Dorsey, George A. 1907. "The Anthropological Exhibits of the American Museum of Natural History." *Science* 25 (641): 584–89.

Douglas, Heather, and Mark Finnane. 2012. *Indigenous Crime and Settler Law: White Sovereignty after Empire*. London: Palgrave Macmillan.

Douglas, Oliver A. 2011. "Folklore, Survivals, and the Neo-Archaic: The Materialist Character of Late Nineteenth-Century Homeland Ethnography." *Museum History Journal* 4 (2): 223–44.

Driver, Felix. 2001. *Geography Militant: Cultures of Exploration and Empire*. Oxford: Blackwell.

Dunn, Leslie Clarence. 1951. *Statement on the Nature of Race and Race Differences*. Paris: UNESCO.

Edwards, Elizabeth. 1990. "Photographic 'Types': The Pursuit of Method." *Visual Anthropology* 3 (2–3): 235–58.

Edwards, Elizabeth. 1998. "Performing Science: Still Photography and the Torres Strait Expedition." In *Cambridge and the Torres Strait*, edited by Anita Herle and Sandra Rouse, 106–35. Cambridge: Cambridge University Press.

Edwards, Elizabeth. 2001. *Raw Histories: Photographs, Anthropology and Museums*. Oxford: Berg.

Edwards, Elizabeth. 2009. "Salvaging Our Past: Photography and Survival." In *Photography, Anthropology and History: Expanding the Frame*, edited by Christopher Morton and Elizabeth Edwards, 67–88. Farnham, UK: Ashgate.

Edwards, Elizabeth. 2012. *The Camera as Historian: Amateur Photographers and Historical Imagination, 1885–1918*. Durham, NC: Duke University Press.

Edwards, Penny. 2007. *Cambodge: The Cultivation of a Nation, 1860–1945*. Honolulu: University of Hawaii Press.

Ellison (Erihana), Edward Pohau. 1931. "The Maori and Hygiene." In *Maori and Education; or, The Education of Natives in New Zealand and Its Dependencies*, edited by Patrick M. Jackson, 282–308. Monograph of the New Zealand Teachers' Summer School 1. Wellington: Ferguson and Osborn.

Engle, Karen. 2001. "From Skepticism to Embrace: Human Rights and the American Anthropological Association from 1947–1999." *Human Rights Quarterly* 23:536–59.

Evans, Brad. 2005. *Before Culture: The Ethnographic Imagination in American Literature, 1865–1920*. Chicago: University of Chicago Press.

Fabre, Daniel. 1997. "L'ethnologie française à la croisée des engagements (1940–45)." In *Résistants et Résistance*, edited by Jean-Yves Boursier, 319–400. Paris: L'Harmattan.

"Fallacies of Racism Exposed: UNESCO Publishes Declaration by World's Scientists." 1950. *UNESCO Courier* 3 (6–7): 1.

Firth, Raymond. 1929. *The Primitive Economics of the New Zealand Māori*. Boston: E. P. Dutton.

Firth, Raymond. 1939. "An Anthropologist's View of Mass-Observation." *Sociological Review* 31 (2): 166–93.

Fleras, Augie, and Paul Spoonley. 1999. *Recalling Aotearoa: Indigenous Politics and Ethnic Relations in New Zealand*. Auckland: Oxford University Press.

Fleure, Herbert J. 1923. *The Races of England and Wales: A Survey of Recent Research*. London: Benn Brothers.

Flinders Petrie, William Matthew. 1922. *The Revolutions of Civilization*. London and New York: Harper & Brothers.

Folklore Society. 1892. "Notes and News." *Folklore* 3:270.

Folklore Society. 1893. "Fifteenth Annual Report of the Council." *Folklore* 4:112–18.

Folklore Society. 1895. "Seventeenth Annual Report of the Council." *Folklore* 6:109–16.

Foucault, Michel. 1972. *The Archaeology of Knowledge*. London: Tavistock.

Foucault, Michel. 1976. *The History of Sexuality*. Vol. 1, *An Introduction*, translated by Robert Hurley. London: Penguin.

Foucault, Michel. 1991. "Governmentality." In *The Foucault Effect: Studies in Governmentality*, edited by Graham Burchell, Colin Gordon, and Peter Miller, 87–104. London: Harvester Wheatsheaf.

Foucault, Michel. 2003. *"Society Must Be Defended": Lectures at the Collège de France 1975–1976*. Vol. 3. Translated by David Macey. Edited by Mauro Bertani and Alessandro Fontana; General Editors: François Ewald and Alessandro Fontana; English Series Editor: Arnold I. Davidson. New York: Picador.

Foucault, Michel. 2007. *Security, Territory, Population: Lectures at the Collège de France 1977–1978*. Vol. 4. Translated by Graham Burchell. Edited by Michel Sennelart. General Editors: François Ewald and Alessandro Fontana. English Series Editor: Arnold I. Davidson. Basingstoke, UK: Palgrave.

Foucault, Michel. 2008. *The Birth of Biopolitics: Lectures at the Collège de France 1978–1979*. Vol. 5. Translated by Graham Burchell. Edited by Michel Sennelart. General Editors: François Ewald and Alessandro Fontana. English Series Editor: Arnold I. Davidson. Basingstoke, UK: Palgrave.

Fowler, Don. 2000. *A Laboratory for Anthropology: Science and Romanticism in the American Southwest, 1846–1930*. Albuquerque: University of New Mexico Press.

Freed, Stanley A. 2012. *Anthropology Unmasked: Museums, Science and Politics in New York City*. 2 vols. Wilmington, OH: Orange Frazer.

Freed, Stanley A., and Ruth S. Freed. 1983. "Clark Wissler and the Development of Anthropology in the United States." *American Anthropologist*, n.s., 85 (4): 800–825.

Freed, Stanley A., and Ruth S. Freed. 1992. "Clark Wissler, 1870–1947." In *Biographical Memoirs* 61, 468–96. Washington, DC: National Academy of Sciences.

Freud, Sigmund. (1921) 1922. *Group Psychology and the Analysis of the Ego*. London: International Psycho-Analytical Press.

Frizzell, Deborah. 1997. *Humphrey Spender's Humanist Landscapes: Photo-Documents, 1932–1942*. New Haven, CT: Yale Center for British Art.

Geismar, Haidy. 2013. *Treasured Possessions: Indigenous Interventions into Cultural and Intellectual Property*. Durham, NC: Duke University Press.

Gilkeson, John. 2010. *Anthropologists and the Discovery of America*. Cambridge: Cambridge University Press.

Gilman, Carolyn, and Mary Jane Schneider. 1987. *The Way to Independence: Memories of a Hidatsa Indian Family, 1840–1920*. St. Paul: Minnesota Historical Society Press.

Goddard, Pliny E. 1919. "San Carlos Apache Texts." *Anthropological Papers of the American Museum of Natural History* 24:141–367.

Goldfrank, Esther S. 1978. *Notes on an Undirected Life: As One Anthropologist Tells It*. Queens College Publications in Anthropology 3. Flushing, NY: Queens College Press.

Golding, Viv, and Wayne Modest, eds. 2013. *Museums and Communities: Curators, Collections and Collaboration*. London: Bloomsbury.

Gomme, George Laurence. 1890. *Handbook of Folklore*. D. Nutt: London.

Goodall, Heather. 1996. *Invasion to Embassy: Land in Aboriginal Politics in New South Wales, 1788–1972*. Sydney: Allen and Unwin.

Gordon, Colin. 1991. "Government Rationality: An Introduction." In *The Foucault Effect: Studies in Governmentality*, edited by Graham Burchell, Colin Gordon, and Peter Miller, 1–51. Chicago: University of Chicago Press.

Gorgus, Nina. 2003. *Le Magicien des Vitrines: Le Muséologue Georges Henri Rivière*. Paris: Éditions de la Maison des Sciences de l'Homme.

Goscha, Christopher E. 1995. *Vietnam or Indochina? Contesting Concepts of Space in Vietnamese Nationalism, 1887–1954*. Copenhagen: Nordic Institute of Asian Studies Press.

Goscha, Christopher E. 2012. *Going Indochinese: Contesting Concepts of Space and Place in French Indochina*. Copenhagen: Nordic Institute of Asian Studies Press.

Gosden, Chris. 1999. *Archaeology and Anthropology: A Changing Relationship*. London: Routledge.

Gosden, Chris, and Frances Larson. 2007. *Knowing Things: Exploring the Collections at the Pitt Rivers Museum, 1884–1945*. With Alison Petch. Oxford: Oxford University Press.

Grant, Madison. 1916. *The Passing of the Great Race; or, The Racial Basis of European History*. New York: Charles Scribner.

Gray, Geoffrey. 1999. "Being Honest to My Science: Reo Fortune and JHP Murray 1927–1930." *Australasian Journal of Anthropology* 10 (1): 56–76.

Gray, Geoffrey. 2007. *A Cautious Silence: The Politics of Australian Anthropology*. Canberra: Aboriginal Studies Press.

Griaule, Marcel. 1933. "Introduction Méthodologique." *Minotaure* 2:7–12.

Griffiths, Alison. 2002. *Wondrous Difference: Cinema, Anthropology and Turn-of-the-Century Visual Culture*. New York: Columbia University Press.

Griffiths, Tom. 1996. *Hunters and Collectors: The Antiquarian Imagination in Australia*. Cambridge: Cambridge University Press.

Grognet, Fabrice. 2010. "Le Concept de Musée: La Patrimonialisation de la Culture des 'Autres': D'une Rive à L'autre, du Trocadéro à Branly." PhD diss., École des Hautes Études en Sciences Sociales.

Gurney, Peter. 1997. " 'Intersex' and 'Dirty Girls': Mass-Observation and Working-Class Sexuality in England in the 1930s." *Journal of the History of Sexuality* 8 (2): 256–90.

Hacking, Ian. 1986. "Making Up People." In *Reconstructing Individualism: Autonomy, Individuality, and the Self in Western Thought*, edited by Thomas C. Heller, Morton Sosna, and David E. Wellbery, 222–36. Stanford, CA: Stanford University Press.

Hacking, Ian. 1995. "The Looping Effect of Human Kinds." In *Causal Cognition: A Multidisciplinary Debate*, edited by Daniel Sperber, David Premack, and Ann James Premack, 351–83. Oxford: Oxford University Press.

Haddad, John. 2006. "'To Inculcate Respect for the Chinese': Berthold Laufer, Franz Boas, and the Chinese Exhibits at the American Museum of Natural History, 1899–1912." *Anthropos* 101:123–44.

Haddon, Alfred Cort. 1895. *Evolution in Art as Illustrated by the Life Histories of Designs*. London: Walter Scott.

Haddon, Alfred Cort. 1921. *The Practical Value of Ethnology*. Conway Memorial Lecture, Delivered at South Place Institute on March 17. London: Watts.

Haddon, Alfred Cort. 1935. *Reports of the Cambridge Anthropological Expedition to Torres Straits*. Vol. 1, *General Ethnology*. Cambridge: Cambridge University Press.

Haddon, Alfred Cort, and Charles R. Browne. 1892. "Ethnography of the Aran Islands." *Proceedings of the Royal Irish Academy* 2: 768–830.

Haeberlin, Herman K. 1916. "The Idea of Fertilization in the Culture of the Pueblo Indians." *American Anthropological Association Memoirs* 3 (1): 1–55.

Hamilton, Augustus. (1898) 2001. *The Art Workmanship of the Maori Race in New Zealand*. Dunedin: New Zealand Institute.

Haraway, Donna. 1992. "Teddy Bear Patriarchy: Taxidermy in the Garden of Eden." In *Primate Visions: Gender, Race and Nature in the World of Modern Science*, 26–58. London: Verso.

Harrison, Rodney. 2013a. *Heritage: Critical Approaches*. Abingdon, UK: Routledge.

Harrison, Rodney. 2013b. "Reassembling Ethnographic Museum Collections." In *Reassembling the Collection: Ethnographic Museums and Indigenous Agency*, edited by Rodney Harrison, Sarah Byrne, and Anne Clarke, 3–35. Santa Fe, NM: SAR Press.

Harrison, Rodney. 2014. "Observing, Collecting and Governing 'Ourselves' and 'Others': Mass-Observation's Fieldwork *Agencements*." *History and Anthropology* 25 (2): 227–45.

Harrisson, Tom H. 1971. "The Mass-Observation Archive at Sussex University." *ASLIB Proceedings* 23 (8): 398–411.

Harrisson, Tom H., Humphrey Jennings, and Charles Madge. 1937. "Anthropology at Home." *The New Statesman and Nation*, January 30, 1937, 155.

Harrisson, Tom H., and Charles Madge. 1940. *War Begins at Home*. London: Chatto and Windus.

Hasenbank, Andrea. 2011. "Mass-Observation and the Praxis of Print." *Inquire: Journal of Comparative Literature* 2(1). http://inquire.streetmag.org/articles/41.

Hasinoff, Erin L. 2010. "The Missionary Exhibit: A Frustration and a Promise for Franz Boas and the American Museum of Natural History." *Museum History Journal* 3 (1): 81–101.

Hasinoff, Erin L. 2013. *Confluences: An American Expedition to Northern Burma, 1935*. New York: Bard Graduate Center.

Havemann, Paul, ed. 1999. *Indigenous Peoples' Rights in Australia, Canada and New Zealand*. Auckland: Oxford University Press.

Hazard, Anthony Q. 2012. *Postwar Anti-Racism: The United States, UNESCO, and "Race," 1945–1968*. London: Palgrave MacMillan.

Hecht, Jennifer M. 2003. *The End of the Soul: Scientific Modernity, Atheism, and Anthropology in France*. New York: Columbia University Press.

Helliwell, Christine, and Barry Hindess. 2002. "The Empire of Uniformity and the Government of Subject Peoples." *Journal for Cultural Research* 6 (1): 139–52.

Henare, Amiria. 2005. *Museums, Anthropology and Imperial Exchange*. Cambridge: Cambridge University Press.

Herle, Anita, and Sandra Rouse. 1998. "Introduction: Cambridge and the Torres Strait." In *Cambridge and the Torres Strait*, edited by Anita Herle and Sandra Rouse, 1–22. Cambridge: Cambridge University Press.

Herskovits, Melville J. 1924. "A Preliminary Consideration of the Culture Areas of Africa." *American Anthropologist* 26:50–64.

Herskovits, Melville J. 1930. "The Culture Areas of Africa." *Africa* 3:59–77.

Herskovits, Melville J. 1938. *Acculturation: The Study of Culture Contact*. New York: J. J. Augustin.

Herskovits, Melville, J. 1953. *Franz Boas: The Science of Man in the Making*. New York: Charles Scribner's Sons.

Higgs, John W. Y. 1956. "Museums of Rural Culture." *Folklore* 67 (1): 34–42.

Highmore, Ben. 2002. *Everyday Life and Cultural Theory: An Introduction*. London: Routledge.

Highmore, Ben. 2006. "Hopscotch Modernism: On Everyday Life and the Blurring of Art and Social Science." *Modernist Cultures* 2 (1): 70–79.

Highmore, Ben. 2007. "Walls without Museums: Anonymous History, Collective Authorship and the Document." *Visual Culture in Britain* 8 (2): 1–20.

Hill, Kate. 2005. *Culture and Class in English Public Museums, 1850–1914*. Aldershot, UK: Ashgate.

Hill, Richard. 2004. *State Authority Indigenous Autonomy: Crown-Māori Relationships in New Zealand/Aotearoa, 1900–1950*. Wellington: Victoria University Press.

Hill, Richard. 2009. "Maori and State Policy." In *The New Oxford History of New Zealand*, edited by Giselle Byrnes, 513–36. Melbourne: Oxford University Press.

Hinkson, Melinda, and Jeremy Beckett, eds. 2008. *An Appreciation of Difference: WEH Stanner and Aboriginal Australia*. Canberra: Aboriginal Studies Press.

Hinton, James. 2008. "'The "Class" Complex': Mass-Observation and Cultural Distinction in Pre-War Britain." *Past and Present* 199:207–36.

Hinton, James. 2013. *The Mass Observers: A History, 1937–1949*. Oxford: Oxford University Press.

Hollier, Denis, and Liesl Ollman. 1991. "The Use-Value of the Impossible." *October* 60:3–24.

Holman, Jeffrey Paparoa. 2010. *Best of Both Worlds: The Story of Elsdon Best and Tutakangahau*. Auckland: Penguin.

Holmes, William Henry. 1919. *Handbook of Aboriginal American Antiquities: Part I: Introductory, The Lithic Industries*. Smithsonian Institution, Bureau of American Ethnology, Bulletin 60. Washington, DC: Government Printing Office.

Horne, Janet Regina. 2002. *A Social Laboratory for Modern France: The Musée Social and the Rise of the Welfare State*. Durham, NC: Duke University Press.

Huard, Pierre. 1940. "À Propos des Métis." *Bulletins et Travaux de l'Institut Indochinois pour l'Étude de l'Homme* 3:15–20.

Huard, Pierre, and Alfred Bigot. 1938. *Caractéristiques anthropologiques des Indochinois à Hanoi*. Hanoi: Imprimerie d'Extrême-Orient.

Huard, Pierre, and Dó-Xuan-Hop. 1943. "Recherches sur L'importance Numérique des Européens et des Eurasiens." *Bulletins et Travaux de l'Institut Indochinois pour l'Étude de l'Homme* 5:163–72.

Huard, Pierre, G. Lanchou, and Tran Anh. 1962. "Les Enquêtes Anthropologiques faites en Indochine et plus particulièrement au Vietnam." *Bulletins et Mémoires de la Société d'Anthropologie de Paris* 3 (4): 372–438.

Hubble, Nick. 2006. *Mass-Observation and Everyday Life: Culture, History, Theory*. London: Palgrave Macmillan.

Hubble, Nick, Margaretta Jolly, and Laura Marcus, eds. 2001. "Mass Observation as Poetics and Science." Special Issue, *New Formations* 44 (autumn).

Humphries, W. R. 1923. *Patrolling in Papua*. Introduced by J. H. P. Murray. London: Unwin.

Hunn, Jack Kent. 1961. *Report on Department of Maori Affairs*. Wellington: Government Printer.

Hurley, Frank. 1924. *Pearls and Savages*. New York: G. P. Putnam's Sons.

Inch, Lawrence Bates. 1936. *History of the Dominion Museum*. The Alexander Turnbull Library, Ms 1070.

Instructions Sommaires pour les Collecteurs d'Objets Ethnographiques. 1931. Musée d'Ethnographie et Mission Scientifique Dakar-Djibouti. Paris: Palais du Trocadéro.

Jacknis, Ira. 1985. "Franz Boas and Exhibits: On the Limitations of the Museum Method of Anthropology." In *Objects and Others: Essays on Museums and Material Culture*, edited by George W. Stocking Jr., 75–111. Madison: University of Wisconsin Press.

Jacknis, Ira. 1988. "Margaret Mead and Gregory Bateson in Bali: Their Use of Photography and Film." *Cultural Anthropology* 3 (2): 160–77.

Jacknis, Ira. 1992. "'The Artist Himself': The Salish Basketry Monograph and the Beginnings of a Boasian Paradigm." In *The Early Years of Native American Art History: The Politics of Scholarship and Collecting*, edited by Janet Catherine Berlo, 134–61. Seattle: University of Washington Press.

Jacknis, Ira. 1996. "The Ethnographic Object and the Object of Ethnology in the Early Career of Franz Boas." In *Volksgeist as Method and Ethic: Essays on Boasian Ethnography and the German Anthropological Tradition*, edited by George W. Stocking Jr., 185–214. Madison: University of Wisconsin Press.

Jacknis, Ira. 2002a. "The First Boasian: Alfred Kroeber and Franz Boas, 1896–1905." *American Anthropologist* 104 (2): 520–32.

Jacknis, Ira. 2002b. *The Storage Box of Tradition: Kwakiutl Art, Anthropologists, and Museums, 1881–1981*. Washington, DC: Smithsonian Institution Press.

Jacknis, Ira. 2004. "'A Magic Place': The Northwest Coast Indian Hall at the American Museum of Natural History." In *Coming Ashore: Northwest Coast Ethnology, Past and Present*, edited by Marie Mauzé, Michael E. Harkin, and Sergei Kan, 221–50. Lincoln: University of Nebraska Press.

Jacknis, Ira. 2015a. "'America Is Our Field': Anthropological Regionalism at the American Museum of Natural History, 1895–1945." *Museums and Society* 13 (1): 52–71.

Jacknis, Ira. 2015b. "In the Field/*En Plein Air*: The Art of Anthropological Display at the American Museum of Natural History, 1905-30." In *The Anthropology of Expeditions: Travel, Visualities, Afterlives*, edited by Joshua A. Bell and Erin L. Hasinoff, 119–73. New York: Bard Graduate Center; Chicago: University of Chicago Press.

Jacknis, Ira. 2016. "Refracting Images: Anthropological Display at the Chicago World's Fair, 1893." In *Coming of Age in Chicago: The 1893 World's Fair and the Coalescence of American Anthropology*, edited by Curtis M. Hinsley and David R. Wilcox, 261–336. Lincoln: University of Nebraska Press.

Jackson, Patrick M., ed. 1931. *Maori and Education; or, The Education of Natives in New Zealand and Its Dependencies*. Monograph of the New Zealand Teachers' Summer School 1. Wellington: Ferguson and Osborn.

Jacobson, Matthew Frye. 1998. *Whiteness of a Different Color: European Immigrants and the Alchemy of Race*. Cambridge, MA: Harvard University Press.

Jamin, Jean. 1982. "Objets trouvés des paradis perdus: À propos de la Mission Dakar-Djibouti." In *Collections: Passion*, edited by Jacques Hainard and Roland Khaer, 69–100. Neuchâtel, Switzerland: Musée d'Ethnographie.

Jamin, Jean. 1986. "L'Ethnographie Mode d'Inemploi: De Quelques Rapports de l'Ethnologie avec le Malaise dans la Civilisation." In *Le Mal et La Douleur*, edited by Jacques Hainard and Roland Khaer, 45–79. Neuchâtel, Switzerland: Musée d'Ethnographie.

Jamin, Jean. 1989. "Le Savant et le Politique: Paul Rivet 1876–1958." *Bulletins de la Société d'Anthropologie de Paris* 3–4:277–94.

Jamin, Jean. 1991. "Anxious Science: Ethnography as a Devil's Dictionary." *Visual Anthropology Review* 7:84–91.

Jeffrey, Tom. 1998. *Mass-Observation: A Short History*. Mass-Observation Archive Occasional Paper 10. Sussex: Mass-Observation Archive, University of Sussex Library.

Jenkins, David. 1994. "Object Lessons and Ethnographic Displays: Museum Exhibitions and the Making of American Anthropology." *Comparative Studies in Society and History* 36 (2): 242–70.

Jennings, Eric T. 2001. *Vichy in the Tropics: Pétain's National Revolution in Madagascar, Guadeloupe, and Indochina, 1940–1944*. Stanford, CA: Stanford University Press.

Jennings, Eric T. 2004a. "Conservative Confluences, 'Nativist' Synergy: Reinscribing Vichy's National Revolution in Indochina, 1940–1945." *French Historical Studies* 27 (3): 601–35.

Jennings, Eric T. 2004b. "L'Indochine de l'Amiral Decoux." In *L'Empire Colonial sous Vichy*, edited by Jacques Cantier and Eric T. Jennings, 29–49. Paris: Odile Jacob.

Jennings, Humphrey, dir. 1939. *Spare Time*. London: General Post Office Film Unit.

Jennings, Humphrey, and Charles Madge. 1937. *May the Twelfth: Mass-Observation Day Surveys*. With T. O. Beachcroft, J. Blackburn, W. Empson, S. Legg, and K. Raine. London: Faber and Faber.

Jennings, Humphrey, and Harry Watt, dir. 1940. *London Can Take It!* London: General Post Office Film Unit.

Jolly, Eric. 2001. "Marcel Griaule, ethnologue: La construction d'une discipline (1925–1956)." *Journal des Africanistes* 7 (1): 149–90.

Jonaitis, Aldona, ed. 1995. *A Wealth of Thought: Franz Boas on Native American Art.* Seattle: University of Washington Press; Vancouver: Douglas and McIntyre.

Jones, Philip G. 1987. "South Australian Anthropological History: The Board for Anthropological Research and Its Early Expeditions." *Records of the South Australian Museum* 20:71–92.

Joyce, Patrick. 1999. "The Politics of the Liberal Archive." *History of the Human Sciences* 12 (2): 35–49.

Joyce, Patrick. 2003. *The Rule of Freedom: Liberalism and the Modern City.* London: Verso.

Joyce, Patrick. 2013. *The State of Freedom: A Social History of the British State since 1800.* Cambridge: Cambridge University Press.

Karp, Ivan, Corrine A. Kratz, Lynn Szwaja, and Tomás Ybarra-Frausto, eds. 2006. *Museum Frictions: Public Cultures, Global Transformations.* Durham, NC: Duke University Press.

Kavanagh, Gaynor. 1990. *History Curatorship.* Leicester: Leicester University Press.

Keesing, Felix. 1928. *The Changing Maori.* New Plymouth, New Zealand: Thomas Avery.

Kehoe, Alice Beck. (1995) 2007. "Introduction to the Bison Books Edition." In *Mythology of the Blackfoot Indians*, compiled and translated by Clark Wissler and D. C. Duvall, xiii–xli. 2nd ed. Lincoln: University of Nebraska Press.

Kehoe, Alice Beck. 1998. *The Land of Prehistory: A Critical History of American Archaeology.* New York: Routledge.

Kendall, Laurel. 2014. " 'China to the Anthropologist': Franz Boas, Berthold Laufer, and a Road Not Taken in Early American Anthropology." In *Anthropologists and Their Traditions across National Borders*, edited by Regna Darnell and Frederic W. Gleach, 1–39. Lincoln: University of Nebraska Press.

Kendall, Laurel, and Igor Krupnik, eds. 2003. *Constructing Cultures Then and Now: Celebrating Franz Boas and the Jesup North Pacific Expedition.* Contributions to Circumpolar Anthropology 4. Washington, DC: Arctic Studies Center, Smithsonian Institution.

Kennedy, John Michael. 1968. "Philanthropy and Science in New York City: The American Museum of Natural History, 1868–1968." PhD diss., Yale University.

Kirshenblatt-Gimblett, Barbara. 1991. "Objects of Ethnography." In *Exhibiting Cultures: The Poetics and Politics of Museum Display*, edited by Ivan Karp and Steven Lavine, 386–443. Washington, DC: Smithsonian Institution Press.

Kirshenblatt-Gimblett, Barbara. 1998. *Destination Culture: Tourism, Museums, and Heritage.* Berkeley: University of California Press.

Knowles, Chantal. 2000. "Reverse Trajectories: Beatrice Blackwood as Collector and Anthropologist." In *Hunting the Gatherers: Ethnographic Collectors, Agents and Agency in Melanesia, 1870s–1930s*, edited by Michael O'Hanlon and Robert Louis Welsch, 251–78. Oxford: Berg.

Kowal, Emma. 2008. "The Politics of the Gap: Indigenous Australians, Liberal Multiculturalism, and the End of the Self-Determination Era." *American Anthropologist* 110 (3): 338–48.

Kramer, Paul A. 2006. *The Blood of Government: Race, Empire, the United States, and the Philippines*. Chapel Hill: University of North Carolina Press.

Kroeber, Alfred L. 1901. "Decorative Symbolism of the Arapaho." *American Anthropologist* 3:308–36.

Kroeber, Alfred L. 1916. "Zuñi Potsherds." *Anthropological Papers of the American Museum of Natural History* 18 (1): 1–37.

Kroeber, Alfred L. 1917a. "The Superorganic." *American Anthropologist* 19 (2): 163–213.

Kroeber, Alfred L. 1917b. "Zuni Kin and Clan." *Anthropological Papers of the American Museum of Natural History* 18 (2): 39–204.

Kroeber, Alfred L. 1923. "The History of Native Culture in California." *University of California Publications in American Anthropology and Ethnology* 20:123–42.

Kroeber, Alfred L., and Clyde Kluckhohn. 1952. *Culture: A Critical Review of Concepts and Definitions*. Papers of the Peabody Museum of American Archaeology and Ethnology, Harvard University, 47 (1). Cambridge, MA: Peabody Museum of American Archaeology and Ethnology, Harvard University.

Krupnik, Igor, and William W. Fitzhugh, eds. 2001. *Gateways: Exploring the Legacy of the Jesup North Pacific Expedition, 1897–1902*. Contributions to Circumpolar Anthropology 1. Washington, DC: Arctic Studies Center, Smithsonian Institution.

Kuklick, Henrika. 1991. *The Savage Within: The Social History of British Anthropology, 1885–1945*. Cambridge: Cambridge University Press.

Kuklick, Henrika. 2006. "'Humanity in the Chrysalis Stage': Indigenous Australians in the Anthropological Imagination, 1899–1926." *British Journal for the History of Science* 39 (4): 535–68.

Kuklick. Henrika. 2009. "The British Tradition." In *New History of Anthropology*, edited by Henrika Kuklick, 52–78. Oxford: Blackwell.

Kuklick, Henrika. 2011. "Personal Equations: Reflections on the History of Fieldwork, with Special Reference to Sociocultural Anthropology." *Isis* 102 (1): 1–33.

Kushner, Tony. 2004. *We Europeans? Mass-Observation, "Race" and British Identity in the Twentieth Century*. London: Ashgate.

Lang, Herbert. 1919. "Nomad Dwarfs and Civilization: A Study of the Pygmies of Central Africa." *Natural History* 19 (6): 697–713.

Langham, Ian. 1981. *The Building of British Social Anthropology: W. H. R. Rivers and His Cambridge Disciples in the Development of Kinship Studies*. London: Reidel.

Larson, Frances. 2011. "'Did He Ever Darn His Stockings?' Beatrice Blackwood and the Ethnographic Authority of Bronislaw Malinowski." *History and Anthropology* 22 (1): 75–92.

Latour, Bruno. 1987. *Science in Action: How to Follow Scientists and Engineers through Society*. Cambridge, MA: Harvard University Press.

Latour, Bruno. 1999. *Pandora's Hope: Essays on the Reality of Science Studies*. Cambridge, MA: Harvard University Press.

Latour, Bruno. 2005. *Reassembling the Social: An Introduction to Actor-Network Theory*. Oxford: Oxford University Press.

Latour, Bruno, and Steve Woolgar. 1979. *Laboratory Life: The Construction of Scientific Facts*. Princeton, NJ: Princeton University Press.

Lattas, Andrew. 1996. "Humanitarianism and Australian Nationalism in Colonial Papua: Hubert Murray and the Project of Caring for the Self of the Coloniser and Colonised." *Australian Journal of Anthropology* 7 (2): 141–64.

Lattas, Andrew, and Knut M. Rio. 2011. "Securing Modernity: Towards an Ethnography of Power in Contemporary Melanesia." *Oceania* 81 (1): 1–21.

Laurière, Christine. 2008. *Paul Rivet le savant et le politique*. Paris: Muséum national d'Histoire naturelle.

Lebovics, Herman. 1992. *True France: The Wars over Cultural Identity, 1900–1945*. Ithaca, NY: Cornell University Press.

Lebovics, Herman. 2004. *Bringing the Empire Back Home: France in the Global Age*. Durham, NC: Duke University Press.

Le Brusq, Arnauld. 2007. "Les Musées de l'Indochine dans le Processus Colonial." *Outre-mers* 94:97–110.

Leighton, Dorothea, and Clyde Kluckhohn. (1947) 1969. *Children of the People: The Navaho Indian and His Development*. New York: Octagon Books.

Leiris, Michel. 1951. *Race and Culture*. Paris: UNESCO.

Lentin, Alana. 2005. "Replacing 'Race,' Historicizing 'Culture' in Multiculturalism." *Patterns of Prejudice* 39 (4): 379–96.

L'Estoile, Benoît de. 2005. "Rationalising Colonial Domination: Anthropology and Native Policy in French-Ruled Africa." In *Empires, Nations, and Natives: Anthropology and State-Making*, edited by Benoît de L'Estoile, Federico Neiburg, and Lygia Sigaud, 30–57. Durham, NC: Duke University Press.

L'Estoile, Benoît de. 2007. *Le Goût des Autres: De l'Exposition coloniale aux Arts premiers*. Paris: Flammarion.

Lévi-Strauss, Claude. 1952. *Race and History*. Paris: UNESCO.

Lévy, Paul. 1939. "Préhistoire et Ethnologie en Indochine." *Cahiers de l'École Française d'Extrême-Orient* 18:47–52.

Lonetree, Amy, and Amanda J. Cobb, eds. 2008. *The National Museum of the American Indian: Critical Conversations*. Lincoln: University of Nebraska Press.

Losche, Diane. 2006. "The Fate of the Senses in Ethnographic Modernity: The Margaret Mead Hall of Pacific Peoples at the American Museum of Natural History." In *Sensible Objects: Colonialism, Museums and Material Culture*, edited by Elizabeth Edwards, Chris Gosden, and Ruth B. Phillips, 223–44. London: Berg.

Lowie, Robert H. 1922. "Crow Indian Art." *Anthropological Papers of the American Museum of Natural History* 21:271–322.

Lowie, Robert H. 1959. *Robert Lowie, Ethnologist: A Personal Record*. Berkeley: University of California Press.

Lucas, Frederic A., ed. 1919. *General Guide to the Exhibition Halls of the American Museum of Natural History*. New York: American Museum of Natural History.

Lydon, Jane. 2005. *Eye Contact: Photographing Indigenous Australians*. Durham, NC: Duke University Press.

Lynd, Robert S., and Helen Merrell Lynd. 1929. *Middletown: A Study in Contemporary American Culture*. New York: Harcourt, Brace.

MacClancy, Jeremy. 1995. "Brief Encounter: The Meeting in Mass-Observation of British Surrealism and Popular Anthropology." *Journal of the Royal Anthropological Institute* 1 (3): 495–512.

MacClancy, Jeremy. 2001. "Mass-Observation, Surrealism, Social Anthropology: A Present-Day Assessment." *New Formations* 44:90–99.

Macoun, Alissa. 2011. "Aboriginality and the Northern Territory Intervention." *Australian Journal of Political Science* 46 (3): 519–34.

Madge, Charles. 1935. "Mass-Observation." *New Verse* 17:16.

Madge, Charles. 1937. "Anthropology at Home." *The New Statesman and Nation* 2 (January): 12.

Madge, Charles. 1943. *War-Time Pattern of Saving and Spending.* Cambridge: Cambridge University Press.

Madge, Charles, and Tom H. Harrisson. 1937. *Mass-Observation.* London: Frederick Muller.

Madge, Charles, and Tom H. Harrisson. 1938. *First Year's Work.* London: Lindsay Drummond.

Madge, Charles, and Humphrey Jennings. 1937. "Poetic Description and Mass-Observation." *New Verse* 24:1–6.

Mandler, Peter. 2013. *Return from the Natives: How Margaret Mead Won the Second World War and Lost the Cold War.* New Haven, CT: Yale University Press.

Marcus, Laura. 2001. "Introduction: The Project of Mass-Observation." *New Formations* 44:5–19.

Markham, S. F., and W. R. B. Oliver. 1933. *A Report on the Museums and Art Galleries of Australia and New Zealand.* London: Museums Association.

Mass-Observation. 1939. *Britain.* Harmondsworth, UK: Penguin.

Mass-Observation. 1940. "In Brief." *Us: Mass-Observation's Weekly Intelligence Service* 2:8.

Mass-Observation. 1941. *Home Propaganda: A Report Prepared by Mass-Observation for the Advertising Services Guild.* London: Advertising Service Guild.

Mauss, Marcel. (1913) 1969. "L'Ethnographie en France et à l'Étranger." In *Oeuvres*, vol. 3: *Cohésion Sociale et Divisions de la Sociologie*, 395–434. Paris: Minuit.

Mauss, Marcel. (1947) 1967. *Manuel d'Ethnographie.* Paris: Payot.

McCarthy, Conal. 2007a. "Before 'Te Maori': A Revolution Deconstructed." In *Museum Revolutions: How Museums Change and Are Changed*, edited by Simon J. Knell, Sheila Watson, and Suzanne MacLeod, 117–33. London: Routledge.

McCarthy, Conal. 2007b. *Exhibiting Māori: A History of Colonial Cultures of Display.* Oxford: Berg.

McCarthy, Conal. 2011. *Museums and Maori: Heritage Professionals, Indigenous Collections, Current Practice.* Wellington: Te Papa Press.

McCarthy, Conal. 2012. "Carving Out a Place in the Better Britain of the South Pacific: Māori in New Zealand Museums and Exhibitions." In *Curating Empire: Museums and the British Imperial Experience*, edited by Sarah Longair and John McAleer, 56–81. Manchester: Manchester University Press.

McCarthy, Conal. 2014a. "'Empirical Anthropologists Advocating Cultural Adjustments': The Anthropological Governance of Āpirana Ngata and the Native Affairs Department." *History and Anthropology* 25 (2): 280–95.

McCarthy, Conal. 2014b. "To Foster and Encourage the Study and Practice of Māori Arts and Crafts: Indigenous Material Culture, Colonial Culture and Museums in New Zealand." In *Craft and Community: The Material Culture of Place and Politics, 19th-20th Century*, edited by Janice Helland, Beverly Lemire, and Alena Buis, 59–82. Aldershot, UK: Ashgate.

McCarthy, Conal, and Joanna Cobley. 2009. "Museums and Museum Studies in New Zealand: A Survey of Historical Developments." *History Compass* 7:1–19.

McFall, Liz. 2009. "The *Agencement* of Industrial Branch Life Assurance." *Journal of Cultural Economy* 2 (1–2): 49–66.

McGregor, Russell. 1997. *Imagined Destinies: Aboriginal Australians and the Doomed Race Theory, 1880–1939*. Melbourne: Melbourne University Press.

McGregor, Russell. 2011. *Indifferent Inclusion: Aboriginal People and the Aboriginal Nation*. Canberra: Aboriginal Studies Press.

McHugh, Paul G. 2004. *Aboriginal Societies and the Common Law: A History of Sovereignty, Status, and Self-Determination*. Oxford: Oxford University Press.

McLaine, Ian. 1979. *Ministry of Morale: Home Front Morale and the Ministry of Information in World War II*. London: Allen and Unwin.

McQueen, Henry C. 1942. *Education in New Zealand Museums*. Wellington: New Zealand Council for Educational Research.

Mead, Margaret. 1928. *An Inquiry into the Question of Cultural Stability in Polynesia*. Columbia University Contributions to Anthropology 9. New York: Columbia University Press.

Mead, Margaret. 1935. *Sex and Temperament in Three Primitive Societies*. New York: William Morrow.

Mead, Margaret. 1938–49. "The Mountain Arapesh." *Anthropological Papers of the American Museum of Natural History* 36 (3): 139–349.

Mead, Margaret. 1942. *And Keep Your Powder Dry: An Anthropologist Looks at America*. New York: William Morrow.

Mead, Margaret. 1947. "Fundamental Education and Cultural Values." In *Fundamental Education: Common Ground for All Peoples. Report of a Special Committee to the Preparatory Committee of UNESCO, Paris 1946*, 150–78. New York: Macmillan.

Mead, Sidney Moko. 1986. *Te Toi Whakairo: The Art of Māori Carving*. Wellington: Reed Methuen.

Mill, John Stuart. 1969. *On Liberty; Representative Government; The Subjection of Women*. Oxford: Oxford University Press.

Miller, Peter, and Nikolas Rose. 1989. "Political Rationalities and Technologies of Government." In *Texts, Concepts, Contexts*, edited by Sakari Hanninen and Kari Palonen, 167–83. Helsinki: Finnish Political Science Association.

Miller, Peter, and Nikolas Rose. 2008. *Governing the Present: Administering Economic, Social and Personal Life*. Cambridge, UK: Polity.

Miller, Tyrus. 2001. "In the Blitz of Dreams: Mass-Observation and the Historical Uses of Dream Reports." *New Formations* 44:34–51.

Mitchell, Timothy. 2002. *Rule of Experts: Egypt, Techno-Politics, Modernity*. Berkeley: University of California Press.

Mitchell, Timothy. 2013. *Carbon Democracy: Political Power in the Age of Oil*. London: Verso.

Montagu, Ashley. 1950. *The Race Question*. Paris: UNESCO.

Morning, Ann. 2011. *The Nature of Race: How Scientists Think and Teach about Human Difference*. Berkeley: University of California Press.

Morphy, Howard. 1997. "Gillen: Man of Science." In *"My Dear Spencer": The Letters of F.J. Gillen to Baldwin Spencer*, edited by John Mulvaney, Howard Morphy, and Alison Petch, 23–50. Melbourne: Hyland House.

Morton, S. R., and Mulvaney, Derek John, eds. 1996. *Exploring Central Australia: Society, Environment and the 1894 Expedition*. Chipping Norton, NSW: Surrey Beatty.

Mosko, Mark S. 2012. "The Making of Chiefs: Hereditary Succession, Personal Agency and Exchange in North Mekeo Chiefdoms." In *The Scope of Anthropology: Maurice Godelier's Work in Context*, edited by Laurent Dousset and Serge Tcherkézoff, 155–86. New York: Berghahn Books.

Moutu, Andrew. 2007. "Collection as Way of Being." In *Thinking through Things: Theorising Artefacts Ethnographically*, edited by Amiria Henare, Martin Holbraad, and Sari Wastell, 93–112. Abingdon, UK: Routledge.

Mulford, Jeremy. 1982. *Worktown People by Humphrey Spender*. Bristol: Falling Wall.

Mulvaney, John, and John Henry Calaby. 1985. *"So Much That Is New": Baldwin Spencer, 186–1929: A Biography*. Melbourne: Melbourne University Press.

Mulvaney, John, Howard Morphy, and Alison Petch, eds. 1997. *"My Dear Spencer": The Letters of F.J. Gillen to Baldwin Spencer*. Melbourne: Hyland House.

Murray, John Hubert Plunkett. 1920. *Review of the Australian Administration in Papua, 1907–1920*. Port Moresby, Territory of Papua: Government Printer.

Murray, John Hubert Plunkett. 1921. *Anthropology and the Government of Subject Races*. Port Moresby, Territory of Papua: Government Printer.

Murray, John Hubert Plunkett. 1923. *The Population Problem in Papua, a Paper Read by JHP Murray, Lieutenant-Governor of Papua, before the Pan-Pacific Conference, at Melbourne, 21st August*. Port Moresby, Territory of Papua: Government Printer.

Murray, John Hubert Plunkett. 1924. Introduction to Francis Edgar Williams, "The Natives of Purari Delta." *Territory of Papua Anthropological Report 5*. Port Moresby, Territory of Papua: Edward George Baker, Government Printer.

Murray, John Hubert Plunkett. 1926. *Native Custom and the Government of Primitive Races with Especial Reference to Papua, a Paper Read at the Third Pan-Pacific Science Congress, Tokyo*. Port Moresby, Territory of Papua: Edward George Baker, Government Printer.

Murray, John Hubert Plunkett. 1929a. *Native Administration in Papua*. Port Moresby, Territory of Papua: Edward George Baker, Government Printer.

Murray, John Hubert Plunkett. 1929b. *The Response of the Natives of Papua to Western Civilisation: A Paper Read before the Pan-Pacific Science Congress*. Port Moresby, Territory of Papua: Edward George Baker, Government Printer.

Murray, John Hubert Plunkett. 1931. *The Scientific Method as Applied to Native Labour Problems in Papua*. Port Moresby, Territory of Papua: Edward George Baker, Government Printer.

Murray, John Hubert Plunkett. 1932. *The Scientific Aspect of the Pacification of Papua: Presidential Address at the Meeting of the Australian and New Zealand Association for the Advancement of Science*. Port Moresby, Territory of Papua: Edward George Baker, Government Printer.

Murray, John Hubert Plunkett. 1932. "Depopulation in Papua." *Oceania* 3:207–13.

Nakata, Martin. 2007. *Disciplining the Savages, Savaging the Disciplines*. Canberra: Aboriginal Studies Press.

Nash, Stephen E., and Gary M. Feinman, eds. 2003. *Curators, Collections, and Contexts: Anthropology at the Field Museum, 1893–2002*. Fieldiana: Anthropology, n.s., 36. Chicago: Field Museum of Natural History.

Nelson, H. 1968. "The Papuan Villager: A National Newspaper." *Journal of the Papua and New Guinea Society* 2 (1): 79–85.

New Zealand Parliamentary Debates. 1936. Vol. 246. Wellington: Government Printer.

Ngata, Āpirana. 1929. "Anthropology and the Government of Native Races in the Pacific." In *New Zealand Affairs*, edited by James Allen, 22–60. Christchurch: Institute of Pacific Relations, New Zealand Branch.

Ngata, Āpirana. 1931. "Maori Land Development." In *Appendices to the Journal of the House of Representatives*, G10, i–xxiii. Wellington: Government Printer.

Ngata, Āpirana. 1943. *The Price of Citizenship*. Wellington: Whitcombe and Tombs.

Norindr, Panivong. 1996. *Phantasmatic Indochina: French Colonial Ideology in Architecture, Film, and Literature*. Durham, NC: Duke University Press.

Northern Territory Board of Inquiry into the Protection of Aboriginal Children from Sexual Abuse. 2007. *Little Children Are Sacred*. Darwin: Northern Territory Government.

Official Guide to the Government Court: New Zealand Centennial Exhibition 1939–40. 1939. Wellington: Centennial Exhibition Company Ltd.

Oliver, W. R. B. 1944. *New Zealand Museums: Present Establishment and Future Policy*. Wellington: Dominion Museum.

Olsen, Bjornar, Michael Shanks, Timothy Webmore, and Christopher Witmore. 2012. *Archaeology: The Discipline of Things*. Berkeley: University of California Press.

O'Neale, Lila M. 1932. "Yurok-Karok Basket Weavers." *University of California Publications in American Archaeology and Ethnology* 32 (1): 1–184.

Orwell, George. (1940) 1998. "Review of *War Begins at Home*, edited by Tom Harrisson and Charles Madge." In *The Complete Works of George Orwell*, vol. 12, *A Patriot After All: 1940–1941*, edited by P. Davison, 17–18. London: Secker and Warburg.

Osborne, Thomas. 1999. "The Ordinariness of the Archive." *History of the Human Sciences* 12 (2): 51–64.

Osborne, Thomas, and Nikolas Rose. 1997. "In the Name of Society: Three Theses on the History of Social Thought." *History of the Human Sciences* 10 (3): 87–104.

Osborne, Thomas, and Nikolas Rose. 1999. "Do the Social Sciences Create Phenomena? The Example of Public Opinion Research." *British Journal of Sociology* 50 (3): 367–96.

Osborne, Thomas, and Nikolas Rose. 2008. "Populating Sociology: Carl Saunders and the Problem of Population." *Sociological Review* 56 (4): 552–78.

Otter, Chris. 2008. *The Victorian Eye: A Political History of Light and Vision in Britain, 1800–1910*. Chicago: University of Chicago Press.

Outram, Dorinda. 1984. *Georges Cuvier: Vocation, Science and Authority in Post-Revolutionary France*. Manchester: Manchester University Press.

Park, Stuart. 1984. "Monocultural Museums?" *AGMANZ Journal* 15 (4): 19–21.

Park, Stuart. 1986. *An Introduction to Auckland Museum*. Auckland: Auckland Institute and Museum.

Peer, Shanny. 1998. *France on Display: Peasants, Provincials, and Folklore in the 1937 World's Fair*. Albany: State University of New York Press.

Pels, Peter. 1997. "The Anthropology of Colonialism: Culture, History, and the Emergence of Western Governmentality." *Annual Review of Anthropology* 26:163–83.

Pels, Peter, and Oscar Salemink. 1999. "Introduction: Locating the Colonial Subjects of Anthropology." In *Colonial Subjects: Essays on the Practical History of Anthropology*, edited by Peter Pels and Oscar Salemink, 1–52. Ann Arbor: University of Michigan Press.

Pels, Peter, and Oscar Salemink, eds. 1999. *Colonial Subjects: Essays on the Practical History of Anthropology*. Ann Arbor: University of Michigan Press.

Penny, H. Glenn. 2002. *Objects of Culture: Ethnology and Ethnographic Museums in Imperial Germany*. Chapel Hill: University of North Carolina Press.

Percy Smith, Stephenson. 1898. *Hawaiki: The Whence of the Maori*. Wellington: Whitcomb and Tombs.

Percy Smith, Stephenson. 1913–15. *The Lore of the Whare Wananga, or Teachings on the Maori College on Religion, Cosmogony and History*. Polynesian Society Monograph 3 and 4. Translated from the original Māori manuscript by H. T. Whatahoro. New Plymouth: Thomas Avery.

Petch, Alison. 2007. "*Notes and Queries* and the Pitt Rivers Museum." *Museum Anthropology* 30 (1): 1548–79.

Petch, Alison. 2009. "Walter Baldwin Spencer and the Pitt Rivers Museum." *Journal of Museum Ethnography* 21:254–65.

Petch, Alison. 2011. "Pitt Rivers and the Ethnographic Survey of the UK." *Rethinking Pitt-Rivers: Analysing the Activities of a Nineteenth-Century Collector*, http://web.prm.ox.ac.uk/rpr/index.php/article-index/12-articles/502-ethnographic-survey/.

Peterson, Nicolas. 2006. "Visual Knowledge: Spencer and Gillen's Use of Photography in *The Native Tribes of Central Australia*." *Australian Aboriginal Studies* 1:12–22.

Petterson, Christina. 2012. "Colonial Subjectification: Foucault, Christianity and Governmentality." *Cultural Studies Review* 18 (2): 89–108.

"The Philippine Exhibit." 1909. *American Museum Journal* 9:126–31.

Phillips, Ruth B. 2011. *Museum Pieces: Toward the Indigenization of Canadian Museums*. Montreal: McGill-Queen's University Press.

Phillips, W. J. 1943. *Maori Designs*. Wellington: Harry Tombs.

Pickering, Michael, and David Chaney. 1986. "Democracy and Communication: Mass-Observation 1937–1943." *Journal of Communication* 36 (1): 41–56.

Pitt-Rivers, A. H. L. F. 1891. "Typological Museums as Exemplified by the Pitt Rivers Museum at Oxford, and His Provincial Museum at Farnham." *Journal of the Society of Arts* 40:115–22.

Pitt-Rivers, A. H. L. F. 1927. *The Clash of Cultures and the Contact of Races.* London: Routledge.

Poovey, Mary. 1994. "Aesthetics and Political Economy in the Eighteenth Century: The Place of Gender in the Social Constitution of Knowledge." In *Aesthetics and Ideology,* edited by George Levine, 79–105. New Brunswick, NJ: Rutgers University Press.

Poulot, Dominique. 1994. "Identity as Self-Discovery: The Eco-Museum in France." In *Museum Culture: Histories, Discourses, Spectacle,* edited by Daniel J. Sherman and Irit Rogoff, 66–84. Minneapolis: University of Minnesota Press.

Poulot, Dominique. 2005. *Une Histoire des Musées de France.* Paris: La Découverte.

Povinelli, Elizabeth A. 2002. *The Cunning of Recognition: Indigenous Alterities and the Making of Australian Multiculturalism.* Durham, NC: Duke University Press.

Price, David H. 2008. *Anthropological Intelligence: The Deployment and Neglect of American Anthropology in the Second World War.* Durham, NC: Duke University Press.

Quinnell, Michael. 2000. "'Before It Has Become Too Late': The Making and Repatriation of Sir William MacGregor's Official Collection from British New Guinea." In *Hunting the Gatherers: Ethnographic Collectors, Agents and Agency in Melanesia 1870s–1930s,* edited by Michael O'Hanlon and Robert Louis Welsch, 81–103. New York: Berghahn Books.

Rader, Karen A., and Victoria E. M. Cain. 2014. *Life on Display: Revolutionizing US Museums of Science and Natural History in the Twentieth Century.* Chicago: University of Chicago Press.

Radin, Paul. (1927) 2008. *Primitive Man as Philosopher.* London: Maudsley.

Raffin, Anne. 2002. "The Integration of Difference in French Indochina during World War II: Organizations and Ideology concerning the Youth." *Theory and Society* 31 (3): 365–90.

Rainger, Ronald. 1991. *An Agenda for Antiquity: Henry Fairfield Osborn and Vertebrate Paleontology at the American Museum of Natural History, 1890–1935.* Tuscaloosa: University of Alabama Press.

Raj, Kapil. 2013. "Beyond Postcolonialism . . . and Postpositivism: Circulation and the Global History of Science." *Isis* 104:337–47.

Regal, Brian. 2002. *Henry Fairfield Osborn: Race, and the Search for the Origins of Man.* Aldershot, UK: Ashgate.

Reichard, Gladys. 1936. *Navajo Shepherd and Weaver.* New York: J. J. Augustin.

Report of the Auckland Institute and Museum. 1889–90. Auckland: H. Brett Star Office.

Reyman, Jonathan E. 1985. "Note on Clark Wissler's Contribution to American Archaeology." *American Anthropologist* 87 (2): 389–90.

Reynolds, Henry. 2013. *Forgotten War.* Sydney: NewSouth Books.

Richards, Graham. 1998. "Getting a Result: The Expedition's Psychological Research 1898–1913." In *Cambridge and the Torres Strait: Centenary Essays on the 1898 Anthropological Expedition,* edited by Anita Herle and Sandra Rouse, 136–57. Cambridge: Cambridge University Press.

Rico, Trinidad. 2014. "The Limits of a 'Heritage at Risk' Framework: The Construction of Post-Disaster Cultural Heritage in Banda Aceh, Indonesia." *Journal of Social Archaeology* 14 (2): 157–76.

Rivers, William Halse Rivers. 1917. "The Government of Subject Peoples." In *Science and the Nation: Essays by Cambridge Graduates,* edited by Albert Charles Seward, 302–28. Cambridge: Cambridge University Press.

Rivers, William Halse Rivers, ed. 1922. *Essays on the Depopulation of Melanesia.* Cambridge: Cambridge University Press.

Rivet, Paul. 1936. "Ce qu'est l'Ethnologie." In *L'Encyclopédie française,* vol. 7, *L'Espèce humaine,* edited by Lucien Febvre and Anatole de Monzie, 7.08.1–7.08.16. Paris: Comité de l'Encyclopédie française, Librairie Larousse.

Rivet, Paul, Paul Lester, and Georges Henri Rivière. 1935. "Le Laboratoire d'Anthropologie du Muséum." *Archives du Muséum d'Histoire Naturelle,* 6th ser., 12:507–31.

Rivet, Paul, and Georges Henri Rivière. 1930. "La réorganisation du Musée d'Ethnographie du Trocadéro." *Bulletin du Muséum National d'Histoire Naturelle* 2:478–87.

Rivière, Georges Henri. 1947. "Recherches et Musées d'Ethnographie Française Depuis 1939." *Man* 47:7–11.

Rivière, Georges Henri, and Suzanne Tardieu. 1953. *Objets Domestiques des Provinces de France dans la Vie Familiale et les Arts Ménagers.* Paris: Musée des Arts et Traditions Populaires, Éditions des Musées Nationaux.

Rivière, Peter. 2010. "Success and Failure: The Tale of Two Museums." *Journal of the History of Collections* 22 (1): 141–51.

Roffman, Karin. 2010. *From the Modernist Annex: American Women Writers in Museums and Libraries.* Tuscaloosa: University of Alabama Press.

Roldán, A. A. 1992. "Looking at Anthropology from a Biological Point of View: A. C. Haddon's Metaphors on Anthropology." *History of the Human Sciences* 5 (4): 21–32.

Roper, Jonathan. 2012. "England—the Land without Folklore?" In *Folklore and Nationalism in Europe during the Long Nineteenth Century,* edited by Timothy P. Baycroft and David Hopkin, 228–54. Leiden: Brill.

Roque, Ricardo. 2011. "Stories, Skulls, and Colonial Collections." *Configurations* 19:1–23.

Rose, Nikolas. 1990. *Governing the Soul: The Shaping of the Private Self.* London: Routledge.

Rose, Nikolas. 1999. *Powers of Freedom: Reframing Political Thought.* Cambridge: Cambridge University Press.

Ross, Dorothy. 1991. *The Origins of American Social Science.* Cambridge: Cambridge University Press.

Ross, Eric B. 1985. "The 'Deceptively Simple' Racism of Clark Wissler." *American Anthropologist* 87 (2): 390–93.

Rouse, Sandra. 1998. "Expedition and Institution: A. C. Haddon and Anthropology at Cambridge." In *Cambridge and the Torres Strait: Centenary Essays on the 1898 Anthropological Expedition,* edited by Anita Herle and Sandra Rouse, 50–76. Cambridge: Cambridge University Press.

Rowse, Tim. 1992. *Remote Possibilities: The Aboriginal Domain and the Administrative Imagination.* Darwin: North Australian Research Unit, Australian National University.

Rowse, Tim. 1998. *White Flour, White Power: From Rations to Citizenship in Central Australia*. Melbourne: Cambridge University Press.

Rowse, Tim. 2000. *Obliged to Be Difficult: Nugget Coombs' Legacy in Indigenous Affairs*. Cambridge: Cambridge University Press.

Rowse, Tim. 2002. *Nugget Coombs: A Reforming Life*. Cambridge: Cambridge University Press.

Rowse, Tim. 2008. "Indigenous Culture: The Politics of Vulnerability and Survival." In *The Sage Handbook of Cultural Analysis*, edited by Tony Bennett and John Frow, 406–26. London: Sage.

Rowse, Tim. 2014. "'Rooted in Demographic Reality': The Contribution of New World Censuses to Indigenous Survival." *History and Anthropology* 25 (2): 246–62.

Ruppert, Evelyn. 2009. "Becoming Peoples: 'Counting Heads in Northern Wilds.'" *Journal of Cultural Economy* 2 (1–2): 11–32.

Saada, Emmanuelle. 2002. "Race and Sociological Reason in the Republic: Inquiries on the *Métis* in the French Empire (1908–1937)." *International Sociology* 17 (3): 361–91.

Saada, Emmanuelle. 2007. *Les Enfants de la Colonie: Les Métis de l'Empire Français entre Sujétion et Citoyenneté*. Paris: La Découverte.

Salemink, Oscar. 1999. "Ethnography as Martial Art: Ethnicizing Vietnam's Montagnards, 1930–1954." In *Colonial Subjects: Essays on the Practical History of Anthropology*, edited by Peter Pels and Oscar Salemink, 282–325. Ann Arbor: University of Michigan Press.

Sapir, Edward. 1916. *Time Perspective in Aboriginal American Culture: A Study in Method*. Geological Survey Memoir 90; Anthropological Series 13. Ottawa: Government Printing Bureau.

Sapir, Edward. (1924) 1949. "Culture, Genuine and Spurious." In *Selected Writings in Language, Culture, and Personality*, edited by David G. Mandelbaum, 308–31. Berkeley: University of California Press.

Savage, Mike. 2008. "Affluence and Social Change in the Making of Technocratic Middle-Class Identities: Britain, 1939–55." *Contemporary British History* 22 (4): 457–76.

Savage, Mike. 2010. *Identities and Social Change in Britain since 1940: The Politics of Method*. Clarendon: Oxford University Press.

Schaffarczyk, Sylvia. 2006. "Australia's Official Papuan Collection: Sir Hubert Murray and the How and Why of a Colonial Collection." *reCollections: Journal of the National Museum of Australia* 1 (1): 41–58. http://recollections.nma.gov.au/issues/vol_1_no_1/papers/the_papuan_collection.

Schaffarczyk, Sylvia. 2011. "A Rara Avis: FE Williams, the Government Anthropologist of Papua, and the Papuan Official Collection." In *Hunting the Collectors: Pacific Collections in Australian Museums, Art Galleries and Archives*, edited by Susan Cochrane and Michael Quanchi, 191–214. Newcastle upon Tyne, UK: Cambridge Scholars.

"A Scheme for the Development of a Museum of English Life and Traditions." 1949. *Man* 49:41–43.

Schieffelin, Edward, and Robert Crittenden, eds. 1991. *Like People You See in a Dream: First Contact in Six Papuan Societies*. Stanford, CA: Stanford University Press.

Schildkrout, Enid. 1998. "Personal Styles and Disciplinary Paradigms: Frederick Starr and Herbert Lang in the Congo." In *The Scramble for Art in Central Africa*, edited by Enid Schildkrout and Curtis Keim, 169–92. Cambridge: Cambridge University Press.

Schumaker, Lynette. 1996. "A Tent with a View: Colonial Officers, Anthropologists, and the Making of the Field in Northern Rhodesia." *OSIRIS*, 2nd ser., 11:237–58.

Schwimmer, Eric. 1968. *The Maori People in the Nineteen Sixties*. Auckland: Blackwood.

Schwimmer, Eric. 1976. "Introduction: F. E. Williams as Ancestor and Rain-Maker." In *Francis Edgar Williams: The Vailala Madness and Other Essays*, edited by Eric Schwimmer, 11–47. London: Hurst.

Scott, David. 1995. "Colonial Governmentality." *Social Text* 43:191–220.

Scott, David. 1999. *Refashioning Futures: Criticism after Postcoloniality*. Princeton, NJ: Princeton University Press.

Seeger, Anthony, and Louise S. Spear, eds. 1987. *Early Field Recordings: A Catalogue of Cylinder Collections at the Indiana University Archives of Traditional Music*. Bloomington: Indiana University Press.

Segalen, Martine. 2001. "Anthropology at Home and in the Museum: The Case of the Musée National des Arts et Traditions Populaires in Paris." In *Academic Anthropology and the Museum: Back to the Future*, edited by Mary Bouquet, 76–91. New York: Berghahn Books.

Segalen, Martine. 2005. *Vie d'un Musée 1937–2005*. Paris: Stock.

Selcer, Perrin. 2012. "Beyond the Cephalic Index: Negotiating Politics to Produce UNESCO's Scientific Statements on Race." *Current Anthropology* 53 (S5): S173–S184.

Shapiro, Harry L. 1945. "A Portrait of the American People." *Natural History* 54 (6): 248–55.

Shapiro, Warren. 1985. "Some Implications of Carl Wissler's Race Theory." *Mankind* 15 (1): 1–17.

Sherman, Daniel J. 2004. "'Peoples Ethnographic': Objects, Museums, and the Colonial Inheritance of French Ethnology." *French Historical Studies* 27 (3): 669–703.

Sibeud, Emmanuelle. 2000. "La Bibliothèque du Musée de l'Homme: Un corpus menacé." *Revue d'Histoire des Sciences Humaines* 2 (3): 185–95.

Sibeud, Emmanuelle. 2012. "A Useless Colonial Science? Practicing Anthropology in the French Colonial Empire, circa 1880–1960." *Current Anthropology* 53 (S5): S83–S94.

Singaravélou, Pierre. 2009. *L'École Française d'Extrême-Orient ou l'institution des marges (1898–1956)*. Paris: L'Harmattan.

Sissons, Jeffrey. 1995. "Tall Trees Need Deep Roots: Biculturalism, Bureaucracy and Tribal Democracy in Aotearoa/New Zealand." *Cultural Studies* 9 (1): 61–73.

Sissons, Jeffrey. 2000. "The Post-Assimilationist Thought of Sir Apirana Ngata: Towards a Genealogy of New Zealand Biculturalism." *New Zealand Journal of History* 34(1): 47–59.

Skinner, Henry D. 1921. "Culture Areas in New Zealand." *Journal of the Polynesian Society* 30 (118): 71–78.

Skinner, Henry D. 1923. *The Moriois of Chatham Islands*. Bishop Museum Memoir, vol. 9, no. 1. Honolulu: Bishop Museum Press.

Skinner, Henry D. 1974. *Comparatively Speaking: Studies in Pacific Material Culture 1921–1972*. Dunedin: University of Otago Press.

Smith, Norman. 1942. *Native Custom and Law Affecting Native Land*. Wellington: Māori Purposes Fund Board.

Sorrenson, Maurice P. K., ed. 1986–88. *Na to Hoa Aroha: From Your Dear Friend. The Correspondence between Sir Apirana Ngata and Sir Peter Buck 1925–1950*. 3 vols. Auckland: Auckland University Press, Maori Purposes Fund Board.

Sorrenson, Maurice P. K. 1992. *Manifest Destiny: The Polynesian Society over 100 Years*. Auckland: The Polynesian Society.

Sapir, Edward. 1985. "Culture, Genuine and Spurious." In *Selected Writings in Language, Culture, and Personality*, edited by David G. Mandelbaum, 308–31. Berkeley: University of California Press.

Specht, Jim. 1979. "Anthropology." In *Rare and Curious Specimens: An Illustrated History of the Australian Museum, 1827–1979*, edited by Ronald Strahan, 141–50. Sydney: The Australian Museum.

Specht, Jim. 2003. *When the Cause of "Science" Is Not Enough: Frank Hurley in Papua*. Armidale: University of New England Press.

Specht, Jim, and John Fields. 1984. *Frank Hurley in Papua: Photographs of the 1920–1923 Expeditions*. Bathurst: R. Brown in association with the Australian Museum Trust.

Spencer, Baldwin. 1901. *Guide to the Australian Ethnographical Collection in the National Museum of Victoria*. Melbourne: Robert S. Bain, Government Printer.

Spencer, Baldwin. 1913. "Preliminary Report on the Aboriginals of the Northern Territory." *Bulletin of the Northern Territory* 7. Melbourne: Government Printer.

Spencer, Baldwin. 1914. "The Aboriginals of Australia." In *Federal Handbook Prepared in Connection with the Eighty-Fourth Meeting of the British Association for the Advancement of Science Held in Australia*, edited by George Handley Knibbs, 33–85. Melbourne: Commonwealth of Australia.

Spencer, Baldwin. (1915) 1922. *Guide to the Ethnological Collection Exhibited at the National Museum of Victoria*. Melbourne: D. W. Paterson.

Spencer, Baldwin. 1921. "Blood and Shade Divisions of Australian Tribes." *Proceedings of the Royal Society of Victoria*, n.s., pt. 1, 34:2–6.

Spencer, Baldwin, and Frank J. Gillen. 1899. *The Native Tribes of Central Australia*. London: Macmillan.

Spencer, Baldwin, and Frank J. Gillen. 1904. *The Northern Tribes of Central Australia*. London: Macmillan.

Spencer, Baldwin, and Frank J. Gillen. 1912. *Across Australia*. 2 vols. London: Macmillan.

Spender, Humphrey. 1987. *Lensman*. London: Chatto and Windus.

Spender, Humphrey, Derek Smith, and Tom Picton. 1978. "Humphrey Spender: M.O. Photographer." *Camerawork*, September, 6–7.

Spieker, Sven. 2008. *The Big Archive: Art from Bureaucracy.* Cambridge, MA: MIT Press.

Spier, Leslie. 1921. "The Sun Dance of the Plains Indians: Its Development and Diffusion." *Anthropological Papers of the American Museum of Natural History* 16 (7): 451–527.

Spiro, Jonathan P. 2002. "Nordic vs. Anti-Nordic: The Galton Society and the American Anthropological Association." *Patterns of Prejudice* 36 (1): 35–48.

Spiro, Jonathan P. 2009. *Defending the Master Race: Conservation, Eugenics, and the Legacy of Madison Grant.* Burlington: University of Vermont Press; Hanover, NH: University Press of New England.

Stanley, Liz. 2001. "Mass-Observation's Fieldwork Methods." In *Handbook of Ethnography*, edited by Paul Atkinson, Amanda Coffey, Sara Delamont, John Lofland, and Lyn Lofland, 92–108. Los Angeles: Sage.

Stanley, Liz. 2008. "It Has Always Known, and We Have Always Been 'Other': Knowing Capitalism and the 'Coming Crisis' of Sociology Confront the Concentration System and Mass-Observation." *Sociological Review* 56 (4): 535–51.

Stanley, Liz. 2009. "The Future for Sociology (and the Tower Will Not Fall)." Edinburgh Working Papers in Sociology 34, University of Edinburgh.

Staum, Martin S. 2011. *Nature and Nurture in French Social Sciences, 1859–1914 and Beyond.* Montreal and Kingston: McGill-Queen's University Press.

Steinmetz, George. 2007. *The Devil's Handwriting: Precoloniality and the German Colonial State in Qingdao, Samoa, and Southwest Africa.* Chicago: University of Chicago Press.

Stocking, George W., Jr. 1968. *Race, Culture, and Evolution: Essays in the History of Anthropology.* Chicago: University of Chicago Press.

Stocking, George W., Jr. 1974. "Clark Wissler." In *Dictionary of American Biography, Supplement*, vol. 4, *1946–50*, edited by John A. Garraty, 906–9. New York: Charles Scribner's Sons.

Stocking, George W., Jr. 1976. "Ideas and Institutions in American Anthropology: Toward a History of the Interwar Period." In *Selected Papers from the American Anthropologist, 1921–1945*, edited by George W. Stocking Jr., 1–53. Washington, DC: American Anthropological Association.

Stocking, George W., Jr. 1983. "The Ethnographer's Magic: Fieldwork in British Anthropology from Tylor to Malinowski." In *Observers Observed: Essays on Ethnographic Fieldwork*, edited by George W. Stocking Jr., 70–120. Madison: University of Wisconsin Press.

Stocking, George W., Jr. 1985. "Philanthropoids and Vanishing Cultures: Rockefeller Funding and the End of the Museum Era in Anglo-American Anthropology." In *Objects and Others: Essays on Museums and Material Culture*, edited by George W. Stocking Jr., 112–45. Madison: University of Wisconsin Press.

Stocking, George W., Jr. 1996. *After Tylor: British Social Anthropology, 1888–1951.* Madison: University of Wisconsin Press.

Stoler, Ann Laura. 1992a. "Sexual Affronts and Racial Frontiers: European Identities and the Cultural Politics of Exclusion in Colonial Southeast Asia." *Comparative Studies in Society and History* 34 (3): 514–51.

Stoler, Ann Laura. 1992b. "Rethinking Colonial Categories: European Communities and the Boundaries of Rule." In *Colonialism and Culture*, edited by Nicholas B. Dirks, 319–52. Ann Arbor: University of Michigan Press.

Stoler, Ann Laura. 1995. *Race and the Education of Desire: Foucault's History of Sexuality and the Colonial Order of Things*. Durham, NC: Duke University Press.

Stoler, Ann Laura. 2009. *Along the Archival Grain: Epistemic Anxieties and Colonial Common Sense*. Princeton, NJ: Princeton University Press.

Street, Brian. n.d. "Mass-Observation and Social Anthropology." Mass Observation Online: Adam Matthew Digital and the University of Sussex. http://www.massobservation.amdigital.co.uk/FurtherResources/Essays/MassObservationAndSocialAnthropology.

Summerfield, Penny. 1985. "Mass-Observation: Social Research or Social Movement?" *Journal of Contemporary History* 20:439–52.

Sussman, Robert Wald. 2014. *The Myth of Race: The Troubling Persistence of an Unscientific Idea*. Cambridge, MA: Harvard University Press.

Sutherland, Ivan G. 1929. "The Study of Maori Mind." *Journal of the Polynesian Society* 38 (150): 127–47.

Sutherland, Ivan G. 1935. *The Māori Situation*. Wellington: Harry H. Tombs.

Sutherland, Ivan G., ed. 1940. *The Māori People Today: A General Survey*. Wellington: New Zealand Institute for International Affairs and the New Zealand Council for Educational Research.

Sutherland, Ivan G. 1950. "Crusade through Parliament." *Journal of the Polynesian Society* 59 (4): 295–318.

Sutherland, Oliver. 2013. *Paikea: The Life of I.L.G. Sutherland*. Christchurch: Canterbury University Press.

Temple, Charles Lindsay. 1918. *Native Races and Their Rulers*. Cape Town: Argus.

Thomas, David Hurst. 1980. "Margaret Mead as a Museum Anthropologist." *American Anthropologist* 82 (2): 354–61.

Thomas, Nicholas. 1991. *Entangled Objects: Exchange, Material Culture and Colonialism in the Pacific*. Cambridge, MA: Harvard University Press.

Thomas, Nicholas. 1994. *Colonialism's Culture: Anthropology, Travel, and Government*. Princeton, NJ: Princeton University Press.

Thomas, Nicholas. 1996. *Out of Time: History and Evolution in Anthropological Discourse*. Ann Arbor: University of Michigan Press.

Thomas, Richard G. 2006. "Philology in Viet Nam and Its Impact on Southeast Asian Cultural History." *Modern Asian Studies* 40 (2): 477–515.

Thompson, Virginia, and Richard Adloff. 1947. "The Cultural Institutions of Indochina Today." *The Far Eastern Quarterly* 4 (4): 414–19.

Thomson, John A. 1915. "Special Reports: Some Principles of Museum Administration Affecting the Future Development of the Dominion Museum." In *Appendices to the Journals of the House of Representatives*, H3: 9–19. Wellington: Government Printer.

Thoresen, Timothy H. H. 1977. "Art, Evolution, and History: A Case Study of Paradigm Change in Anthropology." *Journal of the History of the Behavioral Sciences* 13 (2): 107–25.

Thorpe, William Walford. 1926. "The Ravi or Papuan Club House: A Recent Exhibition." *Australian Museum Magazine*, April–June, 358.

Tindale, Norman B. 1974. *Aboriginal Tribes of Australia: Their Terrain, Environmental Controls, Distribution, Limits, and Proper Names*. Berkeley: University of California Press.

Tomas, David. 1991. "Tools of the Trade: The Production of Ethnographic Observations on the Andaman Islands, 1858–1922." In *Colonial Situations: Essays on the Contextualisation of Ethnographic Knowledge*, edited by George W. Stocking Jr., 75–108. Madison: University of Wisconsin Press.

Treagear, Edward. 1885. *The Aryan Maori*. Wellington: Government Printer.

Trouillot, Michel-Rolph. 2003. *Global Transformations: Anthropology and the Modern World*. New York: Palgrave Macmillan.

UNESCO. 1949. *Records of the General Conference of the United Nations Educational, Scientific and Cultural Organization Fourth Session, Paris, 1949: Resolutions*. Paris: UNESCO.

UNESCO. 1952. *The Race Question: Results of an Inquiry*. Paris: UNESCO.

UNESCO. 1969. *Four Statements on the Race Question*. Paris: UNESCO.

Urry, James. 1984. "Englishmen, Celts and Iberians: The Ethnographic Survey of the United Kingdom, 1892–1899." In *Functionalism Historicized: Essays on British Social Anthropology*, edited by George W. Stocking Jr., 83–105. Madison: University of Wisconsin Press.

Urry, James. 1993. *Before Social Anthropology: Essays on the History of British Anthropology*. Abingdon, UK: Routledge.

Urry, James. 1998. "Making Sense of Diversity and Complexity: The Ethnological Context and Consequences of the Torres Strait Expedition and the Oceanic Phase in British Anthropology, 1890–1935." In *Cambridge and the Torres Strait: Centenary Essays on the 1898 Anthropological Expedition*, edited by Anita Herle and Sandra Rouse, 201–33. Cambridge: Cambridge University Press.

Valverde, Mariana. 1996. "'Despotism' and Ethical Liberal Governance." *Economy and Society* 25 (3): 357–72.

Varagnac, André. 1935. "Une Coopérative de Travail Scientifique: La Commission des Recherches Collectives du Comité de l'Encyclopédie Française." *Annales d'Histoire Économique et Sociale* 7 (33): 302–6.

Vidal, Fernando, and Nélia Dias. 2016. "Introduction: The Endangerment Sensibility." In *Endangerment, Biodiversity and Culture*, edited by Fernando Vidal and Nélia Dias, 1–38. Abingdon, UK: Routledge.

Visweswaran, Kamala. 2010. *Un/common Cultures: Racism and the Rearticulation of Cultural Difference*. Durham, NC: Duke University Press.

Vokes, Richard. 2007. "(Re)constructing the Field through Sound: Actor-Networks, Ethnographic Representation and 'Radio Elicitation' in South-Western Uganda." In *Creativity and Cultural Improvisation*, edited by Elizabeth Halem and Tim Ingold, 285–303. Oxford: Berg.

Walker, Ranginui. 2001. *He Tipua: The Life and Times of Sir Apirana Ngata*. Auckland: Viking.

Walker, Ranginui. 2004. *Ka whawhai tonu matou: Struggle without End*. Rev. ed. Auckland: Penguin.

Weber, Eugene. 1976. *Peasants into Frenchmen: The Modernization of Rural France, 1870–1914*. Stanford, CA: Stanford University Press.

Weber, Florence. 2000. "Le folklore, l'histoire, et l'état en France (1937–1945)." *Revue de synthèse*, 4th ser., 3–4:453–67.

Weber, Florence. 2005. "Vichy France and the End of Scientific Folklore (1937–1954)." In *Empires, Nations, and Natives: Anthropology and State-Making*, edited by Benoît de L'Estoile, Federico Neiburg, and Lygia Sigaud, 88–107. Durham, NC: Duke University Press.

White, Melanie. 2005. "The Liberal Character of Ethological Governance." *Economy and Society* 34 (3): 474–94.

Wilder, Gary. 2005. *The French Imperial Nation-State: Negritude and Colonial Humanism between the Two World Wars*. Chicago: University of Chicago Press.

Willcock, H. D. 1943. "Mass-Observation." *American Journal of Sociology* 48 (4): 445–56.

Williams, Francis Edgar. 1923a. *The Collection of Curios and the Preservation of Native Culture*. Territory of Papua Anthropological Reports 3. Port Moresby, Territory of Papua: Edward George Baker, Government Printer.

Williams, Francis Edgar. 1923b. *The Vailala Madness and the Destruction of Native Ceremonies in the Gulf Division*. Territory of Papua Anthropological Reports 4. Port Moresby, Territory of Papua: Edward George Baker, Government Printer.

Williams, Francis Edgar. 1924. *The Natives of Purari Delta*. Territory of Papua Anthropological Reports 5. Port Moresby, Territory of Papua Edward George Baker, Government Printer.

Williams, Francis Edgar. 1932. "Depopulation and Administration." *Oceania* 3 (2): 218–26.

Williams, Francis Edgar. 1934. "The Vailala Madness in Retrospect." In *Essays Presented to C. G. Seligman*, edited by E. E. Evans-Pritchard, Raymond Firth, Bronislaw Malinowski, and Isaac Schapera, 369–79. London: Kegan Paul, Trench, Trubner.

Williams, Francis Edgar. 1935. *The Blending of Cultures: An Essay on the Aims of Native Education*. Territory of Papua Anthropological Reports 16. Port Moresby, Territory of Papua: Edward George Baker, Government Printer.

Williams, Francis Edgar. 1939. "Presidential Address: The Creed of the Government Anthropologist." *Australian and New Zealand Association for the Advancement of Science* 24:145–59.

Williams, Nancy M. 1986. *The Yolngu and Their Land: A System of Land Tenure and the Fight for Its Recognition*. Canberra: Aboriginal Institute of Aboriginal Studies.

Willis, William S., Jr. (1972) 1999. "Skeletons in the Anthropological Closet." In *Reinventing Anthropology*, edited by Dell Hymes, 121–52. Ann Arbor: University of Michigan Press.

Wingfield, Chris. 2011. "From Greater Britain to Little England: The Pitt Rivers Museum, the Museum of English Rural Life, and Their Six Degrees of Separation." *Museum History Journal* 4 (2): 245–66.

Wingfield, Chris, and Chris Gosden. 2012. "An Imperialist Folklore? Establishing the Folklore Society in London." In *Folklore and Nationalism in Europe during the Long Nineteenth Century*, edited by Timothy P. Baycroft and David Hopkin, 255–74. Leiden: Brill.

Wissler, Clark. 1904. "Decorative Art of the Sioux Indians." *Bulletin of the American Museum of Natural History* 18 (3): 231–77.

Wissler, Clark. 1910. "Material Culture of the Blackfoot Indians." *Anthropological Papers of the American Museum of Natural History* 5 (1): 1–175.

Wissler, Clark, ed. 1912–16. "Societies of the Plains Indians." *Anthropological Papers of the American Museum of Natural History* 11.

Wissler, Clark. 1914. "Material Cultures of the North American Indians." *American Anthropologist* 16 (3): 447–505.

Wissler, Clark, ed. 1915–21. "Sun Dance of the Plains Indians." *Anthropological Papers of the American Museum of Natural History* 16.

Wissler, Clark. 1917. *The American Indian: An Introduction to the Anthropology of the New World*. New York: Douglas C. McMurtrie.

Wissler, Clark. 1923a. *Man and Culture*. New York: Thomas Y. Crowell.

Wissler, Clark. 1923b. "Man as a Museum Subject." *Natural History* 23 (3): 245–57.

Wissler, Clark. 1926. *The Relation of Nature to Man in Aboriginal America*. New York: Oxford University Press.

Wissler, Clark. 1927. "The Culture-Area Concept in Social Anthropology." *American Journal of Sociology* 32 (6): 881–91.

Wolfe, Patrick. 1999. *Settler Colonialism and the Transformation of Anthropology: The Politics and Poetics of an Ethnographic Event*. London: Cassell.

Wright, Gwendolyn. 1987. "Tradition in the Service of Modernity: Architecture and Urbanism in French Colonial Policy, 1900–1930." *Journal of Modern History* 59:291–316.

Yans-McLaughlin, Virginia. 1986. "Science, Democracy, and Ethics: Mobilising Culture and Personality for World War II." In *Malinowski, Rivers, Benedict and Others: Essays on Culture and Personality*, edited by George W. Stocking Jr., 184–219. Madison: University of Wisconsin Press.

Young, Michael, and Julia Clark. 2001. *An Anthropologist in Papua: The Photography of F. E. Williams, 1922–39*. Canberra: National Archives of Australia and Crawford House.

Zimmerman, Andrew. 2001. *Anthropology and Anti-Humanism in Imperial Germany*. Chicago: University of Chicago Press.

Zumwait, Rosemary Lévy. 2008. *Franz Boas and W.E.B. Du Bois at Atlanta University, 1906*. Philadelphia: American Philosophical Society.

TONY BENNETT is a research professor in social and cultural theory in the Institute for Culture and Society at the Western Sydney University, Australia. He is a member of the Australian Academy of the Humanities and of the Academy of the Social Sciences in the United Kingdom. His main books include *Formalism and Marxism* (1979), *Bond and Beyond: The Political Career of a Popular Hero* (1987, with Janet Woollacott), *Outside Literature* (1991), *The Birth of the Museum* (1995), *Culture: A Reformer's Science* (1998), *Pasts beyond Memory: Evolution, Museums, Colonialism* (2004), and *Making Culture, Changing Society* (2013). He is also a coauthor of *Accounting for Tastes: Australian Everyday Cultures* (1999) and *Culture, Class, Distinction* (2009).

FIONA CAMERON is a senior research fellow at the Institute for Culture and Society at Western Sydney University, Australia. Fiona has been a chief investigator on seven Australian Research Council grants and has researched and published widely on topics ranging from museums and their agencies in contemporary societies around "hot topics," most notably climate change, to material culture studies, digital heritage, and the history of museums and engagements with anthropology. Her recent books include three coedited collections, *Theorizing Digital Cultural Heritage: A Critical Discourse* (2007), *Hot Topics, Public Culture, Museums* (2010), and *Climate Change and Museum Futures* (2014), as well as a coauthored monograph, *Compositions, Materialities, Embodiments, Dynamics: Theorizing Digital Cultural Heritage for a Complex World* (2016). Fiona taught museum studies at the University of Sydney and has a professional background as a museum curator.

NÉLIA DIAS is associate professor in the Department of Anthropology (ISCTE-IUL and CRIA). Her research engages the history of anthropology, ethnographical and physical anthropology collections, and French colonialism. She is the author of *Le Musée d'Ethnographie du Trocadéro (1878–1908): Anthropologie et Muséologie en France* (1991) and *La Mesure des Sens: Les Anthropologues et le corps humain* (Aubier, 2004), and she has co-edited the volume *Endangerment, Biodiversity, and Culture* (2015).

BEN DIBLEY is a researcher and writer living in Sydney. He is currently a research fellow at the Institute for Culture and Society at the Western Sydney University, Australia. He has research interests in social and cultural theory, particularly around questions of cultural institutions, colonialism, and the environment. His essays have appeared in the *Australian Humanities Review*, the *Cultural Studies Review*, *History and Anthropology*, the *International Journal of Cultural Studies*, *Museum and Society*, *New Formations*, and *Transformations*.

RODNEY HARRISON is a reader in archaeology, heritage, and museum studies at the Institute of Archaeology at University College London. His research engages the material histories and contemporary sociopolitics of anthropology, archaeology, heritage, material culture, and museums. He is the founding editor of the *Journal of Contemporary Archaeology* and vice president of the Association of Critical Heritage Studies. His recent books include *Heritage: Critical Approaches* (2013) and three coedited volumes: *Reassembling the Collection* (2013), *The Oxford Handbook of the Archaeology of the Contemporary Past* (2013), and *Rethinking Colonial Pasts through Archaeology* (2014).

IRA JACKNIS is a research anthropologist at the Phoebe A. Hearst Museum of Anthropology at the University of California, Berkeley. Before coming to the Hearst in 1991, he worked at the Smithsonian Institution, the Field Museum, Newberry Library, and the Brooklyn Museum. His research specialties include the art and culture of the Native Americans of western North America, nonverbal modes of ethnographic representation (photography, film, and sound recording), museums, and the history of anthropology. Among his publications are *The Storage Box of Tradition: Kwakiutl Art, Anthropologists, and Museums, 1881–1981* (2002) and *Food in California Indian Culture* (2004).

CONAL MCCARTHY is the director of the Museum and Heritage Studies program at Victoria University of Wellington, Aotearoa/New Zealand, where he is an associate professor. Conal has degrees in English, art history, Māori language, and museum studies and has worked in galleries and museums in a variety of professional roles. Among his current research projects are the history of museum visitation in Australia and New Zealand; "Indigenising Museologies" in Australia, New Zealand, the United States, and Canada; and "Te Ao Hou," a study of Māori leaders and their Pakeha associates in 1900–50, who imagined a "new world" for themselves within modern New Zealand. He has published on museum history and practice, including the books *Exhibiting Māori: A History of Colonial Cultures of Display* (2007) and *Museums and Māori: Heritage Professionals, Indigenous Collections, Current Practice* (2011). His latest book, *Museum Practice*, an edited collection on contemporary museum practice, was published in the series International Handbooks of Museum Studies in 2015.

compulsion, 126
Congo, 144, 230
Conklin, Alice, 17, 225, 227, 288n19
Conn, Steven, 39
contact zones, 32
Cooke Daniels Expedition, 62
Cook Islands, 204
Coombes, H. C. "Nugget," 262, 263
Cowlishaw, Gillian, 262
Cro-Magnon man, 157
cross-cultural exchange, 60
Crow Indians, 138
cultural adaptation, 197, 203, 269
cultural anthropology, 132
cultural creativity, 133
cultural difference: culture areas as, 146–52;
    displays of, 153–61
cultural diffusion, 132, 133, 148
cultural diversity, 82, 172, 229, 257–59
cultural economy, 30
cultural governance, 49
cultural junk, 83
cultural patterning, 7
cultural relativism, 156, 161, 227, 256
cultural rights, 289n4
culture: aesthetic conceptions of, 133–35,
    170, 171, 285; living, 210; mass, 121, 128;
    Polynesian, 166; settler, 35; universal pattern
    of, 163–66. See also material culture; native
    culture
culture-areas, 6, 132, 133, 163–66, 178, 256, 263,
    265, 266; Best and, 186; Boas and, 7; as cul-
    tural difference, 146–52; Kroeber and, 7, 44;
    Māori and, 184, 193–96, 269, 270; for Native
    Americans, 150–51, 265–67
culture concept, 1, 2, 6, 7, 49, 98, 131–35, 178,
    210, 256, 271; Native Americans and, 15–16,
    167; race and, 167–73; as race repellent, 132
Cunningham, Daniel J., 91, 96
curatorial logics, 84–87
customs, 82

Dakar-Djibouti mission, 28, 38, 230
Dakota Sioux Indians, 136
Darnell, Regna, 135
Daston, Lorraine, 113
Davenport, Charles, 161
day surveys, 100, 104, 105, 112, 113, 119

Decoux, Jean, 248
dehistoricization, of subject, 15
Deleuze, Gilles, 30
demarcation, 118
democracy, 79
demoralization, 76
Department of External Affairs (AUS), 61
Department of Internal Affairs (NZ),
    201
Department of Native Affairs (NZ), 24, 177,
    181, 197, 203, 204, 214
Department of Tourism and Health Resorts
    (NZ), 198, 200
Derrida, Jacques, 36
Dewey, John, 171
Dexter, Barrie, 262, 263
diaries, 100, 102; dream, 121; war, 105, 112;
    writing of, 113. See also Mass-Observation
Dias, Nélia, 276n40
Dickinson, Robert Latou, 168
difference: cultural, 146–52, 153–61; race as
    explanation of, 135, 161–63, 226; rule of
    colonial difference, 42
différents pays, 243
diffusion, cultural, 132, 133, 148
Direction des Musées de France, 227
directives, 100, 105, 111, 114, 115
direct observation, 104, 113
Dirks, Nicholas, 41, 42
discrimination, 118
DM. See Dominion Museum
documentary filmmaking, 113, 119. See also
    film
Dominion Museum (DM) Wellington, 5, 9, 20,
    23, 38, 175–76, 187–92, 287n24
Dorsey, George, 145, 156
Douglas, Heather, 268
Douglas, Oliver, 98, 99
Douglass, A. E., 149
dream diaries, 121
Drummond, I. Wyman, 145
Du Bois, W. E. B., 271
Duvall, David C., 138

École des Hautes Études, 27
École Française d'Extrême-Orient (EFEO),
    219, 224, 225, 231, 235, 240, 244
eco-museums, 49

Nigrescence, 93

NMV. *See* National Museum of Victoria

Nordic race, 133, 157, 162, 165, 172

Norindr, Panivong, 224

Norma (statue), 167, 169

Normman (statue), 167, 168

Northern Territory, 51, 52, 67, 69, 74–78, 85

Northern Territory Intervention (NTI), 8, 256, 267, 268

The Northern Tribes of Central Australia (Spencer and Gillen), 57

Northwest Coast Indians, 5, 9, 13, 15, 47

Notes and Queries on Anthropology, 29, 54, 93, 96, 97, 105, 112, 113

NTI. *See* Northern Territory Intervention

Nuie, 204

object-types, 139

objet trouvé, 119, 120

Oceania, 144–46

Oeser, Oscar, 101, 104

Office of Indian Affairs (USA), 173

oligoptic technologies, 109–18

oligoptic vision, 6, 89, 129

OM. *See* Otago Museum

O'Neale, Lila, 164

oral testimony, 38, 275n29

oral tradition, 196

Orwell, George, 283n21

Osborn, Henry Fairfield, 7, 15, 134, 157, 161

Osborne, Thomas, 36, 41

Otago Museum (OM), 39, 177, 193–96, 211

Otter, Chris, 89, 109

Overland Telegraph line, 58, 60

pacification campaigns, 230

Pacific Hall (AMNH), 166

Pagan Peoples (Philippines), 144

Pakeha, 178, 179, 180, 186, 191, 196, 211

Papago Indians, 173

Papua, 1, 5, 51, 52; centers of collection and calculation and, 66–74; fieldwork agencements and, 61–66; native culture and, 78–84. *See also* New Guinea

Papuan Official Collection (POC), 1, 52, 62, 66, 70–74, 85

The Papuan Villager (newspaper), 71

Parsons, Elsie Clews, 138

participant observation, 53, 57, 100, 138

Parti Populaire Français, 220

The Passing of the Great Race (Grant), 161

Pearson, Noel, 268

Peer, Shanny, 229

Pels, Peter, 29, 42

perambulatory laboratory, 53, 91

persuasion, 126

Pétain, Marshall, 246, 248, 249, 253

Peterson, Nicholas, 34

petites patries, 8, 229, 248, 249

petits pays, 229, 252

Petrie, Flinders, 194

Philippine Hall (AMNH), 160, 163, 166

Philippines, 144, 157

photography, 34, 37, 93, 108, 137, 142

piforu (preserved human heads), 64, 81

Pitt Rivers, A. H. L. F., 10, 68, 96, 280n36

POC. *See* Papuan Official Collection

Political and Economic Planning (UK), 102

"The Political and Educational Development under American Influence," 157

Polynesian cultures, 166

Polynesian Society, 177, 197, 200–201

Pōmare, Māui, 200

Poovey, Mary, 277n41

Popular Front, 217, 220, 227, 241, 253

populations, 41–49

Port Moresby, 62, 66, 70, 86

Port Moresby Museum, 71

Poulot, Dominique, 253

Povinelli, Elizabeth, 35, 43, 262

Powell, John Wesley, 135

practical anthropology, 63–64

practical histories, 42

practice anthropology, 53

preserved human heads (*piforu*), 64, 81

préterrain, 29

primitive art, 164

Primitive Man as Philosopher (Radlin), 211

primitives, 132

primitivism, 99

private opinion, 124–25

Progressive Era, 167

propaganda, 127; wartime, 122

protégés français, 228, 246

CPSIA information can be obtained
at www.ICGtesting.com
Printed in the USA
LVHW082352120122
708470LV00014B/897